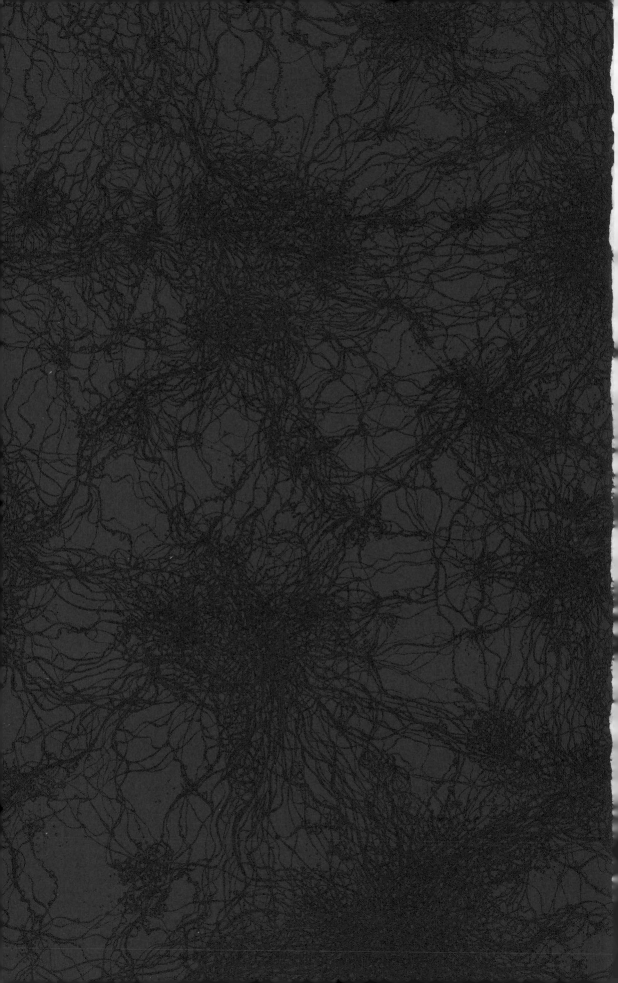

STRANGE ATTRACTORS

ARCHAIA ENTERTAINMENT LLC
WWW.ARCHAIA.COM

CREATED BY CHARLES SOULE

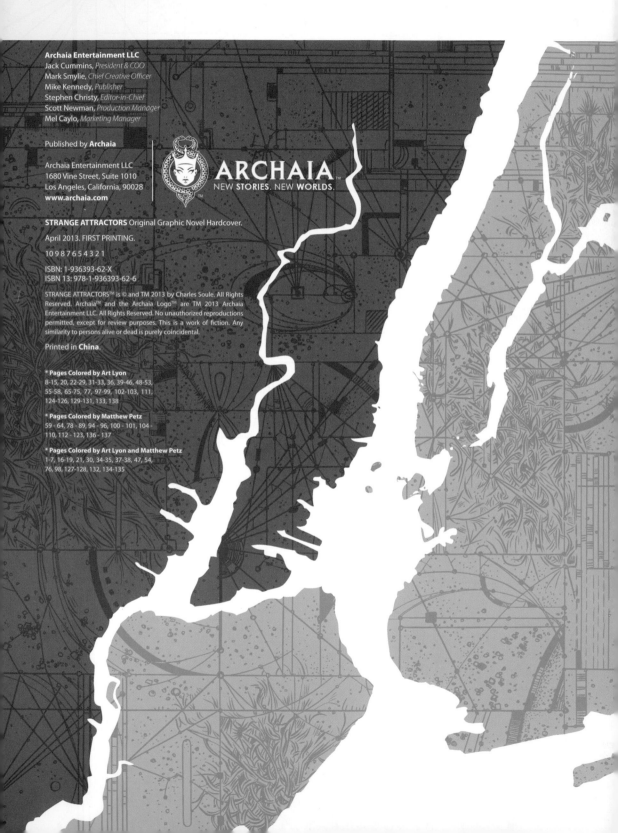

Archaia Entertainment LLC

Jack Cummins, *President & COO*
Mark Smylie, *Chief Creative Officer*
Mike Kennedy, *Publisher*
Stephen Christy, *Editor-in-Chief*
Scott Newman, *Production Manager*
Mel Caylo, *Marketing Manager*

Published by **Archaia**

Archaia Entertainment LLC
1680 Vine Street, Suite 1010
Los Angeles, California, 90028
www.archaia.com

ARCHAIA
NEW STORIES. NEW WORLDS.

STRANGE ATTRACTORS Original Graphic Novel Hardcover.

April 2013. FIRST PRINTING.

10 9 8 7 6 5 4 3 2 1

ISBN: 1-936393-62-X
ISBN 13: 978-1-936393-62-6

* **Pages Colored by Art Lyon**
8-15, 20, 22-29, 31-33, 36, 39-46, 48-53, 55-58, 65-75, 77, 97-99, 102-103, 111, 124-126, 129-131, 133, 138

* **Pages Colored by Matthew Petz**
59 - 64, 78 - 89, 94 - 96, 100 - 101, 104 - 110, 112 - 123, 136 - 137

* **Pages Colored by Art Lyon and Matthew Petz**
1-7, 16-19, 21, 30, 34-35, 37-38, 47, 54, 76, 98, 127-128, 132, 134-135

STRANGE ATTRACTORS

WRITTEN BY
CHARLES SOULE

ILLUSTRATED BY
GREG SCOTT

COVER BY
DAN DUNCAN

COLORED BY
ART LYON &
MATTHEW PETZ'

LETTERED BY
THOMAS MAUER

COMPLEXITY MAPS BY
ROBERT SAYWITZ

EDITED BY
REBECCA TAYLOR

DESIGN BY
SCOTT NEWMAN

INTRODUCTION THE KEY TO THE ENGINE

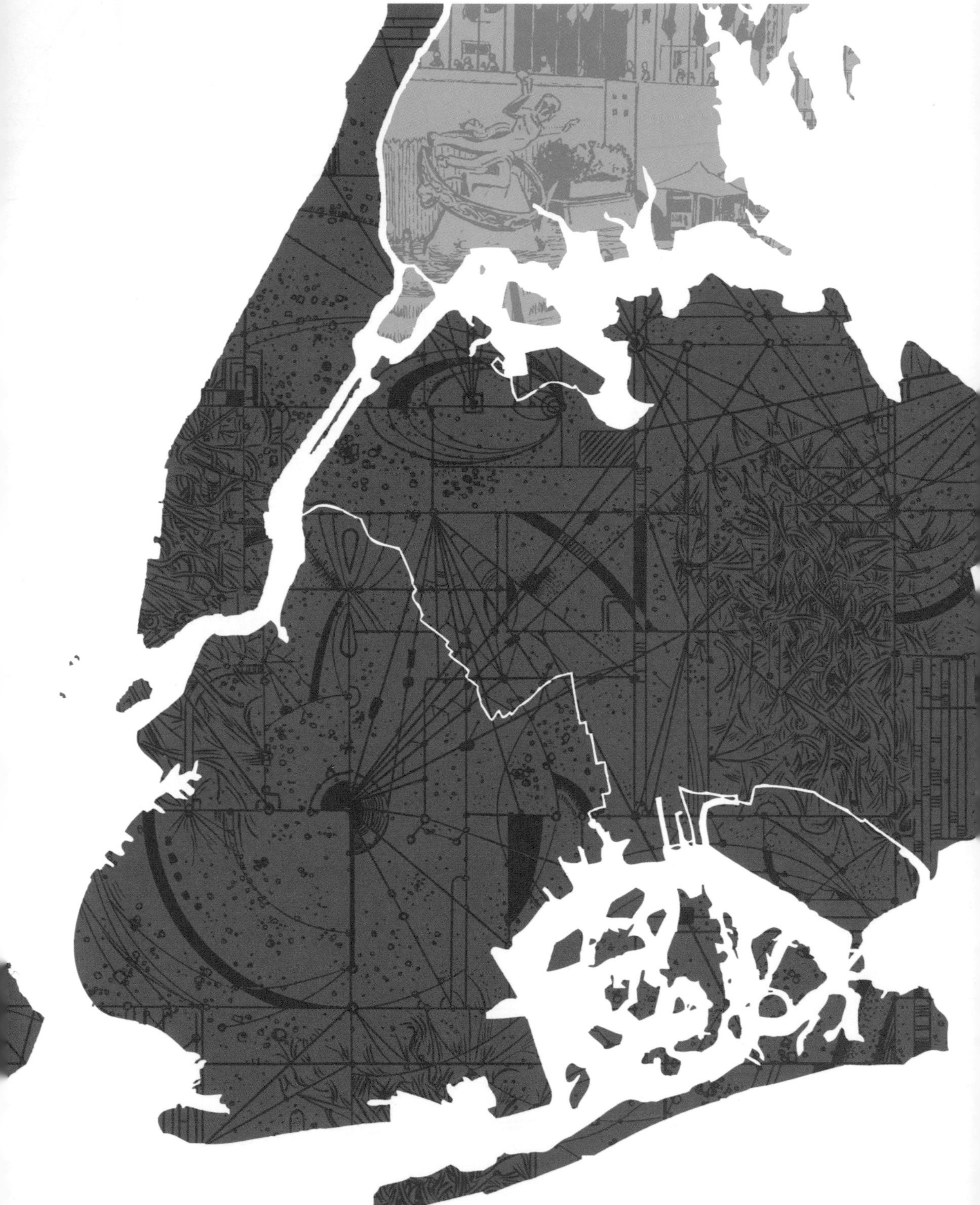

I ♥ New York. I mean, I really, truly love it. As of this writing, I've lived in NYC for almost sixteen years, the longest stretch I've lived anywhere. The first ten were in Manhattan, and the past six or so have been in Brooklyn. I've been extremely fortunate to travel quite a bit in my life - as a kid, my family lived in Asia, and my dad's job took us to a bunch of different places all over the world. While I haven't been to all of the world's great cities (South America and Africa remain galling blank spots in my travel history, along with India and the Middle East), I've gotten around. I can therefore unequivocally say that nowhere else I've been comes close to New York City.

The complexity here is unbelievable. You could spend a lifetime just trying to eat at each restaurant *once*. I think of it as fractal - the deeper you dig into any one aspect of the city, the more layers are revealed, each a reflection of the whole. Let's take music as just one example. New York has always had a thriving music scene. National acts come through and play the Garden or the all-new, all-shiny (except on the outside) Barclay's Center, slightly smaller bands might play the Beacon. Then you get down to the clubs, and then, down at the local level, it gets wild. There are thousands of bands in New York, featuring every genre you can think of, with literally some of the best musicians in the world. If you know what you're about, you can find music on any given Monday night in New York City that would... well, it would change things for you. You'd have to think things over a bit. There's so much music here that you can't get your head around the entirety of what's available. Even the music critics I know have to spend their careers focusing on one genre or another. It's incredible.

Now, take that level of fractal complexity and add in food, and art, and fashion, and finance, and infrastructure, and politics, and architecture, and any number of other things, layered up together like some sort of soufflé composed entirely of dreams, money, intensity, and despair. Amazing.

You can't fight New York. It will roll right over you if you try. The best you can hope for is to sort of surf the wave of the city's complexity. You can choose a piece of NYC and make it your emotional or literal home, but you can't understand this place. Not all of it at once. No one can do that.

But what if someone could?

That single idea was the impetus behind *Strange Attractors*. This city can be a hard place to live, even though it's an easy place to love. I wanted to write a story about a man who takes his immense love for New York City and uses his equally immense talents to make this place a little easier, a little safer. This city always seems to be teetering on the edge of one form of collapse or another (Hurricane Sandy having been just the most recent example of "NYC as disaster magnet"), and there are days where I really want to believe in Dr. Spencer Brownfield, grinding away, thankless, just keeping this marvelous machine going.

I don't think you have to love NYC or know it as well as I do to enjoy *Strange Attractors*. I do hope, however, that my love for this wonderful, terrifying place comes through in the book - and not just mine. Of the six creators who worked on this project, four are currently living in New York, and the editor went to college here (even though she abandoned us to go live in Los Angeles, of all places - my god). This is a New York book, through and through.

We ♥ NYC, and I'd like to think that despite everything, NYC ♥ us right back.

CHARLES SOULE
Brooklyn, NY
January, 2013

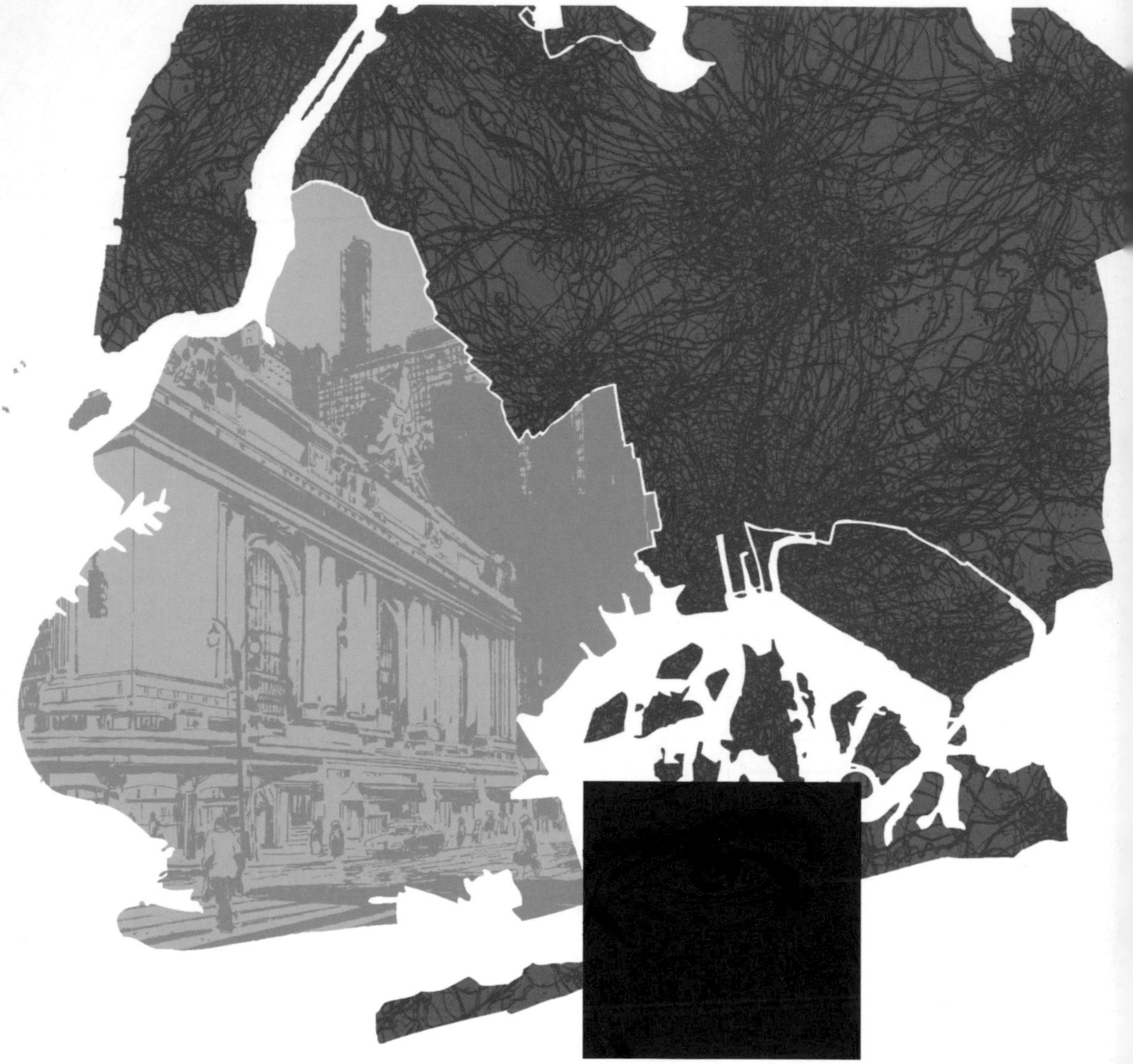

PART ONE

TANGLES IN THE TAPESTRY

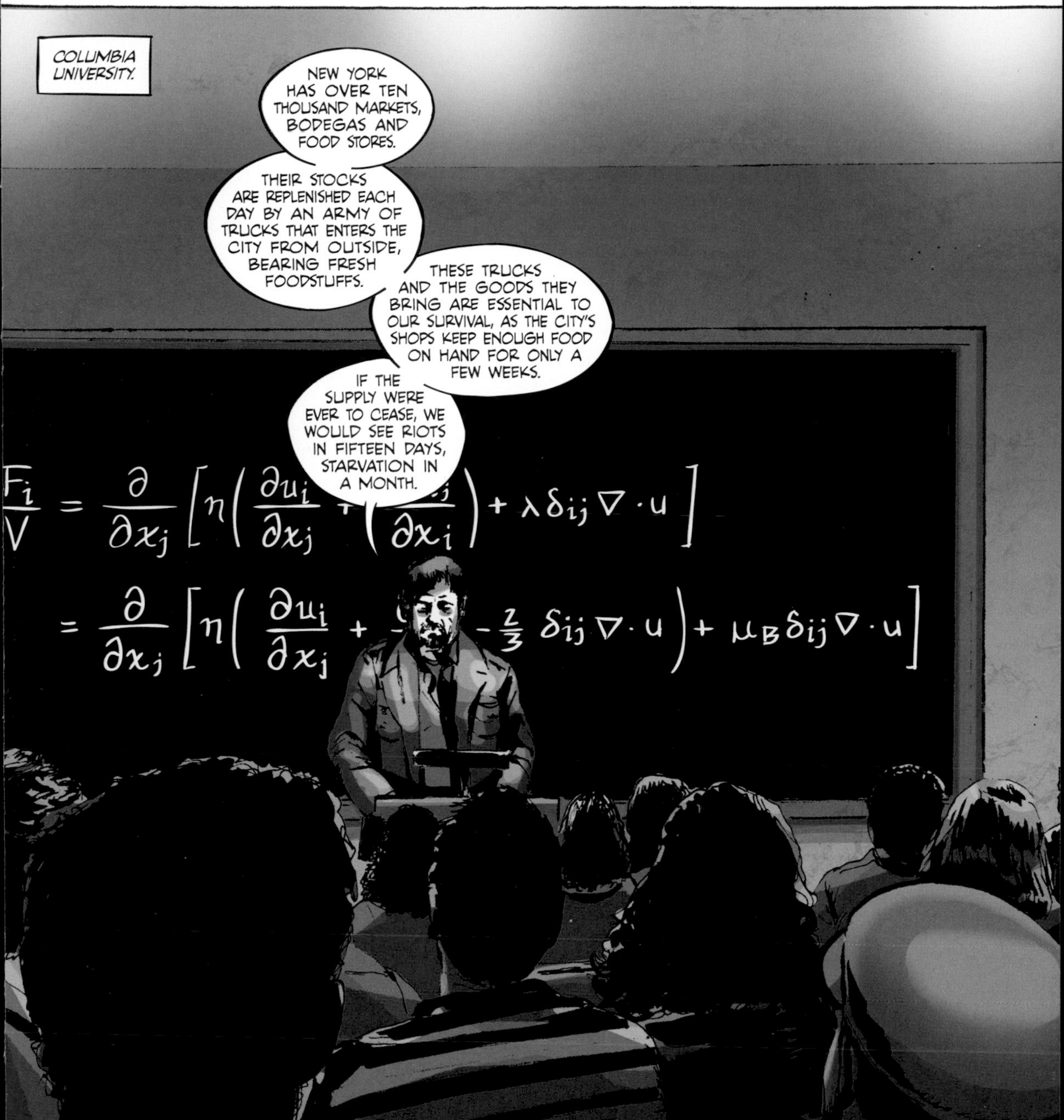
COLUMBIA UNIVERSITY.
NEW YORK HAS OVER TEN THOUSAND MARKETS, BODEGAS AND FOOD STORES.
THEIR STOCKS ARE REPLENISHED EACH DAY BY AN ARMY OF TRUCKS THAT ENTERS THE CITY FROM OUTSIDE, BEARING FRESH FOODSTUFFS.
THESE TRUCKS AND THE GOODS THEY BRING ARE ESSENTIAL TO OUR SURVIVAL, AS THE CITY'S SHOPS KEEP ENOUGH FOOD ON HAND FOR ONLY A FEW WEEKS.
IF THE SUPPLY WERE EVER TO CEASE, WE WOULD SEE RIOTS IN FIFTEEN DAYS, STARVATION IN A MONTH.

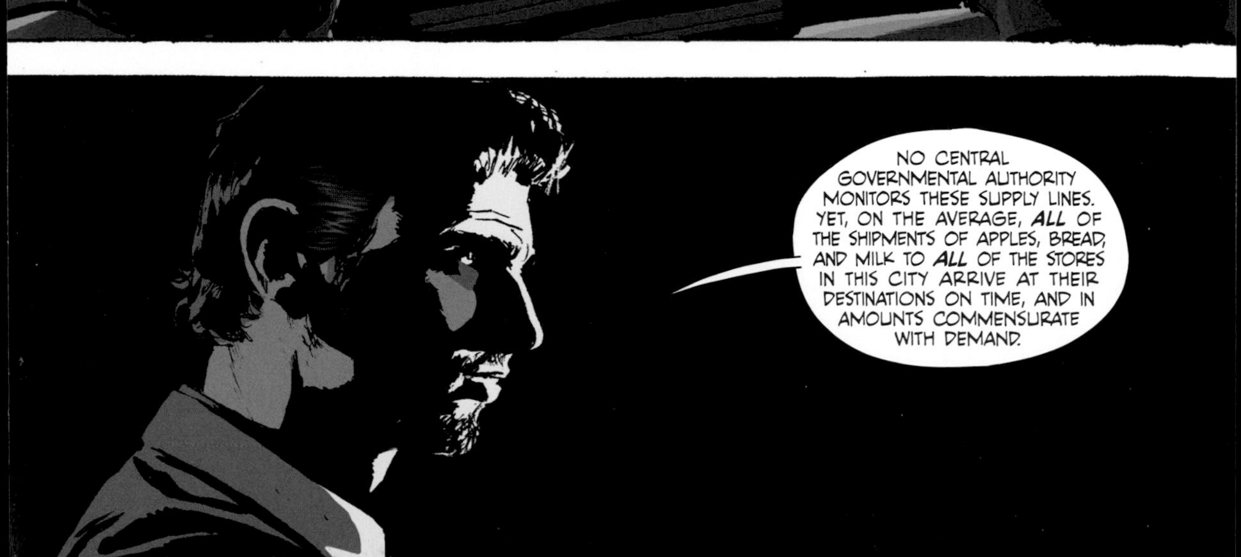
NO CENTRAL GOVERNMENTAL AUTHORITY MONITORS THESE SUPPLY LINES. YET, ON THE AVERAGE, ALL OF THE SHIPMENTS OF APPLES, BREAD, AND MILK TO ALL OF THE STORES IN THIS CITY ARRIVE AT THEIR DESTINATIONS ON TIME, AND IN AMOUNTS COMMENSURATE WITH DEMAND.

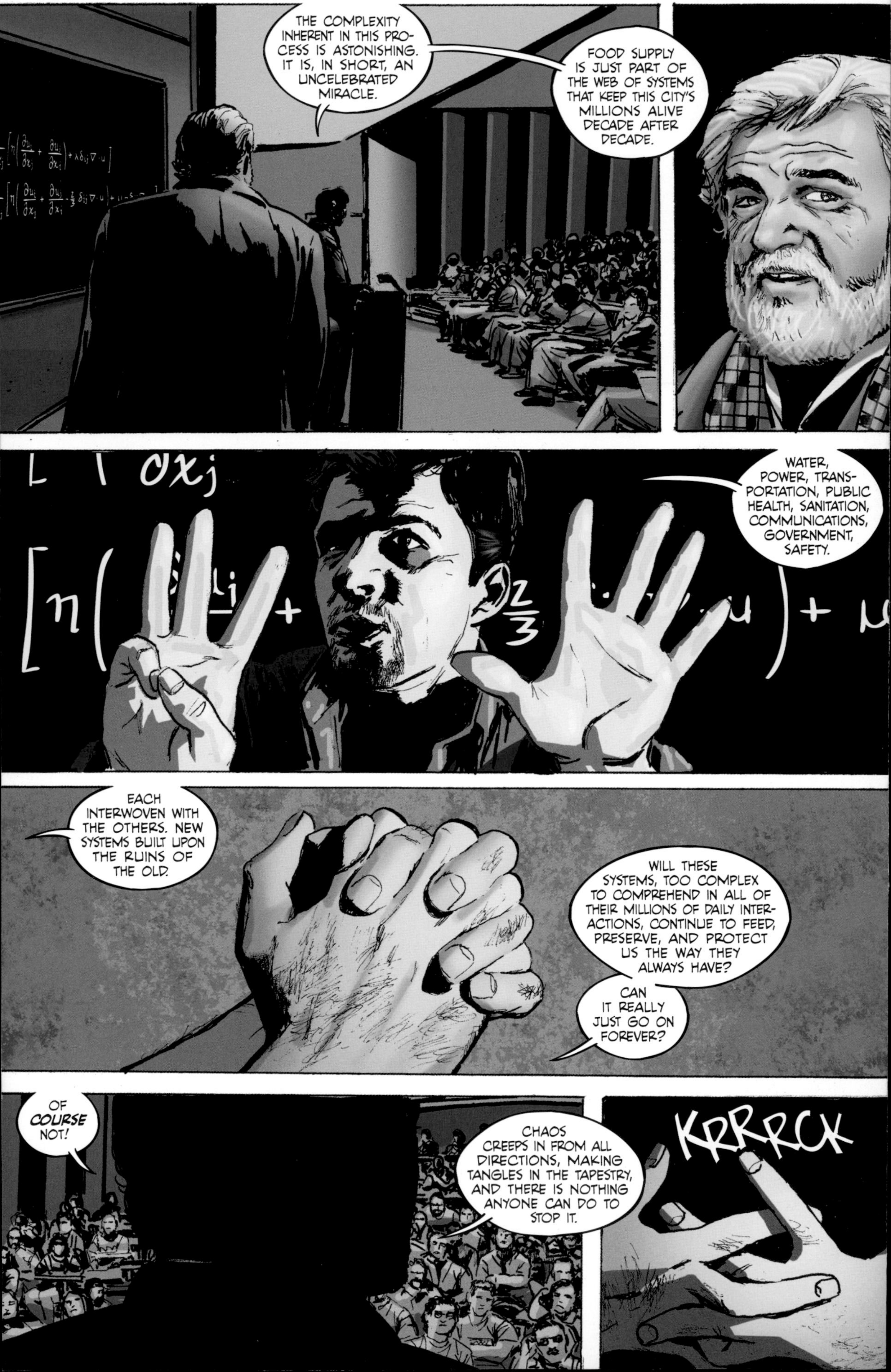
THE COMPLEXITY INHERENT IN THIS PROCESS IS ASTONISHING. IT IS, IN SHORT, AN UNCELEBRATED MIRACLE.
FOOD SUPPLY IS JUST PART OF THE WEB OF SYSTEMS THAT KEEP THIS CITY'S MILLIONS ALIVE DECADE AFTER DECADE.
WATER, POWER, TRANSPORTATION, PUBLIC HEALTH, SANITATION, COMMUNICATIONS, GOVERNMENT, SAFETY.
EACH INTERWOVEN WITH THE OTHERS. NEW SYSTEMS BUILT UPON THE RUINS OF THE OLD.
WILL THESE SYSTEMS, TOO COMPLEX TO COMPREHEND IN ALL OF THEIR MILLIONS OF DAILY INTERACTIONS, CONTINUE TO FEED, PRESERVE, AND PROTECT US THE WAY THEY ALWAYS HAVE?
CAN IT REALLY JUST GO ON FOREVER?
OF *COURSE* NOT!
CHAOS CREEPS IN FROM ALL DIRECTIONS, MAKING TANGLES IN THE TAPESTRY, AND THERE IS NOTHING ANYONE CAN DO TO STOP IT.
KRRRCK

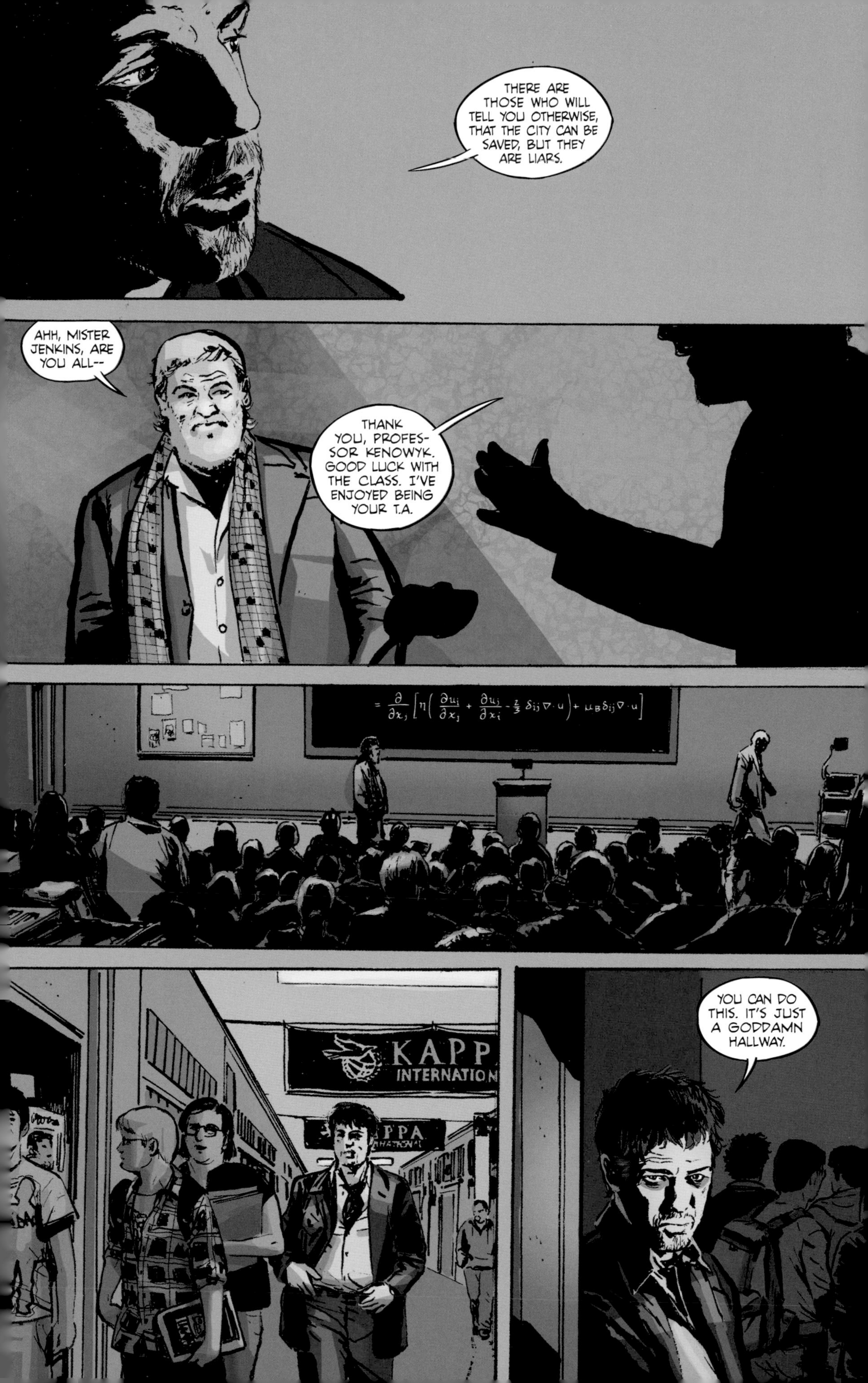
THERE ARE THOSE WHO WILL TELL YOU OTHERWISE, THAT THE CITY CAN BE SAVED, BUT THEY ARE LIARS.
AHH, MISTER JENKINS, ARE YOU ALL--
THANK YOU, PROFESSOR KENOWYK. GOOD LUCK WITH THE CLASS. I'VE ENJOYED BEING YOUR T.A.
$= \frac{\partial}{\partial x_j}\left[\eta\left(\frac{\partial u_i}{\partial x_j} + \frac{\partial u_j}{\partial x_i} - \frac{2}{3}\delta_{ij}\nabla\cdot u\right) + \mu_B \delta_{ij}\nabla\cdot u\right]$
KAPPA INTERNATION
YOU CAN DO THIS. IT'S JUST A GODDAMN HALLWAY.

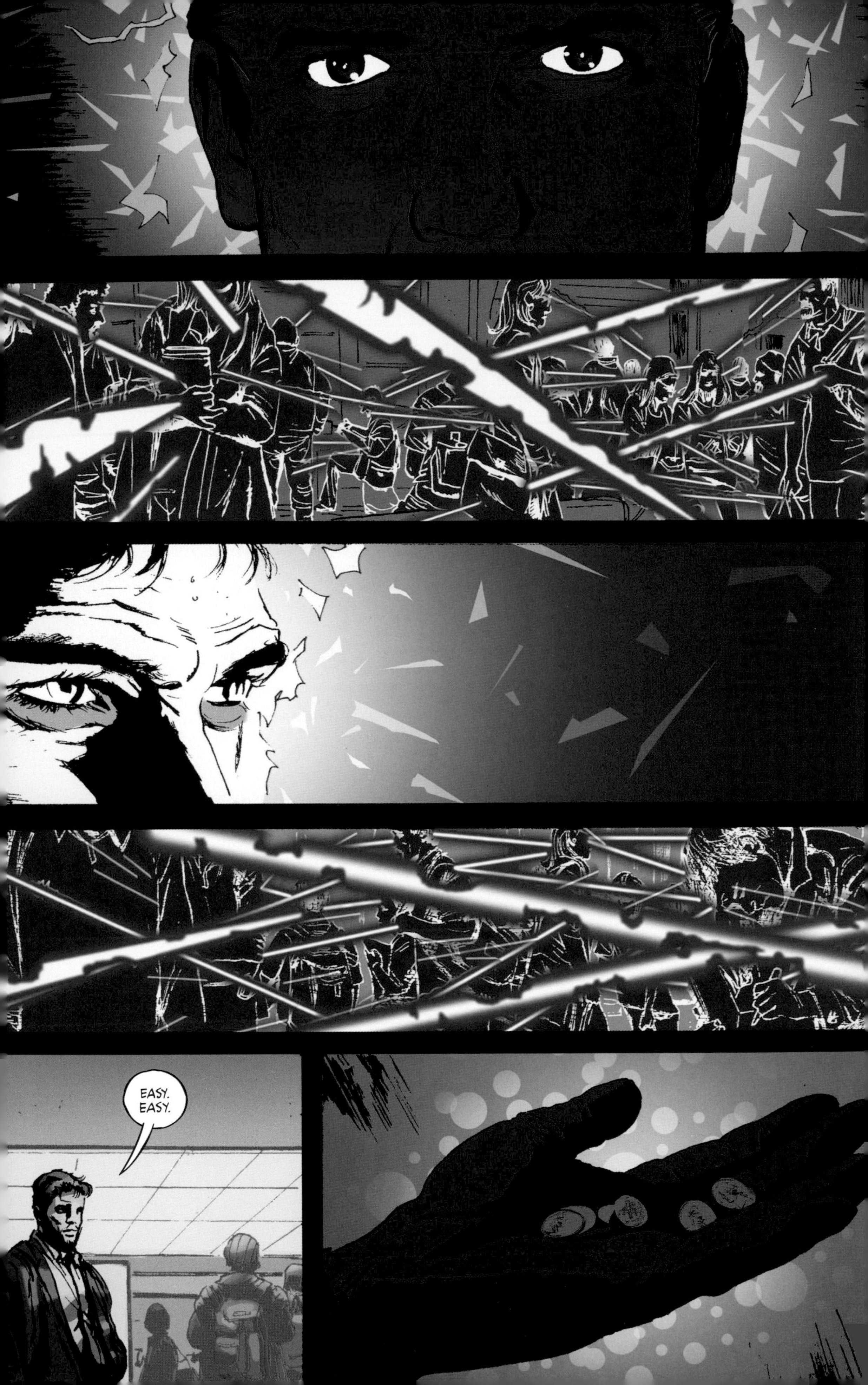
EASY. EASY.

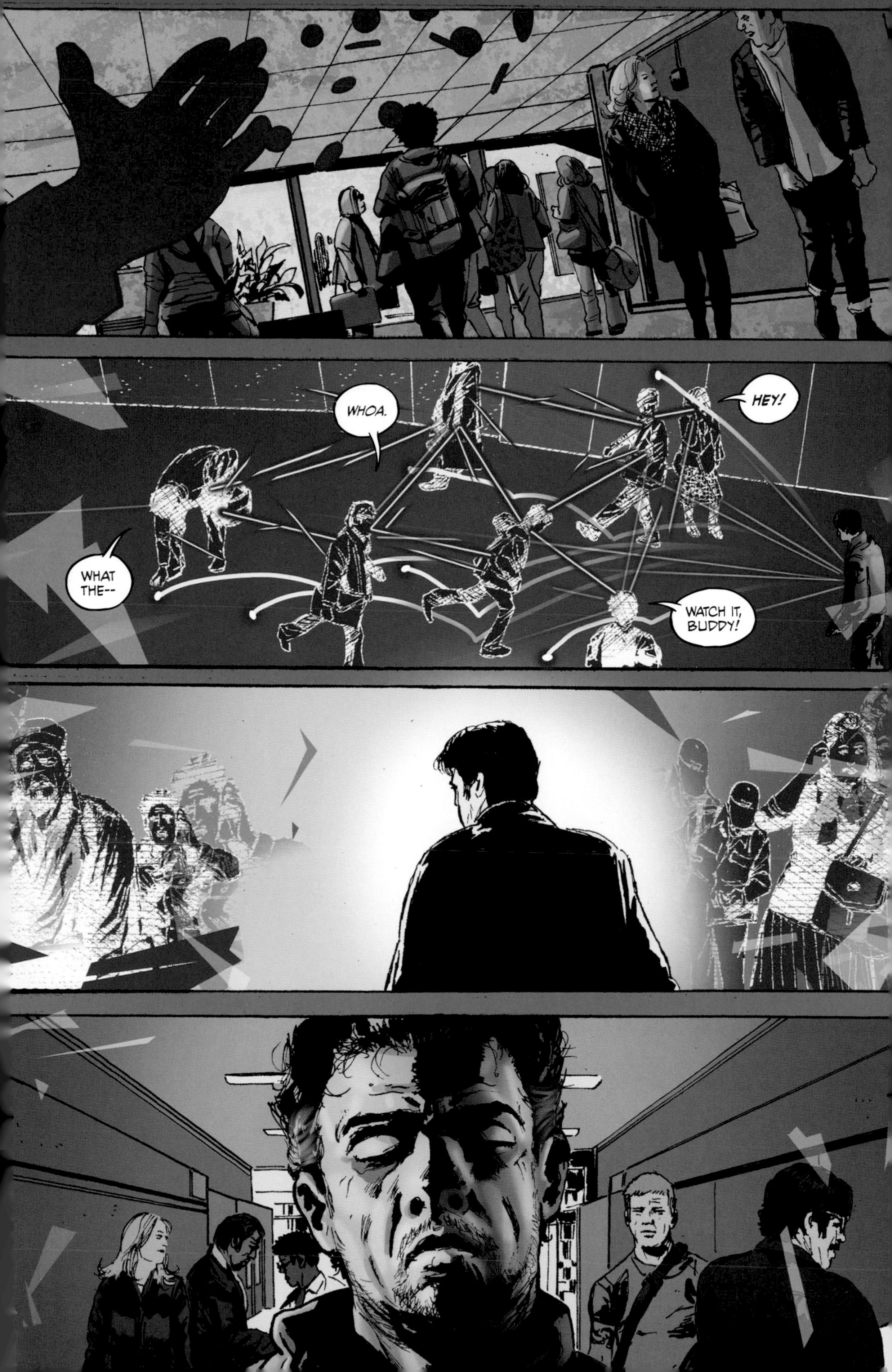
WHOA.
HEY!
WHAT THE--
WATCH IT, BUDDY!

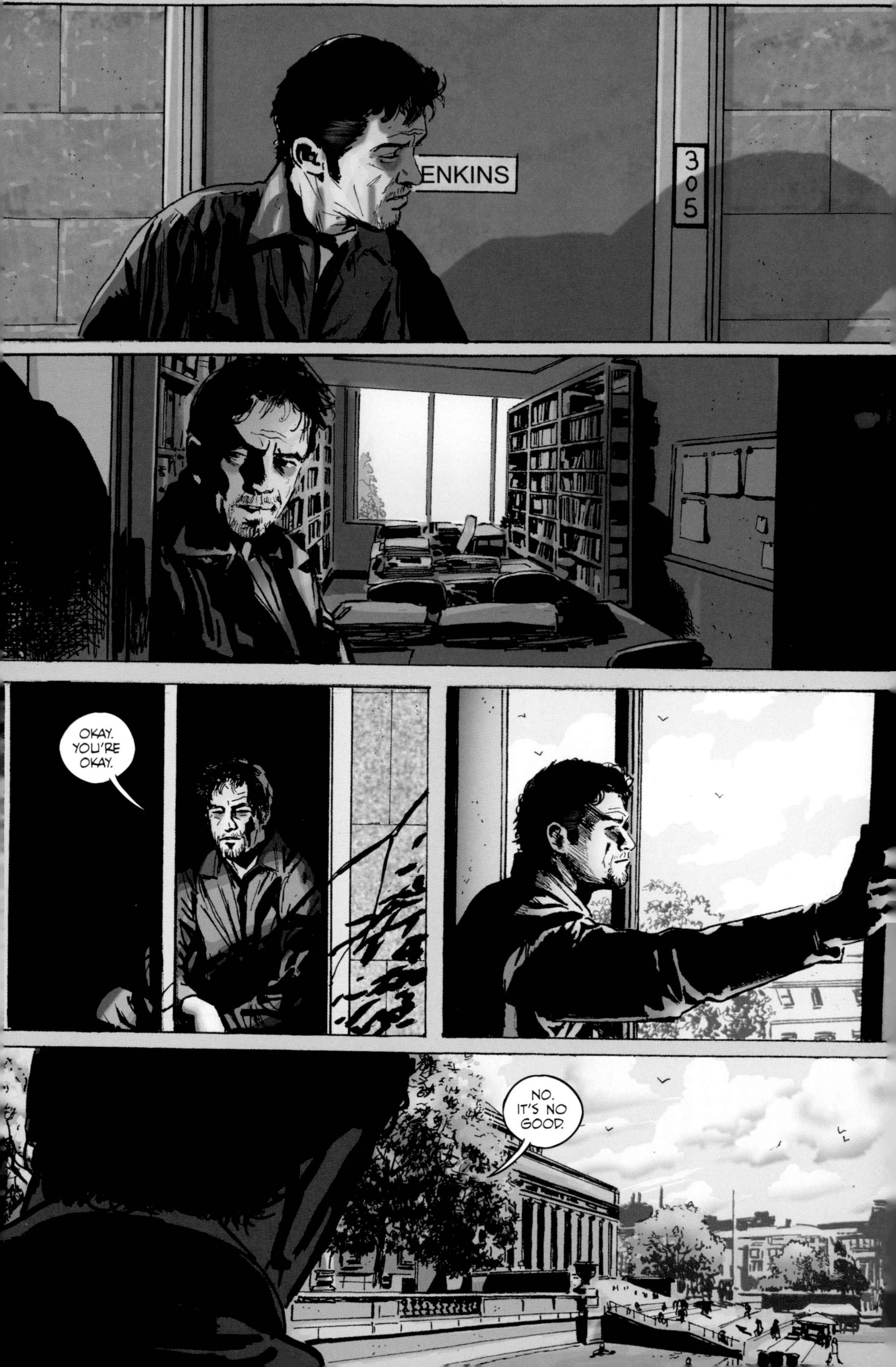
ENKINS
305
OKAY. YOU'RE OKAY.
NO. IT'S NO GOOD.

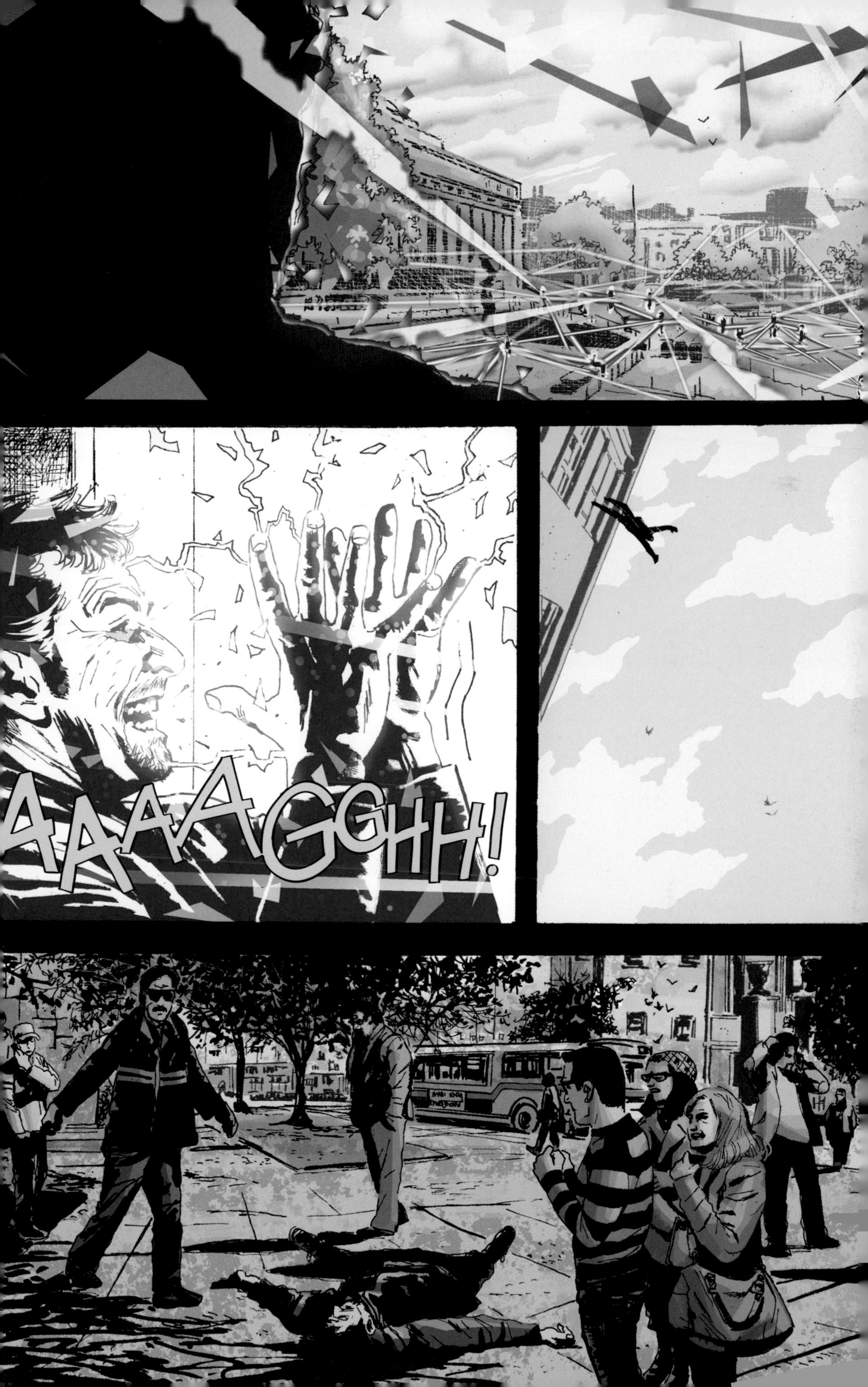
AAAAGGHH!

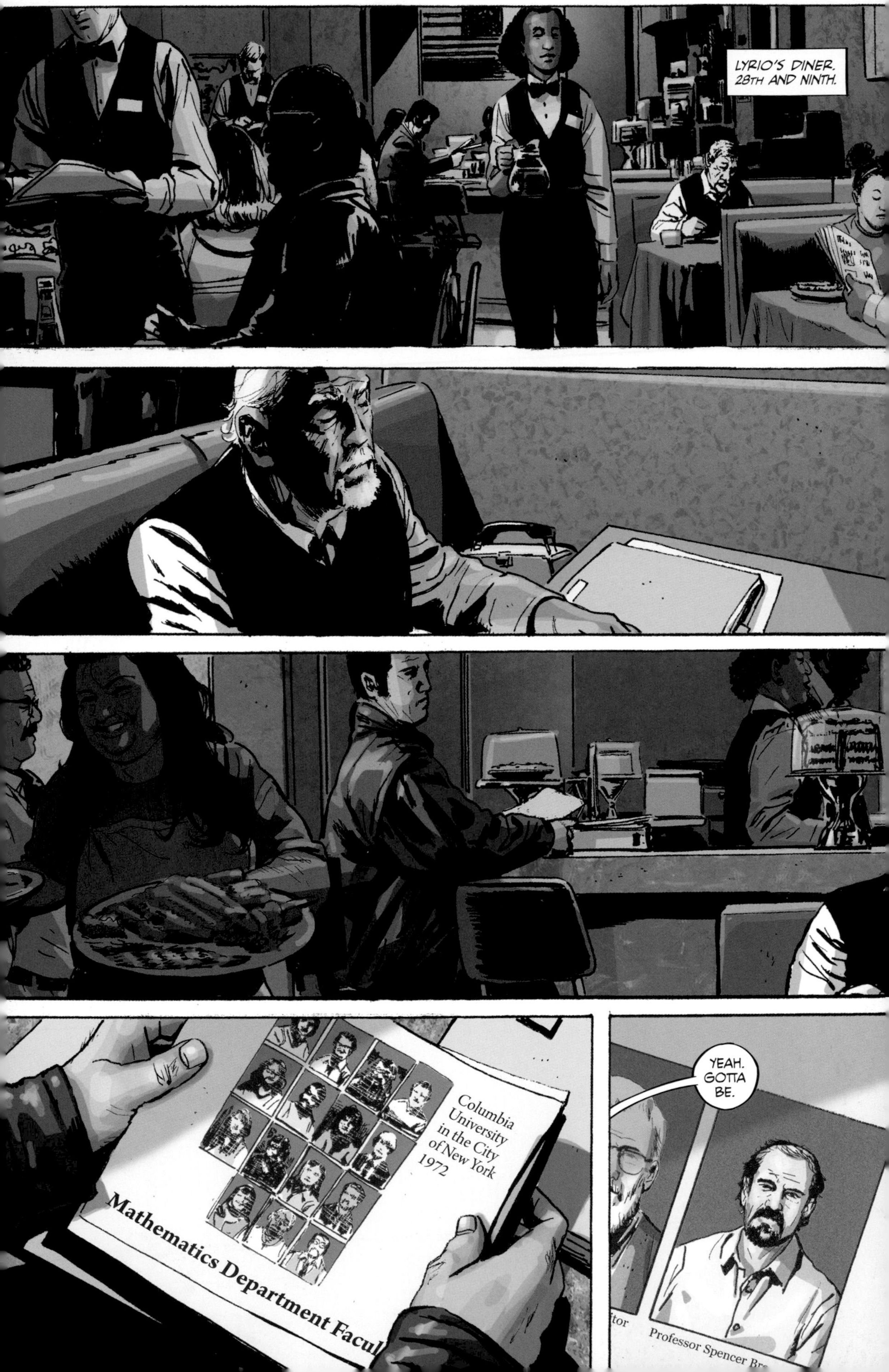
LYRIO'S DINER. 28TH AND NINTH.
Columbia University in the City of New York 1972
Mathematics Department Facul
YEAH. GOTTA BE.
tor
Professor Spencer Br

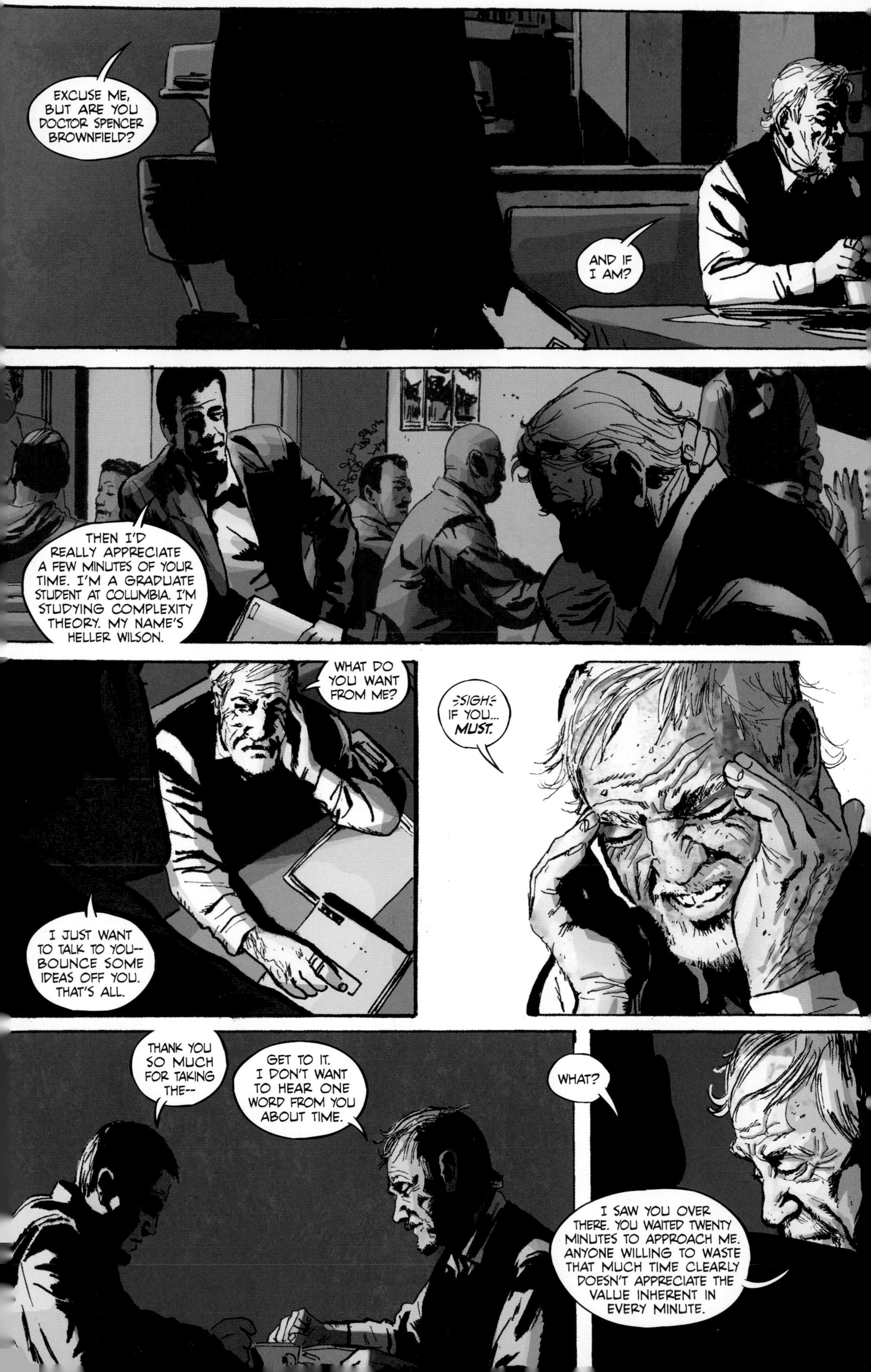
EXCUSE ME, BUT ARE YOU DOCTOR SPENCER BROWNFIELD?
AND IF I AM?
THEN I'D REALLY APPRECIATE A FEW MINUTES OF YOUR TIME. I'M A GRADUATE STUDENT AT COLUMBIA. I'M STUDYING COMPLEXITY THEORY. MY NAME'S HELLER WILSON.
WHAT DO YOU WANT FROM ME?
I JUST WANT TO TALK TO YOU-- BOUNCE SOME IDEAS OFF YOU. THAT'S ALL.
SIGH IF YOU... MUST.
THANK YOU SO MUCH FOR TAKING THE--
GET TO IT. I DON'T WANT TO HEAR ONE WORD FROM YOU ABOUT TIME.
WHAT?
I SAW YOU OVER THERE. YOU WAITED TWENTY MINUTES TO APPROACH ME. ANYONE WILLING TO WASTE THAT MUCH TIME CLEARLY DOESN'T APPRECIATE THE VALUE INHERENT IN EVERY MINUTE.

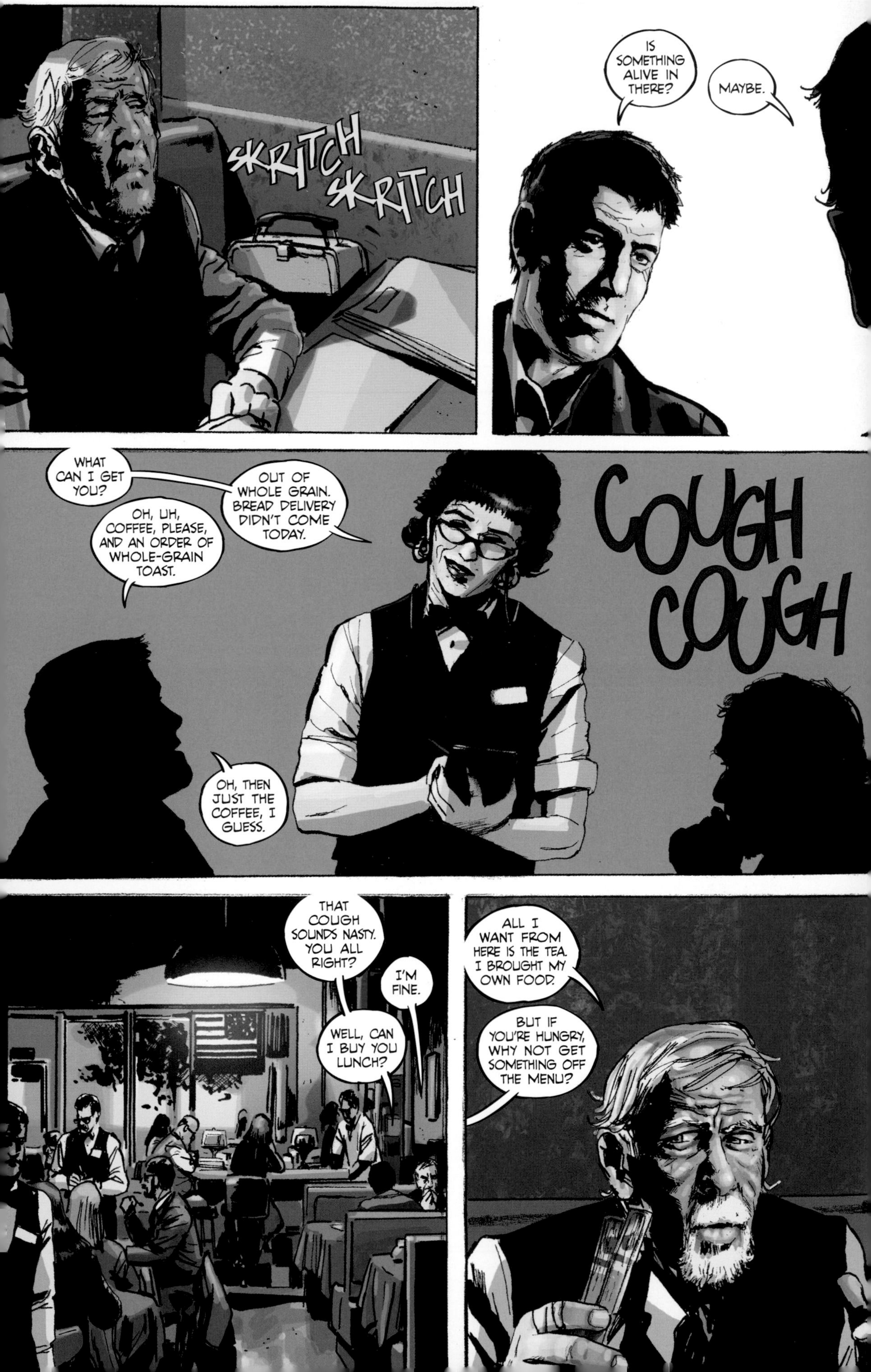
SKRITCH SKRITCH
IS SOMETHING ALIVE IN THERE?
MAYBE.
WHAT CAN I GET YOU?
OH, UH, COFFEE, PLEASE, AND AN ORDER OF WHOLE-GRAIN TOAST.
OUT OF WHOLE GRAIN. BREAD DELIVERY DIDN'T COME TODAY.
OH, THEN JUST THE COFFEE, I GUESS.
COUGH COUGH
THAT COUGH SOUNDS NASTY. YOU ALL RIGHT?
I'M FINE.
WELL, CAN I BUY YOU LUNCH?
ALL I WANT FROM HERE IS THE TEA. I BROUGHT MY OWN FOOD.
BUT IF YOU'RE HUNGRY, WHY NOT GET SOMETHING OFF THE MENU?

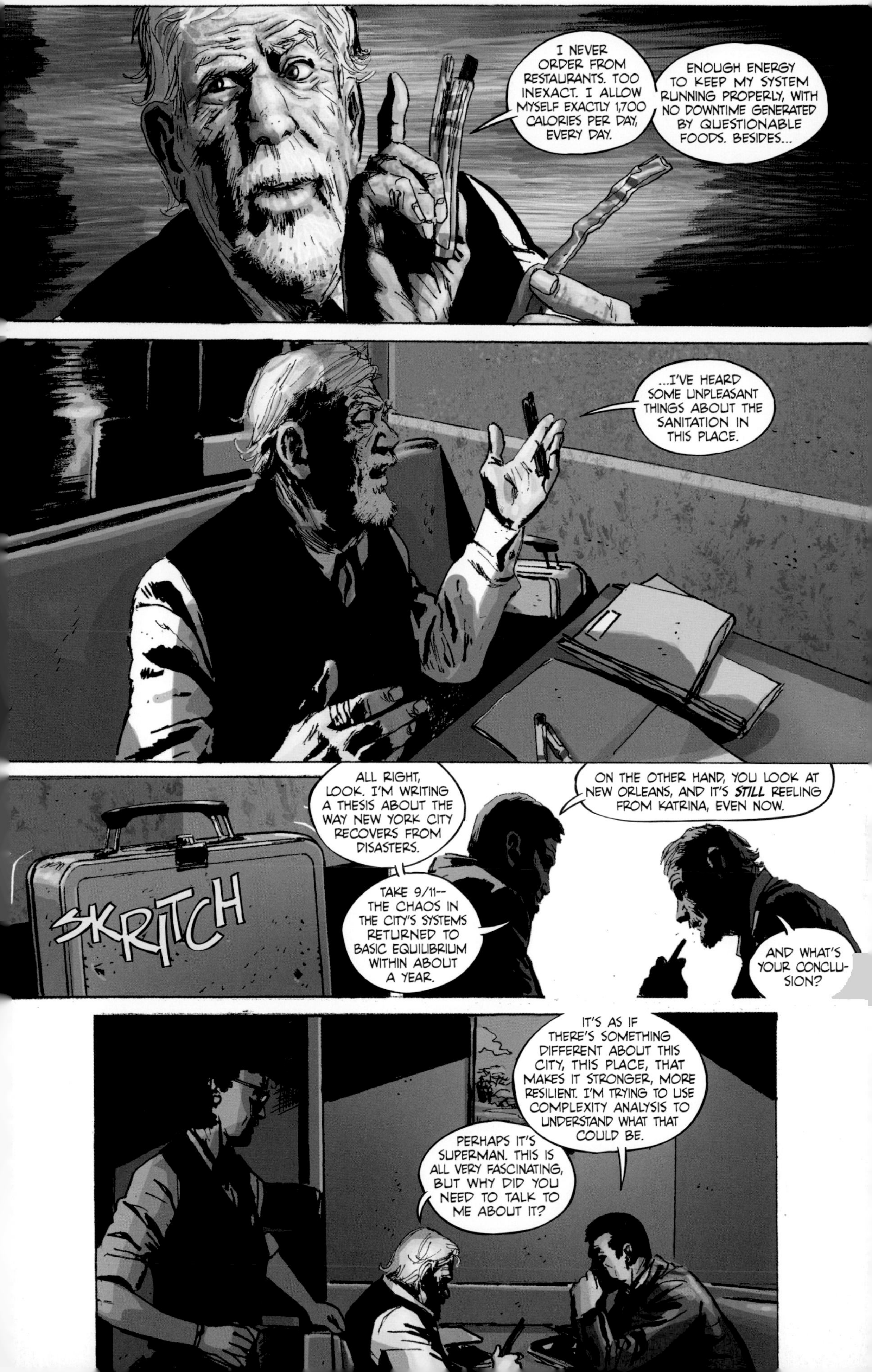
I NEVER ORDER FROM RESTAURANTS. TOO INEXACT. I ALLOW MYSELF EXACTLY 1,700 CALORIES PER DAY, EVERY DAY.
ENOUGH ENERGY TO KEEP MY SYSTEM RUNNING PROPERLY, WITH NO DOWNTIME GENERATED BY QUESTIONABLE FOODS. BESIDES...
...I'VE HEARD SOME UNPLEASANT THINGS ABOUT THE SANITATION IN THIS PLACE.
ALL RIGHT, LOOK. I'M WRITING A THESIS ABOUT THE WAY NEW YORK CITY RECOVERS FROM DISASTERS.
TAKE 9/11-- THE CHAOS IN THE CITY'S SYSTEMS RETURNED TO BASIC EQUILIBRIUM WITHIN ABOUT A YEAR.
SKRITCH
ON THE OTHER HAND, YOU LOOK AT NEW ORLEANS, AND IT'S *STILL* REELING FROM KATRINA, EVEN NOW.
AND WHAT'S YOUR CONCLU-SION?
IT'S AS IF THERE'S SOMETHING DIFFERENT ABOUT THIS CITY, THIS PLACE, THAT MAKES IT STRONGER, MORE RESILIENT. I'M TRYING TO USE COMPLEXITY ANALYSIS TO UNDERSTAND WHAT THAT COULD BE.
PERHAPS IT'S SUPERMAN. THIS IS ALL VERY FASCINATING, BUT WHY DID YOU NEED TO TALK TO ME ABOUT IT?

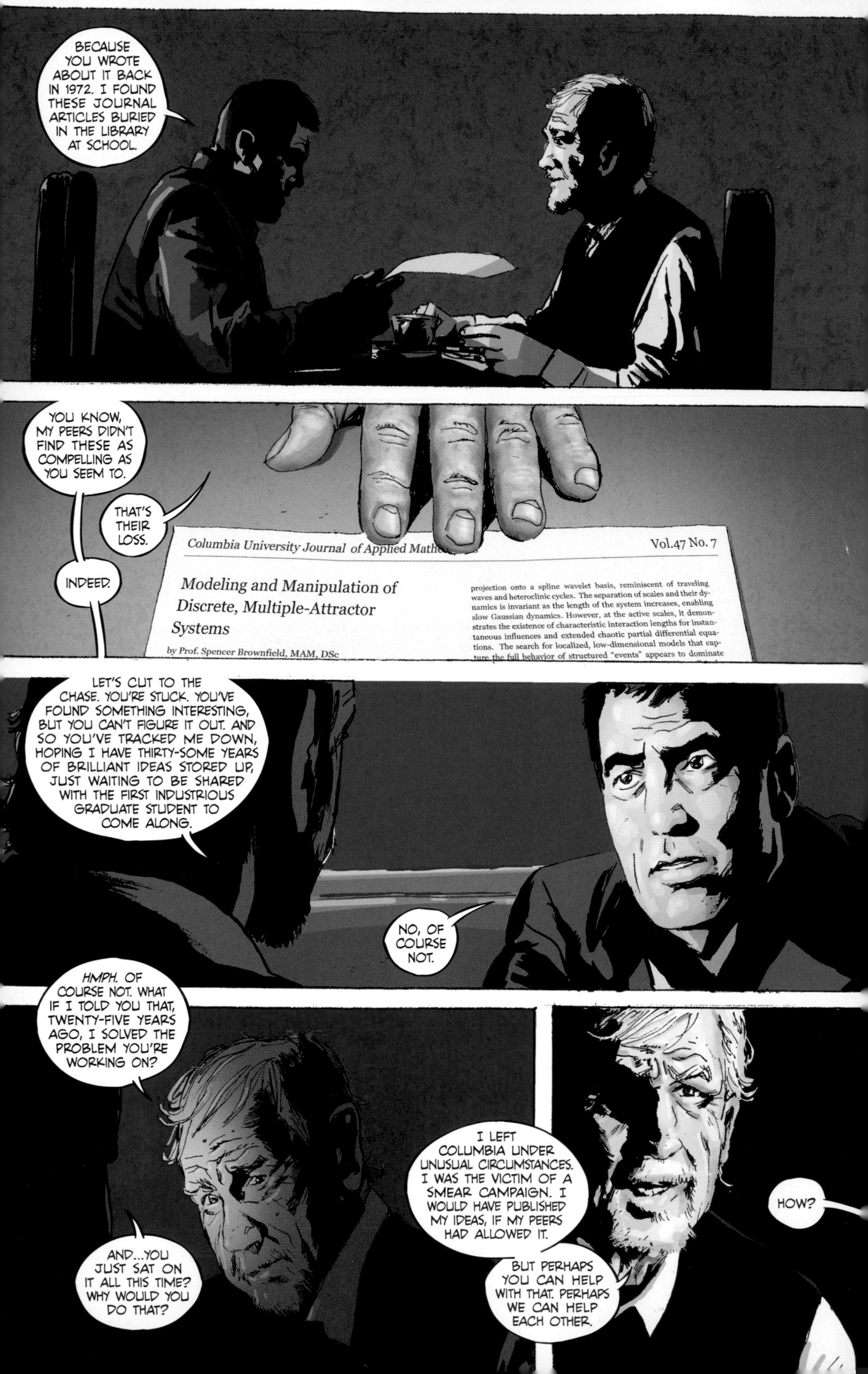
BECAUSE YOU WROTE ABOUT IT BACK IN 1972. I FOUND THESE JOURNAL ARTICLES BURIED IN THE LIBRARY AT SCHOOL.
YOU KNOW, MY PEERS DIDN'T FIND THESE AS COMPELLING AS YOU SEEM TO.
THAT'S THEIR LOSS.
INDEED.
Columbia University Journal of Applied Mathe
Vol.47 No. 7
Modeling and Manipulation of Discrete, Multiple-Attractor Systems
by Prof. Spencer Brownfield, MAM, DSc
projection onto a spline wavelet basis, reminiscent of traveling waves and heteroclinic cycles. The separation of scales and their dynamics is invariant as the length of the system increases, enabling slow Gaussian dynamics. However, at the active scales, it demonstrates the existence of characteristic interaction lengths for instantaneous influences and extended chaotic partial differential equations. The search for localized, low-dimensional models that capture the full behavior of structured "events" appears to dominate
LET'S CUT TO THE CHASE. YOU'RE STUCK. YOU'VE FOUND SOMETHING INTERESTING, BUT YOU CAN'T FIGURE IT OUT. AND SO YOU'VE TRACKED ME DOWN, HOPING I HAVE THIRTY-SOME YEARS OF BRILLIANT IDEAS STORED UP, JUST WAITING TO BE SHARED WITH THE FIRST INDUSTRIOUS GRADUATE STUDENT TO COME ALONG.
NO, OF COURSE NOT.
HMPH. OF COURSE NOT. WHAT IF I TOLD YOU THAT, TWENTY-FIVE YEARS AGO, I SOLVED THE PROBLEM YOU'RE WORKING ON?
AND...YOU JUST SAT ON IT ALL THIS TIME? WHY WOULD YOU DO THAT?
I LEFT COLUMBIA UNDER UNUSUAL CIRCUMSTANCES. I WAS THE VICTIM OF A SMEAR CAMPAIGN. I WOULD HAVE PUBLISHED MY IDEAS, IF MY PEERS HAD ALLOWED IT.
HOW?
BUT PERHAPS YOU CAN HELP WITH THAT. PERHAPS WE CAN HELP EACH OTHER.

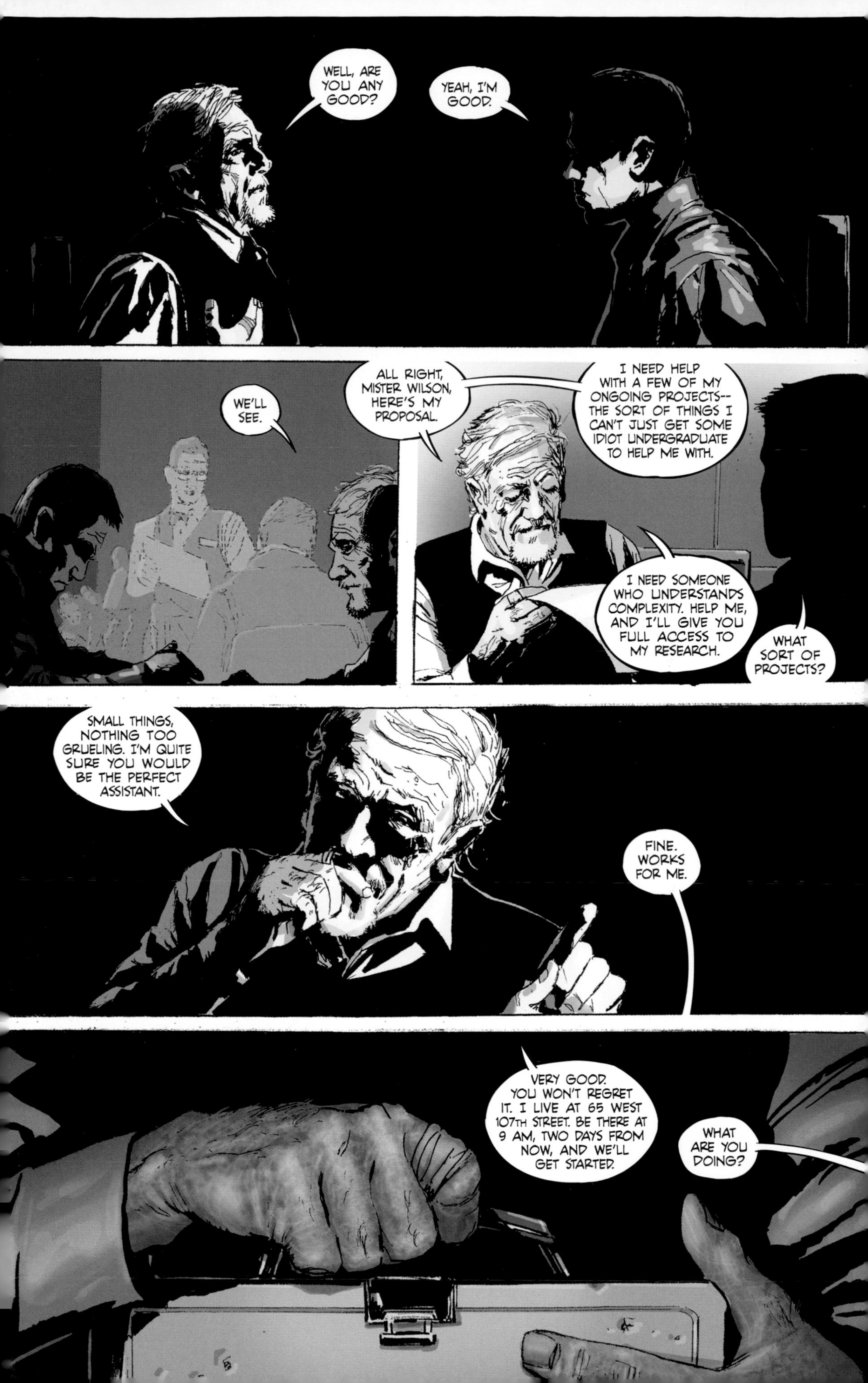
WELL, ARE YOU ANY GOOD?
YEAH, I'M GOOD.
WE'LL SEE.
ALL RIGHT, MISTER WILSON, HERE'S MY PROPOSAL.
I NEED HELP WITH A FEW OF MY ONGOING PROJECTS-- THE SORT OF THINGS I CAN'T JUST GET SOME IDIOT UNDERGRADUATE TO HELP ME WITH.
I NEED SOMEONE WHO UNDERSTANDS COMPLEXITY. HELP ME, AND I'LL GIVE YOU FULL ACCESS TO MY RESEARCH.
WHAT SORT OF PROJECTS?
SMALL THINGS, NOTHING TOO GRUELING. I'M QUITE SURE YOU WOULD BE THE PERFECT ASSISTANT.
FINE. WORKS FOR ME.
VERY GOOD. YOU WON'T REGRET IT. I LIVE AT 65 WEST 107TH STREET. BE THERE AT 9 AM, TWO DAYS FROM NOW, AND WE'LL GET STARTED.
WHAT ARE YOU DOING?

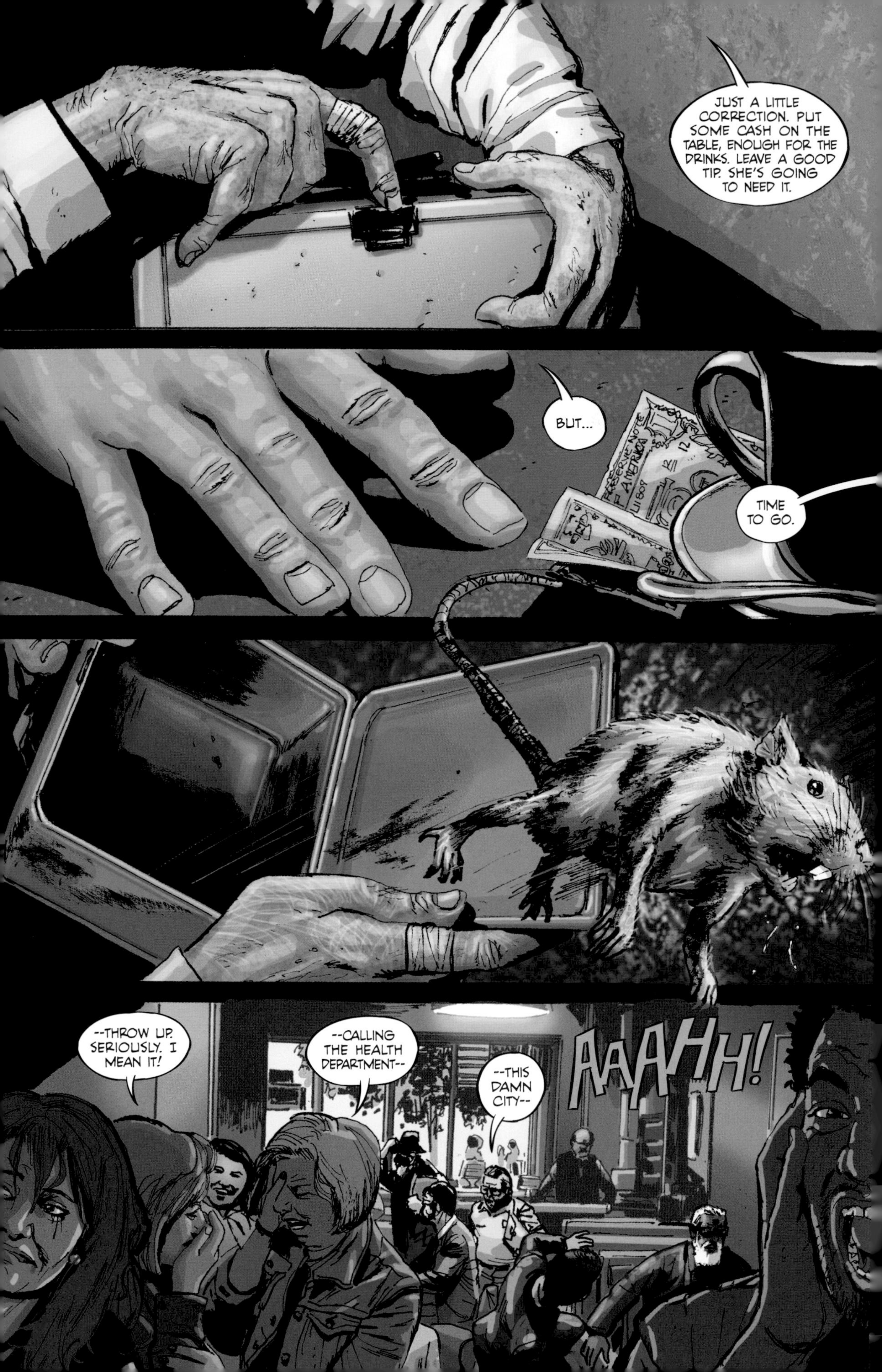

JUST A LITTLE CORRECTION. PUT SOME CASH ON THE TABLE, ENOUGH FOR THE DRINKS. LEAVE A GOOD TIP. SHE'S GOING TO NEED IT.
BUT...
TIME TO GO.
--THROW UP. SERIOUSLY. I MEAN IT!
--CALLING THE HEALTH DEPARTMENT--
--THIS DAMN CITY--
AAAHH!

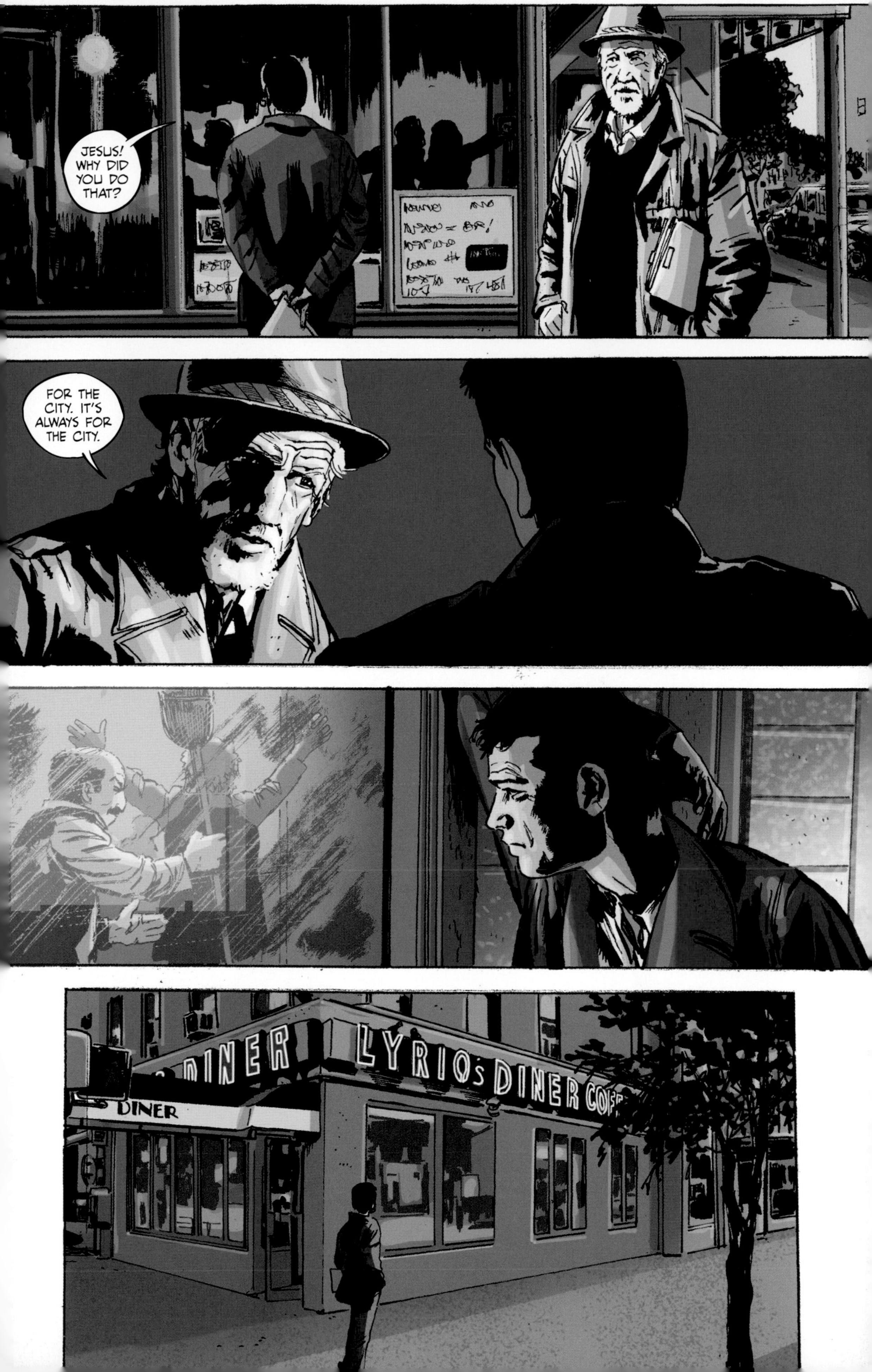
JESUS! WHY DID YOU DO THAT?
FOR THE CITY. IT'S ALWAYS FOR THE CITY.
DINER
LYRIO'S DINER COF
DINER

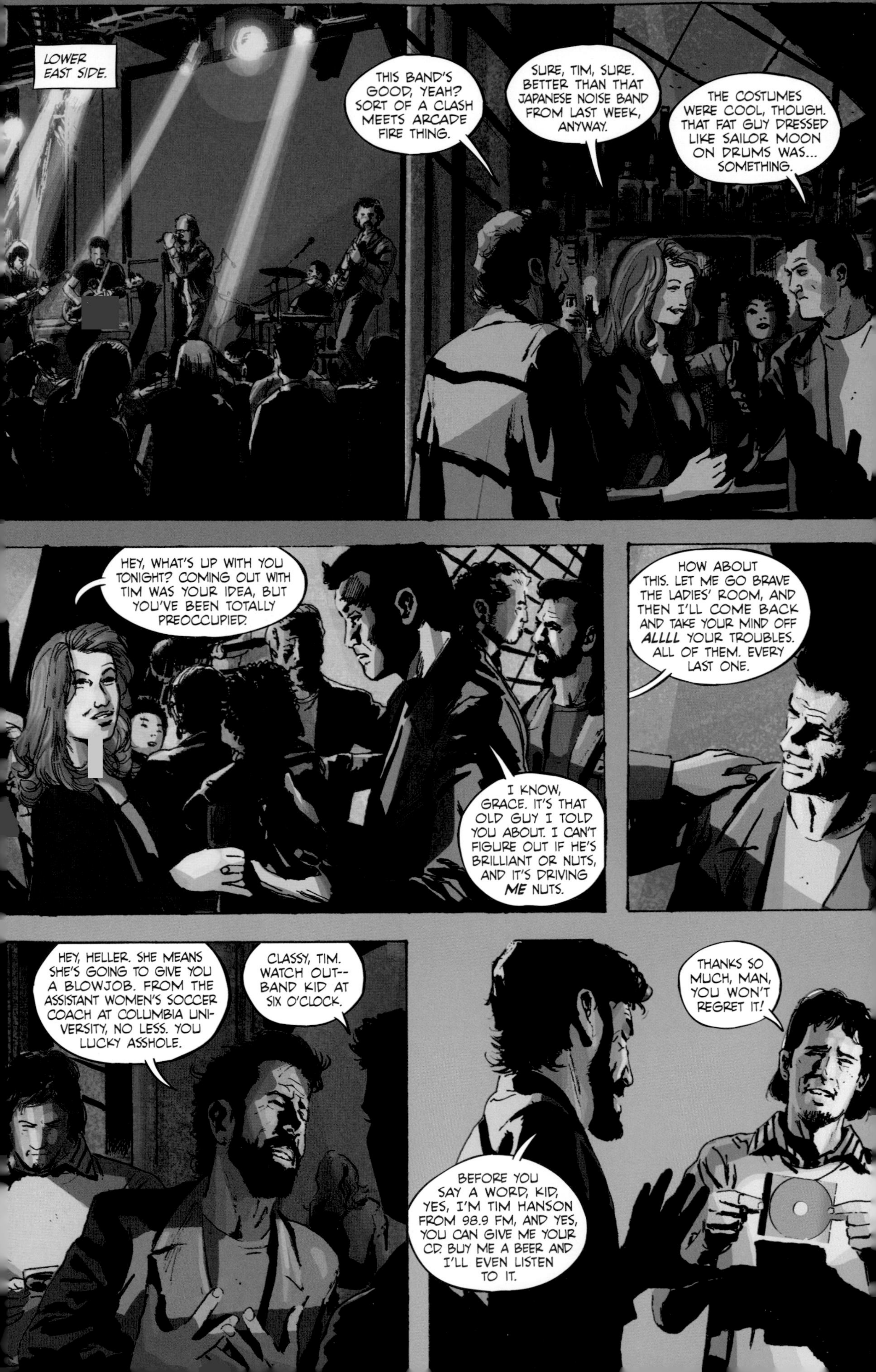
LOWER EAST SIDE.
THIS BAND'S GOOD, YEAH? SORT OF A CLASH MEETS ARCADE FIRE THING.
SURE, TIM, SURE. BETTER THAN THAT JAPANESE NOISE BAND FROM LAST WEEK, ANYWAY.
THE COSTUMES WERE COOL, THOUGH. THAT FAT GUY DRESSED LIKE SAILOR MOON ON DRUMS WAS... SOMETHING.
HEY, WHAT'S UP WITH YOU TONIGHT? COMING OUT WITH TIM WAS YOUR IDEA, BUT YOU'VE BEEN TOTALLY PREOCCUPIED.
I KNOW, GRACE. IT'S THAT OLD GUY I TOLD YOU ABOUT. I CAN'T FIGURE OUT IF HE'S BRILLIANT OR NUTS, AND IT'S DRIVING ME NUTS.
HOW ABOUT THIS. LET ME GO BRAVE THE LADIES' ROOM, AND THEN I'LL COME BACK AND TAKE YOUR MIND OFF ALLLL YOUR TROUBLES. ALL OF THEM. EVERY LAST ONE.
HEY, HELLER. SHE MEANS SHE'S GOING TO GIVE YOU A BLOWJOB. FROM THE ASSISTANT WOMEN'S SOCCER COACH AT COLUMBIA UNIVERSITY, NO LESS. YOU LUCKY ASSHOLE.
CLASSY, TIM. WATCH OUT-- BAND KID AT SIX O'CLOCK.
THANKS SO MUCH, MAN, YOU WON'T REGRET IT!
BEFORE YOU SAY A WORD, KID, YES, I'M TIM HANSON FROM 98.9 FM, AND YES, YOU CAN GIVE ME YOUR CD. BUY ME A BEER AND I'LL EVEN LISTEN TO IT.

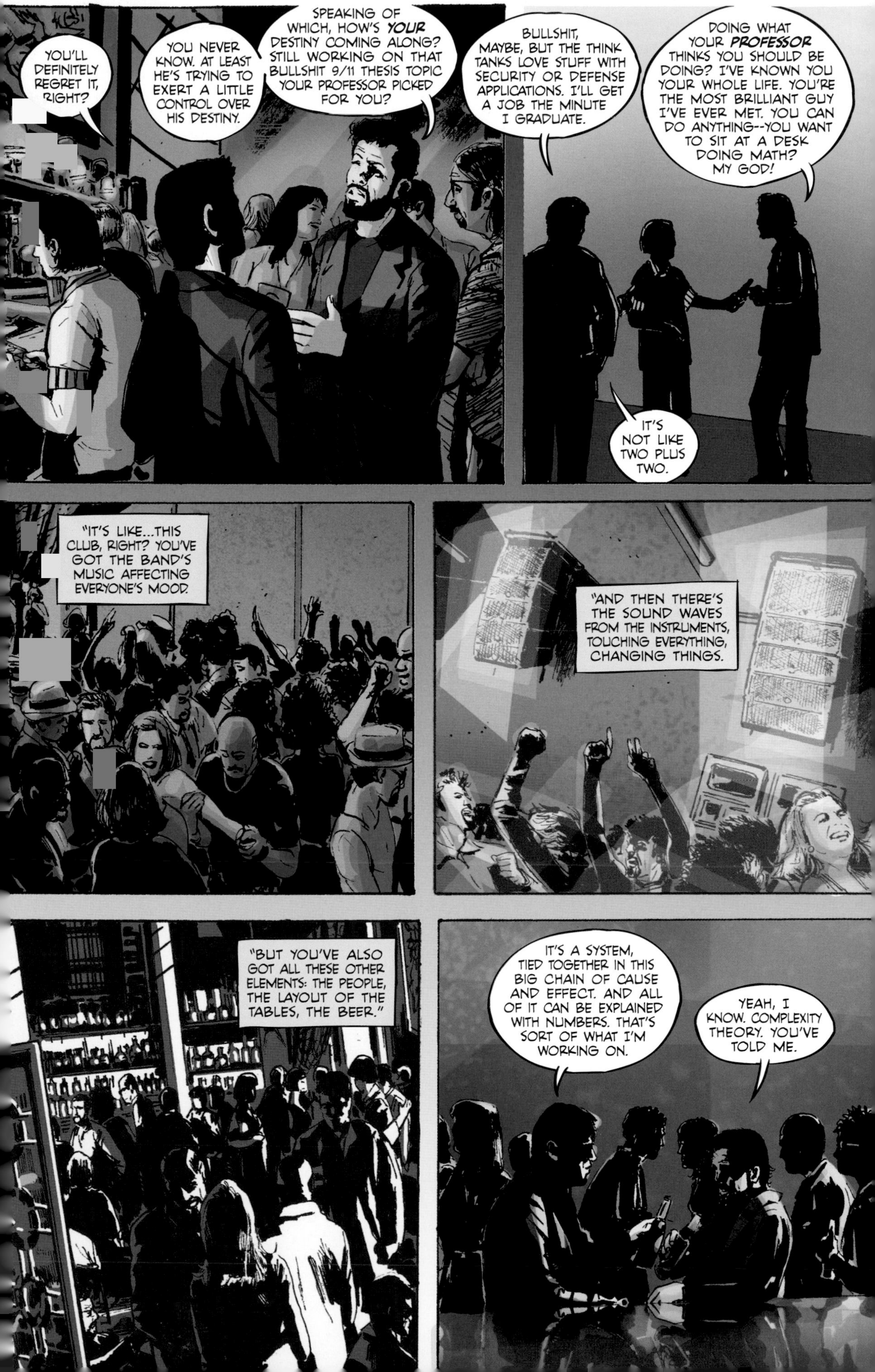
YOU'LL DEFINITELY REGRET IT, RIGHT?
YOU NEVER KNOW. AT LEAST HE'S TRYING TO EXERT A LITTLE CONTROL OVER HIS DESTINY.
SPEAKING OF WHICH, HOW'S YOUR DESTINY COMING ALONG? STILL WORKING ON THAT BULLSHIT 9/11 THESIS TOPIC YOUR PROFESSOR PICKED FOR YOU?
BULLSHIT, MAYBE, BUT THE THINK TANKS LOVE STUFF WITH SECURITY OR DEFENSE APPLICATIONS. I'LL GET A JOB THE MINUTE I GRADUATE.
DOING WHAT YOUR PROFESSOR THINKS YOU SHOULD BE DOING? I'VE KNOWN YOU YOUR WHOLE LIFE. YOU'RE THE MOST BRILLIANT GUY I'VE EVER MET. YOU CAN DO ANYTHING--YOU WANT TO SIT AT A DESK DOING MATH? MY GOD!
IT'S NOT LIKE TWO PLUS TWO.
"IT'S LIKE...THIS CLUB, RIGHT? YOU'VE GOT THE BAND'S MUSIC AFFECTING EVERYONE'S MOOD.
"AND THEN THERE'S THE SOUND WAVES FROM THE INSTRUMENTS, TOUCHING EVERYTHING, CHANGING THINGS.
"BUT YOU'VE ALSO GOT ALL THESE OTHER ELEMENTS: THE PEOPLE, THE LAYOUT OF THE TABLES, THE BEER."
IT'S A SYSTEM, TIED TOGETHER IN THIS BIG CHAIN OF CAUSE AND EFFECT. AND ALL OF IT CAN BE EXPLAINED WITH NUMBERS. THAT'S SORT OF WHAT I'M WORKING ON.
YEAH, I KNOW. COMPLEXITY THEORY. YOU'VE TOLD ME.

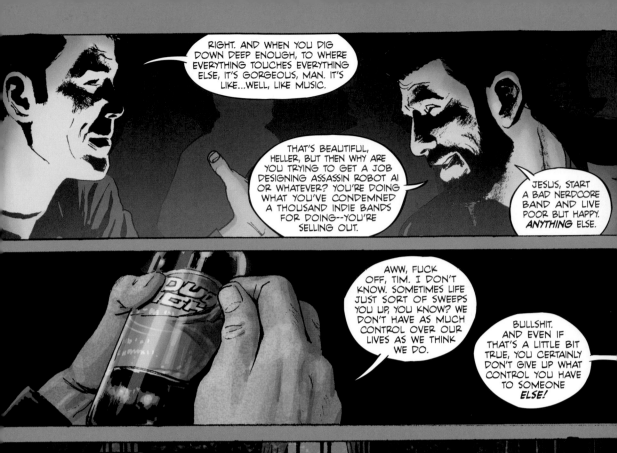

RIGHT. AND WHEN YOU DIG DOWN DEEP ENOUGH, TO WHERE EVERYTHING TOUCHES EVERYTHING ELSE, IT'S GORGEOUS, MAN. IT'S LIKE...WELL, LIKE MUSIC.

THAT'S BEAUTIFUL, HELLER, BUT THEN WHY ARE YOU TRYING TO GET A JOB DESIGNING ASSASSIN ROBOT AI OR WHATEVER? YOU'RE DOING WHAT YOU'VE CONDEMNED A THOUSAND INDIE BANDS FOR DOING--YOU'RE SELLING OUT.

JESUS, START A BAD NERDCORE BAND AND LIVE POOR BUT HAPPY. *ANYTHING* ELSE.

AWW, FUCK OFF, TIM. I DON'T KNOW. SOMETIMES LIFE JUST SORT OF SWEEPS YOU UP, YOU KNOW? WE DON'T HAVE AS MUCH CONTROL OVER OUR LIVES AS WE THINK WE DO.

BULLSHIT. AND EVEN IF THAT'S A LITTLE BIT TRUE, YOU CERTAINLY DON'T GIVE UP WHAT CONTROL YOU HAVE TO SOMEONE *ELSE!*

"YOU'RE TELLING ME YOU NEVER WANTED TO TAKE THE PATH OF LEAST RESISTANCE? RESISTANCE SUCKS."

"SAYS WHO? VIVE LA RESISTANCE! ANYWAY, IF YOU'RE TAKING THE *EASY* PATH, WHY CAN'T YOU FINISH THAT BRILLIANT THESIS WITH ALL THOSE AMAZING DEFENSE APPLICATIONS?"

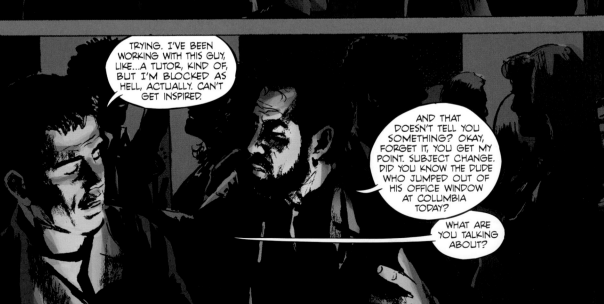

TRYING. I'VE BEEN WORKING WITH THIS GUY, LIKE...A TUTOR, KIND OF, BUT I'M BLOCKED AS HELL, ACTUALLY. CAN'T GET INSPIRED.

AND THAT DOESN'T TELL YOU SOMETHING? OKAY, FORGET IT, YOU GET MY POINT. SUBJECT CHANGE. DID YOU KNOW THE DUDE WHO JUMPED OUT OF HIS OFFICE WINDOW AT COLUMBIA TODAY?

WHAT ARE YOU TALKING ABOUT?

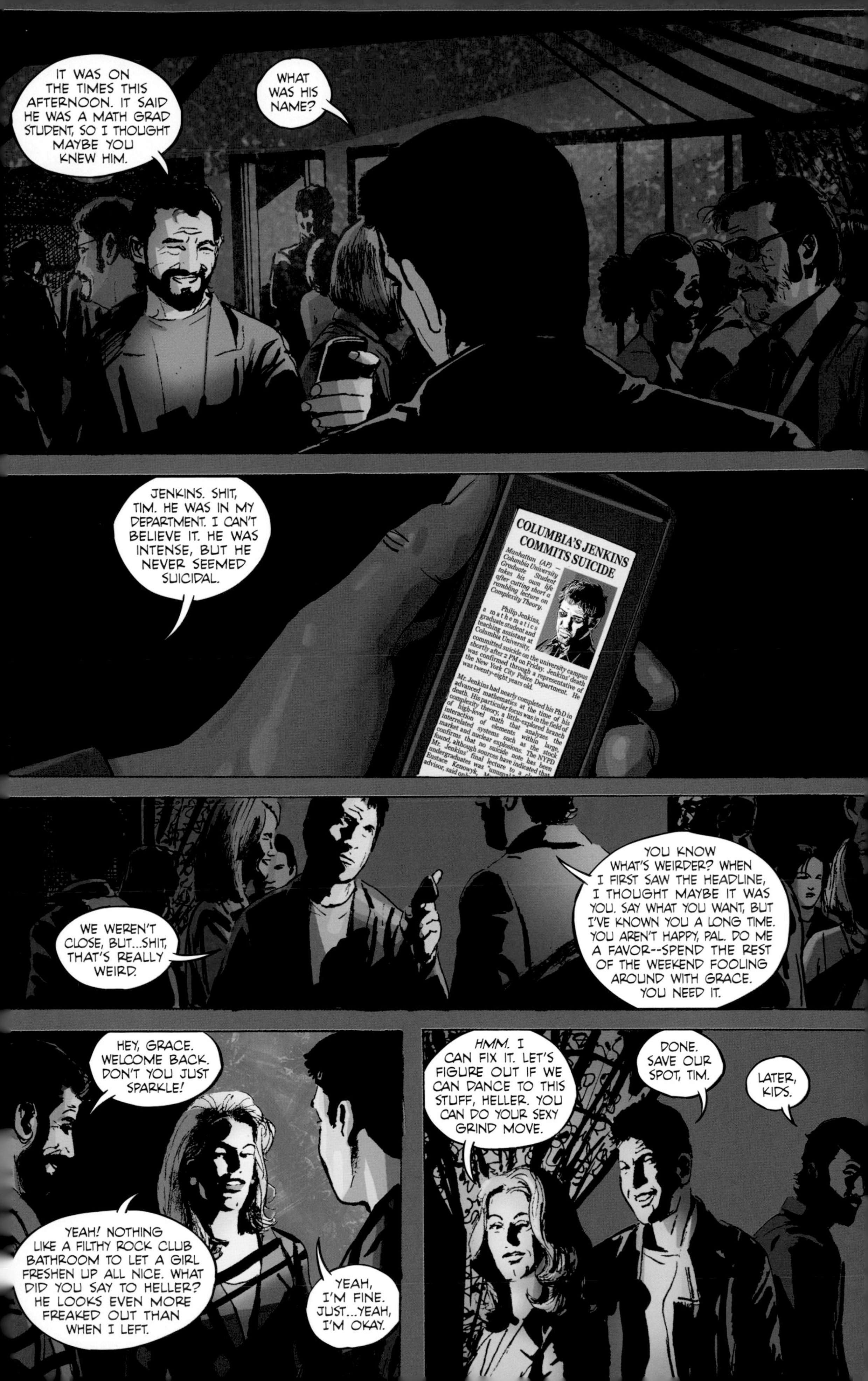
IT WAS ON THE TIMES THIS AFTERNOON. IT SAID HE WAS A MATH GRAD STUDENT, SO I THOUGHT MAYBE YOU KNEW HIM.
WHAT WAS HIS NAME?
JENKINS. SHIT, TIM. HE WAS IN MY DEPARTMENT. I CAN'T BELIEVE IT. HE WAS INTENSE, BUT HE NEVER SEEMED SUICIDAL.
COLUMBIA'S JENKINS COMMITS SUICIDE
Manhattan (AP) — Columbia University Graduate Student takes his own life after cutting short a rambling lecture on Complexity Theory.
Philip Jenkins, a mathematics graduate student and teaching assistant at Columbia University, committed suicide on the university campus shortly after 2 PM on Friday. Jenkins' death was confirmed through a representative of the New York City Police Department. He was twenty-eight years old.
Mr. Jenkins had nearly completed his PhD in advanced mathematics at the time of his death. His particular focus was in the field of complexity theory, a little-explored branch of high-level math that analyzes the interaction of elements within large, interrelated systems such as the stock market and nuclear explosions. The NYPD confirms that no suicide note has been found, although sources have indicated that
WE WEREN'T CLOSE, BUT...SHIT, THAT'S REALLY WEIRD.
YOU KNOW WHAT'S WEIRDER? WHEN I FIRST SAW THE HEADLINE, I THOUGHT MAYBE IT WAS YOU. SAY WHAT YOU WANT, BUT I'VE KNOWN YOU A LONG TIME. YOU AREN'T HAPPY, PAL. DO ME A FAVOR--SPEND THE REST OF THE WEEKEND FOOLING AROUND WITH GRACE. YOU NEED IT.
HEY, GRACE. WELCOME BACK. DON'T YOU JUST SPARKLE!
YEAH! NOTHING LIKE A FILTHY ROCK CLUB BATHROOM TO LET A GIRL FRESHEN UP ALL NICE. WHAT DID YOU SAY TO HELLER? HE LOOKS EVEN MORE FREAKED OUT THAN WHEN I LEFT.
YEAH, I'M FINE. JUST...YEAH, I'M OKAY.
HMM. I CAN FIX IT. LET'S FIGURE OUT IF WE CAN DANCE TO THIS STUFF, HELLER. YOU CAN DO YOUR SEXY GRIND MOVE.
DONE. SAVE OUR SPOT, TIM.
LATER, KIDS.

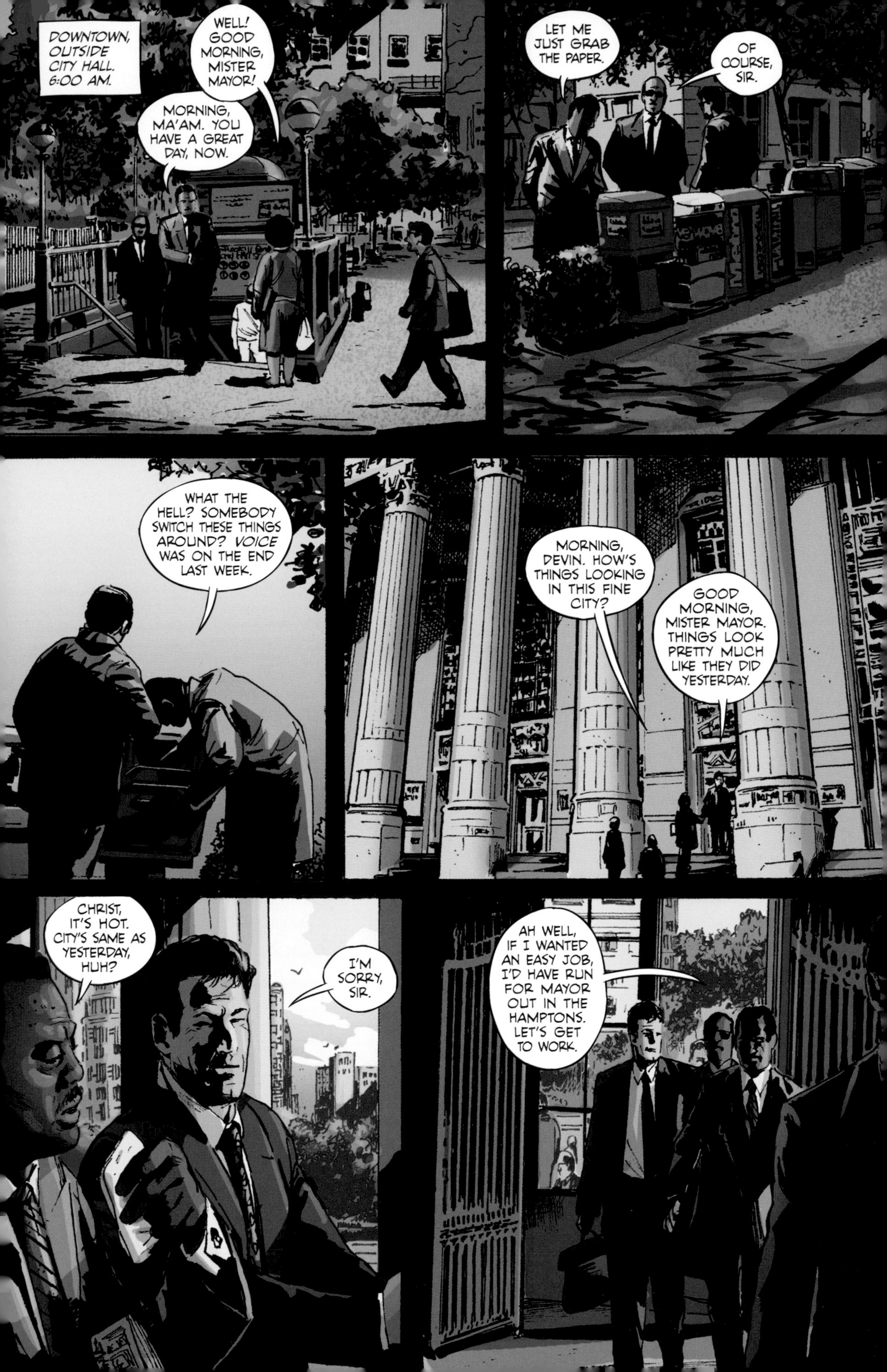
DOWNTOWN, OUTSIDE CITY HALL. 6:00 AM.
WELL! GOOD MORNING, MISTER MAYOR!
MORNING, MA'AM. YOU HAVE A GREAT DAY, NOW.
LET ME JUST GRAB THE PAPER.
OF COURSE, SIR.
WHAT THE HELL? SOMEBODY SWITCH THESE THINGS AROUND? *VOICE* WAS ON THE END LAST WEEK.
MORNING, DEVIN. HOW'S THINGS LOOKING IN THIS FINE CITY?
GOOD MORNING, MISTER MAYOR. THINGS LOOK PRETTY MUCH LIKE THEY DID YESTERDAY.
CHRIST, IT'S HOT. CITY'S SAME AS YESTERDAY, HUH?
I'M SORRY, SIR.
AH WELL, IF I WANTED AN EASY JOB, I'D HAVE RUN FOR MAYOR OUT IN THE HAMPTONS. LET'S GET TO WORK.

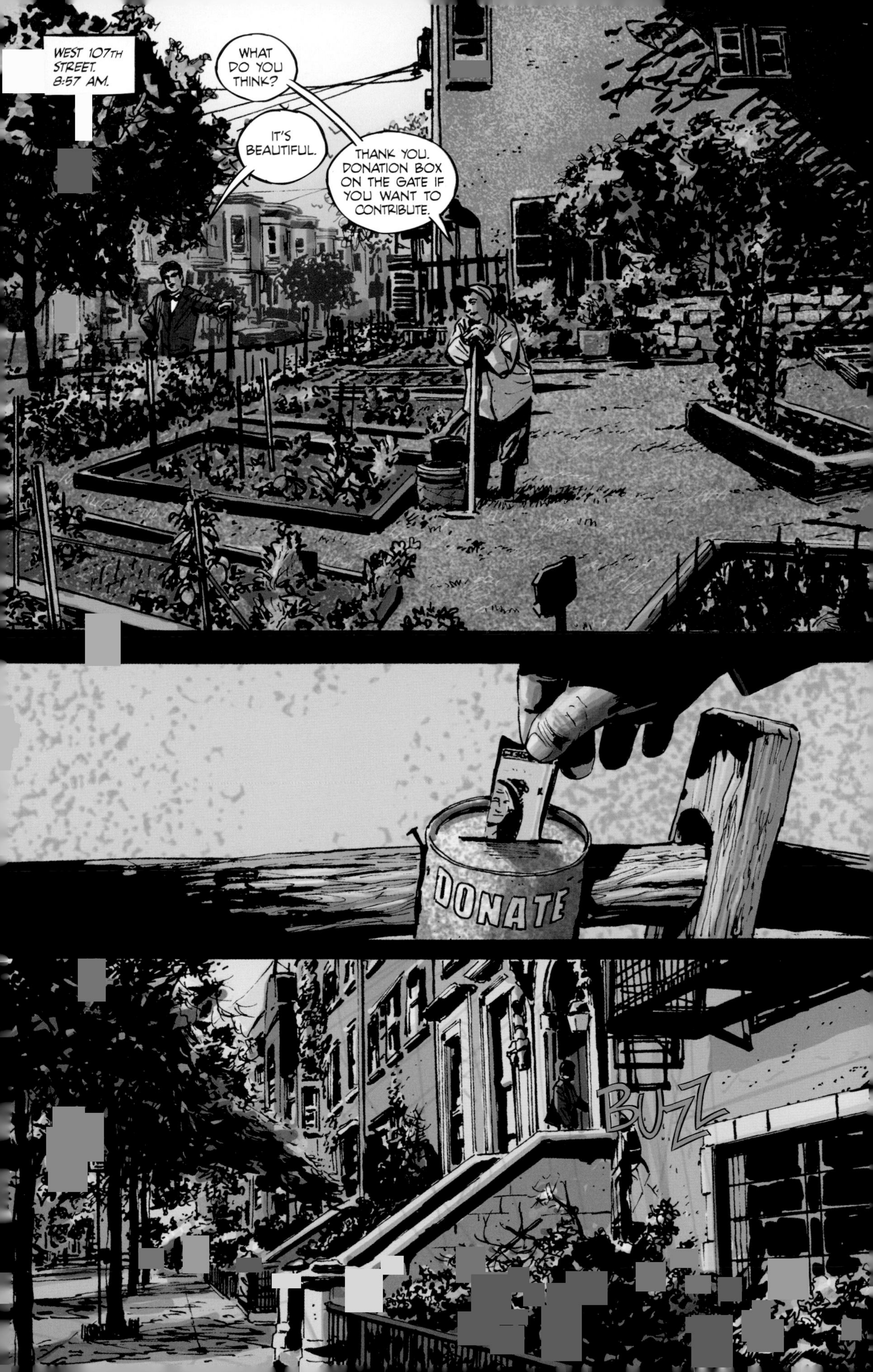
WEST 107TH STREET. 8:57 AM.
WHAT DO YOU THINK?
IT'S BEAUTIFUL.
THANK YOU. DONATION BOX ON THE GATE IF YOU WANT TO CONTRIBUTE.
DONATE
BUZZ

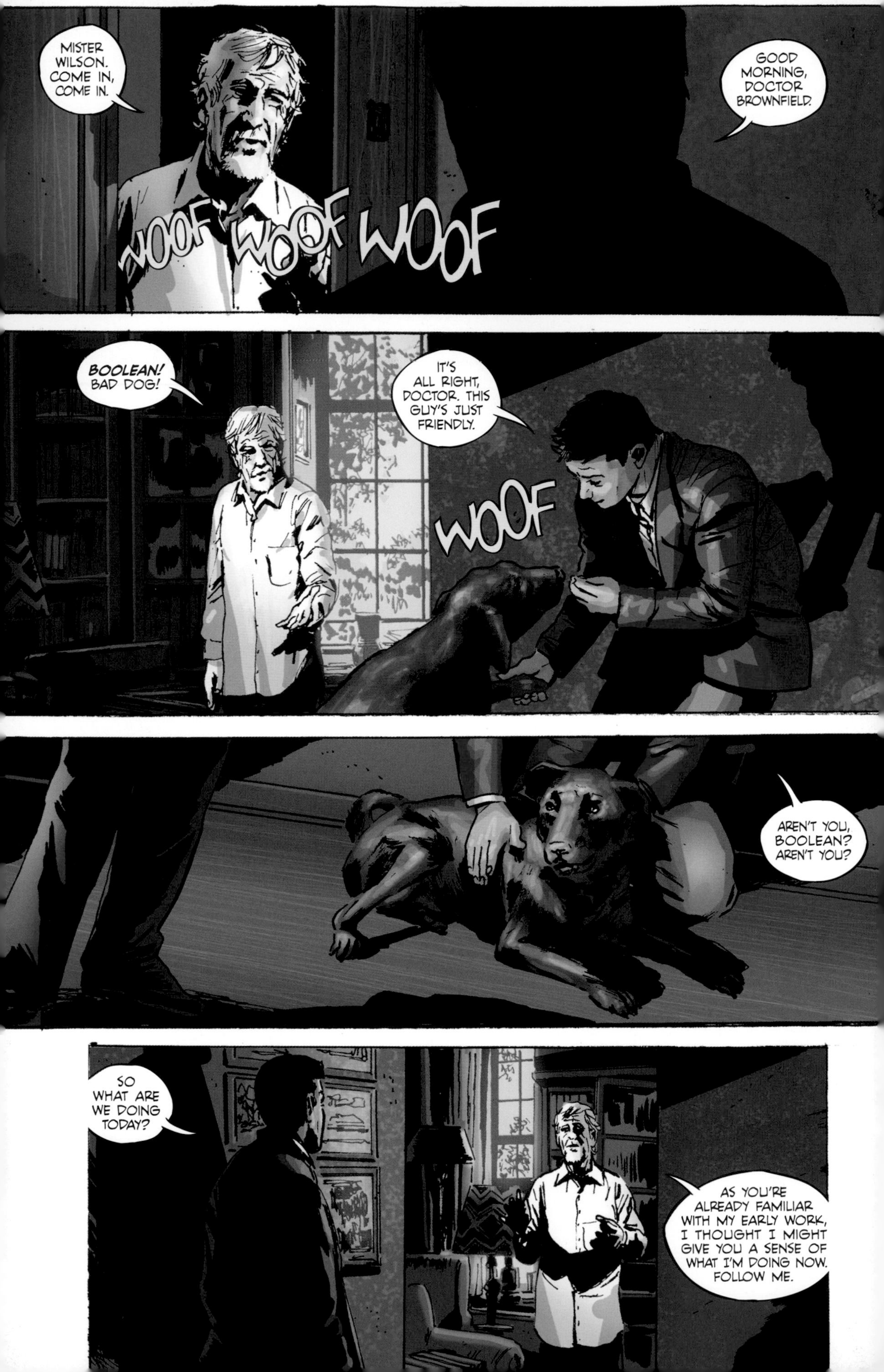
MISTER WILSON. COME IN, COME IN.
GOOD MORNING, DOCTOR BROWNFIELD.
WOOF WOOF WOOF
BOOLEAN! BAD DOG!
IT'S ALL RIGHT, DOCTOR. THIS GUY'S JUST FRIENDLY.
WOOF
AREN'T YOU, BOOLEAN? AREN'T YOU?
SO WHAT ARE WE DOING TODAY?
AS YOU'RE ALREADY FAMILIAR WITH MY EARLY WORK, I THOUGHT I MIGHT GIVE YOU A SENSE OF WHAT I'M DOING NOW. FOLLOW ME.

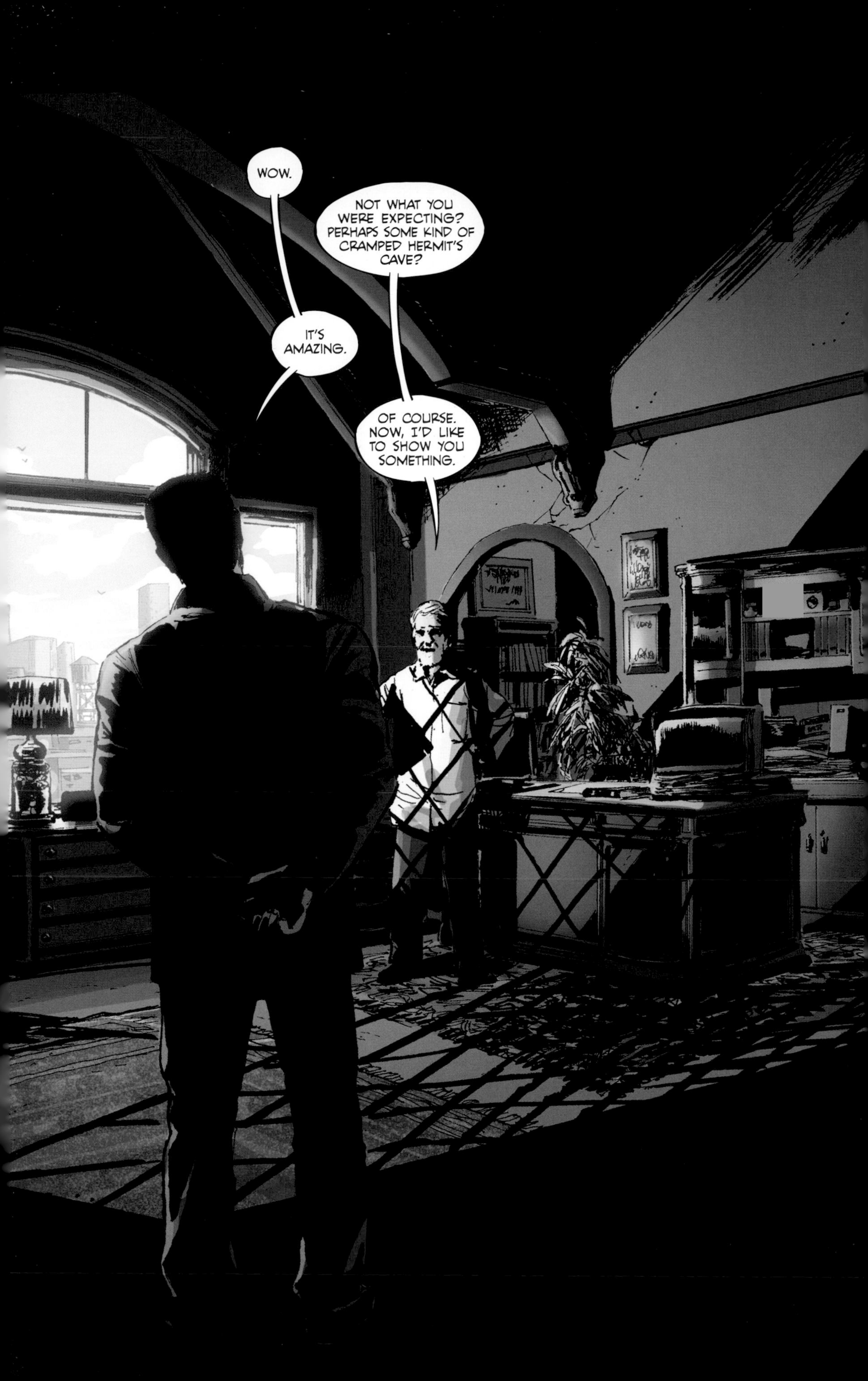
WOW.
NOT WHAT YOU WERE EXPECTING? PERHAPS SOME KIND OF CRAMPED HERMIT'S CAVE?
IT'S AMAZING.
OF COURSE. NOW, I'D LIKE TO SHOW YOU SOMETHING.

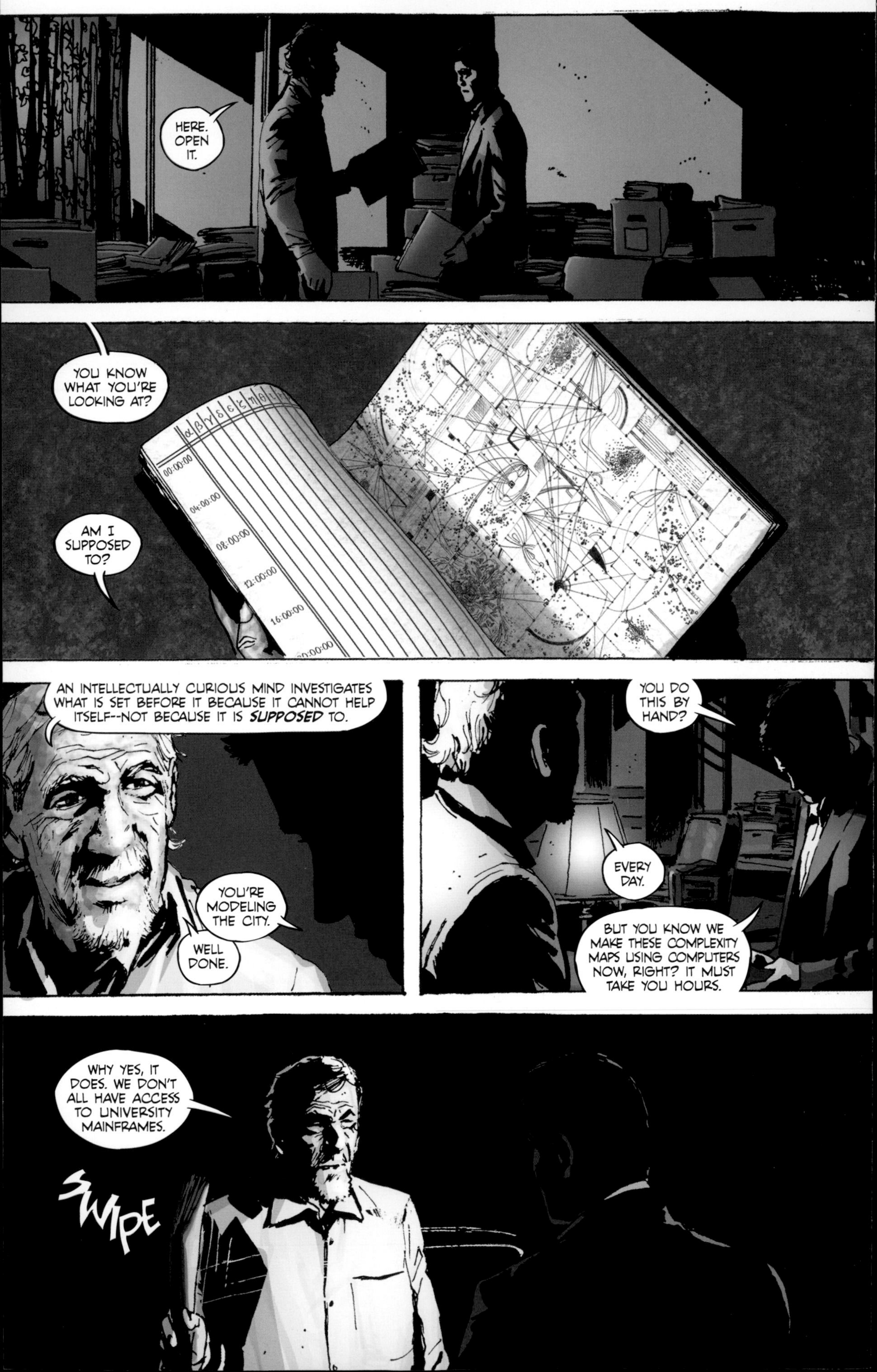
HERE. OPEN IT.
YOU KNOW WHAT YOU'RE LOOKING AT?
AM I SUPPOSED TO?
AN INTELLECTUALLY CURIOUS MIND INVESTIGATES WHAT IS SET BEFORE IT BECAUSE IT CANNOT HELP ITSELF--NOT BECAUSE IT IS SUPPOSED TO.
YOU'RE MODELING THE CITY.
WELL DONE.
YOU DO THIS BY HAND?
EVERY DAY.
BUT YOU KNOW WE MAKE THESE COMPLEXITY MAPS USING COMPUTERS NOW, RIGHT? IT MUST TAKE YOU HOURS.
WHY YES, IT DOES. WE DON'T ALL HAVE ACCESS TO UNIVERSITY MAINFRAMES.
SWIPE

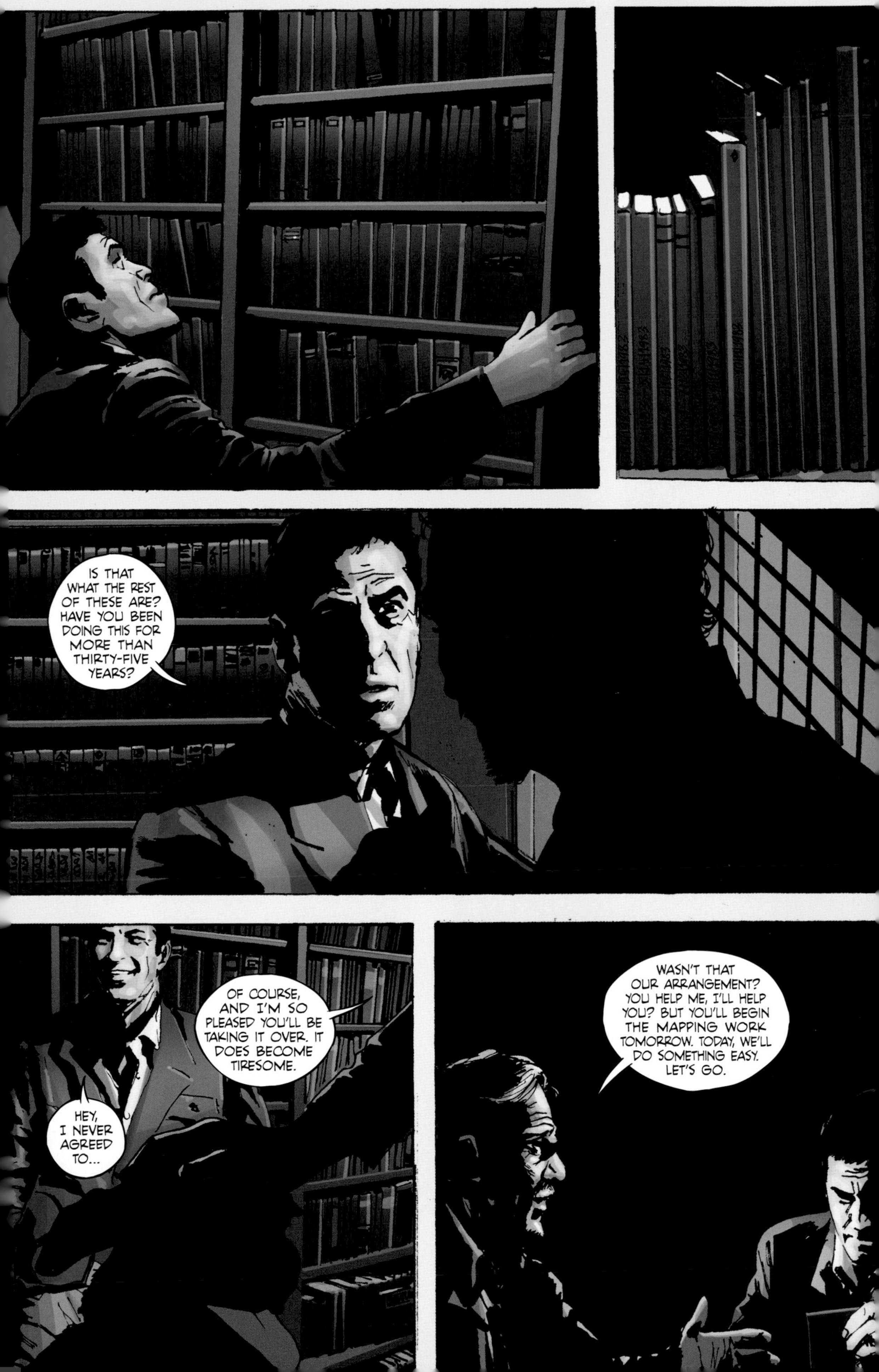
IS THAT WHAT THE REST OF THESE ARE? HAVE YOU BEEN DOING THIS FOR MORE THAN THIRTY-FIVE YEARS?
OF COURSE, AND I'M SO PLEASED YOU'LL BE TAKING IT OVER. IT DOES BECOME TIRESOME.
HEY, I NEVER AGREED TO...
WASN'T THAT OUR ARRANGEMENT? YOU HELP ME, I'LL HELP YOU? BUT YOU'LL BEGIN THE MAPPING WORK TOMORROW. TODAY, WE'LL DO SOMETHING EASY. LET'S GO.

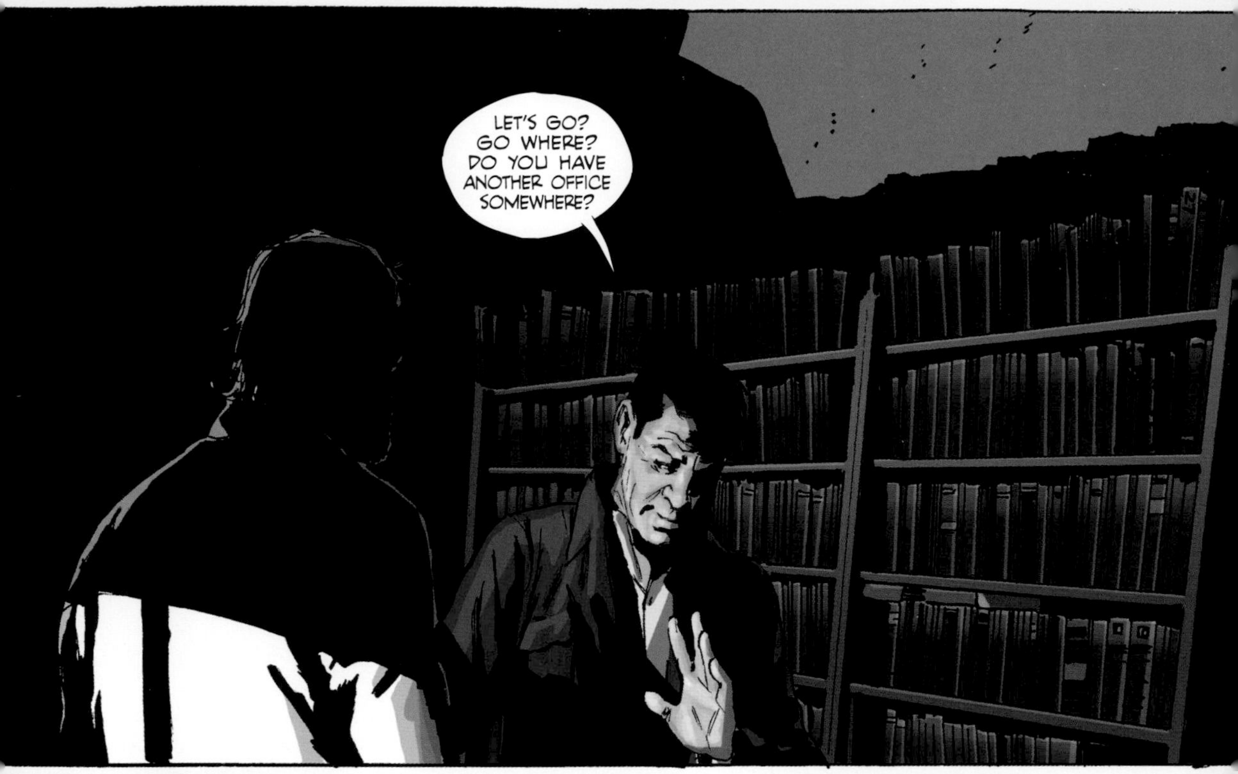
LET'S GO? GO WHERE? DO YOU HAVE ANOTHER OFFICE SOMEWHERE?

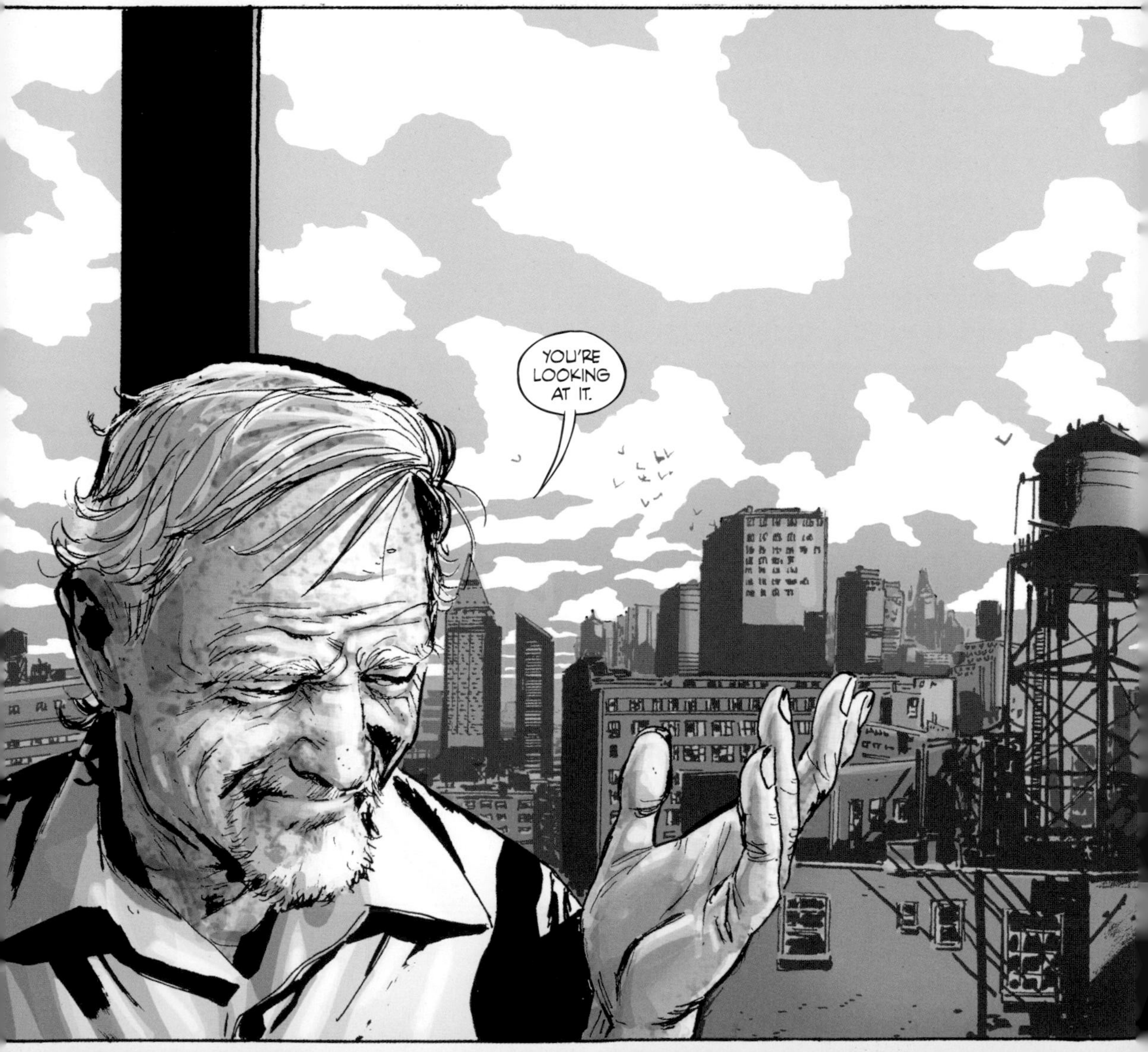
YOU'RE LOOKING AT IT.

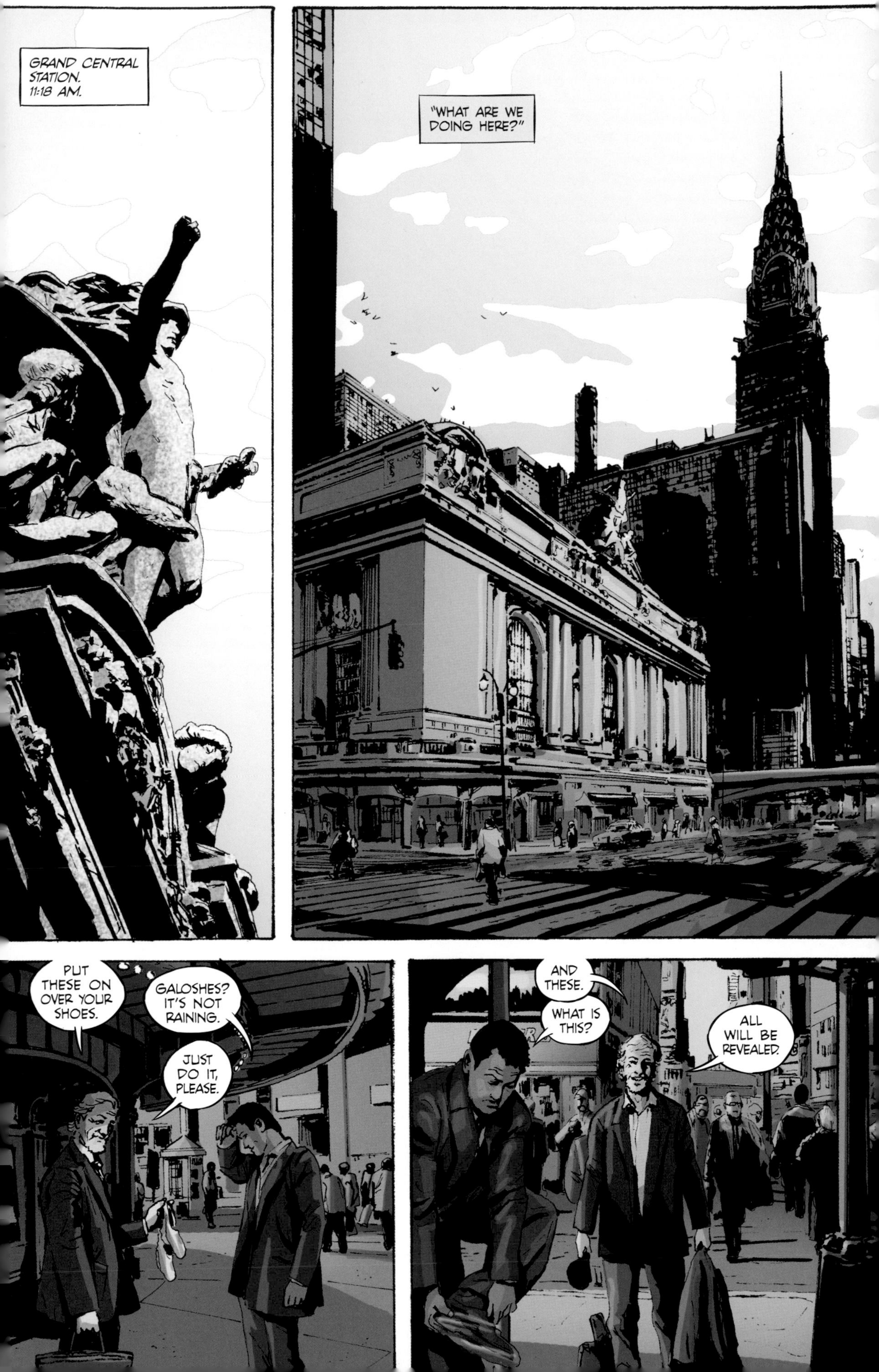
GRAND CENTRAL STATION. 11:18 AM.
"WHAT ARE WE DOING HERE?"
PUT THESE ON OVER YOUR SHOES.
GALOSHES? IT'S NOT RAINING.
JUST DO IT, PLEASE.
AND THESE.
WHAT IS THIS?
ALL WILL BE REVEALED.

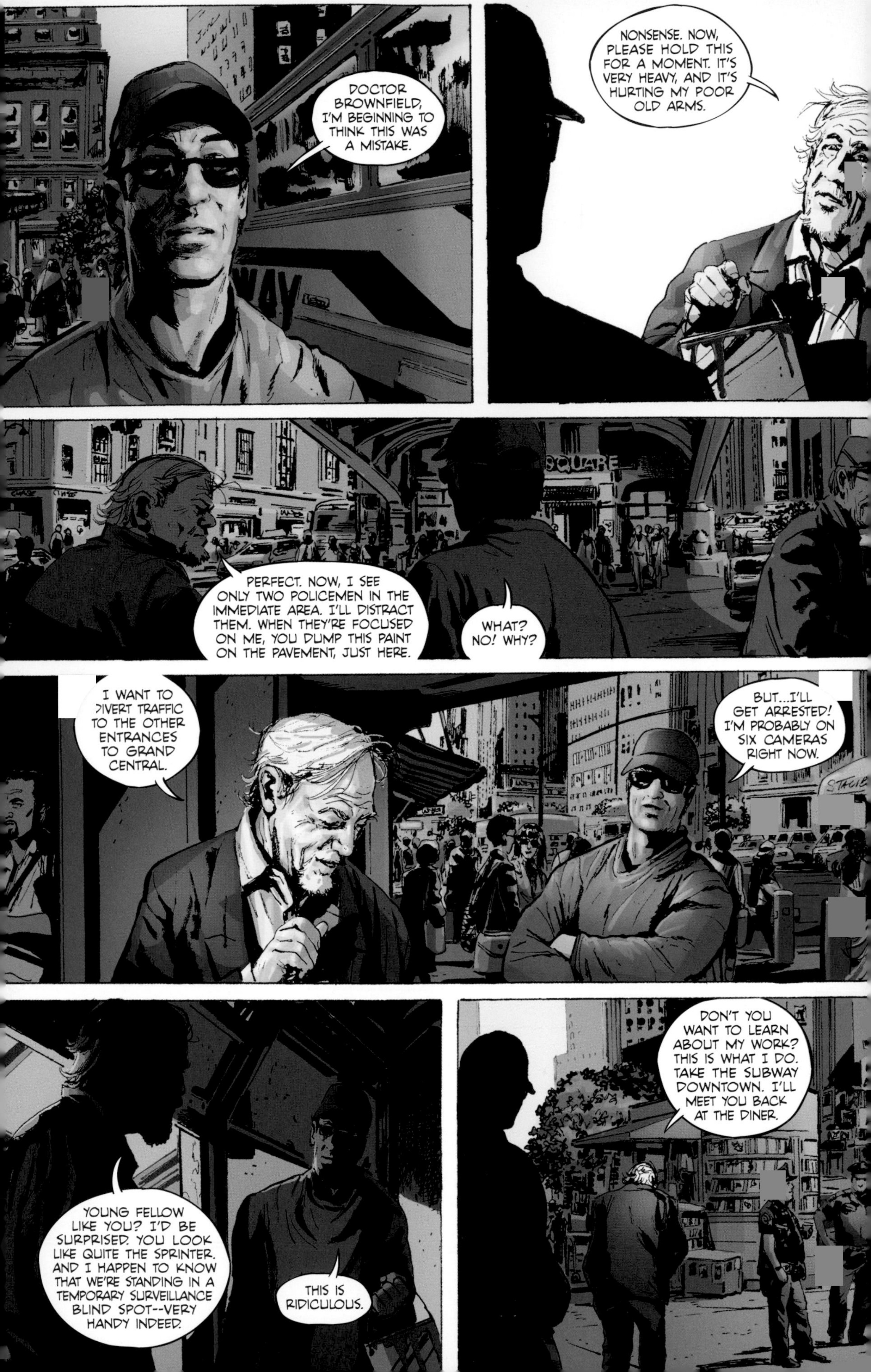
DOCTOR BROWNFIELD, I'M BEGINNING TO THINK THIS WAS A MISTAKE.
NONSENSE. NOW, PLEASE HOLD THIS FOR A MOMENT. IT'S VERY HEAVY, AND IT'S HURTING MY POOR OLD ARMS.
PERFECT. NOW, I SEE ONLY TWO POLICEMEN IN THE IMMEDIATE AREA. I'LL DISTRACT THEM. WHEN THEY'RE FOCUSED ON ME, YOU DUMP THIS PAINT ON THE PAVEMENT, JUST HERE.
WHAT? NO! WHY?
I WANT TO DIVERT TRAFFIC TO THE OTHER ENTRANCES TO GRAND CENTRAL.
BUT...I'LL GET ARRESTED! I'M PROBABLY ON SIX CAMERAS RIGHT NOW.
YOUNG FELLOW LIKE YOU? I'D BE SURPRISED. YOU LOOK LIKE QUITE THE SPRINTER. AND I HAPPEN TO KNOW THAT WE'RE STANDING IN A TEMPORARY SURVEILLANCE BLIND SPOT--VERY HANDY INDEED.
THIS IS RIDICULOUS.
DON'T YOU WANT TO LEARN ABOUT MY WORK? THIS IS WHAT I DO. TAKE THE SUBWAY DOWNTOWN. I'LL MEET YOU BACK AT THE DINER.

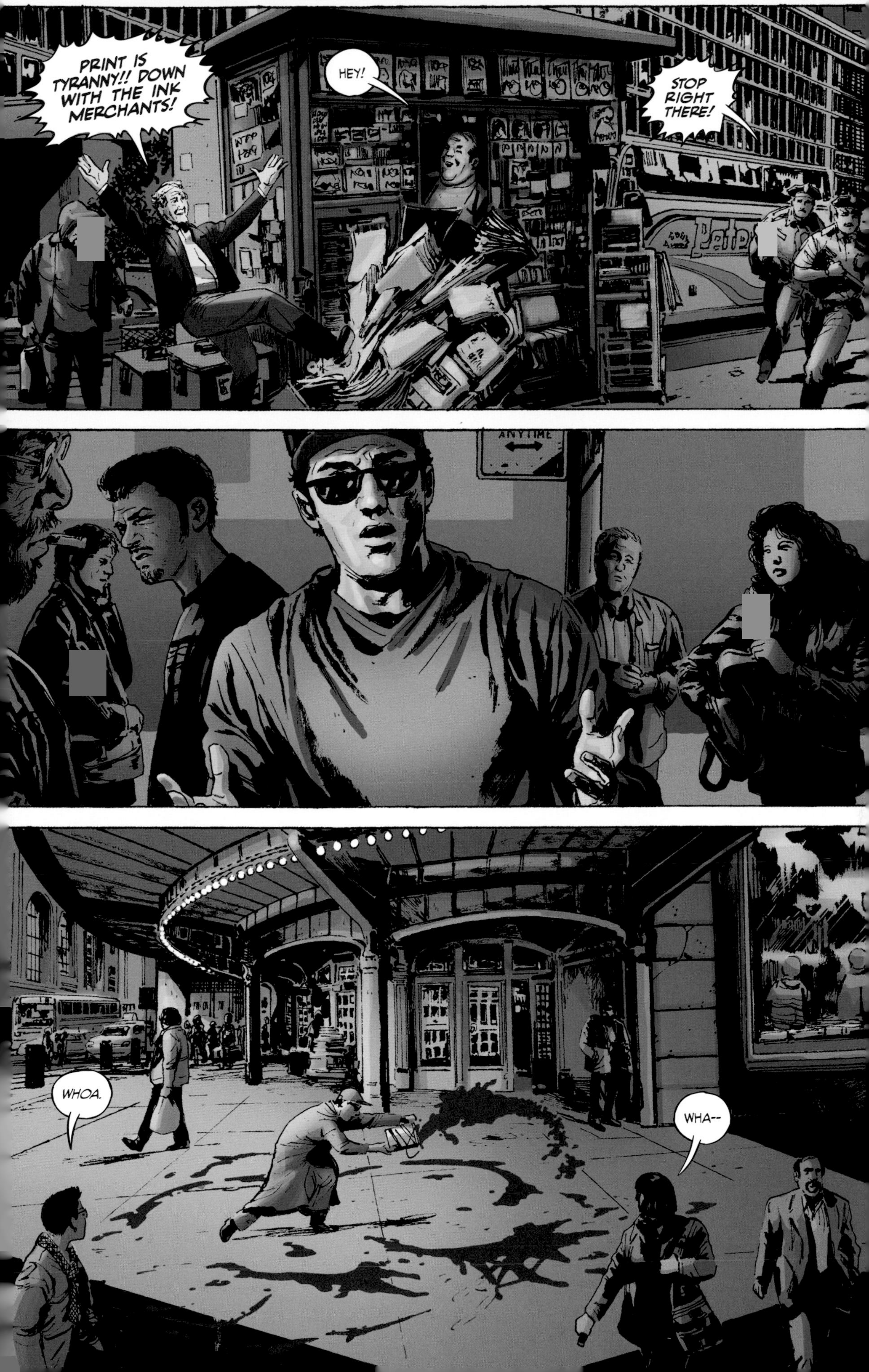
PRINT IS TYRANNY!! DOWN WITH THE INK MERCHANTS!
HEY!
STOP RIGHT THERE!
ANYTIME
WHOA.
WHA--

28TH & NINTH. LATER.

MISTER WILSON! WELL DONE.

I THOUGHT YOU SAID WE WERE DOING SOMETHING EASY TODAY!

I THOUGHT IT WAS EASY, DIDN'T YOU? BUT I AM SORRY ABOUT YOUR PANTS--I THOUGHT THE PONCHO WOULD COVER A BIT BETTER. LET ME BUY YOU A CUP OF COFFEE.

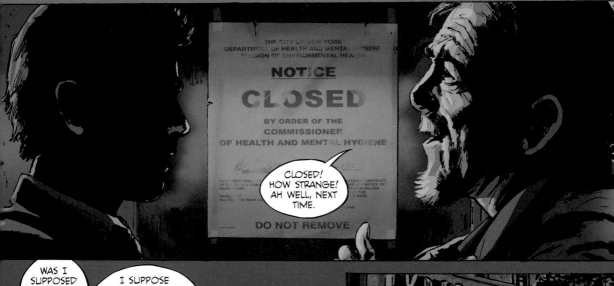

THE CITY OF NEW YORK
DEPARTMENT OF HEALTH AND MENTAL HYGIENE
DIVISION OF ENVIRONMENTAL HEALTH

NOTICE

CLOSED

BY ORDER OF THE COMMISSIONER OF HEALTH AND MENTAL HYGIENE

DO NOT REMOVE

CLOSED! HOW STRANGE! AH WELL, NEXT TIME.

WAS I SUPPOSED TO LEARN SOMETHING FROM ALL OF THAT?

I SUPPOSE YOU *COULD* HAVE, BUT I'M NOT SURE YOU ACTUALLY *DID*. NOW, I'M OFF. I'LL SEE YOU TOMORROW, 9 AM. I'M SURE WE'LL BE ABLE TO DO SOME MORE WORK ON MY THEORIES THEN.

ARE YOU *KIDDING* ME?

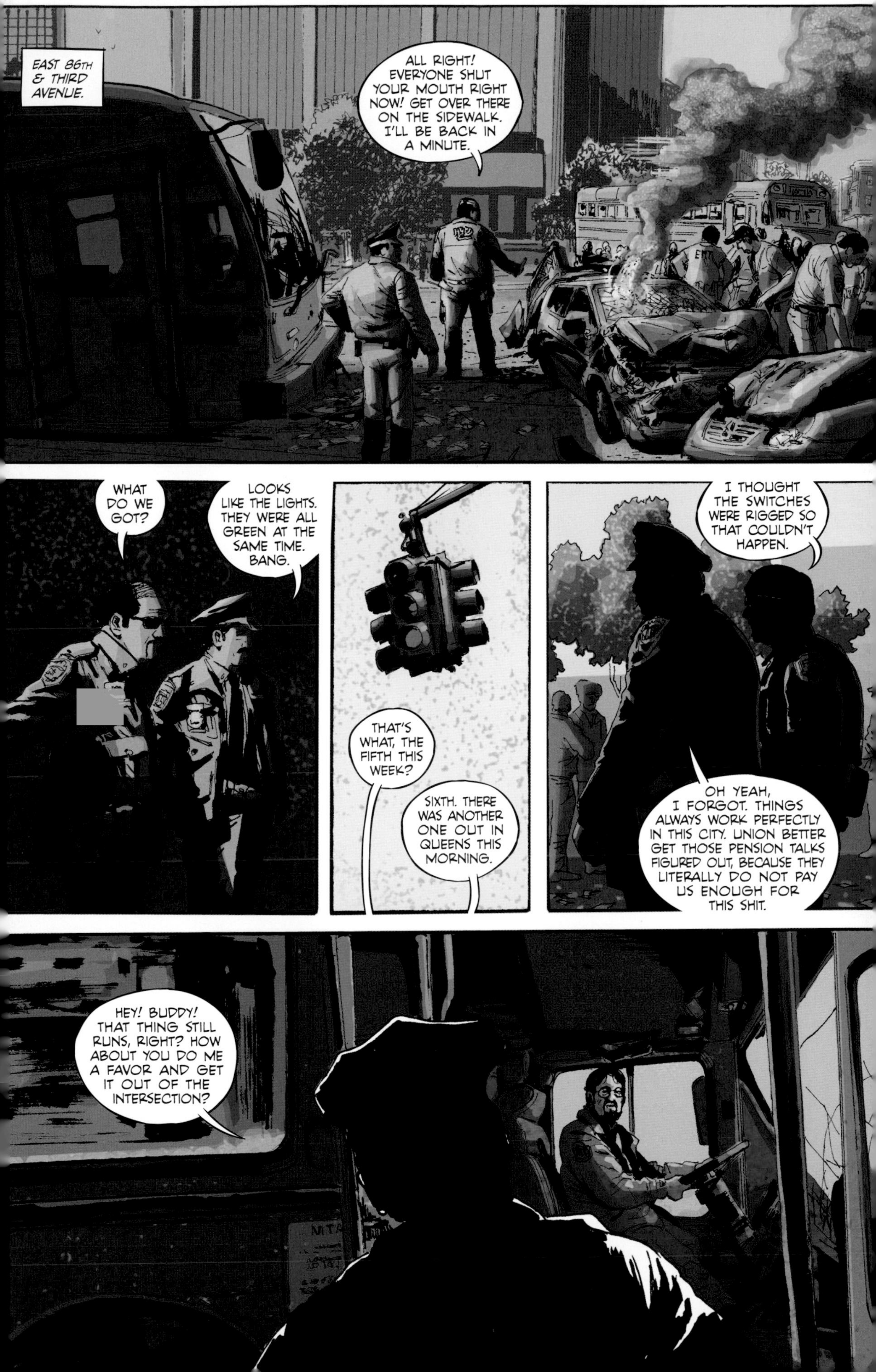
EAST 86TH & THIRD AVENUE.
ALL RIGHT! EVERYONE SHUT YOUR MOUTH RIGHT NOW! GET OVER THERE ON THE SIDEWALK. I'LL BE BACK IN A MINUTE.
WHAT DO WE GOT?
LOOKS LIKE THE LIGHTS. THEY WERE ALL GREEN AT THE SAME TIME. BANG.
THAT'S WHAT, THE FIFTH THIS WEEK?
SIXTH. THERE WAS ANOTHER ONE OUT IN QUEENS THIS MORNING.
I THOUGHT THE SWITCHES WERE RIGGED SO THAT COULDN'T HAPPEN.
OH YEAH, I FORGOT. THINGS ALWAYS WORK PERFECTLY IN THIS CITY. UNION BETTER GET THOSE PENSION TALKS FIGURED OUT, BECAUSE THEY LITERALLY DO NOT PAY US ENOUGH FOR THIS SHIT.
HEY! BUDDY! THAT THING STILL RUNS, RIGHT? HOW ABOUT YOU DO ME A FAVOR AND GET IT OUT OF THE INTERSECTION?

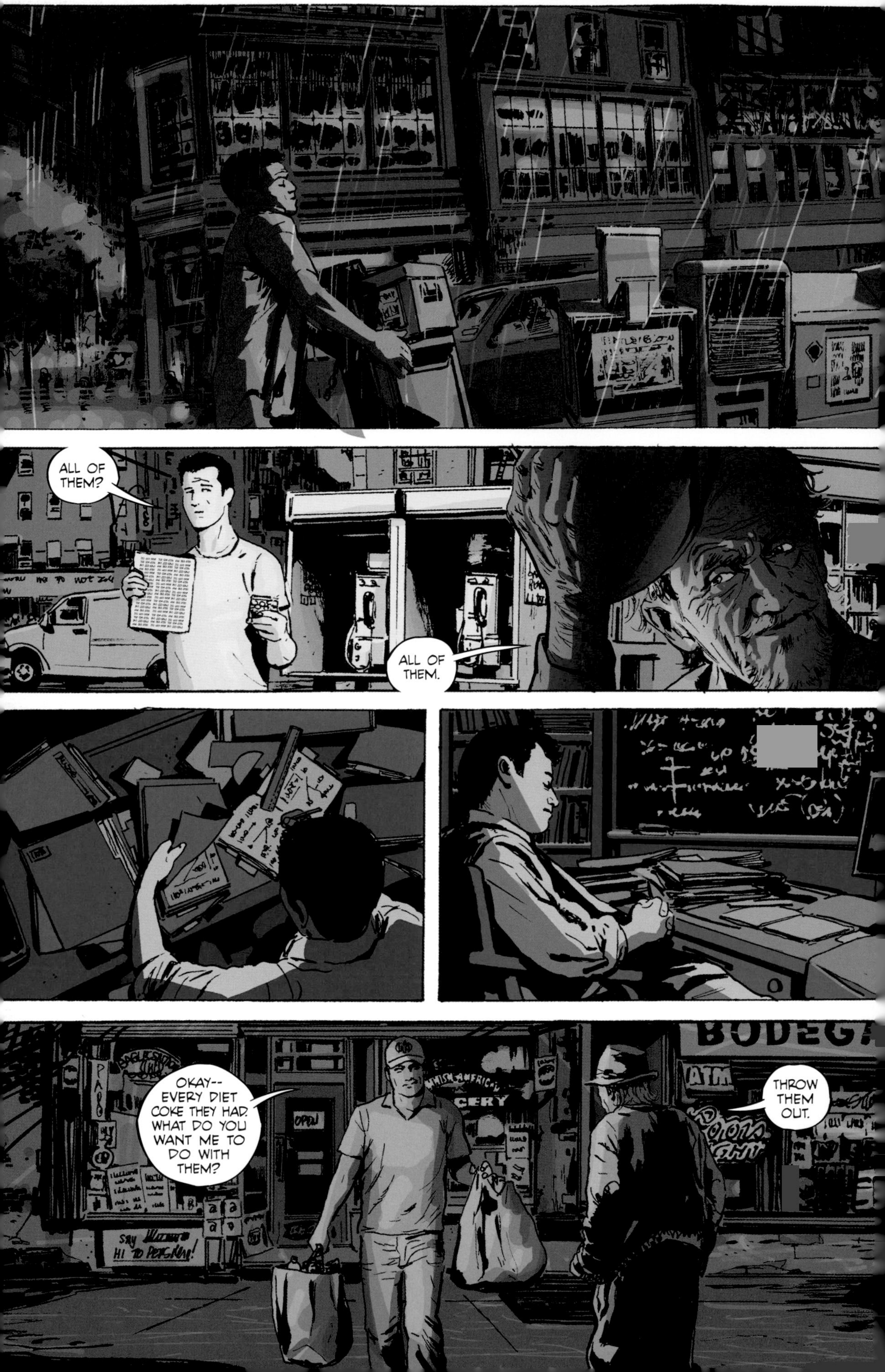
ALL OF THEM?
ALL OF THEM.
BODEGA
ATM
OPEN
OKAY-- EVERY DIET COKE THEY HAD. WHAT DO YOU WANT ME TO DO WITH THEM?
THROW THEM OUT.

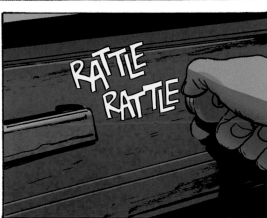

RATTLE
RATTLE

PLEASE TELL ME THERE'S A POINT TO ALL THIS? THAT IT'S SOME SORT OF KARATE KID THING, AND I'M GOING TO GET INTO A BAR FIGHT AND IT WILL ALL PAY OFF? BECAUSE I'VE GOT TO TELL YOU, I'M GETTING PRETTY GODDAMN SICK OF IT. THIS ISN'T COMPLEXITY. I DON'T KNOW WHAT THIS IS.

KARATE KID? NEVER SAW IT.

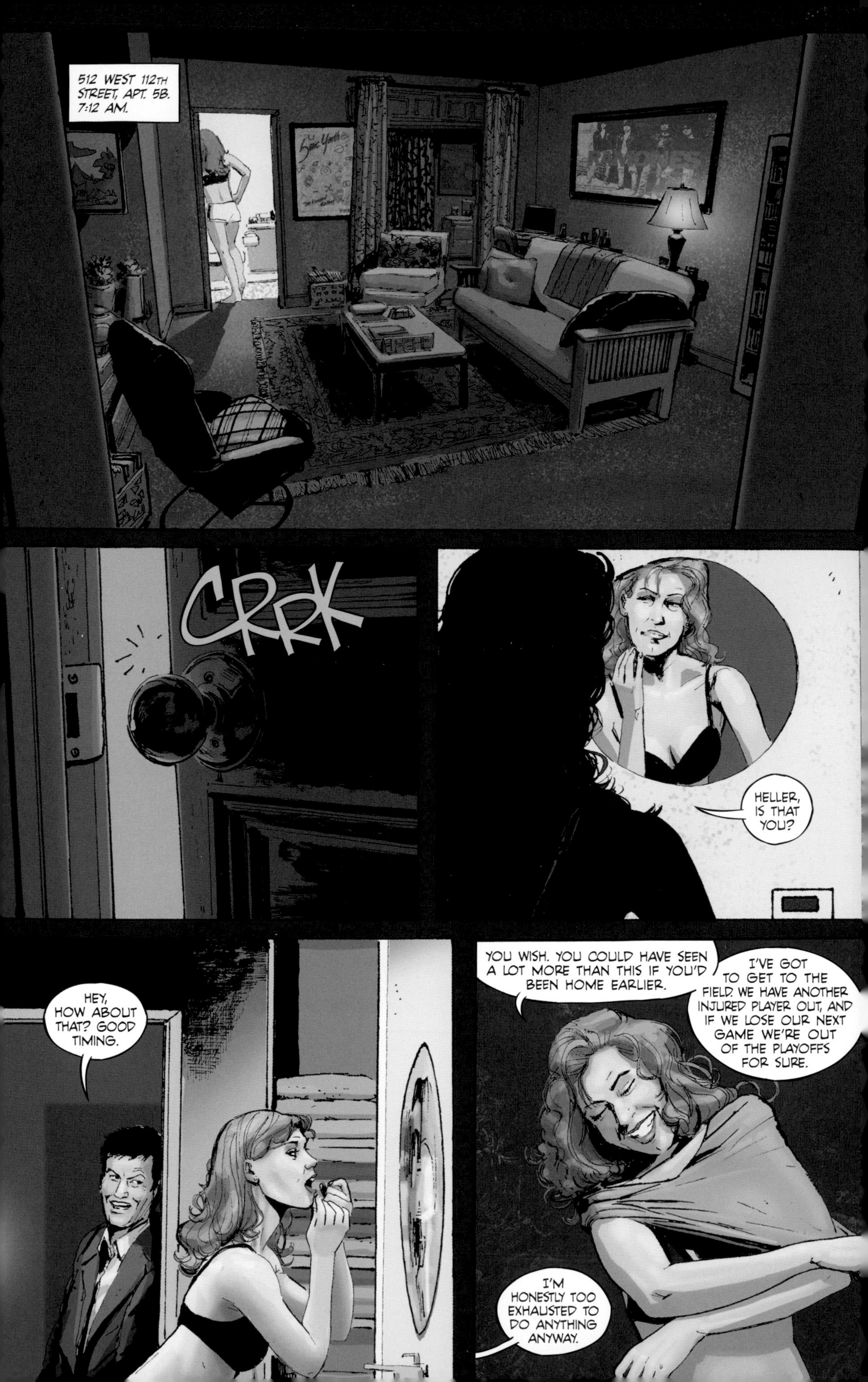

512 WEST 112TH STREET, APT. 5B. 7:12 AM.
CRRK
HELLER, IS THAT YOU?
HEY, HOW ABOUT THAT? GOOD TIMING.
YOU WISH. YOU COULD HAVE SEEN A LOT MORE THAN THIS IF YOU'D BEEN HOME EARLIER.
I'VE GOT TO GET TO THE FIELD. WE HAVE ANOTHER INJURED PLAYER OUT, AND IF WE LOSE OUR NEXT GAME WE'RE OUT OF THE PLAYOFFS FOR SURE.
I'M HONESTLY TOO EXHAUSTED TO DO ANYTHING ANYWAY.

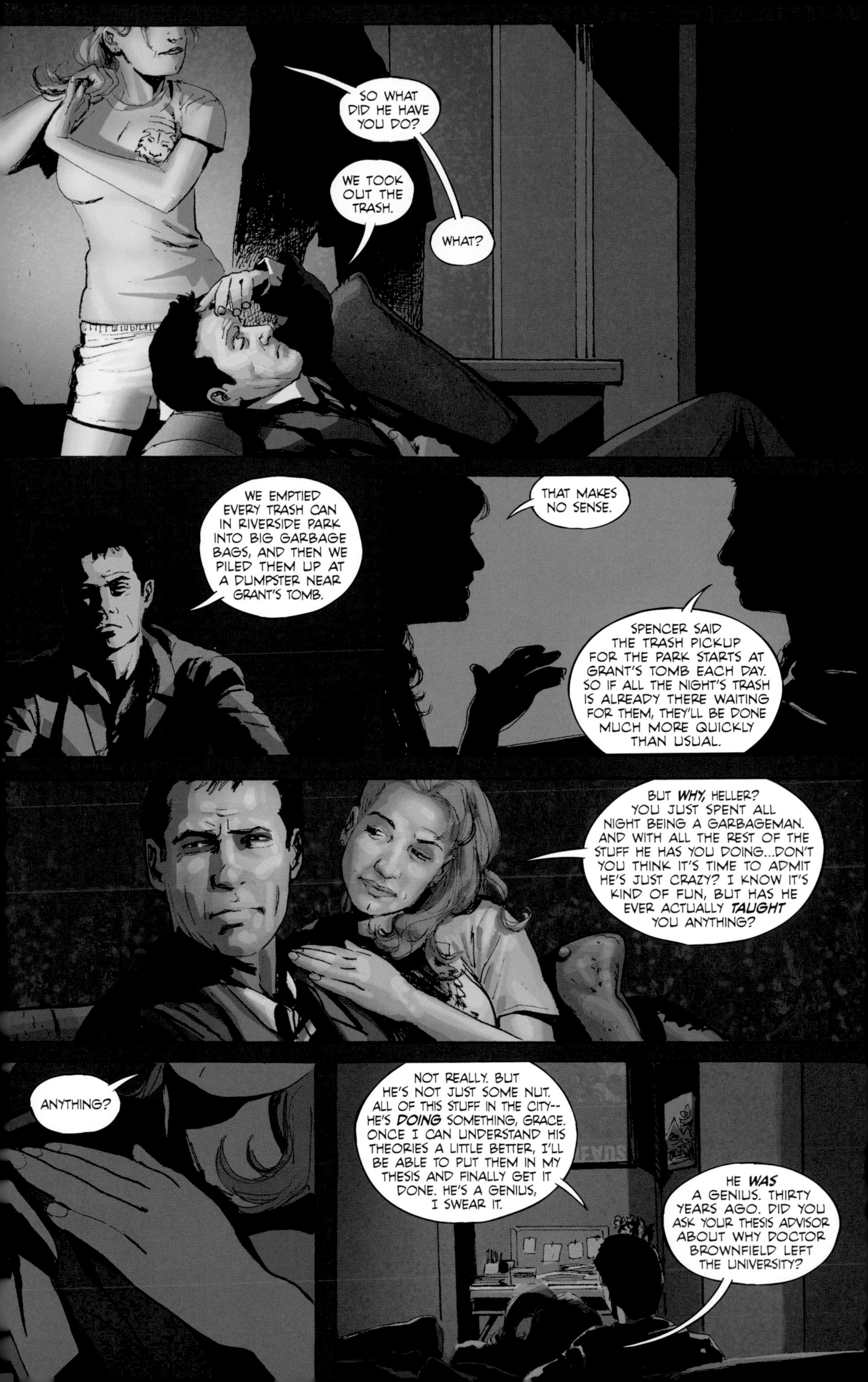
SO WHAT DID HE HAVE YOU DO?
WE TOOK OUT THE TRASH.
WHAT?
WE EMPTIED EVERY TRASH CAN IN RIVERSIDE PARK INTO BIG GARBAGE BAGS, AND THEN WE PILED THEM UP AT A DUMPSTER NEAR GRANT'S TOMB.
THAT MAKES NO SENSE.
SPENCER SAID THE TRASH PICKUP FOR THE PARK STARTS AT GRANT'S TOMB EACH DAY. SO IF ALL THE NIGHT'S TRASH IS ALREADY THERE WAITING FOR THEM, THEY'LL BE DONE MUCH MORE QUICKLY THAN USUAL.
BUT *WHY,* HELLER? YOU JUST SPENT ALL NIGHT BEING A GARBAGEMAN. AND WITH ALL THE REST OF THE STUFF HE HAS YOU DOING...DON'T YOU THINK IT'S TIME TO ADMIT HE'S JUST CRAZY? I KNOW IT'S KIND OF FUN, BUT HAS HE EVER ACTUALLY *TAUGHT* YOU ANYTHING?
ANYTHING?
NOT REALLY. BUT HE'S NOT JUST SOME NUT. ALL OF THIS STUFF IN THE CITY-- HE'S *DOING* SOMETHING, GRACE. ONCE I CAN UNDERSTAND HIS THEORIES A LITTLE BETTER, I'LL BE ABLE TO PUT THEM IN MY THESIS AND FINALLY GET IT DONE. HE'S A GENIUS, I SWEAR IT.
HE *WAS* A GENIUS. THIRTY YEARS AGO. DID YOU ASK YOUR THESIS ADVISOR ABOUT WHY DOCTOR BROWNFIELD LEFT THE UNIVERSITY?

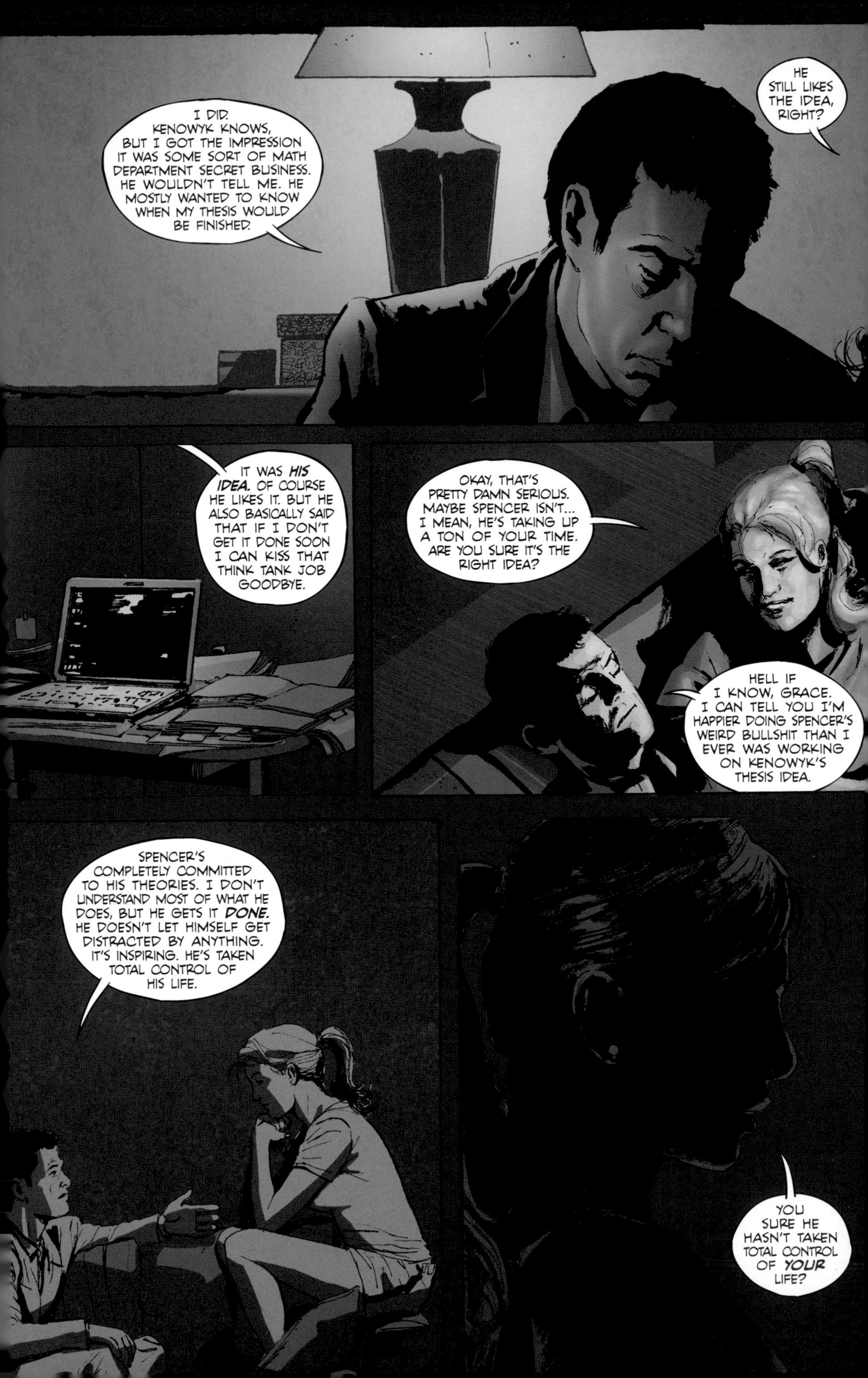
I DID. KENOWYK KNOWS, BUT I GOT THE IMPRESSION IT WAS SOME SORT OF MATH DEPARTMENT SECRET BUSINESS. HE WOULDN'T TELL ME. HE MOSTLY WANTED TO KNOW WHEN MY THESIS WOULD BE FINISHED.
HE STILL LIKES THE IDEA, RIGHT?
IT WAS ***HIS IDEA.*** OF COURSE HE LIKES IT. BUT HE ALSO BASICALLY SAID THAT IF I DON'T GET IT DONE SOON I CAN KISS THAT THINK TANK JOB GOODBYE.
OKAY, THAT'S PRETTY DAMN SERIOUS. MAYBE SPENCER ISN'T... I MEAN, HE'S TAKING UP A TON OF YOUR TIME. ARE YOU SURE IT'S THE RIGHT IDEA?
HELL IF I KNOW, GRACE. I CAN TELL YOU I'M HAPPIER DOING SPENCER'S WEIRD BULLSHIT THAN I EVER WAS WORKING ON KENOWYK'S THESIS IDEA.
SPENCER'S COMPLETELY COMMITTED TO HIS THEORIES. I DON'T UNDERSTAND MOST OF WHAT HE DOES, BUT HE GETS IT ***DONE.*** HE DOESN'T LET HIMSELF GET DISTRACTED BY ANYTHING. IT'S INSPIRING. HE'S TAKEN TOTAL CONTROL OF HIS LIFE.
YOU SURE HE HASN'T TAKEN TOTAL CONTROL OF ***YOUR*** LIFE?

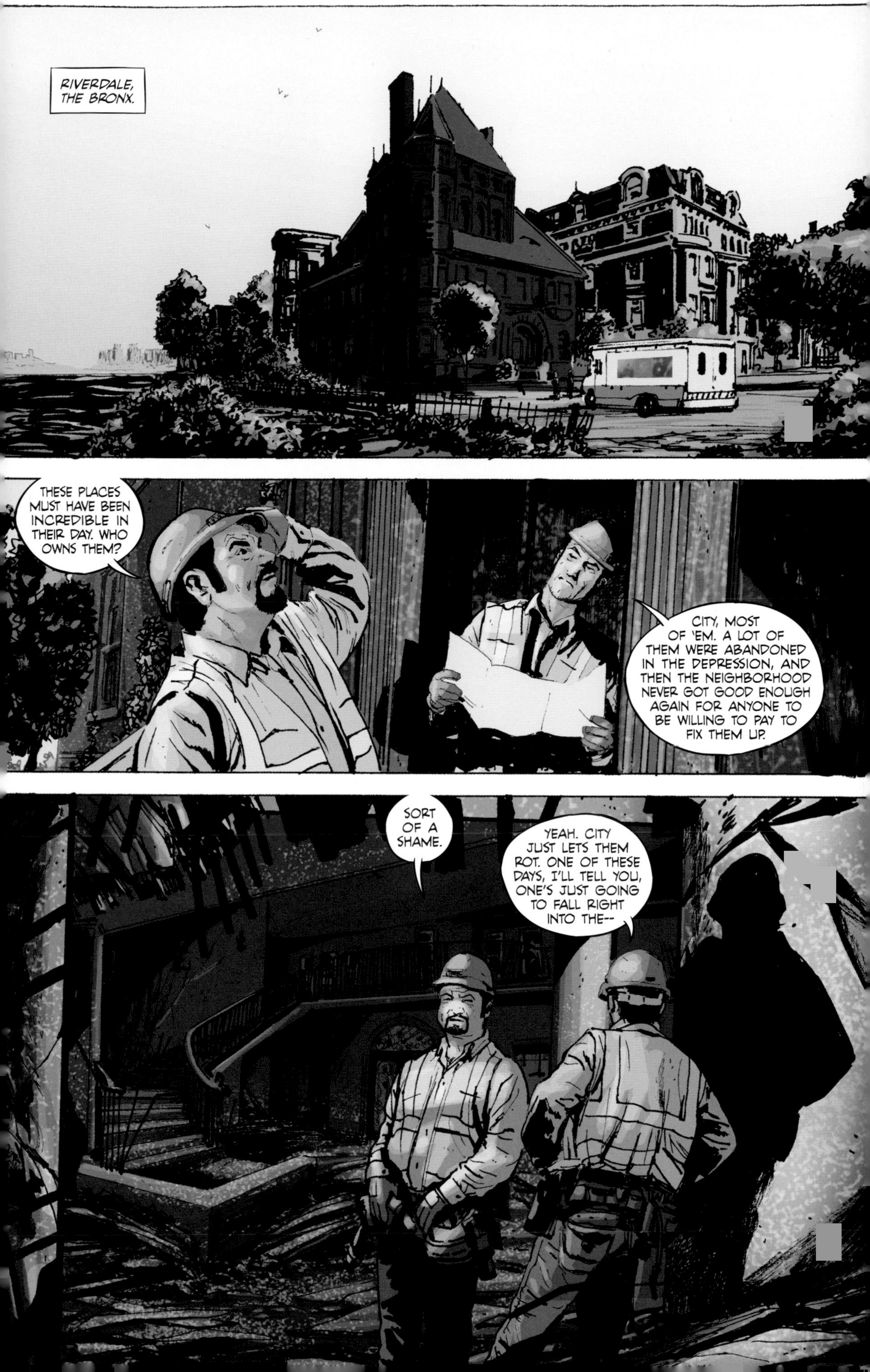
RIVERDALE, THE BRONX.
THESE PLACES MUST HAVE BEEN INCREDIBLE IN THEIR DAY. WHO OWNS THEM?
CITY, MOST OF 'EM. A LOT OF THEM WERE ABANDONED IN THE DEPRESSION, AND THEN THE NEIGHBORHOOD NEVER GOT GOOD ENOUGH AGAIN FOR ANYONE TO BE WILLING TO PAY TO FIX THEM UP.
SORT OF A SHAME.
YEAH. CITY JUST LETS THEM ROT. ONE OF THESE DAYS, I'LL TELL YOU, ONE'S JUST GOING TO FALL RIGHT INTO THE--

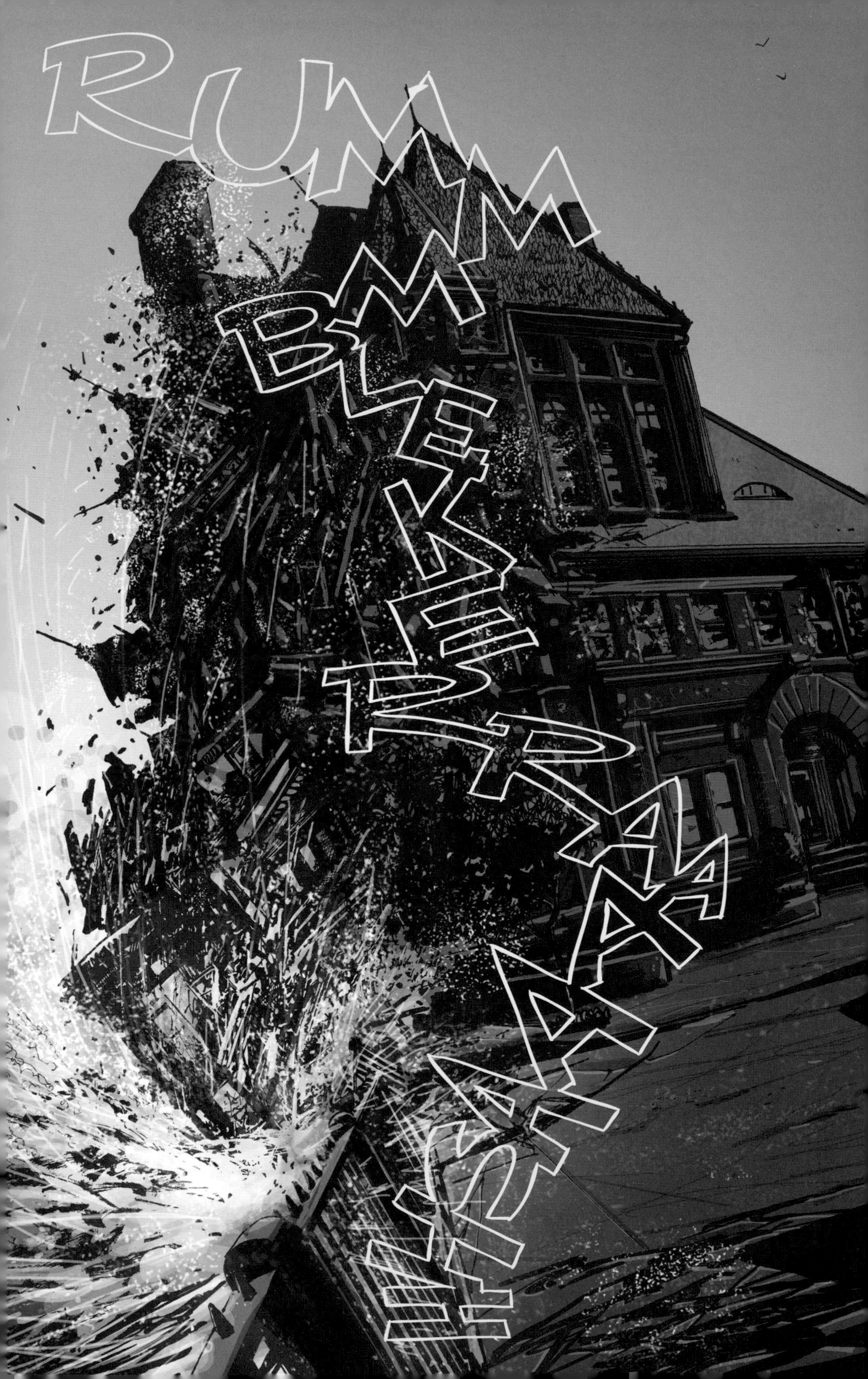
RUMMMMM
BLEKERRAAAAASH

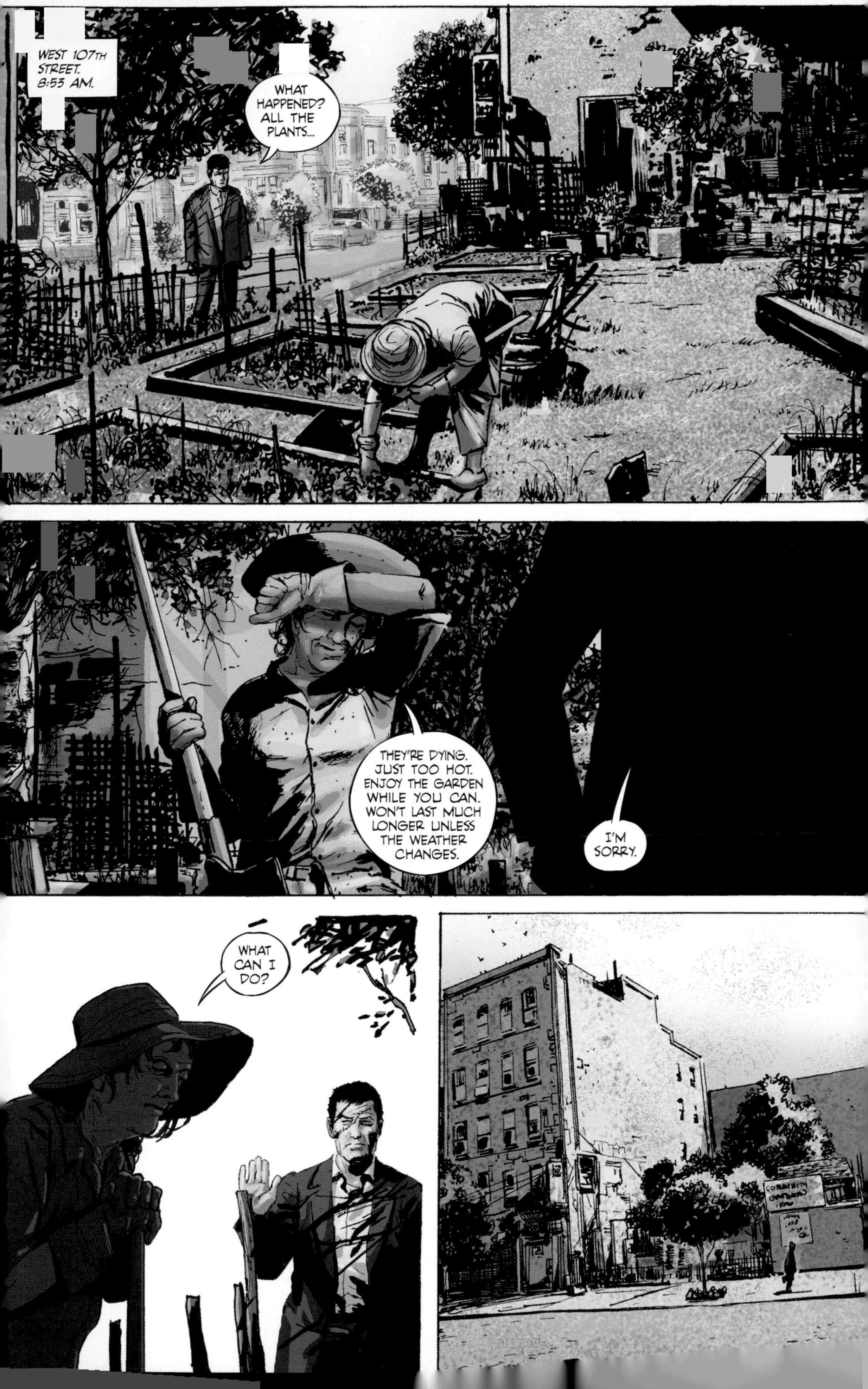
WEST 107TH STREET. 8:53 AM.
WHAT HAPPENED? ALL THE PLANTS...
THEY'RE DYING. JUST TOO HOT. ENJOY THE GARDEN WHILE YOU CAN. WON'T LAST MUCH LONGER UNLESS THE WEATHER CHANGES.
I'M SORRY.
WHAT CAN I DO?

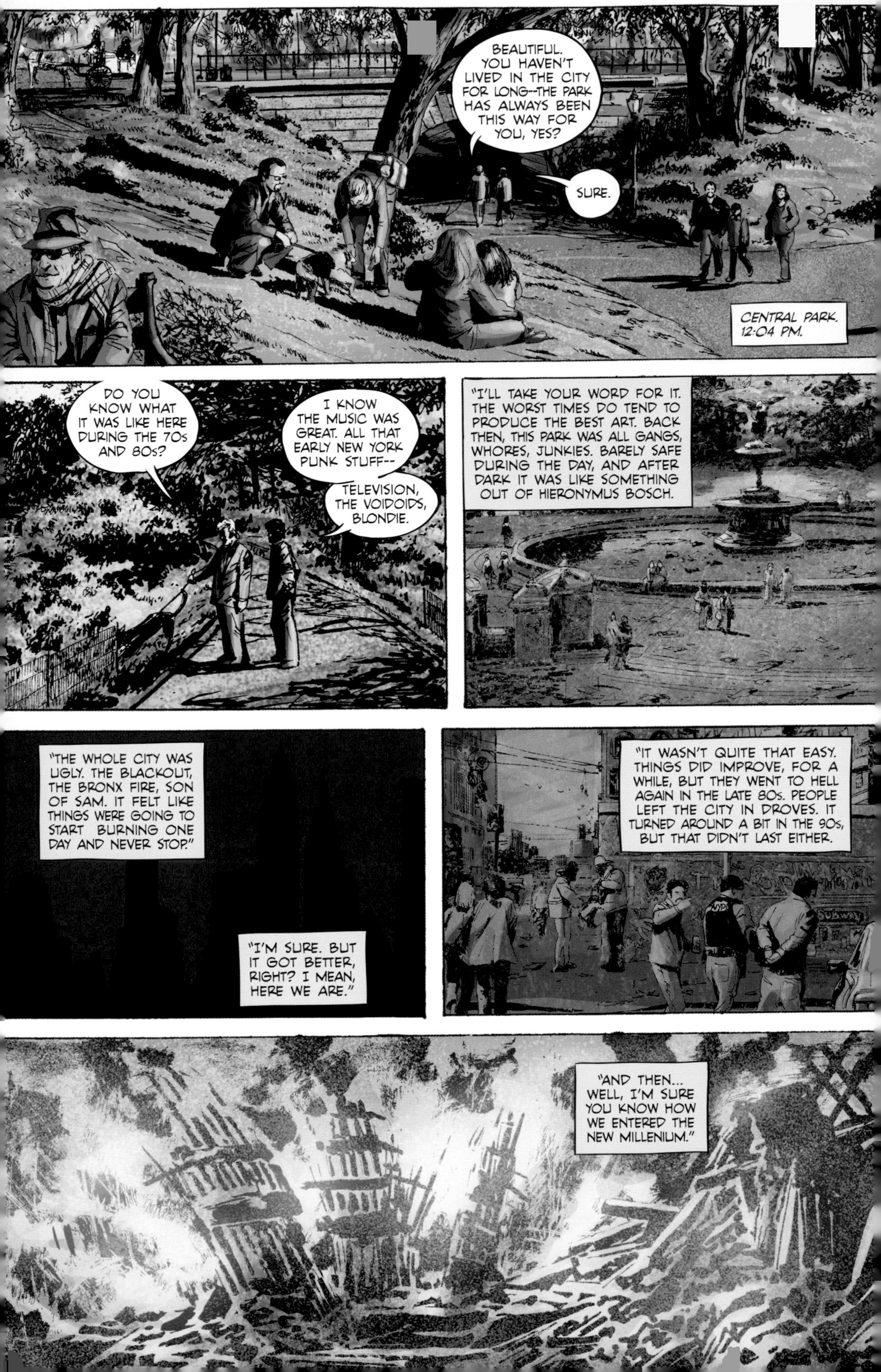
BEAUTIFUL. YOU HAVEN'T LIVED IN THE CITY FOR LONG--THE PARK HAS ALWAYS BEEN THIS WAY FOR YOU, YES?
SURE.
CENTRAL PARK. 12:04 PM.
DO YOU KNOW WHAT IT WAS LIKE HERE DURING THE 70s AND 80s?
I KNOW THE MUSIC WAS GREAT. ALL THAT EARLY NEW YORK PUNK STUFF--
TELEVISION, THE VOIDOIDS, BLONDIE.
"I'LL TAKE YOUR WORD FOR IT. THE WORST TIMES DO TEND TO PRODUCE THE BEST ART. BACK THEN, THIS PARK WAS ALL GANGS, WHORES, JUNKIES. BARELY SAFE DURING THE DAY, AND AFTER DARK IT WAS LIKE SOMETHING OUT OF HIERONYMUS BOSCH.
"THE WHOLE CITY WAS UGLY. THE BLACKOUT, THE BRONX FIRE, SON OF SAM. IT FELT LIKE THINGS WERE GOING TO START BURNING ONE DAY AND NEVER STOP."
"I'M SURE. BUT IT GOT BETTER, RIGHT? I MEAN, HERE WE ARE."
"IT WASN'T QUITE THAT EASY. THINGS DID IMPROVE, FOR A WHILE, BUT THEY WENT TO HELL AGAIN IN THE LATE 80s. PEOPLE LEFT THE CITY IN DROVES. IT TURNED AROUND A BIT IN THE 90s, BUT THAT DIDN'T LAST EITHER.
"AND THEN... WELL, I'M SURE YOU KNOW HOW WE ENTERED THE NEW MILLENIUM."

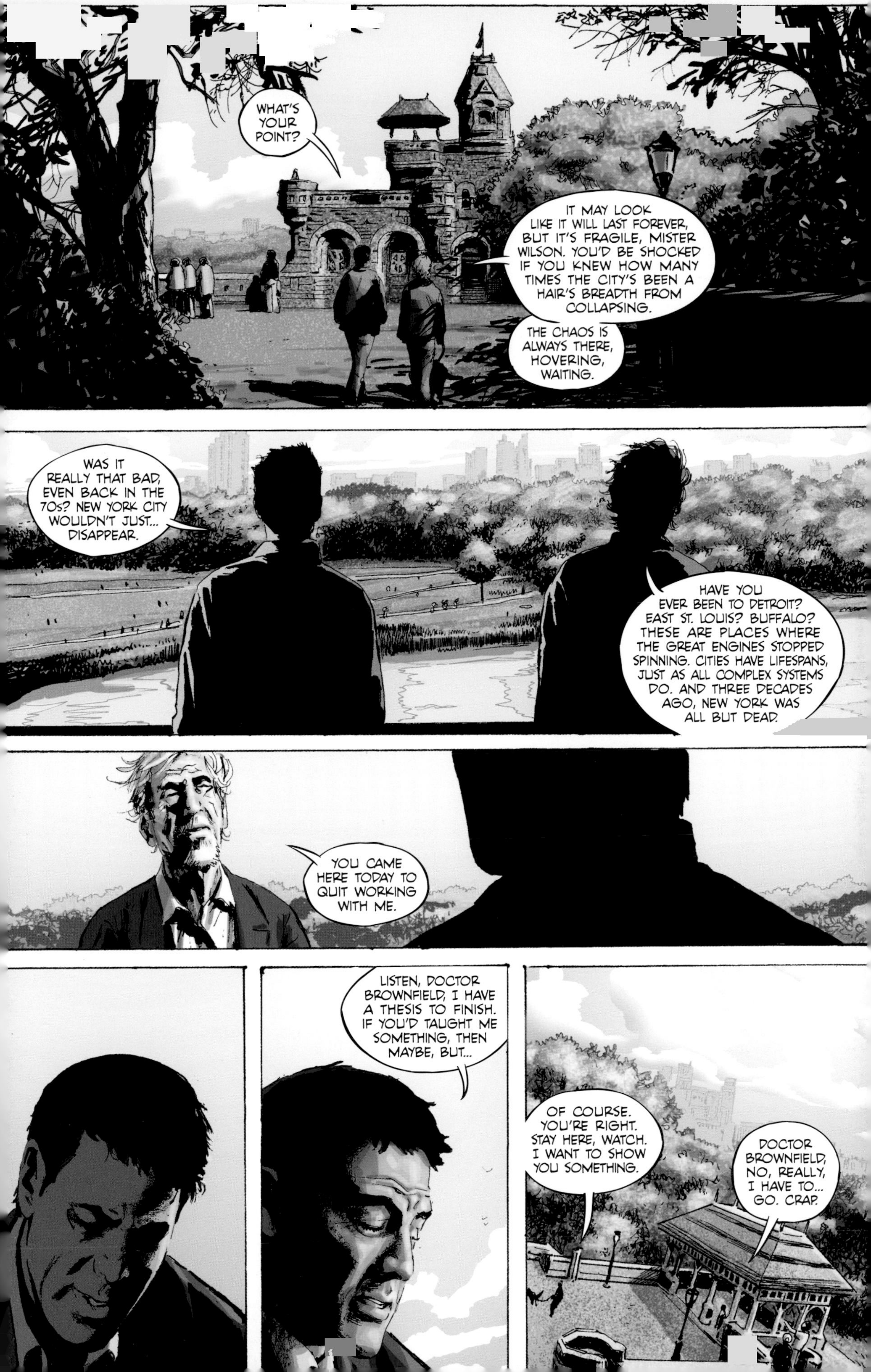
WHAT'S YOUR POINT?
IT MAY LOOK LIKE IT WILL LAST FOREVER, BUT IT'S FRAGILE, MISTER WILSON. YOU'D BE SHOCKED IF YOU KNEW HOW MANY TIMES THE CITY'S BEEN A HAIR'S BREADTH FROM COLLAPSING.
THE CHAOS IS ALWAYS THERE, HOVERING, WAITING.
WAS IT REALLY THAT BAD, EVEN BACK IN THE 70s? NEW YORK CITY WOULDN'T JUST... DISAPPEAR.
HAVE YOU EVER BEEN TO DETROIT? EAST ST. LOUIS? BUFFALO? THESE ARE PLACES WHERE THE GREAT ENGINES STOPPED SPINNING. CITIES HAVE LIFESPANS, JUST AS ALL COMPLEX SYSTEMS DO. AND THREE DECADES AGO, NEW YORK WAS ALL BUT DEAD.
YOU CAME HERE TODAY TO QUIT WORKING WITH ME.
LISTEN, DOCTOR BROWNFIELD, I HAVE A THESIS TO FINISH. IF YOU'D TAUGHT ME SOMETHING, THEN MAYBE, BUT...
OF COURSE. YOU'RE RIGHT. STAY HERE, WATCH. I WANT TO SHOW YOU SOMETHING.
DOCTOR BROWNFIELD, NO, REALLY, I HAVE TO... GO. CRAP.

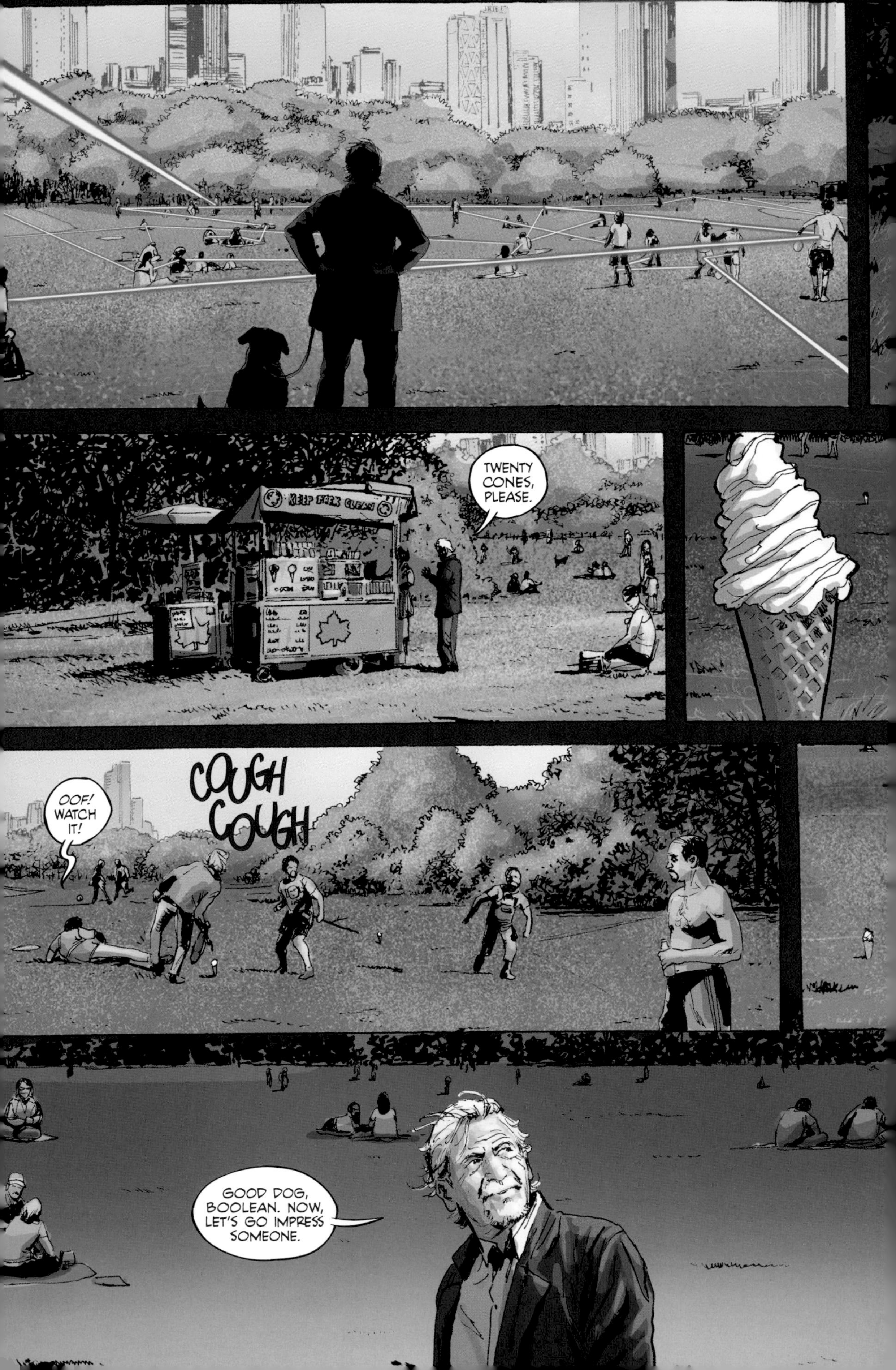
KEEP PARK CLEAN
TWENTY CONES, PLEASE.
COUGH COUGH
OOF! WATCH IT!
GOOD DOG, BOOLEAN. NOW, LET'S GO IMPRESS SOMEONE.

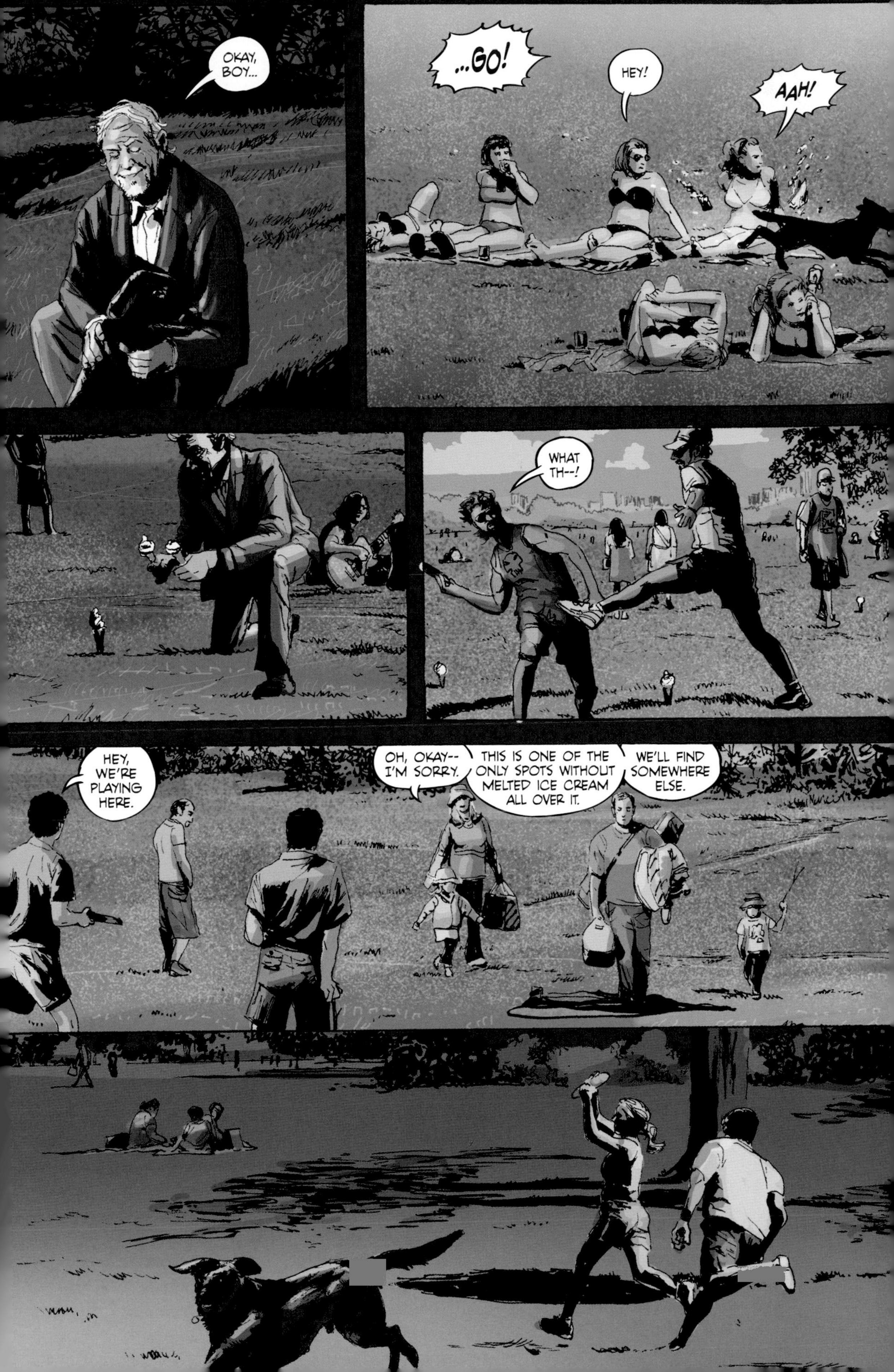
OKAY, BOY...
...GO!
HEY!
AAH!
WHAT TH--!
HEY, WE'RE PLAYING HERE.
OH, OKAY-- I'M SORRY.
THIS IS ONE OF THE ONLY SPOTS WITHOUT MELTED ICE CREAM ALL OVER IT.
WE'LL FIND SOMEWHERE ELSE.

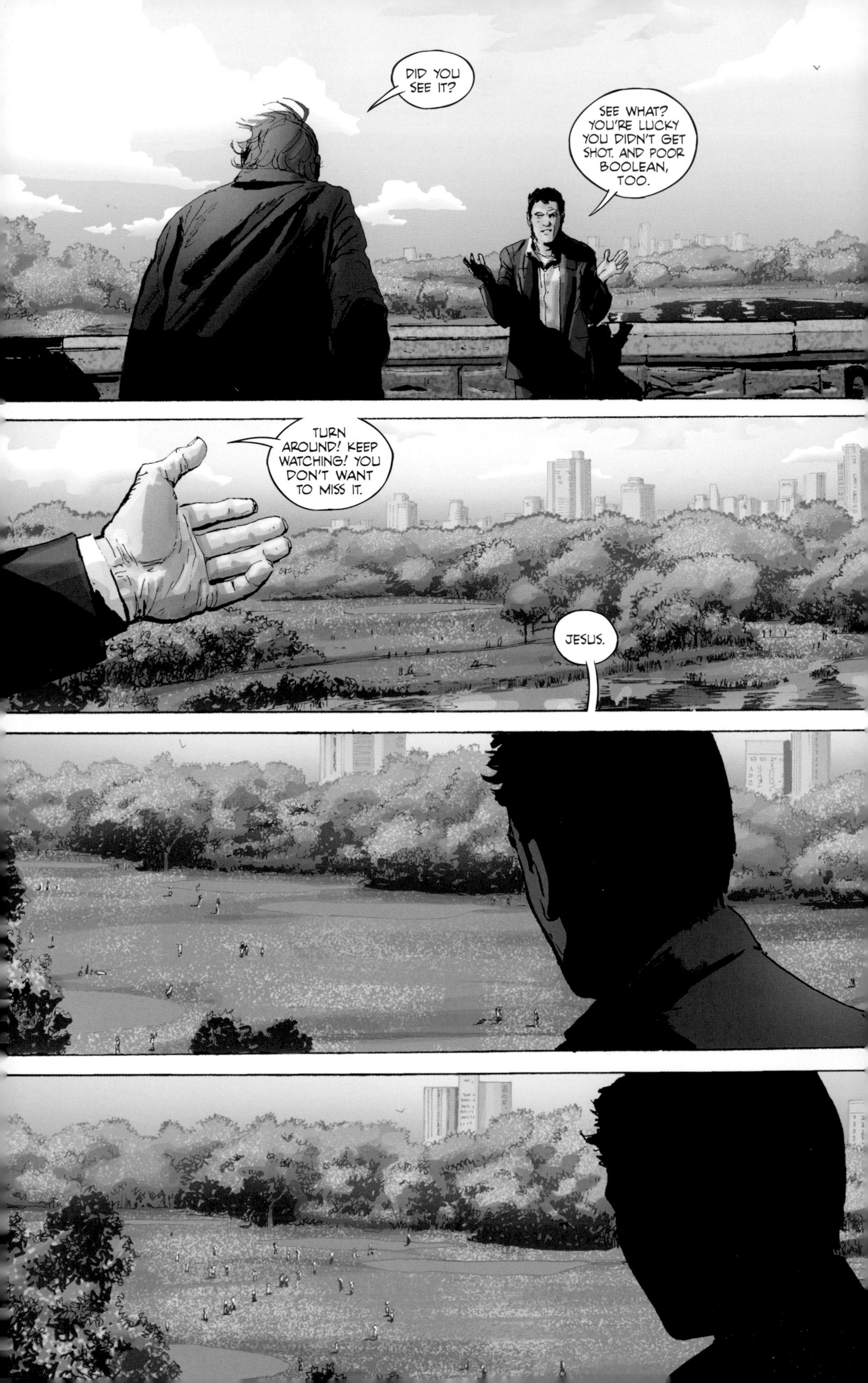
DID YOU SEE IT?
SEE WHAT? YOU'RE LUCKY YOU DIDN'T GET SHOT. AND POOR BOOLEAN, TOO.
TURN AROUND! KEEP WATCHING! YOU DON'T WANT TO MISS IT.
JESUS.

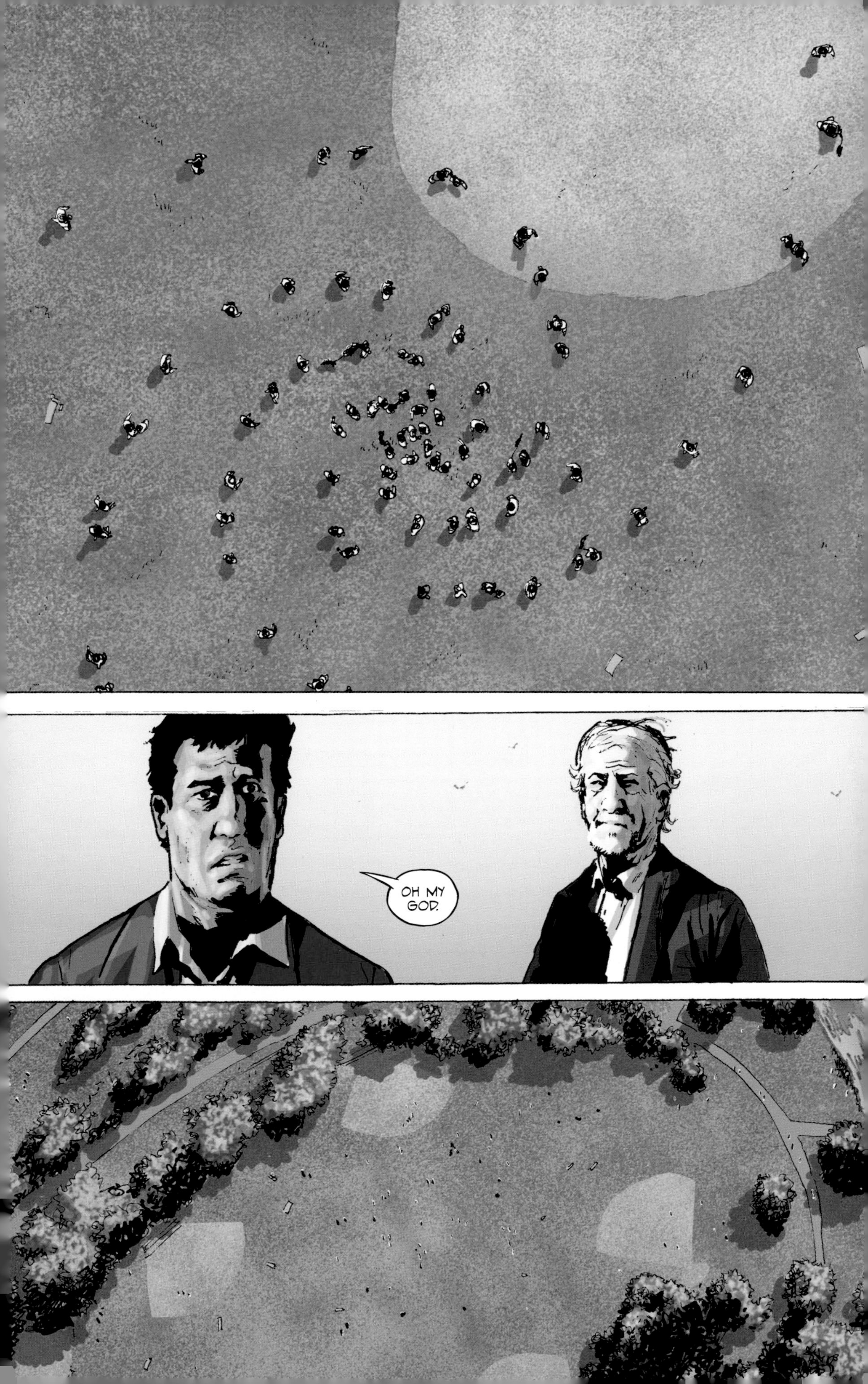
OH MY GOD.

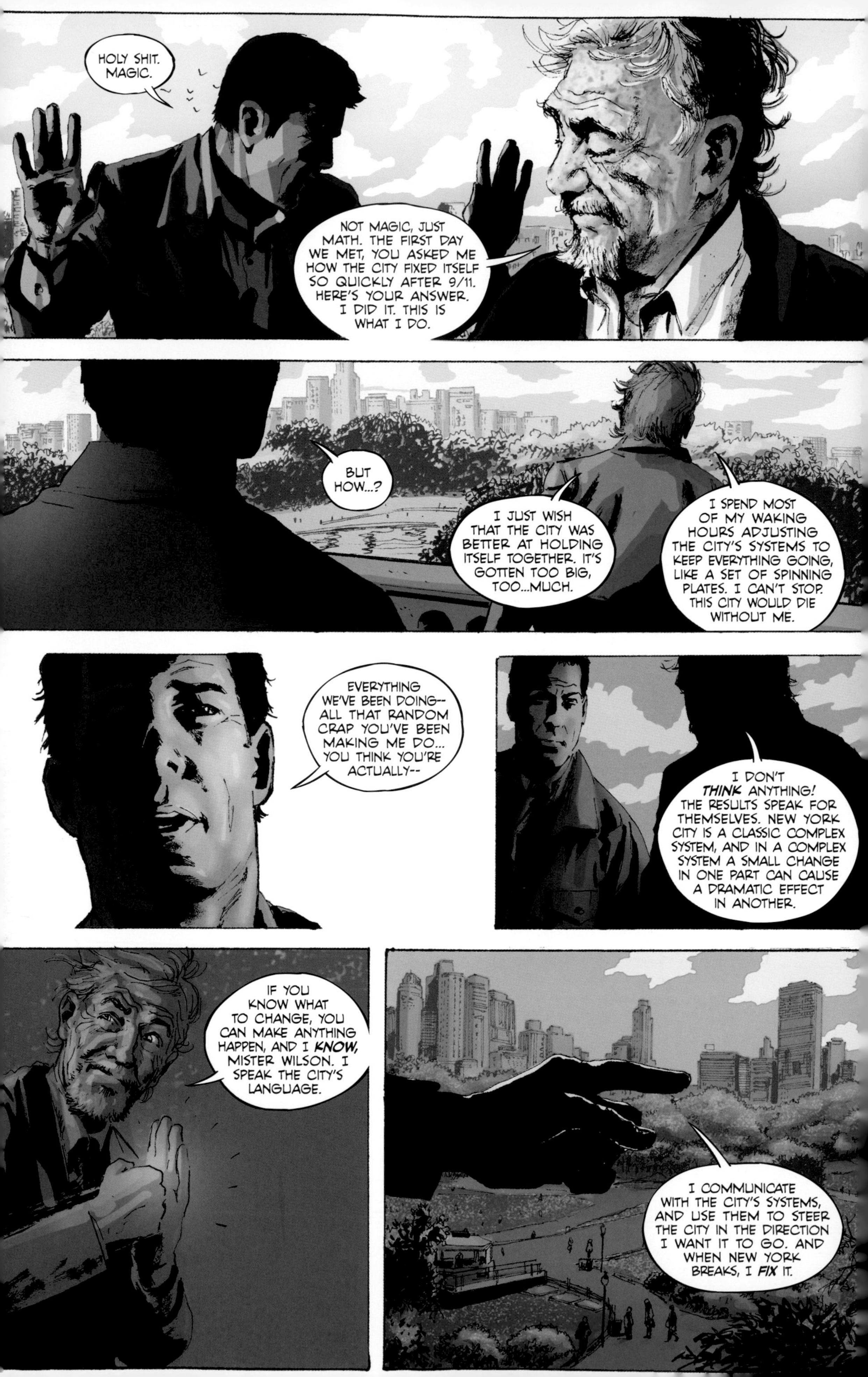
HOLY SHIT. MAGIC.
NOT MAGIC, JUST MATH. THE FIRST DAY WE MET, YOU ASKED ME HOW THE CITY FIXED ITSELF SO QUICKLY AFTER 9/11. HERE'S YOUR ANSWER. I DID IT. THIS IS WHAT I DO.
BUT HOW...?
I JUST WISH THAT THE CITY WAS BETTER AT HOLDING ITSELF TOGETHER. IT'S GOTTEN TOO BIG, TOO...MUCH.
I SPEND MOST OF MY WAKING HOURS ADJUSTING THE CITY'S SYSTEMS TO KEEP EVERYTHING GOING, LIKE A SET OF SPINNING PLATES. I CAN'T STOP. THIS CITY WOULD DIE WITHOUT ME.
EVERYTHING WE'VE BEEN DOING-- ALL THAT RANDOM CRAP YOU'VE BEEN MAKING ME DO... YOU THINK YOU'RE ACTUALLY--
I DON'T THINK ANYTHING! THE RESULTS SPEAK FOR THEMSELVES. NEW YORK CITY IS A CLASSIC COMPLEX SYSTEM, AND IN A COMPLEX SYSTEM A SMALL CHANGE IN ONE PART CAN CAUSE A DRAMATIC EFFECT IN ANOTHER.
IF YOU KNOW WHAT TO CHANGE, YOU CAN MAKE ANYTHING HAPPEN, AND I KNOW, MISTER WILSON. I SPEAK THE CITY'S LANGUAGE.
I COMMUNICATE WITH THE CITY'S SYSTEMS, AND USE THEM TO STEER THE CITY IN THE DIRECTION I WANT IT TO GO. AND WHEN NEW YORK BREAKS, I FIX IT.

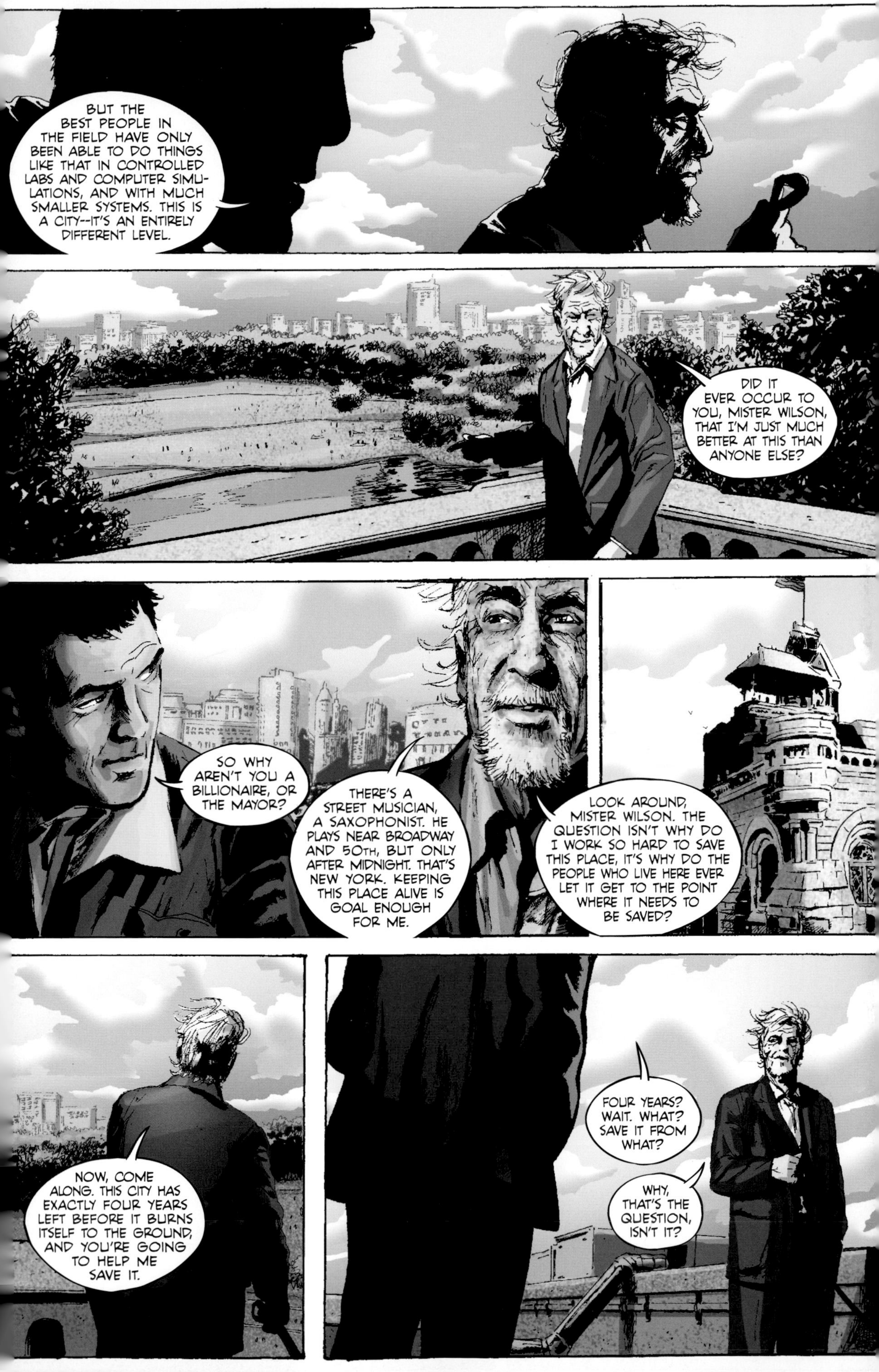
BUT THE BEST PEOPLE IN THE FIELD HAVE ONLY BEEN ABLE TO DO THINGS LIKE THAT IN CONTROLLED LABS AND COMPUTER SIMULATIONS, AND WITH MUCH SMALLER SYSTEMS. THIS IS A CITY--IT'S AN ENTIRELY DIFFERENT LEVEL.
DID IT EVER OCCUR TO YOU, MISTER WILSON, THAT I'M JUST MUCH BETTER AT THIS THAN ANYONE ELSE?
SO WHY AREN'T YOU A BILLIONAIRE, OR THE MAYOR?
THERE'S A STREET MUSICIAN, A SAXOPHONIST. HE PLAYS NEAR BROADWAY AND 50TH, BUT ONLY AFTER MIDNIGHT. THAT'S NEW YORK. KEEPING THIS PLACE ALIVE IS GOAL ENOUGH FOR ME.
LOOK AROUND, MISTER WILSON. THE QUESTION ISN'T WHY DO I WORK SO HARD TO SAVE THIS PLACE, IT'S WHY DO THE PEOPLE WHO LIVE HERE EVER LET IT GET TO THE POINT WHERE IT NEEDS TO BE SAVED?
NOW, COME ALONG. THIS CITY HAS EXACTLY FOUR YEARS LEFT BEFORE IT BURNS ITSELF TO THE GROUND, AND YOU'RE GOING TO HELP ME SAVE IT.
FOUR YEARS? WAIT. WHAT? SAVE IT FROM WHAT?
WHY, THAT'S THE QUESTION, ISN'T IT?

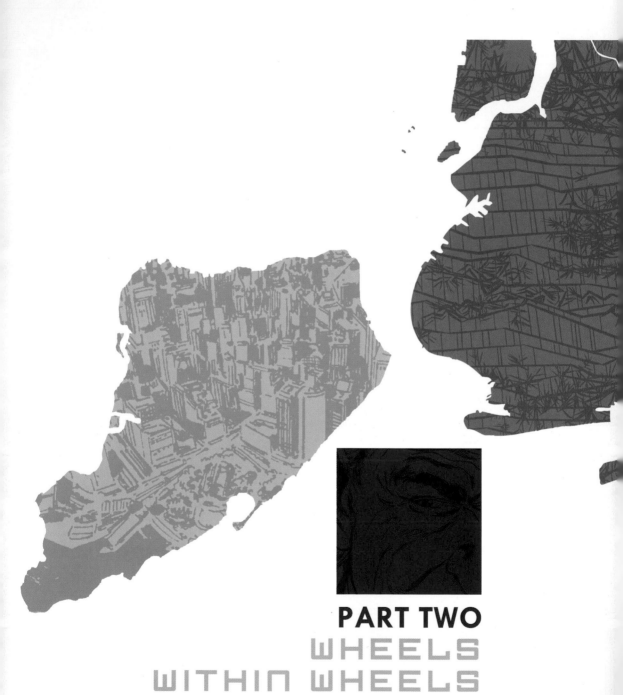

PART TWO
WHEELS
WITHIN WHEELS

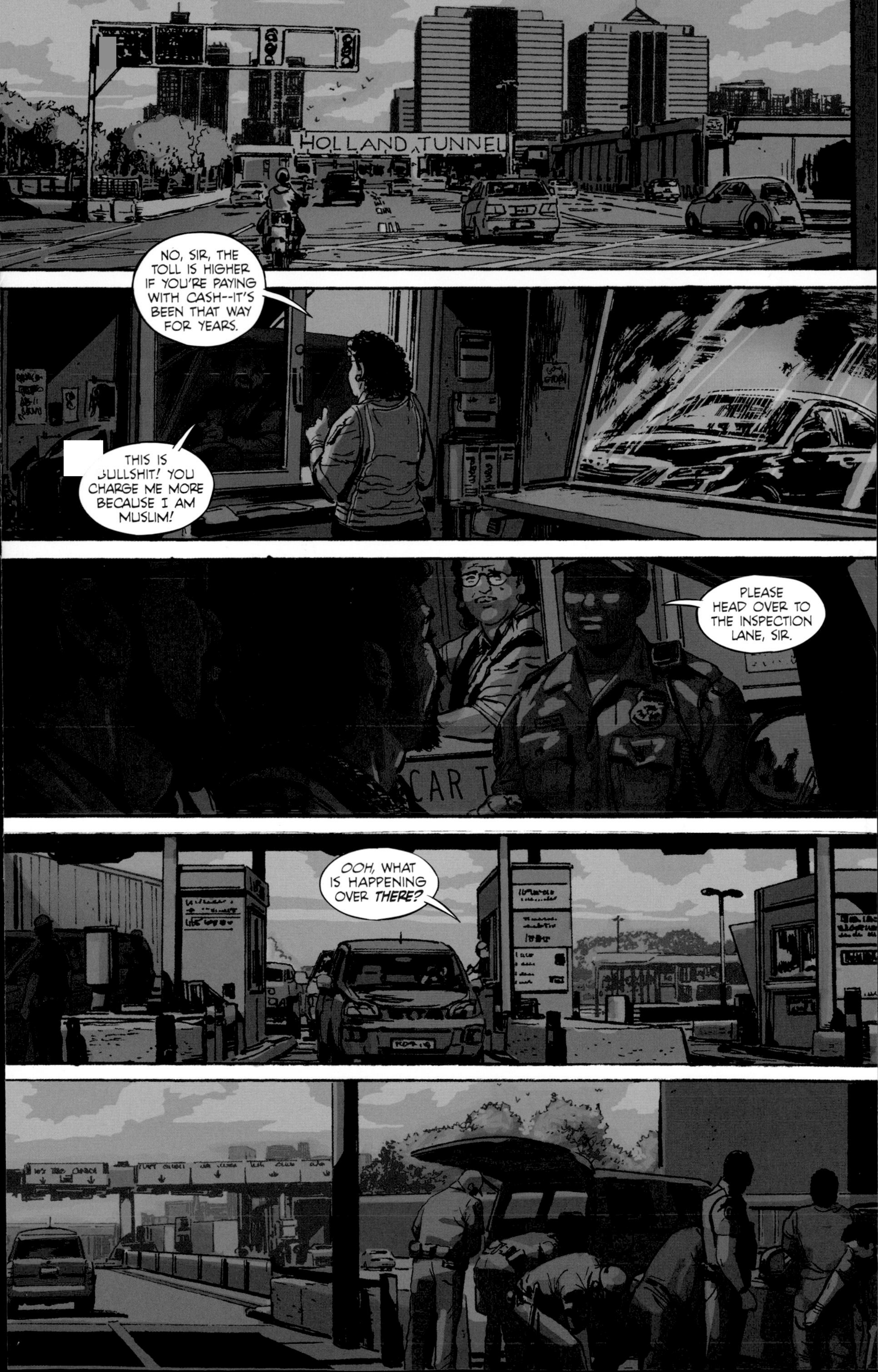
HOLLAND TUNNEL
NO, SIR, THE TOLL IS HIGHER IF YOU'RE PAYING WITH CASH--IT'S BEEN THAT WAY FOR YEARS.
THIS IS BULLSHIT! YOU CHARGE ME MORE BECAUSE I AM MUSLIM!
PLEASE HEAD OVER TO THE INSPECTION LANE, SIR.
OOH, WHAT IS HAPPENING OVER ***THERE?***

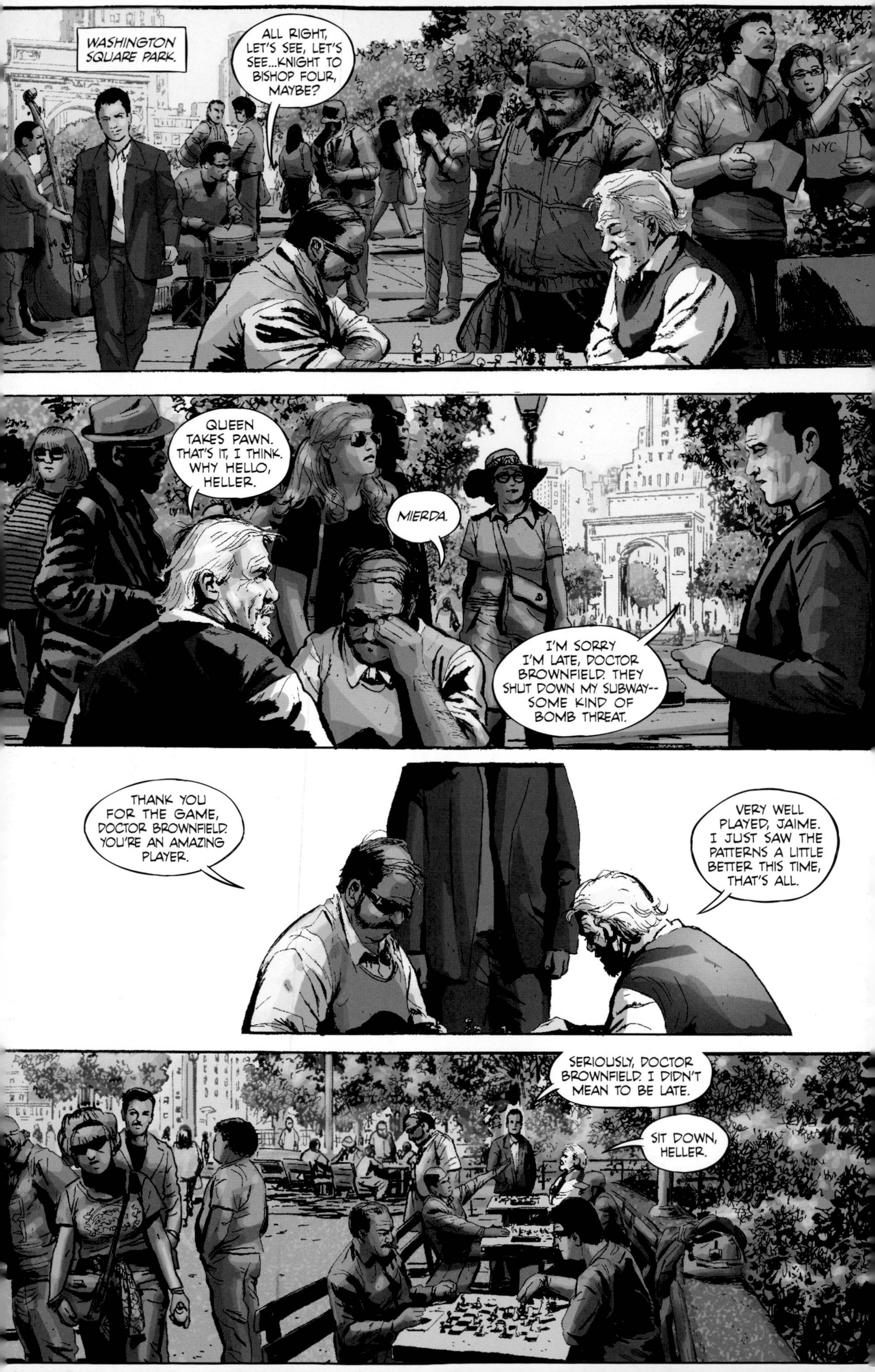
WASHINGTON SQUARE PARK.
ALL RIGHT, LET'S SEE, LET'S SEE...KNIGHT TO BISHOP FOUR, MAYBE?
NYC
QUEEN TAKES PAWN. THAT'S IT, I THINK. WHY HELLO, HELLER.
MIERDA.
I'M SORRY I'M LATE, DOCTOR BROWNFIELD. THEY SHUT DOWN MY SUBWAY-- SOME KIND OF BOMB THREAT.
THANK YOU FOR THE GAME, DOCTOR BROWNFIELD. YOU'RE AN AMAZING PLAYER.
VERY WELL PLAYED, JAIME. I JUST SAW THE PATTERNS A LITTLE BETTER THIS TIME, THAT'S ALL.
SERIOUSLY, DOCTOR BROWNFIELD. I DIDN'T MEAN TO BE LATE.
SIT DOWN, HELLER.

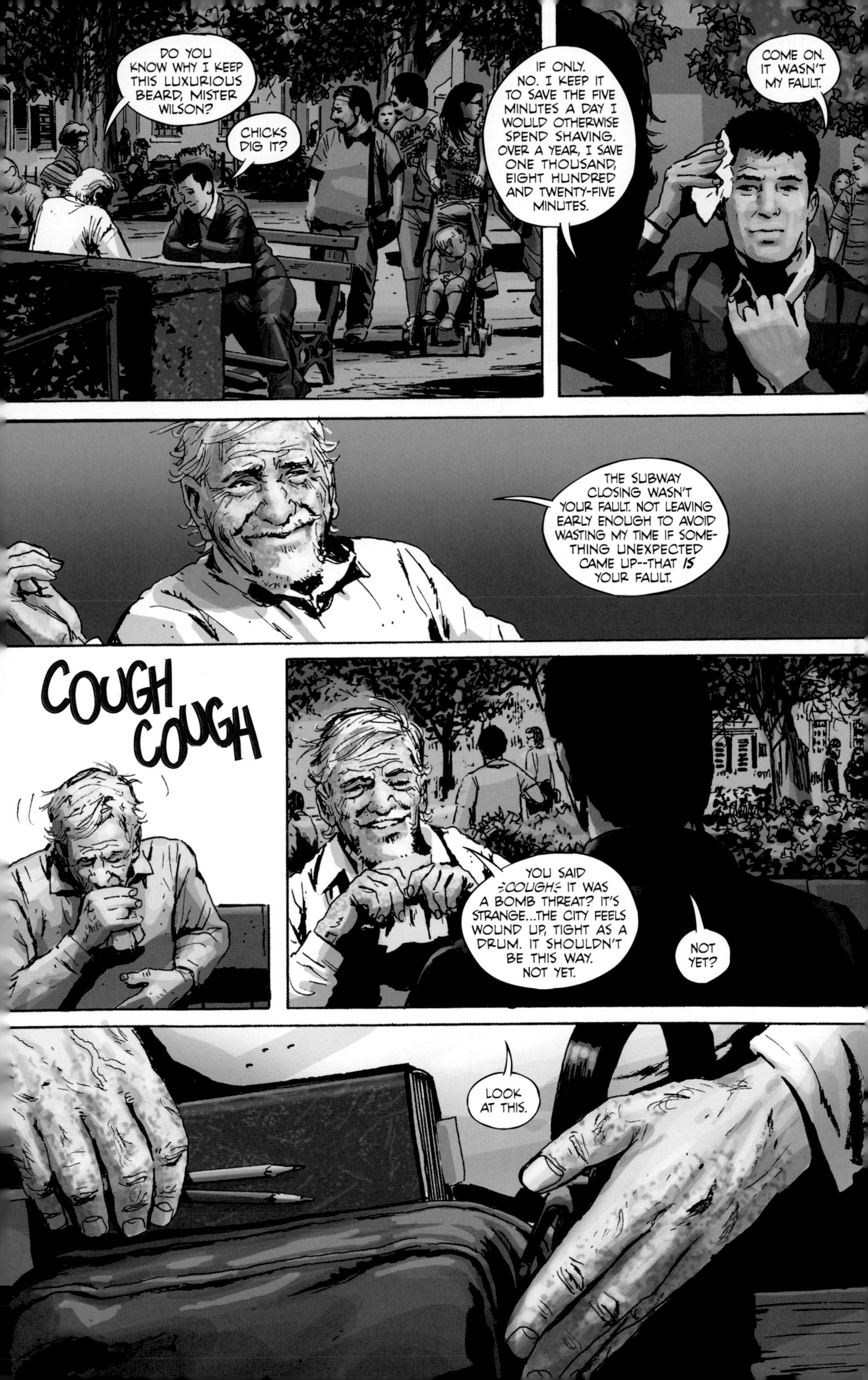
DO YOU KNOW WHY I KEEP THIS LUXURIOUS BEARD, MISTER WILSON?
CHICKS DIG IT?
IF ONLY. NO. I KEEP IT TO SAVE THE FIVE MINUTES A DAY I WOULD OTHERWISE SPEND SHAVING. OVER A YEAR, I SAVE ONE THOUSAND, EIGHT HUNDRED AND TWENTY-FIVE MINUTES.
COME ON. IT WASN'T MY FAULT.
THE SUBWAY CLOSING WASN'T YOUR FAULT. NOT LEAVING EARLY ENOUGH TO AVOID WASTING MY TIME IF SOME-THING UNEXPECTED CAME UP--THAT IS YOUR FAULT.
COUGH COUGH
YOU SAID =COUGH= IT WAS A BOMB THREAT? IT'S STRANGE...THE CITY FEELS WOUND UP, TIGHT AS A DRUM. IT SHOULDN'T BE THIS WAY. NOT YET.
NOT YET?
LOOK AT THIS.

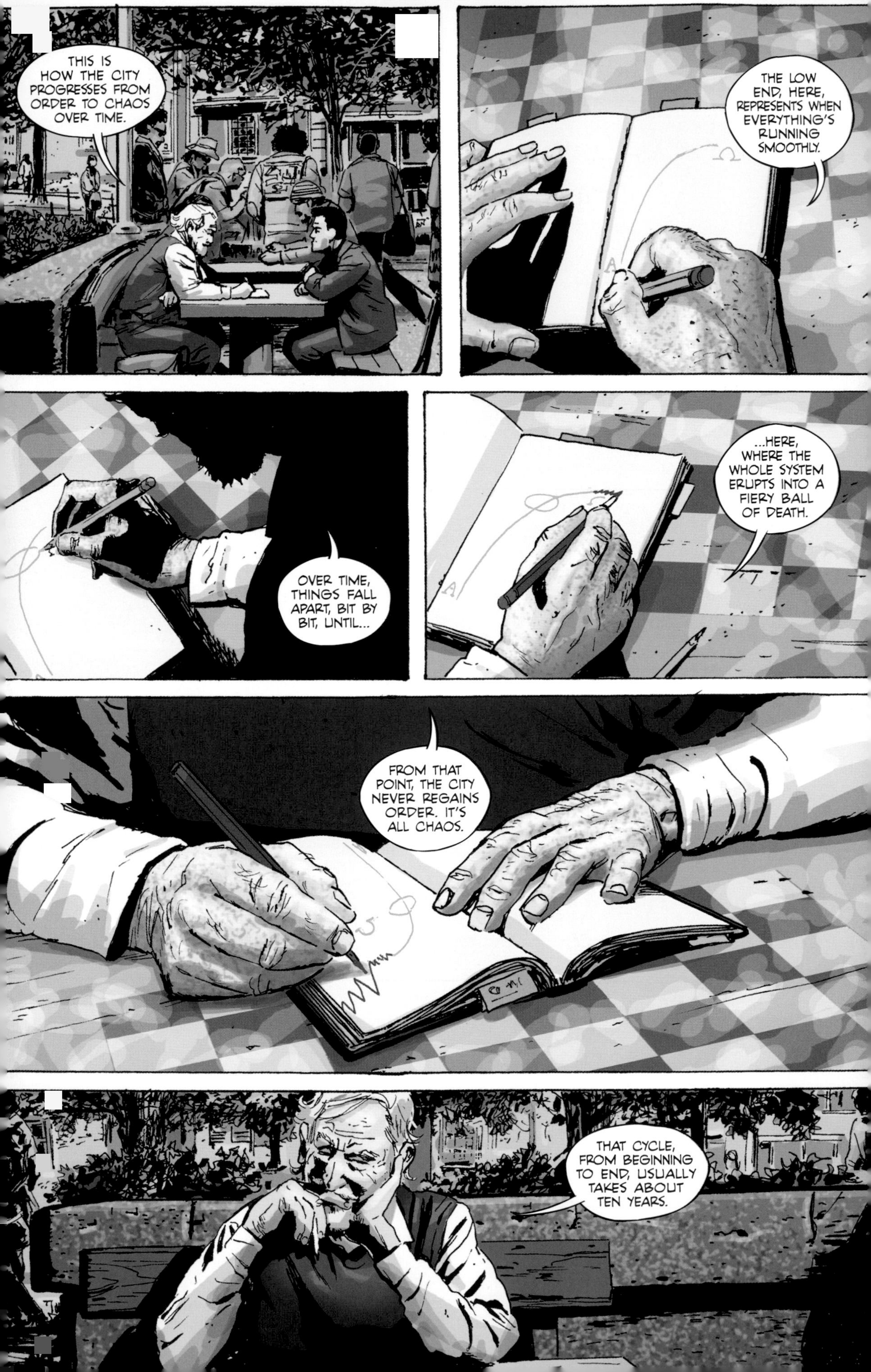
THIS IS HOW THE CITY PROGRESSES FROM ORDER TO CHAOS OVER TIME.
THE LOW END, HERE, REPRESENTS WHEN EVERYTHING'S RUNNING SMOOTHLY.
OVER TIME, THINGS FALL APART, BIT BY BIT, UNTIL...
...HERE, WHERE THE WHOLE SYSTEM ERUPTS INTO A FIERY BALL OF DEATH.
FROM THAT POINT, THE CITY NEVER REGAINS ORDER. IT'S ALL CHAOS.
THAT CYCLE, FROM BEGINNING TO END, USUALLY TAKES ABOUT TEN YEARS.

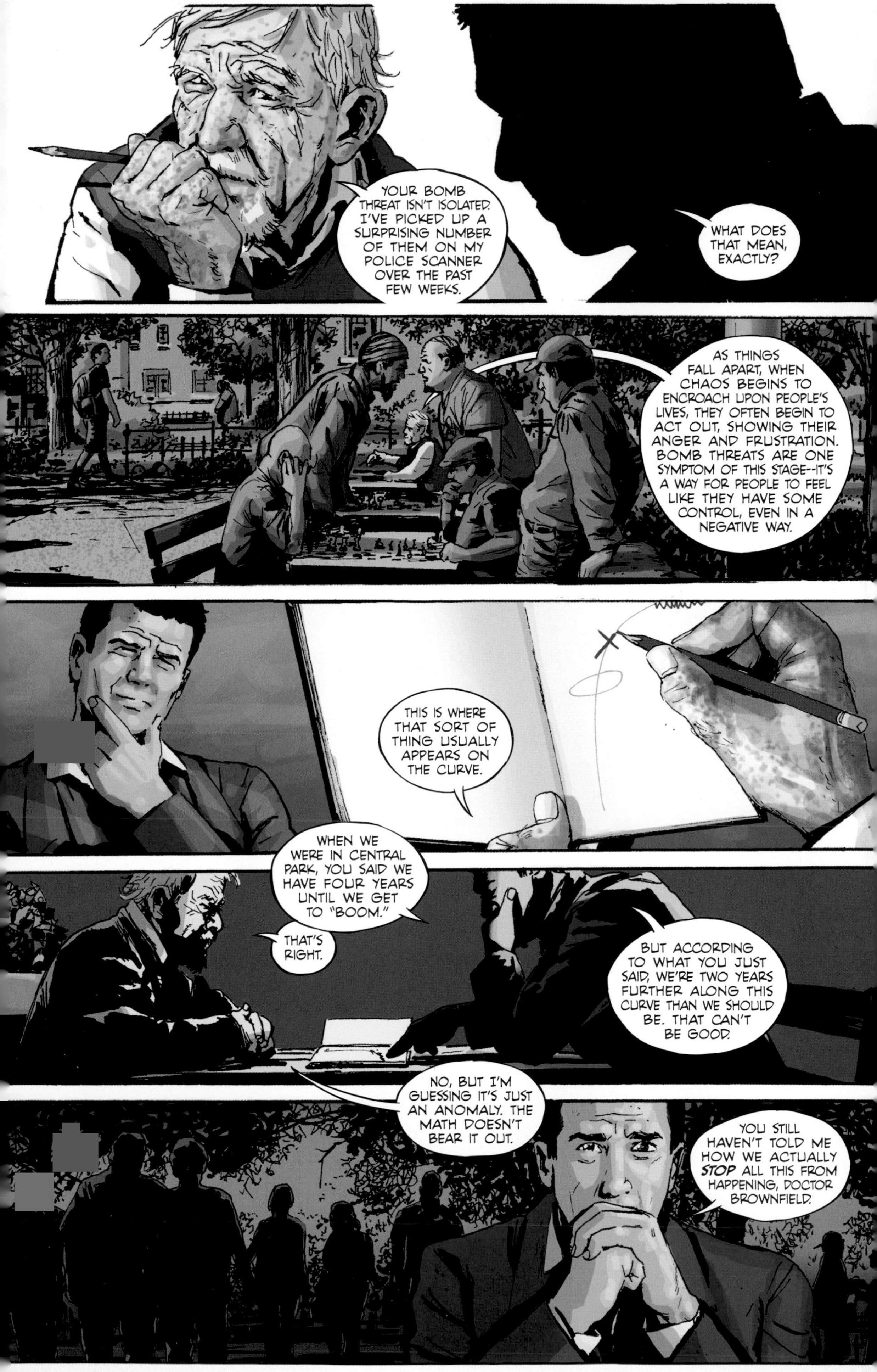
YOUR BOMB THREAT ISN'T ISOLATED. I'VE PICKED UP A SURPRISING NUMBER OF THEM ON MY POLICE SCANNER OVER THE PAST FEW WEEKS.
WHAT DOES THAT MEAN, EXACTLY?
AS THINGS FALL APART, WHEN CHAOS BEGINS TO ENCROACH UPON PEOPLE'S LIVES, THEY OFTEN BEGIN TO ACT OUT, SHOWING THEIR ANGER AND FRUSTRATION. BOMB THREATS ARE ONE SYMPTOM OF THIS STAGE--IT'S A WAY FOR PEOPLE TO FEEL LIKE THEY HAVE SOME CONTROL, EVEN IN A NEGATIVE WAY.
THIS IS WHERE THAT SORT OF THING USUALLY APPEARS ON THE CURVE.
WHEN WE WERE IN CENTRAL PARK, YOU SAID WE HAVE FOUR YEARS UNTIL WE GET TO "BOOM."
THAT'S RIGHT.
BUT ACCORDING TO WHAT YOU JUST SAID, WE'RE TWO YEARS FURTHER ALONG THIS CURVE THAN WE SHOULD BE. THAT CAN'T BE GOOD.
NO, BUT I'M GUESSING IT'S JUST AN ANOMALY. THE MATH DOESN'T BEAR IT OUT.
YOU STILL HAVEN'T TOLD ME HOW WE ACTUALLY *STOP* ALL THIS FROM HAPPENING, DOCTOR BROWNFIELD.

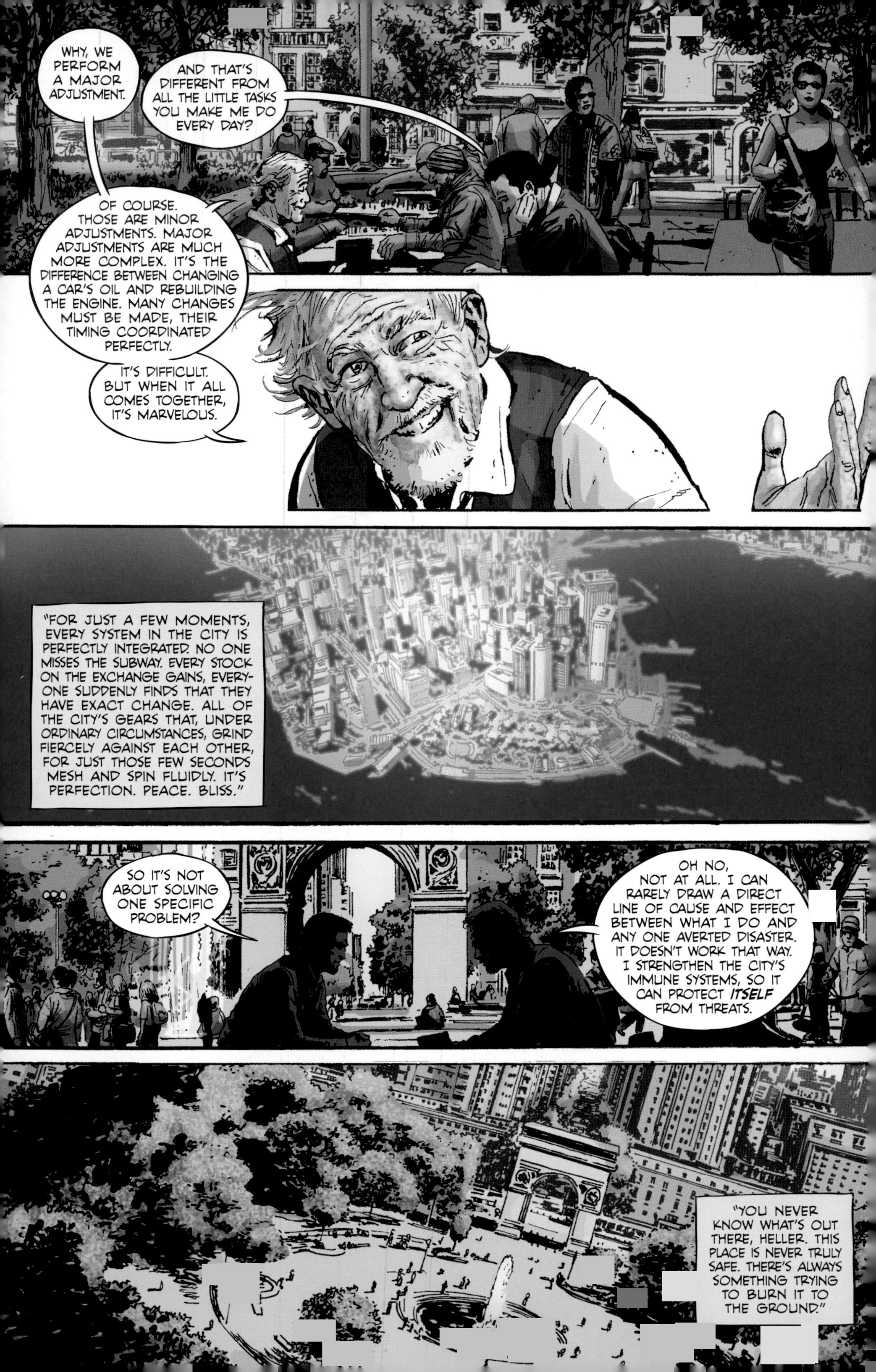
WHY, WE PERFORM A MAJOR ADJUSTMENT.
AND THAT'S DIFFERENT FROM ALL THE LITTLE TASKS YOU MAKE ME DO EVERY DAY?
OF COURSE. THOSE ARE MINOR ADJUSTMENTS. MAJOR ADJUSTMENTS ARE MUCH MORE COMPLEX. IT'S THE DIFFERENCE BETWEEN CHANGING A CAR'S OIL AND REBUILDING THE ENGINE. MANY CHANGES MUST BE MADE, THEIR TIMING COORDINATED PERFECTLY.
IT'S DIFFICULT. BUT WHEN IT ALL COMES TOGETHER, IT'S MARVELOUS.
"FOR JUST A FEW MOMENTS, EVERY SYSTEM IN THE CITY IS PERFECTLY INTEGRATED. NO ONE MISSES THE SUBWAY. EVERY STOCK ON THE EXCHANGE GAINS, EVERYONE SUDDENLY FINDS THAT THEY HAVE EXACT CHANGE. ALL OF THE CITY'S GEARS THAT, UNDER ORDINARY CIRCUMSTANCES, GRIND FIERCELY AGAINST EACH OTHER, FOR JUST THOSE FEW SECONDS MESH AND SPIN FLUIDLY. IT'S PERFECTION. PEACE. BLISS."
SO IT'S NOT ABOUT SOLVING ONE SPECIFIC PROBLEM?
OH NO, NOT AT ALL. I CAN RARELY DRAW A DIRECT LINE OF CAUSE AND EFFECT BETWEEN WHAT I DO AND ANY ONE AVERTED DISASTER. IT DOESN'T WORK THAT WAY. I STRENGTHEN THE CITY'S IMMUNE SYSTEMS, SO IT CAN PROTECT *ITSELF* FROM THREATS.
"YOU NEVER KNOW WHAT'S OUT THERE, HELLER. THIS PLACE IS NEVER TRULY SAFE. THERE'S ALWAYS SOMETHING TRYING TO BURN IT TO THE GROUND."

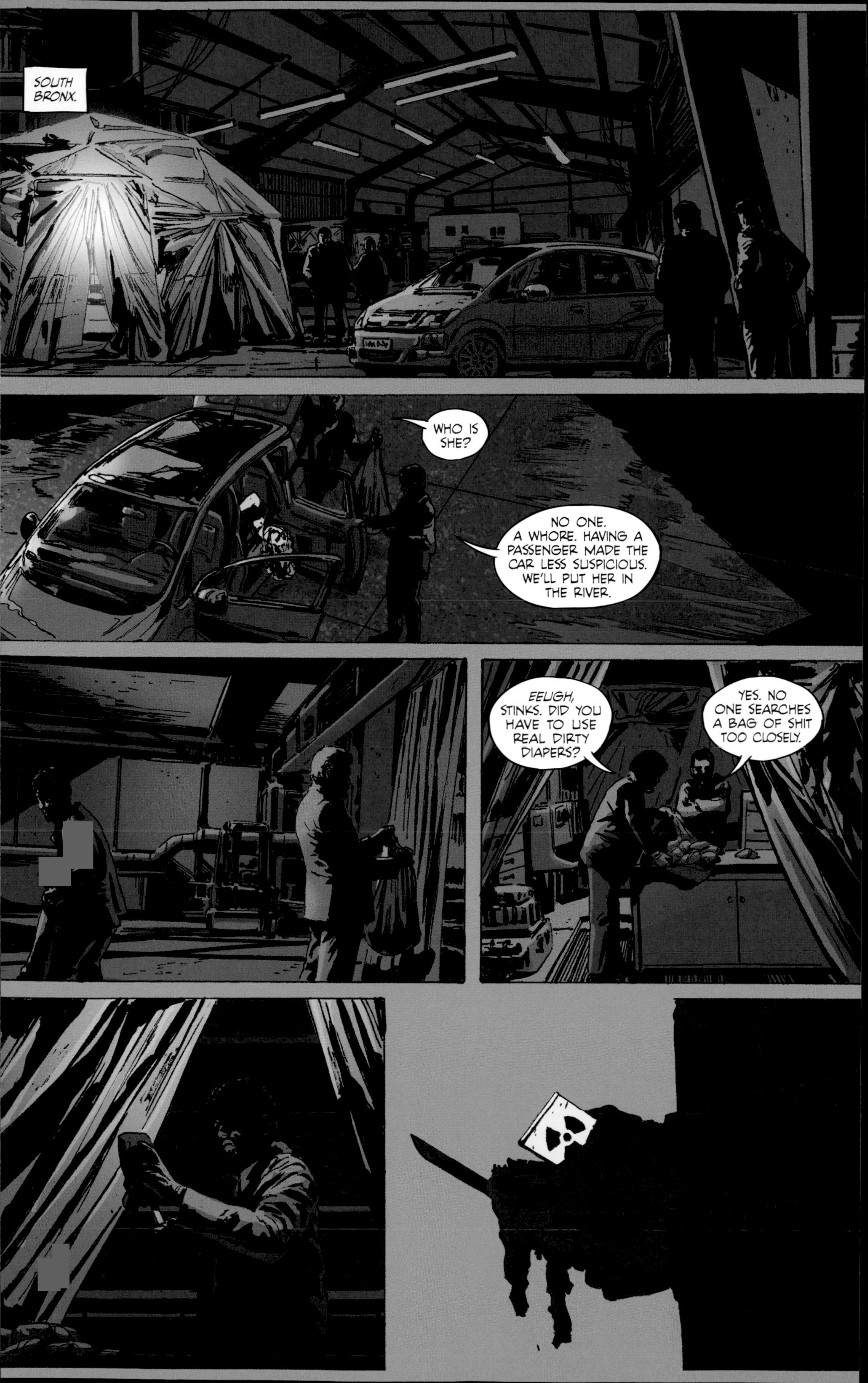
SOUTH BRONX.
WHO IS SHE?
NO ONE. A WHORE. HAVING A PASSENGER MADE THE CAR LESS SUSPICIOUS. WE'LL PUT HER IN THE RIVER.
EEUGH, STINKS. DID YOU HAVE TO USE REAL DIRTY DIAPERS?
YES. NO ONE SEARCHES A BAG OF SHIT TOO CLOSELY.

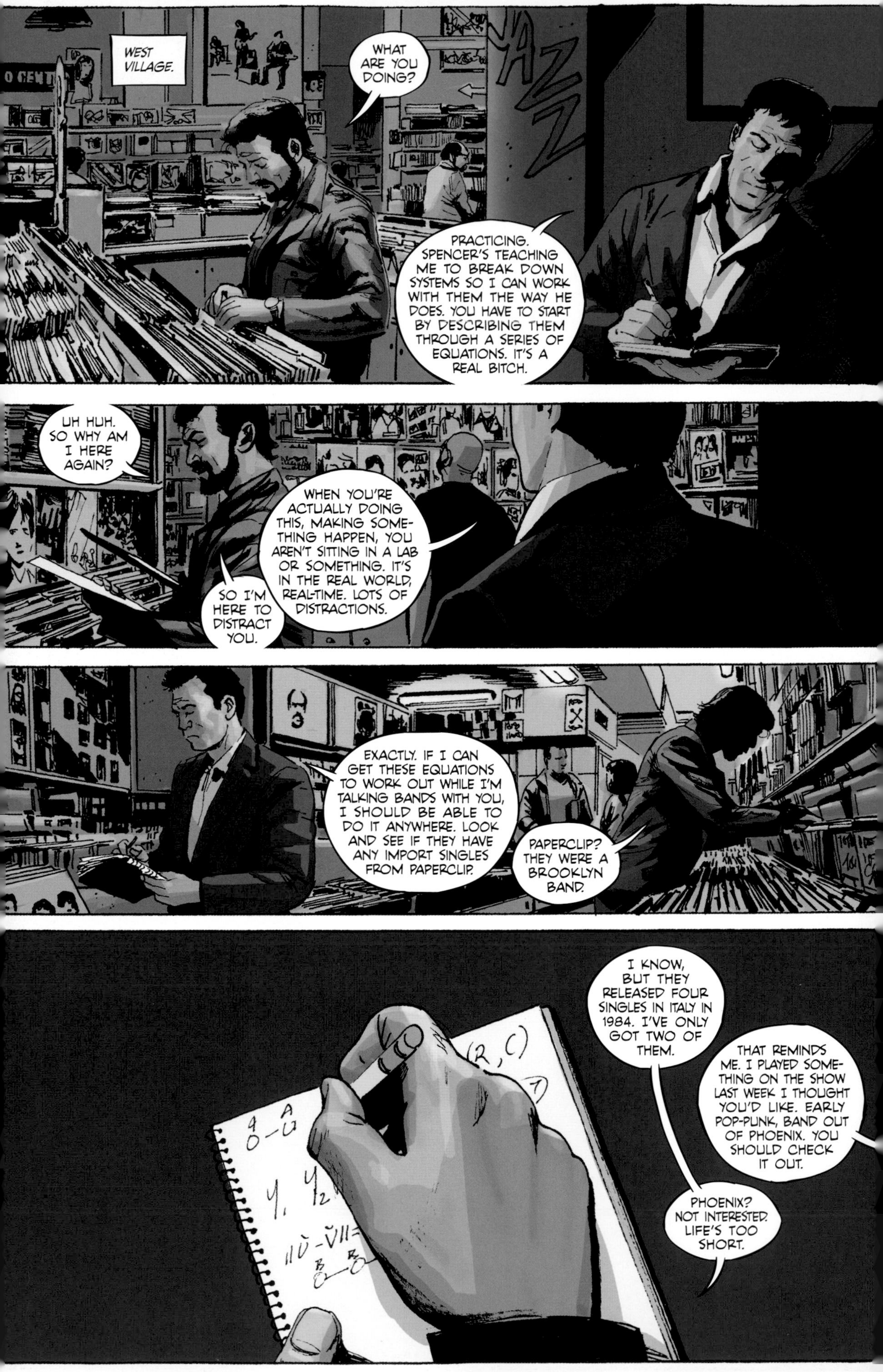

WEST VILLAGE.
WHAT ARE YOU DOING?
PRACTICING. SPENCER'S TEACHING ME TO BREAK DOWN SYSTEMS SO I CAN WORK WITH THEM THE WAY HE DOES. YOU HAVE TO START BY DESCRIBING THEM THROUGH A SERIES OF EQUATIONS. IT'S A REAL BITCH.
UH HUH. SO WHY AM I HERE AGAIN?
WHEN YOU'RE ACTUALLY DOING THIS, MAKING SOME-THING HAPPEN, YOU AREN'T SITTING IN A LAB OR SOMETHING. IT'S IN THE REAL WORLD, REAL-TIME. LOTS OF DISTRACTIONS.
SO I'M HERE TO DISTRACT YOU.
EXACTLY. IF I CAN GET THESE EQUATIONS TO WORK OUT WHILE I'M TALKING BANDS WITH YOU, I SHOULD BE ABLE TO DO IT ANYWHERE. LOOK AND SEE IF THEY HAVE ANY IMPORT SINGLES FROM PAPERCLIP.
PAPERCLIP? THEY WERE A BROOKLYN BAND.
I KNOW, BUT THEY RELEASED FOUR SINGLES IN ITALY IN 1984. I'VE ONLY GOT TWO OF THEM.
THAT REMINDS ME. I PLAYED SOME-THING ON THE SHOW LAST WEEK I THOUGHT YOU'D LIKE. EARLY POP-PUNK, BAND OUT OF PHOENIX. YOU SHOULD CHECK IT OUT.
PHOENIX? NOT INTERESTED. LIFE'S TOO SHORT.

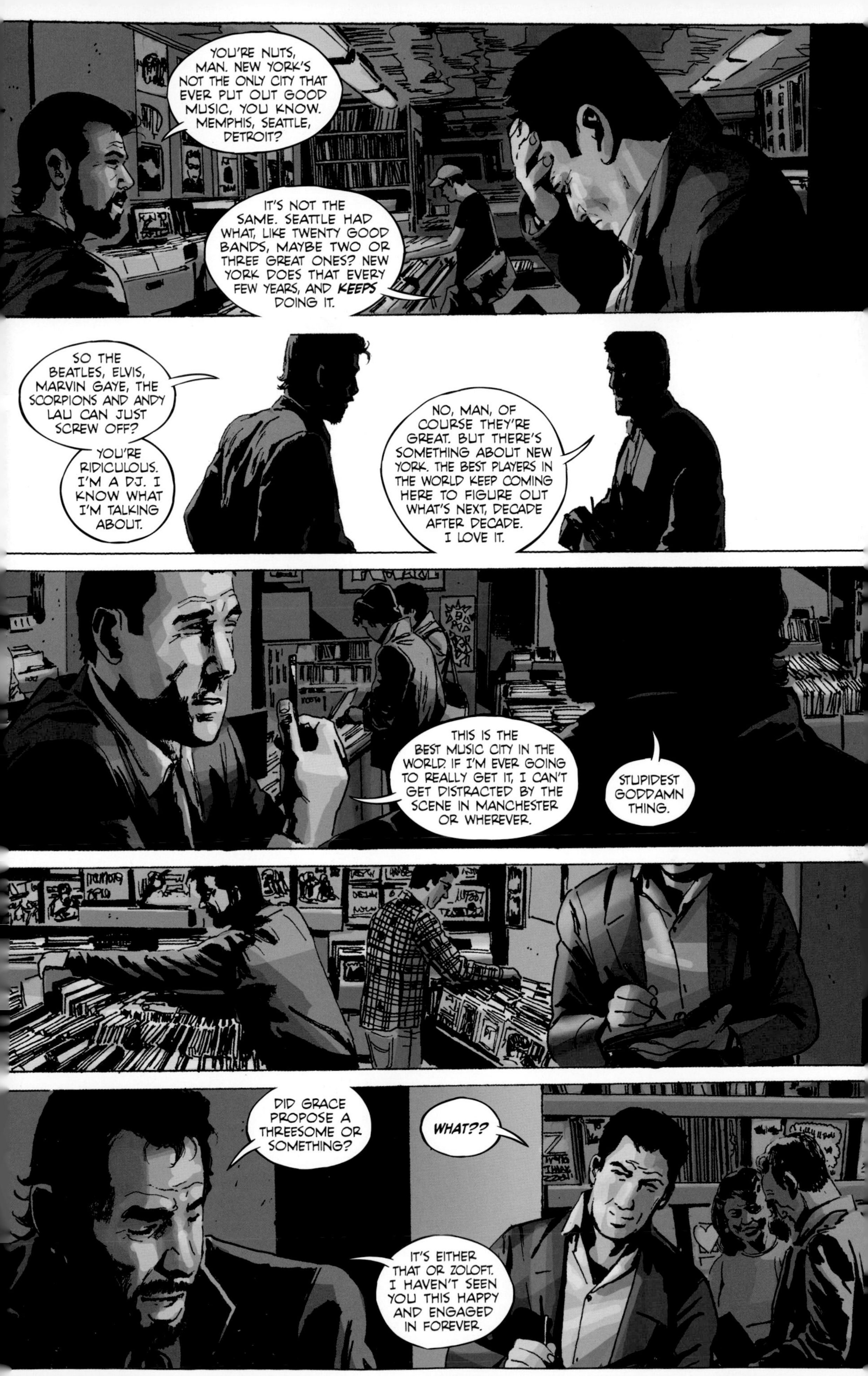
YOU'RE NUTS, MAN. NEW YORK'S NOT THE ONLY CITY THAT EVER PUT OUT GOOD MUSIC, YOU KNOW. MEMPHIS, SEATTLE, DETROIT?
IT'S NOT THE SAME. SEATTLE HAD WHAT, LIKE TWENTY GOOD BANDS, MAYBE TWO OR THREE GREAT ONES? NEW YORK DOES THAT EVERY FEW YEARS, AND KEEPS DOING IT.
SO THE BEATLES, ELVIS, MARVIN GAYE, THE SCORPIONS AND ANDY LAU CAN JUST SCREW OFF?
YOU'RE RIDICULOUS. I'M A DJ. I KNOW WHAT I'M TALKING ABOUT.
NO, MAN, OF COURSE THEY'RE GREAT. BUT THERE'S SOMETHING ABOUT NEW YORK. THE BEST PLAYERS IN THE WORLD KEEP COMING HERE TO FIGURE OUT WHAT'S NEXT, DECADE AFTER DECADE. I LOVE IT.
THIS IS THE BEST MUSIC CITY IN THE WORLD. IF I'M EVER GOING TO REALLY GET IT, I CAN'T GET DISTRACTED BY THE SCENE IN MANCHESTER OR WHEREVER.
STUPIDEST GODDAMN THING.
DID GRACE PROPOSE A THREESOME OR SOMETHING?
WHAT??
IT'S EITHER THAT OR ZOLOFT. I HAVEN'T SEEN YOU THIS HAPPY AND ENGAGED IN FOREVER.

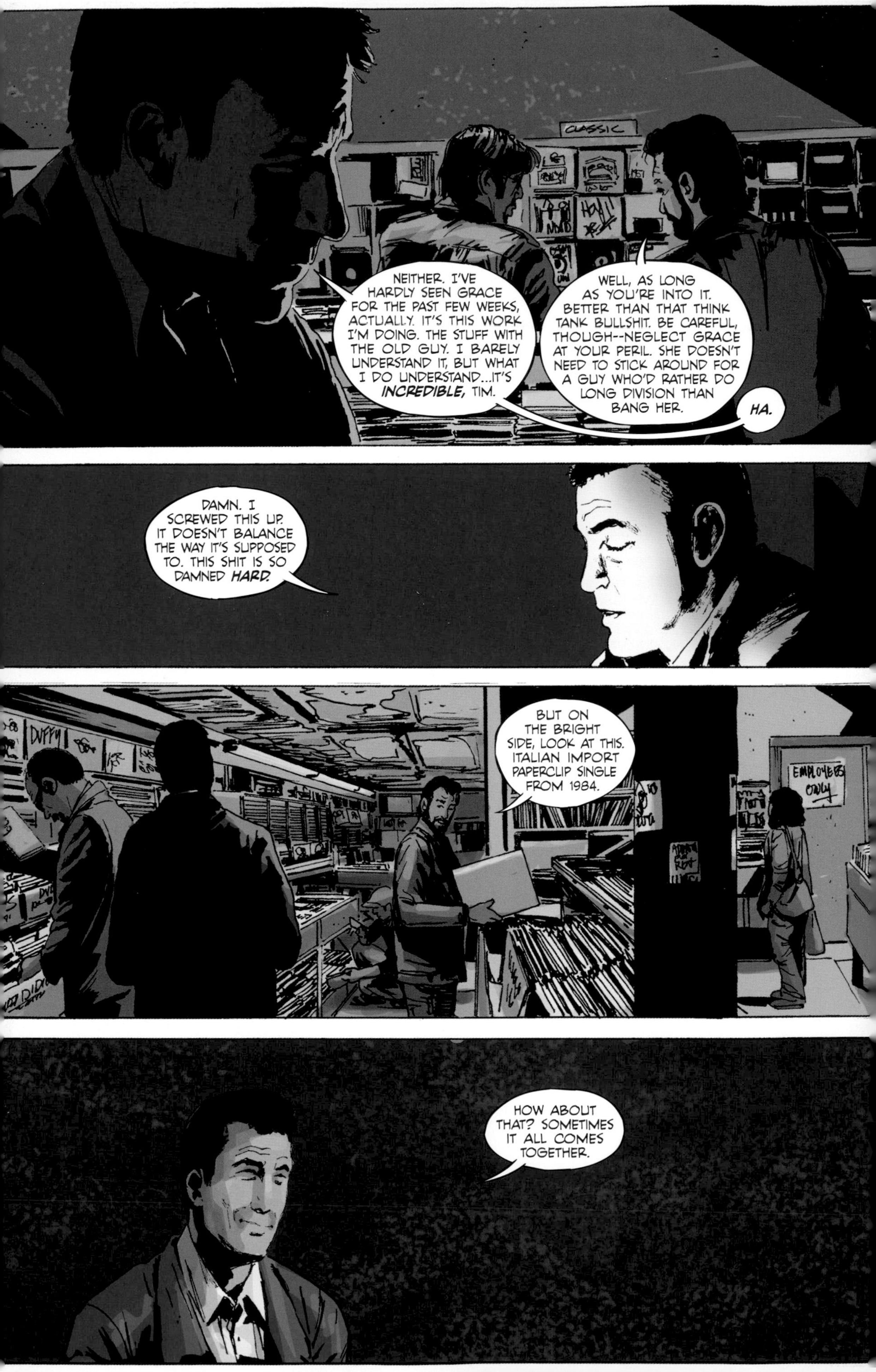
NEITHER. I'VE HARDLY SEEN GRACE FOR THE PAST FEW WEEKS, ACTUALLY. IT'S THIS WORK I'M DOING. THE STUFF WITH THE OLD GUY. I BARELY UNDERSTAND IT, BUT WHAT I DO UNDERSTAND...IT'S *INCREDIBLE,* TIM.
WELL, AS LONG AS YOU'RE INTO IT. BETTER THAN THAT THINK TANK BULLSHIT. BE CAREFUL, THOUGH--NEGLECT GRACE AT YOUR PERIL. SHE DOESN'T NEED TO STICK AROUND FOR A GUY WHO'D RATHER DO LONG DIVISION THAN BANG HER.
HA.
CLASSIC
DAMN. I SCREWED THIS UP. IT DOESN'T BALANCE THE WAY IT'S SUPPOSED TO. THIS SHIT IS SO DAMNED *HARD.*
BUT ON THE BRIGHT SIDE, LOOK AT THIS. ITALIAN IMPORT PAPERCLIP SINGLE FROM 1984.
EMPLOYEES ONLY
HOW ABOUT THAT? SOMETIMES IT ALL COMES TOGETHER.

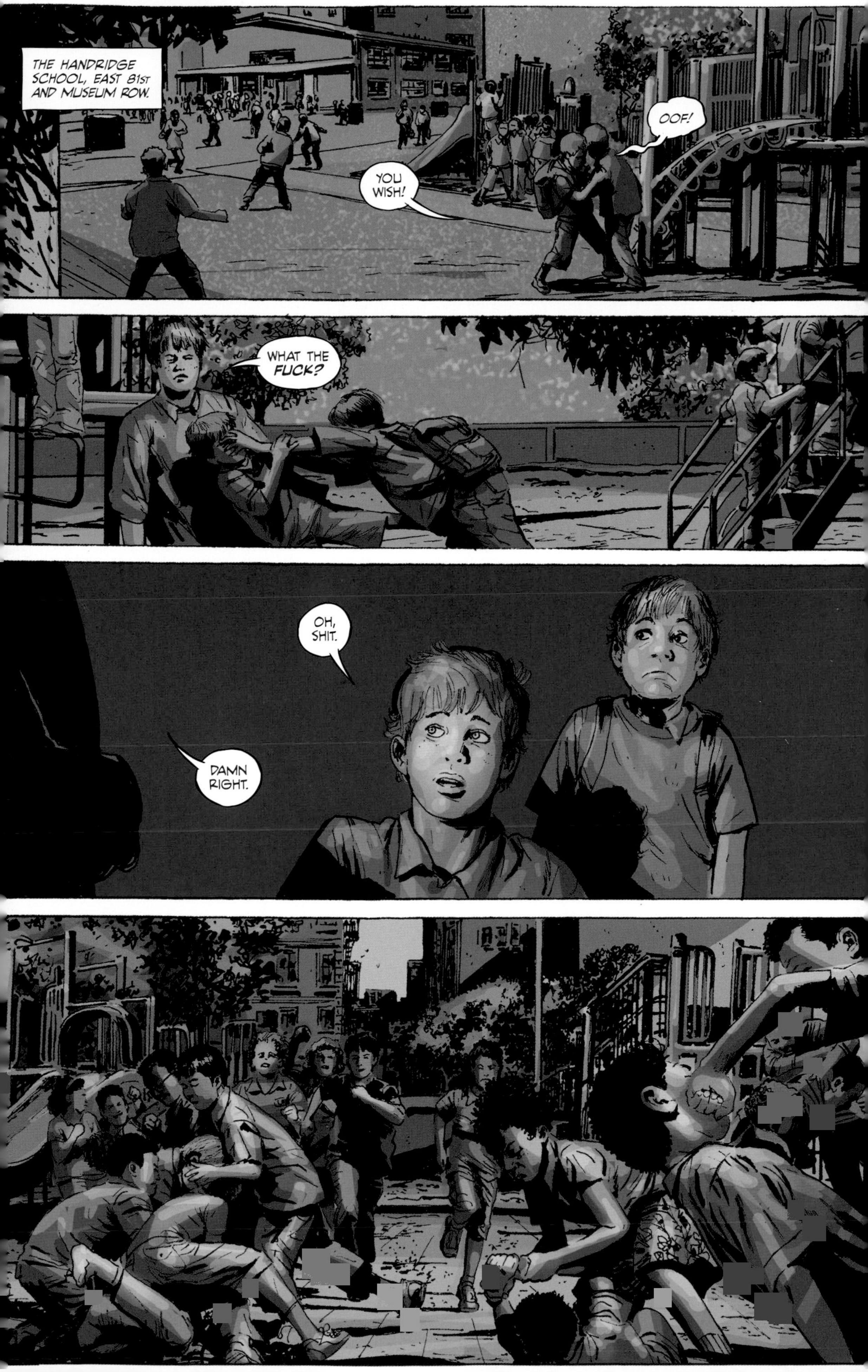
THE HANDRIDGE SCHOOL, EAST 81ST AND MUSEUM ROW.
YOU WISH!
OOF!
WHAT THE FUCK?
OH, SHIT.
DAMN RIGHT.

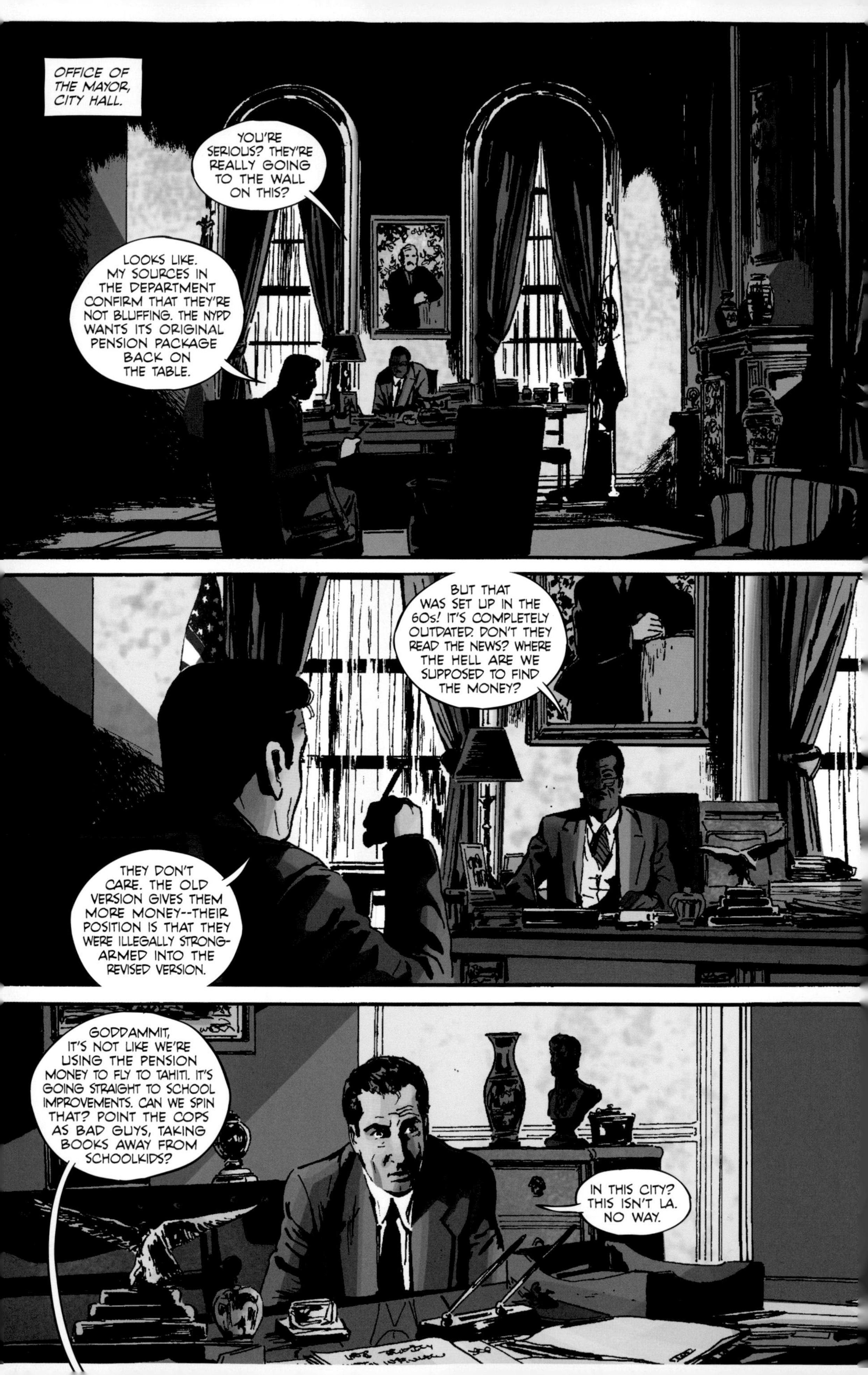

OFFICE OF THE MAYOR, CITY HALL.
YOU'RE SERIOUS? THEY'RE REALLY GOING TO THE WALL ON THIS?
LOOKS LIKE. MY SOURCES IN THE DEPARTMENT CONFIRM THAT THEY'RE NOT BLUFFING. THE NYPD WANTS ITS ORIGINAL PENSION PACKAGE BACK ON THE TABLE.
BUT THAT WAS SET UP IN THE 60s! IT'S COMPLETELY OUTDATED. DON'T THEY READ THE NEWS? WHERE THE HELL ARE WE SUPPOSED TO FIND THE MONEY?
THEY DON'T CARE. THE OLD VERSION GIVES THEM MORE MONEY--THEIR POSITION IS THAT THEY WERE ILLEGALLY STRONG-ARMED INTO THE REVISED VERSION.
GODDAMMIT, IT'S NOT LIKE WE'RE USING THE PENSION MONEY TO FLY TO TAHITI. IT'S GOING STRAIGHT TO SCHOOL IMPROVEMENTS. CAN WE SPIN THAT? POINT THE COPS AS BAD GUYS, TAKING BOOKS AWAY FROM SCHOOLKIDS?
IN THIS CITY? THIS ISN'T LA. NO WAY.

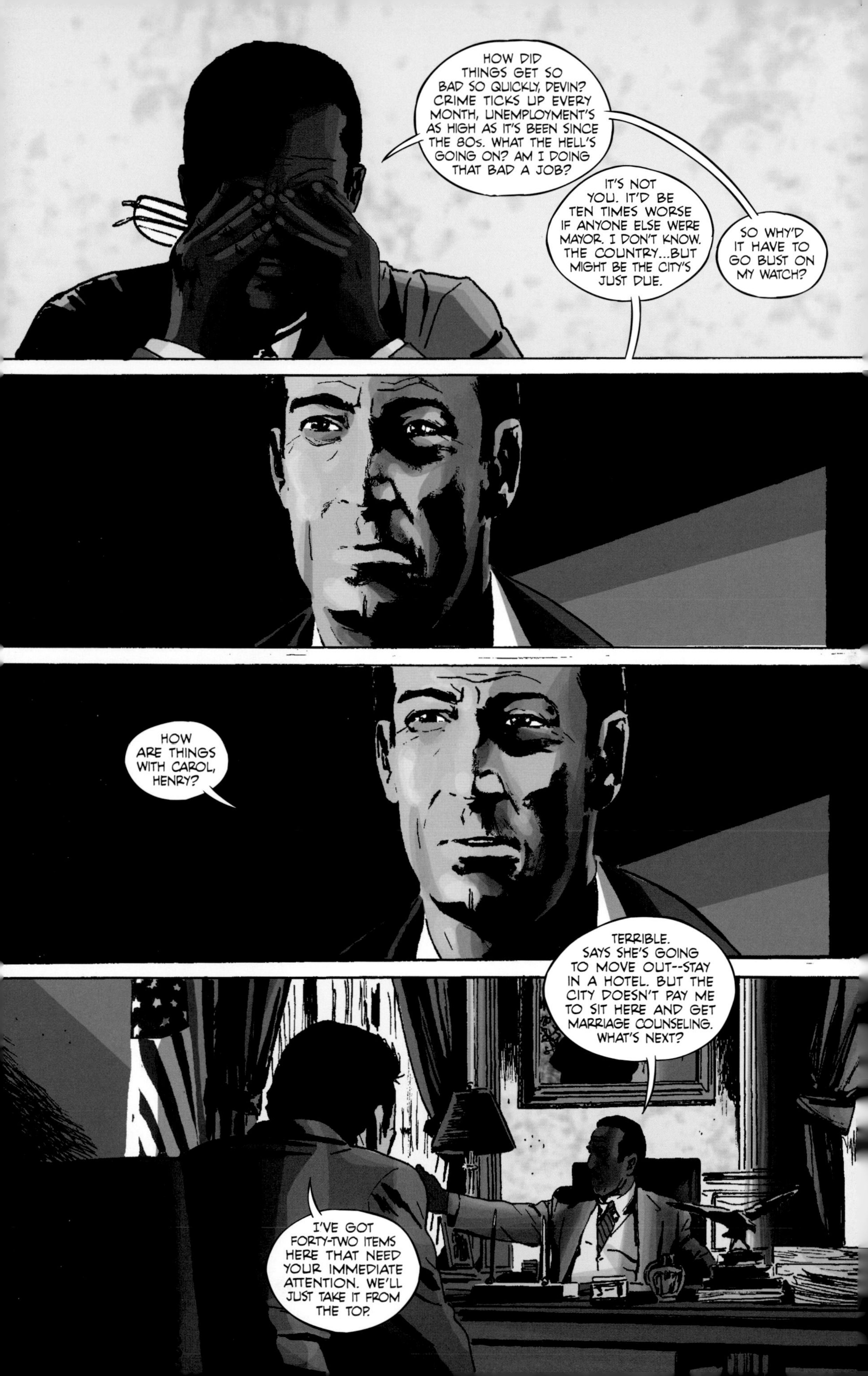
HOW DID THINGS GET SO BAD SO QUICKLY, DEVIN? CRIME TICKS UP EVERY MONTH, UNEMPLOYMENT'S AS HIGH AS IT'S BEEN SINCE THE 80s. WHAT THE HELL'S GOING ON? AM I DOING THAT BAD A JOB?
IT'S NOT YOU. IT'D BE TEN TIMES WORSE IF ANYONE ELSE WERE MAYOR. I DON'T KNOW. THE COUNTRY...BUT MIGHT BE THE CITY'S JUST DUE.
SO WHY'D IT HAVE TO GO BUST ON MY WATCH?
HOW ARE THINGS WITH CAROL, HENRY?
TERRIBLE. SAYS SHE'S GOING TO MOVE OUT--STAY IN A HOTEL. BUT THE CITY DOESN'T PAY ME TO SIT HERE AND GET MARRIAGE COUNSELING. WHAT'S NEXT?
I'VE GOT FORTY-TWO ITEMS HERE THAT NEED YOUR IMMEDIATE ATTENTION. WE'LL JUST TAKE IT FROM THE TOP.

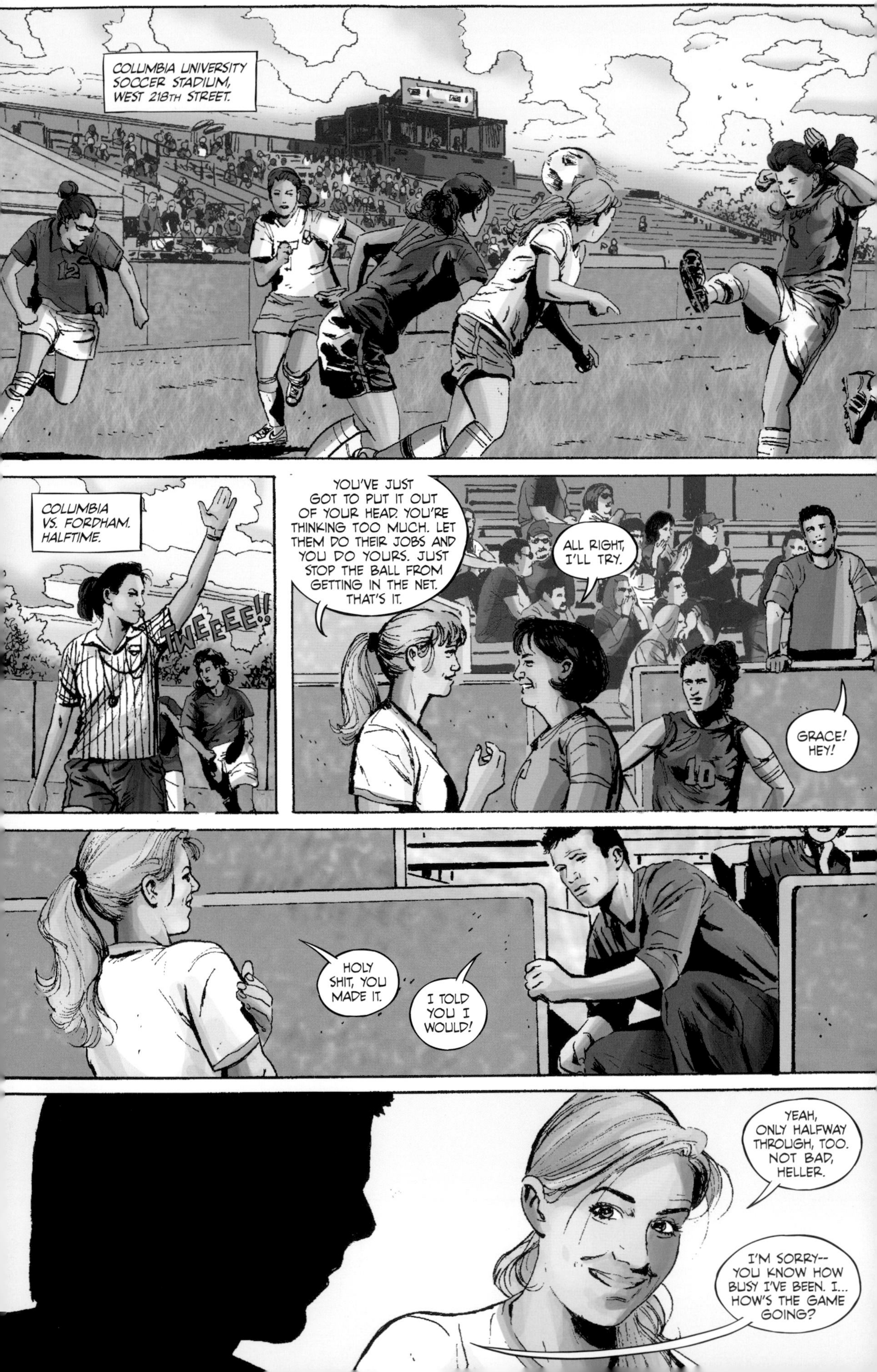
COLUMBIA UNIVERSITY SOCCER STADIUM, WEST 218TH STREET.
COLUMBIA VS. FORDHAM. HALFTIME.
TWEEEEE!!
YOU'VE JUST GOT TO PUT IT OUT OF YOUR HEAD. YOU'RE THINKING TOO MUCH. LET THEM DO THEIR JOBS AND YOU DO YOURS. JUST STOP THE BALL FROM GETTING IN THE NET. THAT'S IT.
ALL RIGHT, I'LL TRY.
GRACE! HEY!
HOLY SHIT, YOU MADE IT.
I TOLD YOU I WOULD!
YEAH, ONLY HALFWAY THROUGH, TOO. NOT BAD, HELLER.
I'M SORRY-- YOU KNOW HOW BUSY I'VE BEEN. I... HOW'S THE GAME GOING?

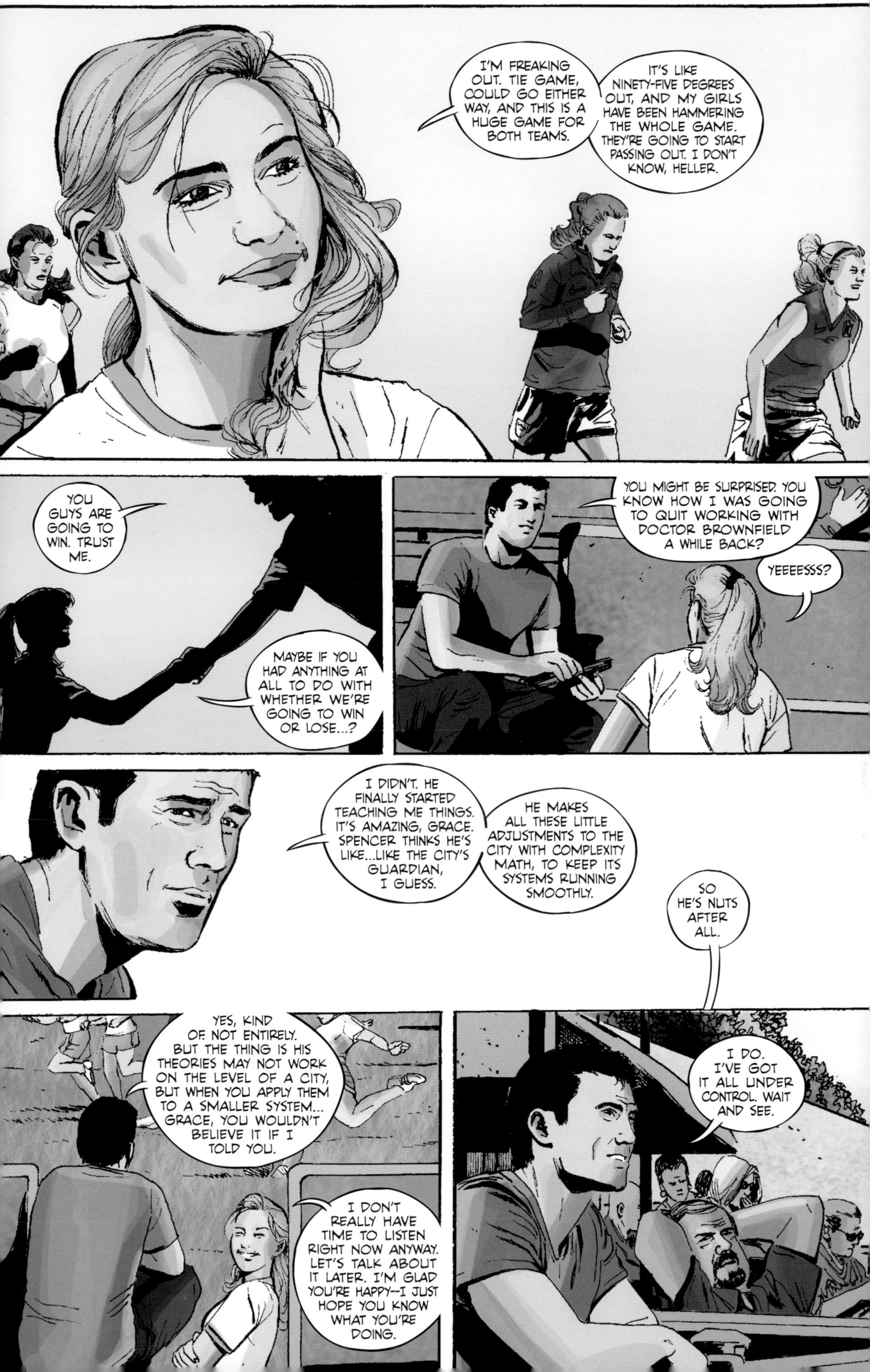
I'M FREAKING OUT. TIE GAME, COULD GO EITHER WAY, AND THIS IS A HUGE GAME FOR BOTH TEAMS.
IT'S LIKE NINETY-FIVE DEGREES OUT, AND MY GIRLS HAVE BEEN HAMMERING THE WHOLE GAME. THEY'RE GOING TO START PASSING OUT. I DON'T KNOW, HELLER.
YOU GUYS ARE GOING TO WIN. TRUST ME.
MAYBE IF YOU HAD ANYTHING AT ALL TO DO WITH WHETHER WE'RE GOING TO WIN OR LOSE...?
YOU MIGHT BE SURPRISED. YOU KNOW HOW I WAS GOING TO QUIT WORKING WITH DOCTOR BROWNFIELD A WHILE BACK?
YEEEESSS?
I DIDN'T. HE FINALLY STARTED TEACHING ME THINGS. IT'S AMAZING, GRACE. SPENCER THINKS HE'S LIKE...LIKE THE CITY'S GUARDIAN, I GUESS.
HE MAKES ALL THESE LITTLE ADJUSTMENTS TO THE CITY WITH COMPLEXITY MATH, TO KEEP ITS SYSTEMS RUNNING SMOOTHLY.
SO HE'S NUTS AFTER ALL.
YES, KIND OF. NOT ENTIRELY. BUT THE THING IS HIS THEORIES MAY NOT WORK ON THE LEVEL OF A CITY, BUT WHEN YOU APPLY THEM TO A SMALLER SYSTEM... GRACE, YOU WOULDN'T BELIEVE IT IF I TOLD YOU.
I DON'T REALLY HAVE TIME TO LISTEN RIGHT NOW ANYWAY. LET'S TALK ABOUT IT LATER. I'M GLAD YOU'RE HAPPY--I JUST HOPE YOU KNOW WHAT YOU'RE DOING.
I DO. I'VE GOT IT ALL UNDER CONTROL. WAIT AND SEE.

OKAY.

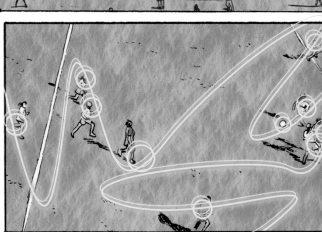

SPLOOSH

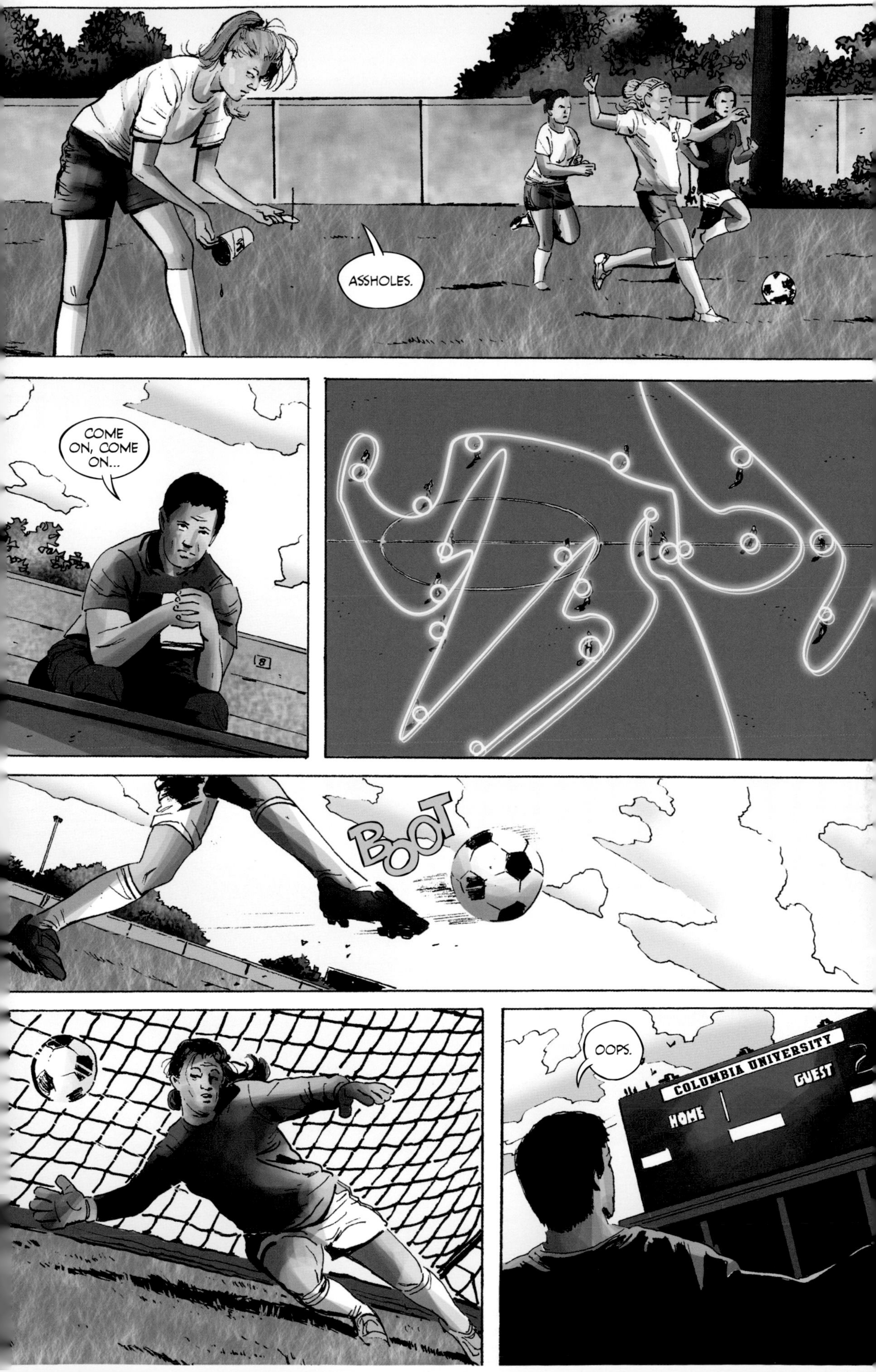
ASSHOLES.
COME ON, COME ON...
BOOT
OOPS.
COLUMBIA UNIVERSITY
HOME
GUEST

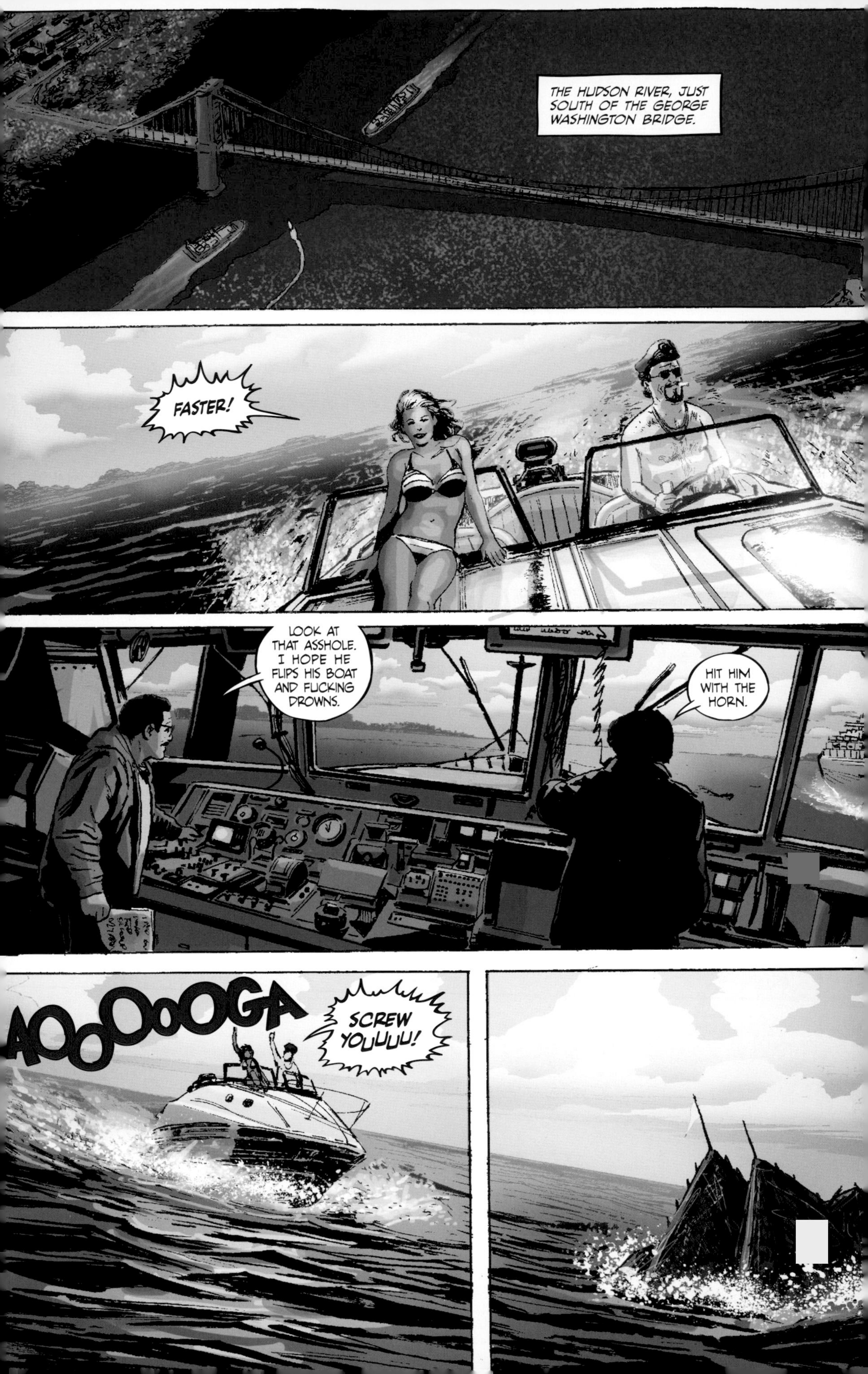

THE HUDSON RIVER, JUST SOUTH OF THE GEORGE WASHINGTON BRIDGE.
FASTER!
LOOK AT THAT ASSHOLE. I HOPE HE FLIPS HIS BOAT AND FUCKING DROWNS.
HIT HIM WITH THE HORN.
AOOOOOOGA
SCREW YOUUUU!

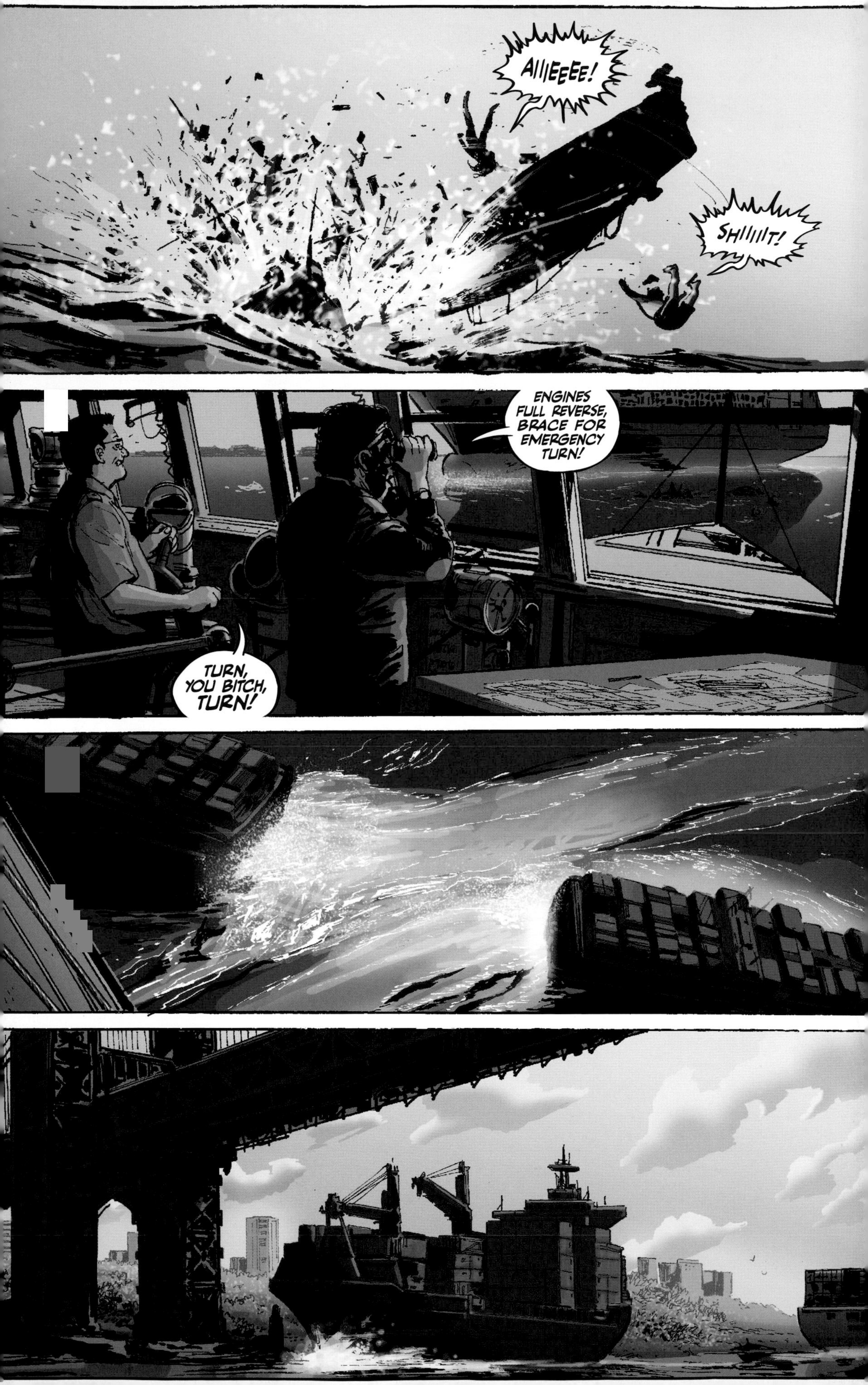
AIIIEEEE!
SHIIIIIT!
ENGINES FULL REVERSE, BRACE FOR EMERGENCY TURN!
TURN, YOU BITCH, TURN!

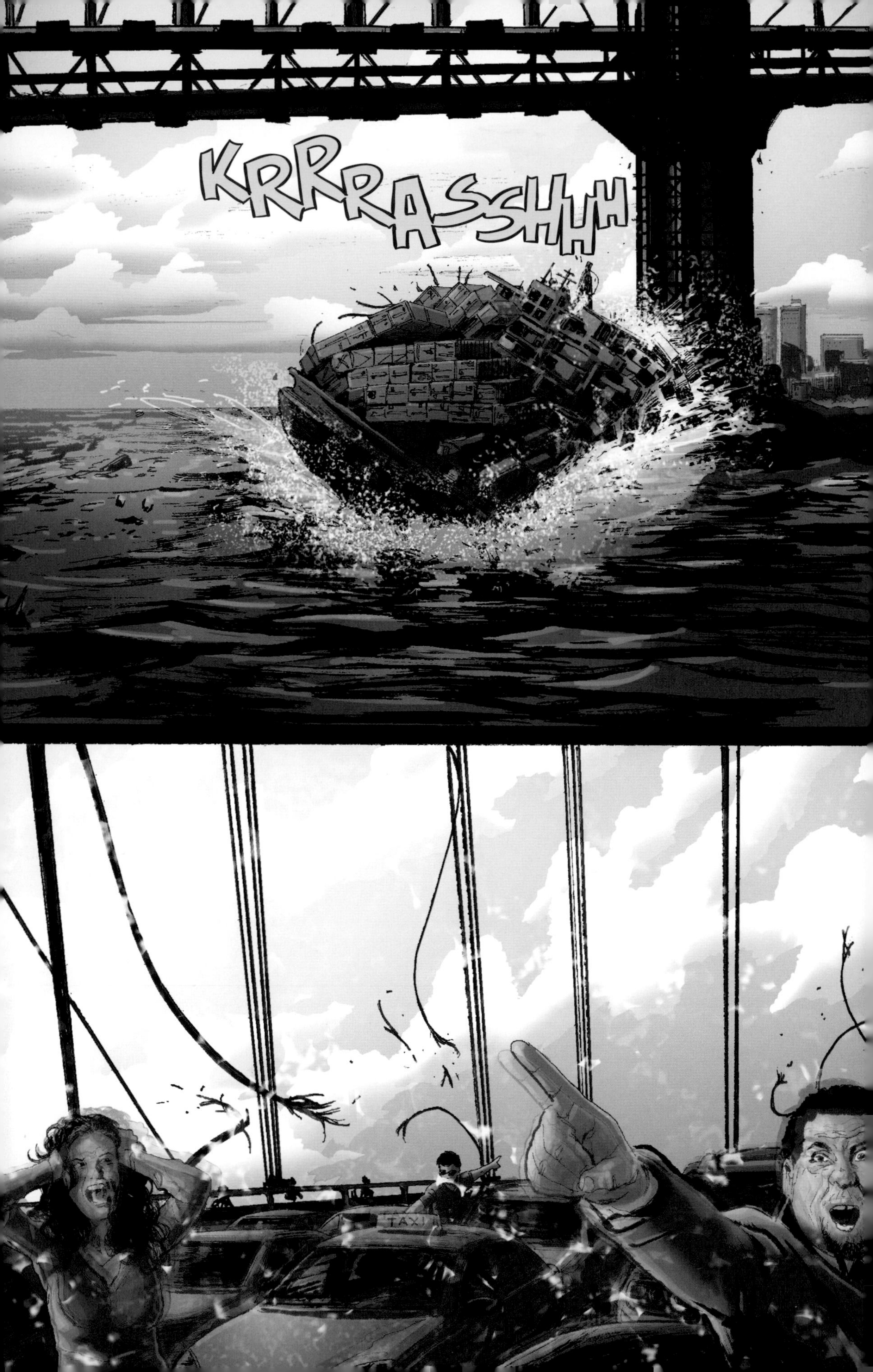
KRRRASSHHH
TAXI

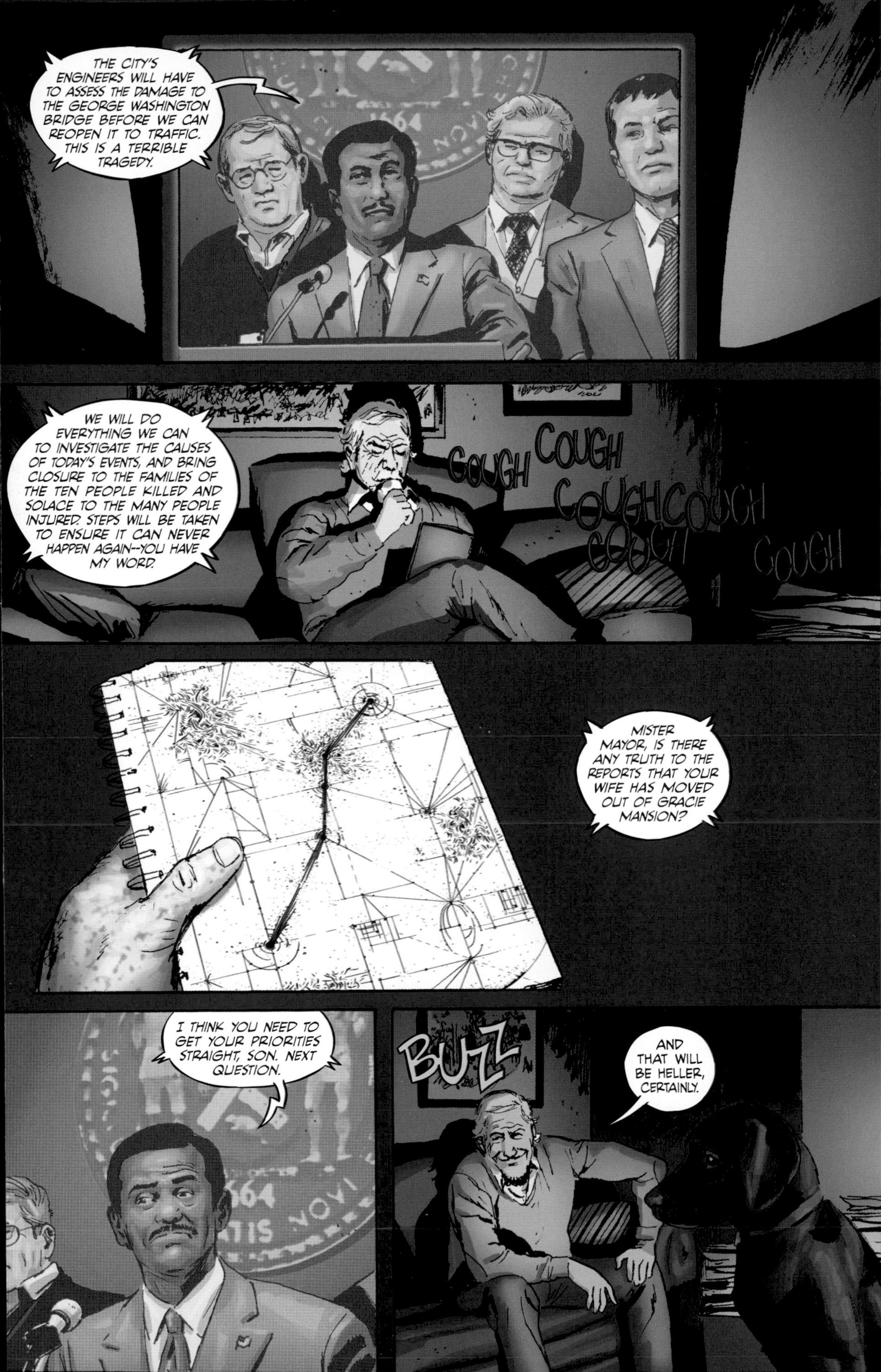
THE CITY'S ENGINEERS WILL HAVE TO ASSESS THE DAMAGE TO THE GEORGE WASHINGTON BRIDGE BEFORE WE CAN REOPEN IT TO TRAFFIC. THIS IS A TERRIBLE TRAGEDY.
1664
WE WILL DO EVERYTHING WE CAN TO INVESTIGATE THE CAUSES OF TODAY'S EVENTS, AND BRING CLOSURE TO THE FAMILIES OF THE TEN PEOPLE KILLED AND SOLACE TO THE MANY PEOPLE INJURED. STEPS WILL BE TAKEN TO ENSURE IT CAN NEVER HAPPEN AGAIN--YOU HAVE MY WORD.
COUGH COUGH
COUGHCOUGH
COUGH
COUGH
MISTER MAYOR, IS THERE ANY TRUTH TO THE REPORTS THAT YOUR WIFE HAS MOVED OUT OF GRACIE MANSION?
I THINK YOU NEED TO GET YOUR PRIORITIES STRAIGHT, SON. NEXT QUESTION.
1664
BUZZ
AND THAT WILL BE HELLER, CERTAINLY.

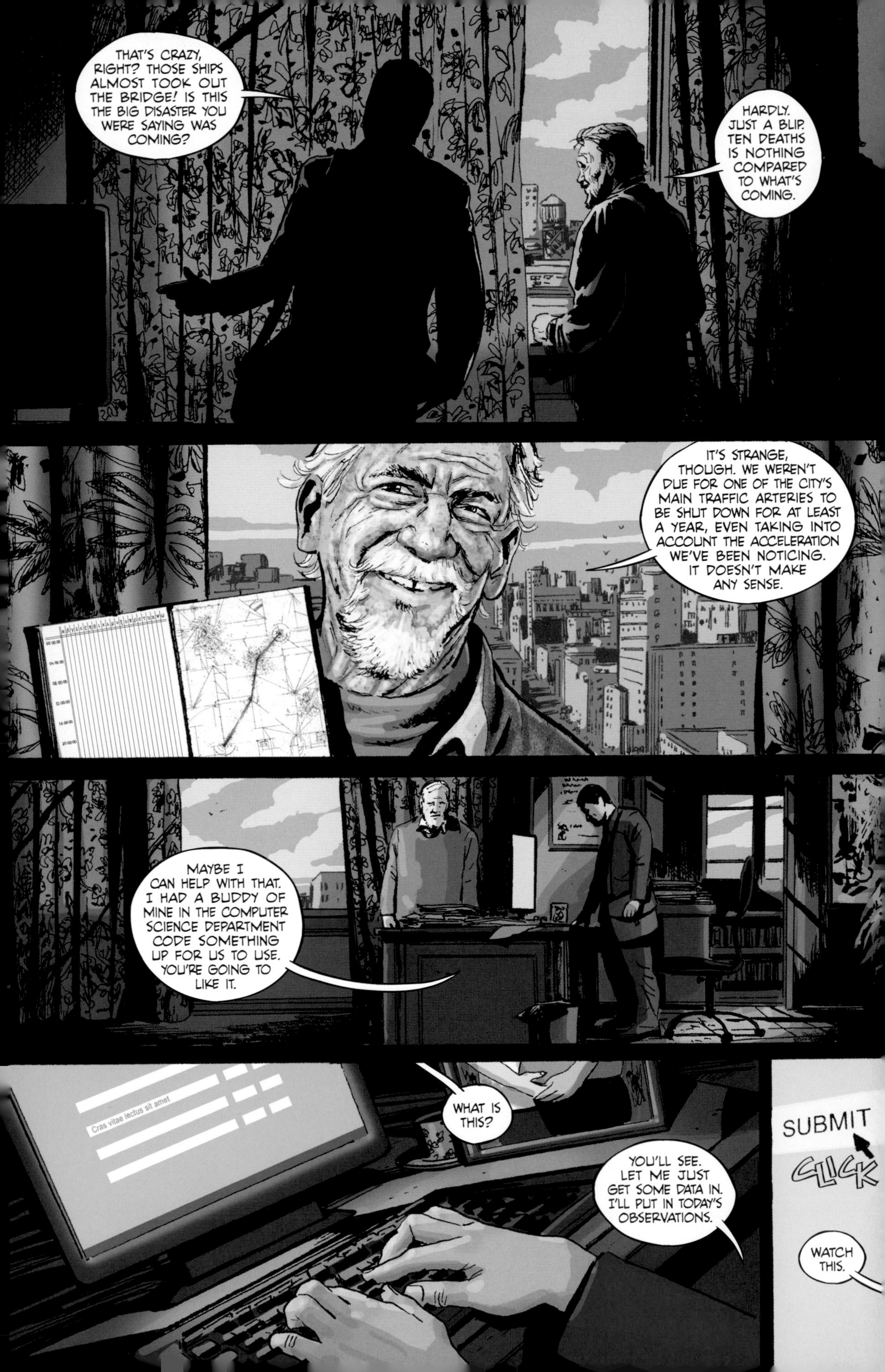
THAT'S CRAZY, RIGHT? THOSE SHIPS ALMOST TOOK OUT THE BRIDGE! IS THIS THE BIG DISASTER YOU WERE SAYING WAS COMING?
HARDLY. JUST A BLIP. TEN DEATHS IS NOTHING COMPARED TO WHAT'S COMING.
IT'S STRANGE, THOUGH. WE WEREN'T DUE FOR ONE OF THE CITY'S MAIN TRAFFIC ARTERIES TO BE SHUT DOWN FOR AT LEAST A YEAR, EVEN TAKING INTO ACCOUNT THE ACCELERATION WE'VE BEEN NOTICING. IT DOESN'T MAKE ANY SENSE.
MAYBE I CAN HELP WITH THAT. I HAD A BUDDY OF MINE IN THE COMPUTER SCIENCE DEPARTMENT CODE SOMETHING UP FOR US TO USE. YOU'RE GOING TO LIKE IT.
Cras vitae lectus sit amet
WHAT IS THIS?
YOU'LL SEE. LET ME JUST GET SOME DATA IN. I'LL PUT IN TODAY'S OBSERVATIONS.
SUBMIT
CLICK
WATCH THIS.

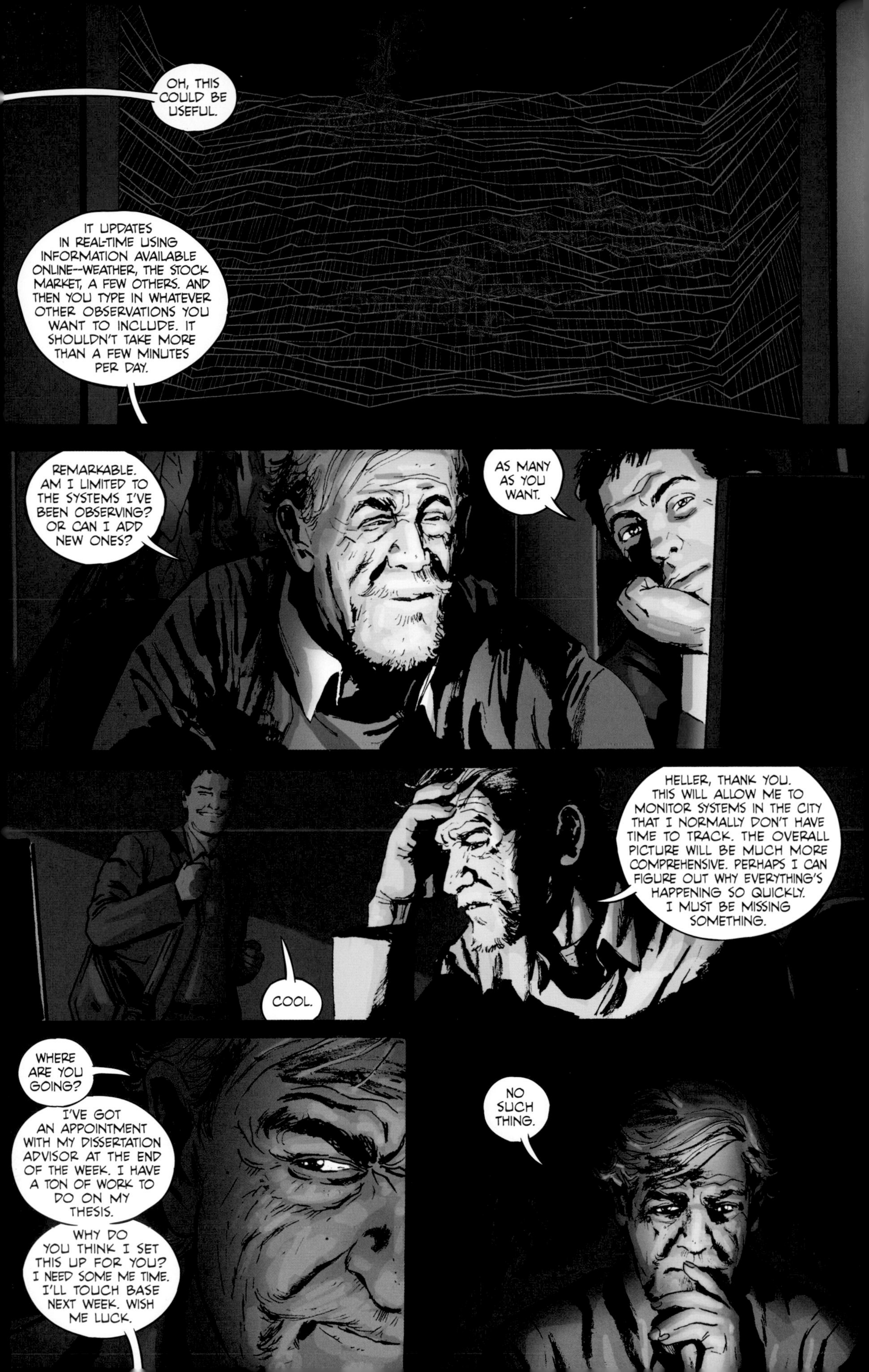
OH, THIS COULD BE USEFUL.
IT UPDATES IN REAL-TIME USING INFORMATION AVAILABLE ONLINE--WEATHER, THE STOCK MARKET, A FEW OTHERS. AND THEN YOU TYPE IN WHATEVER OTHER OBSERVATIONS YOU WANT TO INCLUDE. IT SHOULDN'T TAKE MORE THAN A FEW MINUTES PER DAY.
REMARKABLE. AM I LIMITED TO THE SYSTEMS I'VE BEEN OBSERVING? OR CAN I ADD NEW ONES?
AS MANY AS YOU WANT.
HELLER, THANK YOU. THIS WILL ALLOW ME TO MONITOR SYSTEMS IN THE CITY THAT I NORMALLY DON'T HAVE TIME TO TRACK. THE OVERALL PICTURE WILL BE MUCH MORE COMPREHENSIVE. PERHAPS I CAN FIGURE OUT WHY EVERYTHING'S HAPPENING SO QUICKLY. I MUST BE MISSING SOMETHING.
COOL.
WHERE ARE YOU GOING?
I'VE GOT AN APPOINTMENT WITH MY DISSERTATION ADVISOR AT THE END OF THE WEEK. I HAVE A TON OF WORK TO DO ON MY THESIS.
WHY DO YOU THINK I SET THIS UP FOR YOU? I NEED SOME ME TIME. I'LL TOUCH BASE NEXT WEEK. WISH ME LUCK.
NO SUCH THING.

DISSERTATION
Real-time Manipulation
Systems Through Spatial
by: H. Wilson
Advisor: E. Kenowyk, Chair of
Mathematics, Columbia University

Presented for consideration of a
doctoral degree in Mathematics

THANK YOU FOR COMING IN, HELLER.

NOT AT ALL, DOCTOR KENOWYK. I WAS HAPPY TO GET YOUR CALL.

I'M A LITTLE SURPRISED YOU READ THROUGH MY DISSERTATION SO QUICKLY. I ONLY GAVE IT TO YOU A FEW HOURS AGO.

I APOLOGIZE, HELLER. I THINK YOU'VE MISUNDER-STOOD. I HAVEN'T READ THE WHOLE THESIS, JUST THE ABSTRACT AND YOUR INITIAL ARGUMENTS.

IS THERE... SOME SORT OF PROBLEM?

I SUPPOSE THAT'S WHAT WE'RE HERE TO FIND OUT.

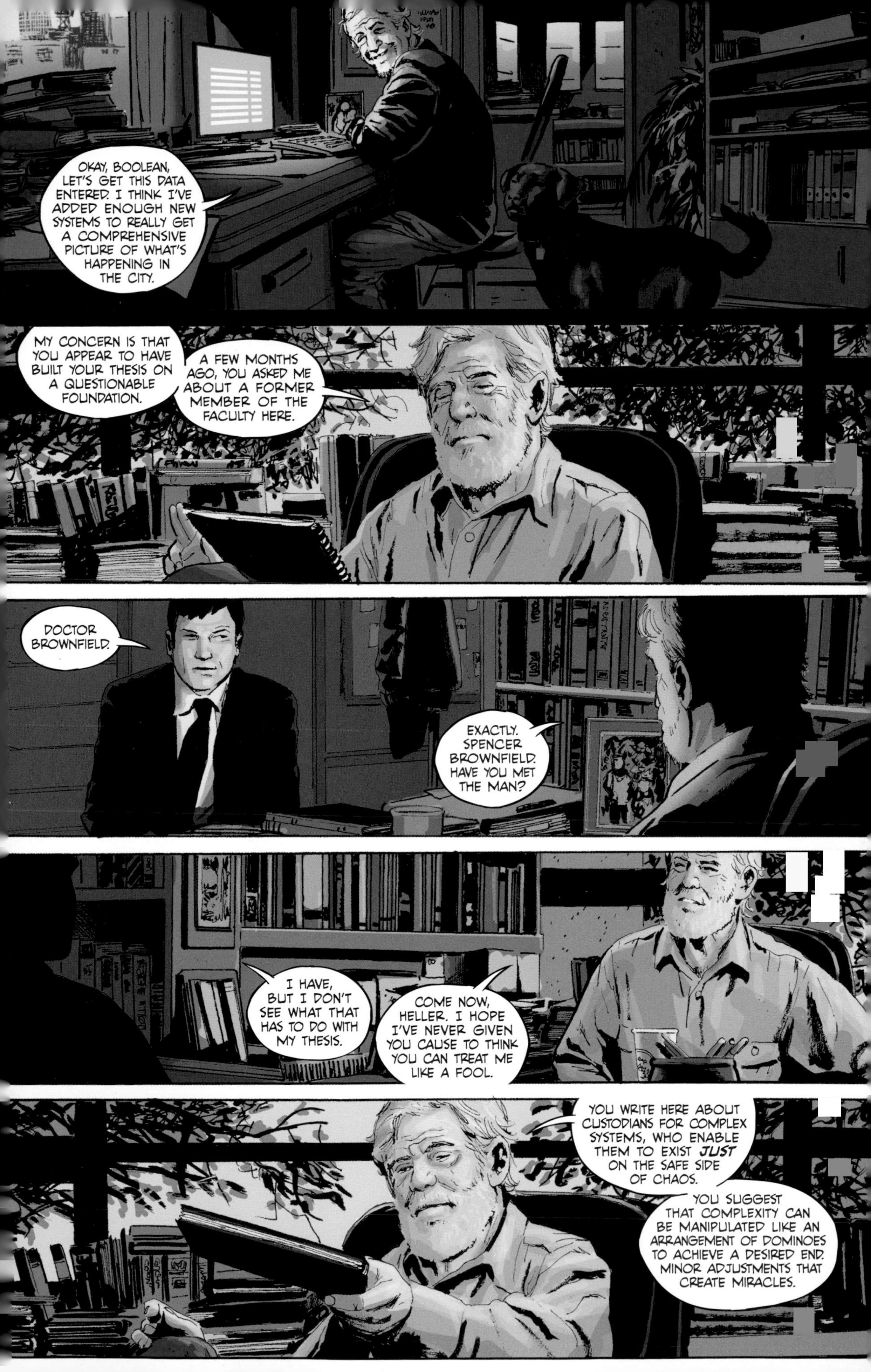
OKAY, BOOLEAN, LET'S GET THIS DATA ENTERED. I THINK I'VE ADDED ENOUGH NEW SYSTEMS TO REALLY GET A COMPREHENSIVE PICTURE OF WHAT'S HAPPENING IN THE CITY.
MY CONCERN IS THAT YOU APPEAR TO HAVE BUILT YOUR THESIS ON A QUESTIONABLE FOUNDATION.
A FEW MONTHS AGO, YOU ASKED ME ABOUT A FORMER MEMBER OF THE FACULTY HERE.
DOCTOR BROWNFIELD.
EXACTLY. SPENCER BROWNFIELD. HAVE YOU MET THE MAN?
I HAVE, BUT I DON'T SEE WHAT THAT HAS TO DO WITH MY THESIS.
COME NOW, HELLER. I HOPE I'VE NEVER GIVEN YOU CAUSE TO THINK YOU CAN TREAT ME LIKE A FOOL.
YOU WRITE HERE ABOUT CUSTODIANS FOR COMPLEX SYSTEMS, WHO ENABLE THEM TO EXIST *JUST* ON THE SAFE SIDE OF CHAOS.
YOU SUGGEST THAT COMPLEXITY CAN BE MANIPULATED LIKE AN ARRANGEMENT OF DOMINOES TO ACHIEVE A DESIRED END. MINOR ADJUSTMENTS THAT CREATE MIRACLES.

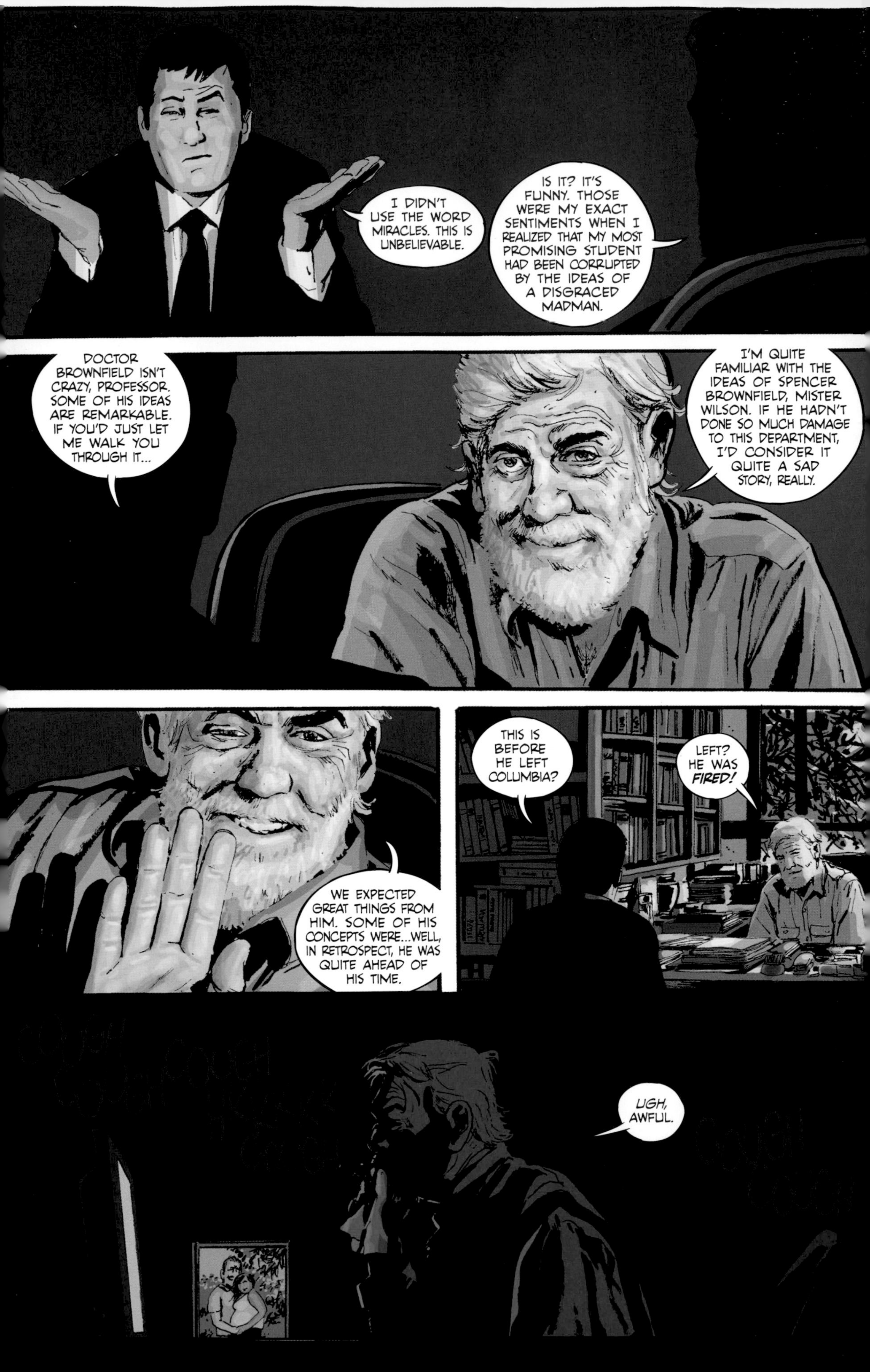
I DIDN'T USE THE WORD MIRACLES. THIS IS UNBELIEVABLE.
IS IT? IT'S FUNNY. THOSE WERE MY EXACT SENTIMENTS WHEN I REALIZED THAT MY MOST PROMISING STUDENT HAD BEEN CORRUPTED BY THE IDEAS OF A DISGRACED MADMAN.
DOCTOR BROWNFIELD ISN'T CRAZY, PROFESSOR. SOME OF HIS IDEAS ARE REMARKABLE. IF YOU'D JUST LET ME WALK YOU THROUGH IT...
I'M QUITE FAMILIAR WITH THE IDEAS OF SPENCER BROWNFIELD, MISTER WILSON. IF HE HADN'T DONE SO MUCH DAMAGE TO THIS DEPARTMENT, I'D CONSIDER IT QUITE A SAD STORY, REALLY.
WE EXPECTED GREAT THINGS FROM HIM. SOME OF HIS CONCEPTS WERE...WELL, IN RETROSPECT, HE WAS QUITE AHEAD OF HIS TIME.
THIS IS BEFORE HE LEFT COLUMBIA?
LEFT? HE WAS *FIRED!*
UGH, AWFUL.

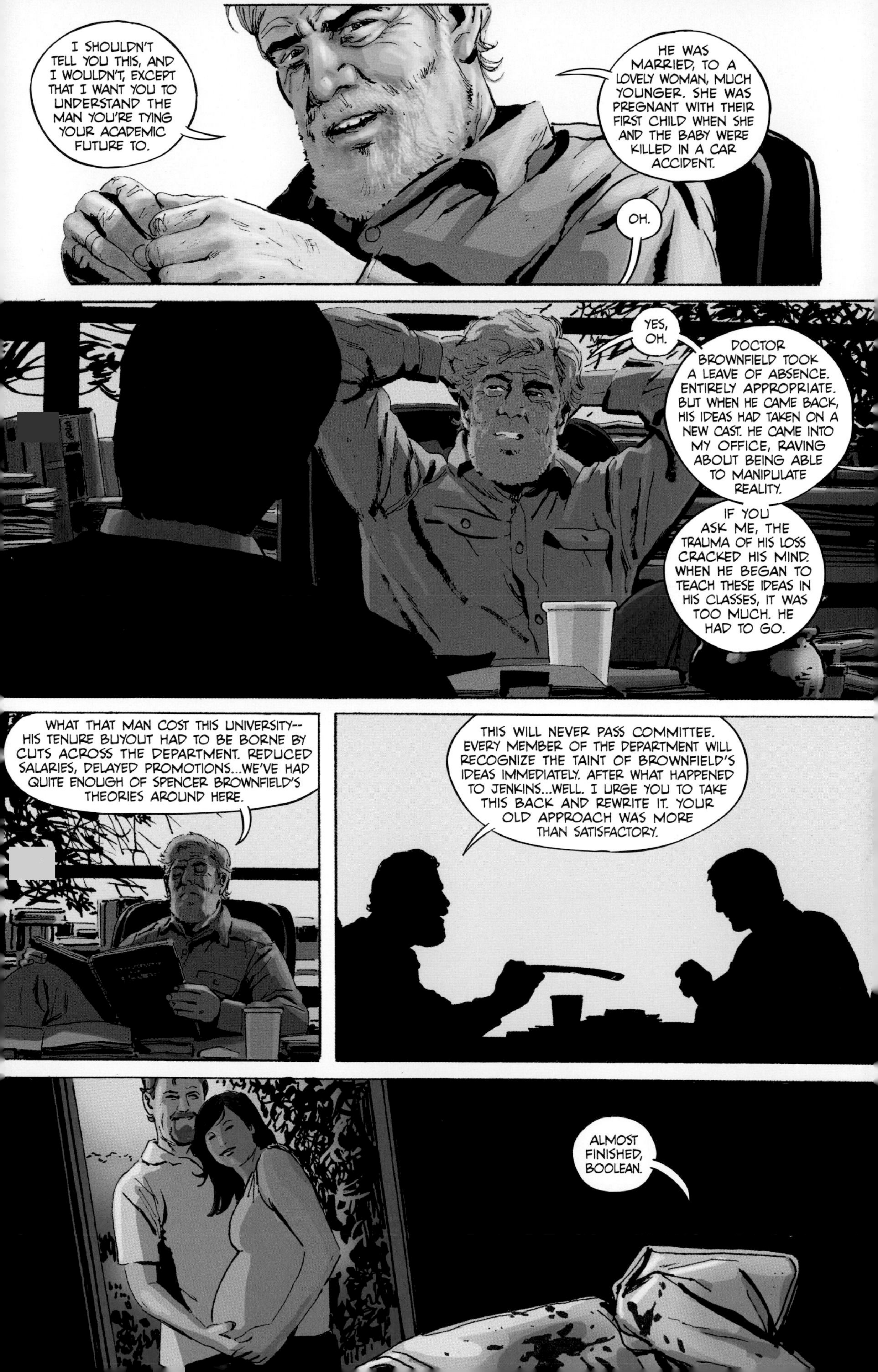
I SHOULDN'T TELL YOU THIS, AND I WOULDN'T, EXCEPT THAT I WANT YOU TO UNDERSTAND THE MAN YOU'RE TYING YOUR ACADEMIC FUTURE TO.
HE WAS MARRIED, TO A LOVELY WOMAN, MUCH YOUNGER. SHE WAS PREGNANT WITH THEIR FIRST CHILD WHEN SHE AND THE BABY WERE KILLED IN A CAR ACCIDENT.
OH.
YES, OH.
DOCTOR BROWNFIELD TOOK A LEAVE OF ABSENCE. ENTIRELY APPROPRIATE. BUT WHEN HE CAME BACK, HIS IDEAS HAD TAKEN ON A NEW CAST. HE CAME INTO MY OFFICE, RAVING ABOUT BEING ABLE TO MANIPULATE REALITY.
IF YOU ASK ME, THE TRAUMA OF HIS LOSS CRACKED HIS MIND. WHEN HE BEGAN TO TEACH THESE IDEAS IN HIS CLASSES, IT WAS TOO MUCH. HE HAD TO GO.
WHAT THAT MAN COST THIS UNIVERSITY-- HIS TENURE BUYOUT HAD TO BE BORNE BY CUTS ACROSS THE DEPARTMENT. REDUCED SALARIES, DELAYED PROMOTIONS...WE'VE HAD QUITE ENOUGH OF SPENCER BROWNFIELD'S THEORIES AROUND HERE.
THIS WILL NEVER PASS COMMITTEE. EVERY MEMBER OF THE DEPARTMENT WILL RECOGNIZE THE TAINT OF BROWNFIELD'S IDEAS IMMEDIATELY. AFTER WHAT HAPPENED TO JENKINS...WELL. I URGE YOU TO TAKE THIS BACK AND REWRITE IT. YOUR OLD APPROACH WAS MORE THAN SATISFACTORY.
ALMOST FINISHED, BOOLEAN.

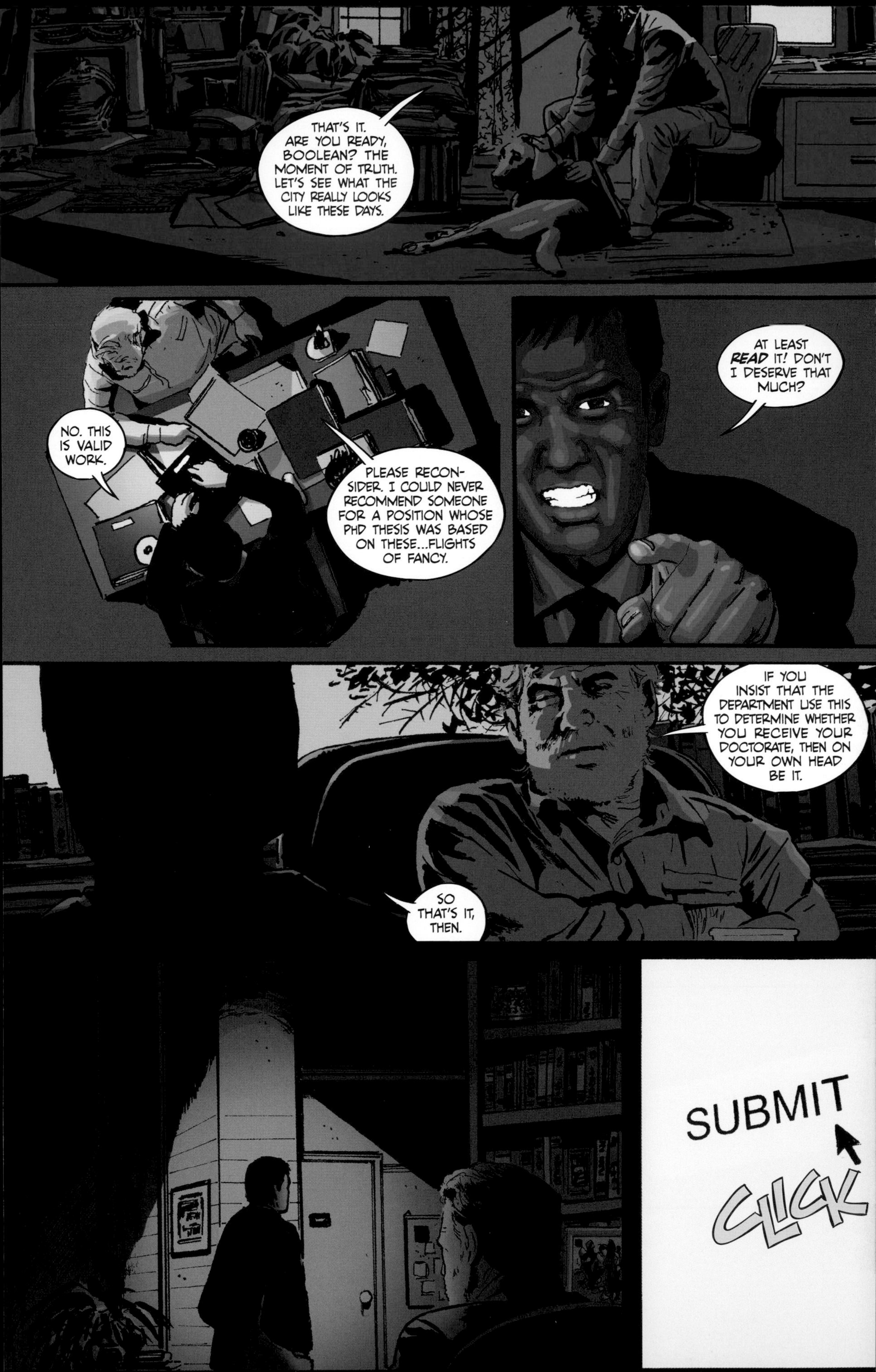
THAT'S IT. ARE YOU READY, BOOLEAN? THE MOMENT OF TRUTH. LET'S SEE WHAT THE CITY REALLY LOOKS LIKE THESE DAYS.
NO. THIS IS VALID WORK.
PLEASE RECON-SIDER. I COULD NEVER RECOMMEND SOMEONE FOR A POSITION WHOSE PHD THESIS WAS BASED ON THESE...FLIGHTS OF FANCY.
AT LEAST READ IT! DON'T I DESERVE THAT MUCH?
IF YOU INSIST THAT THE DEPARTMENT USE THIS TO DETERMINE WHETHER YOU RECEIVE YOUR DOCTORATE, THEN ON YOUR OWN HEAD BE IT.
SO THAT'S IT, THEN.
SUBMIT
CLICK

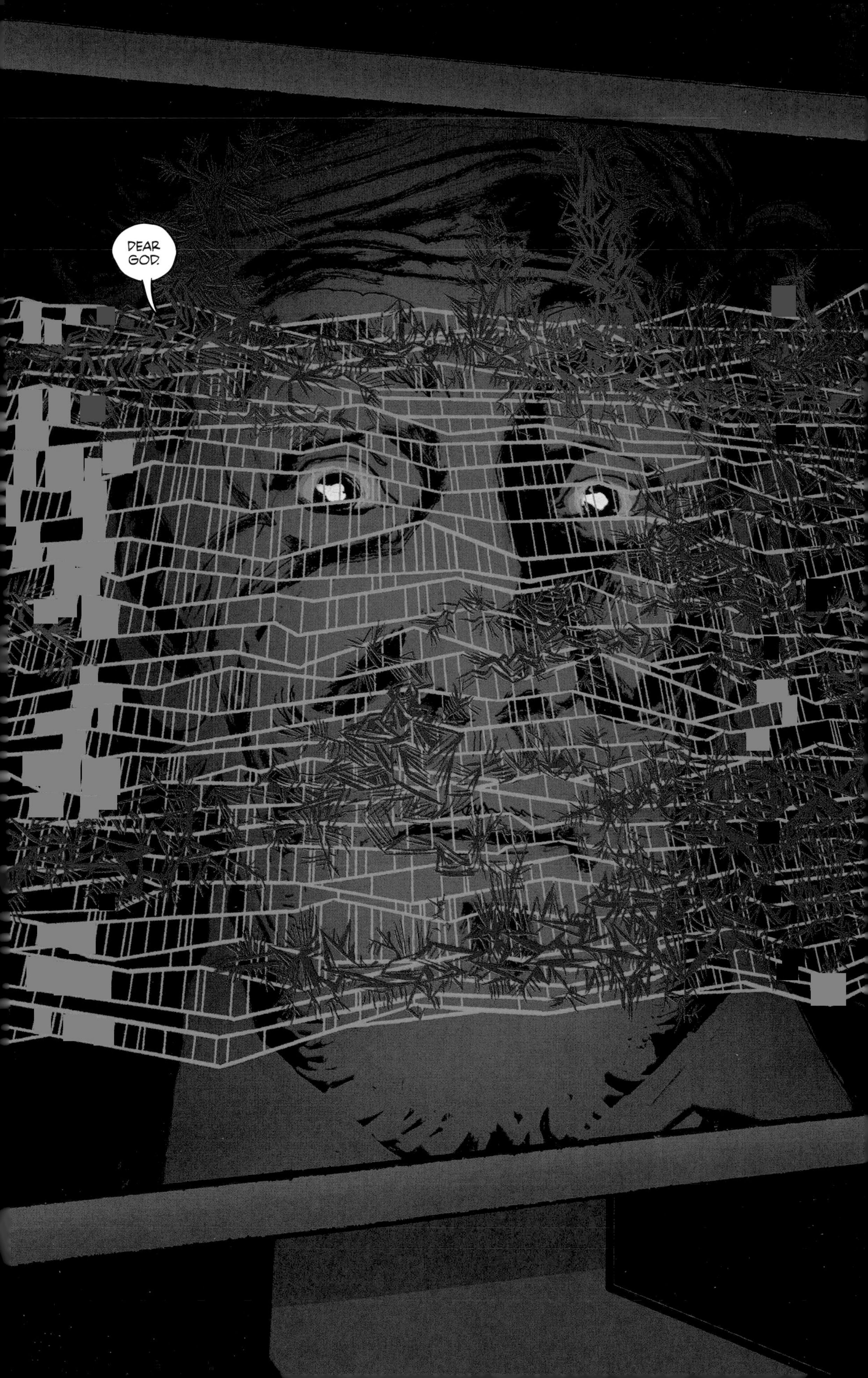
DEAR GOD.

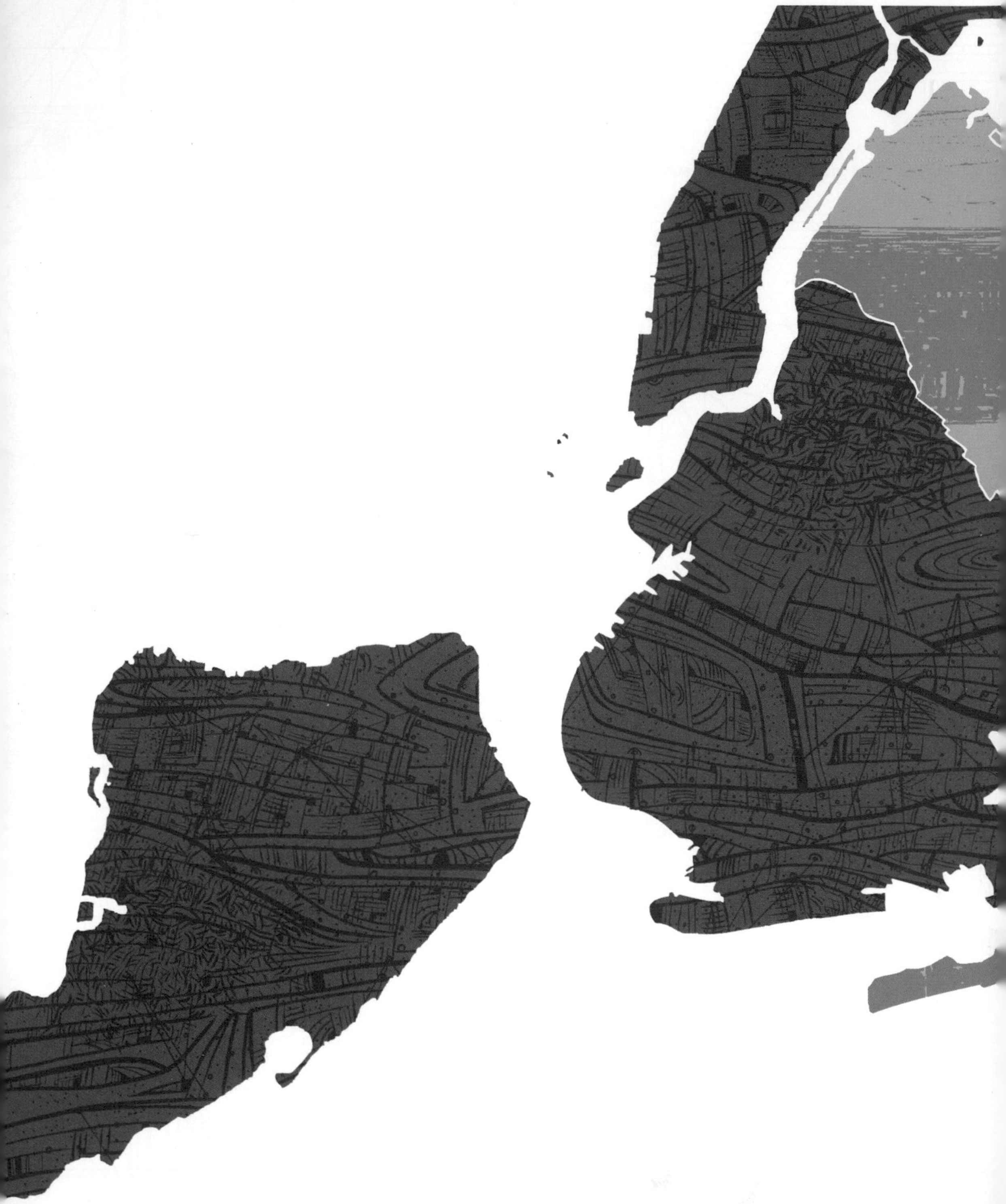

PART THREE
THE CENTER
CANNOT HOLD

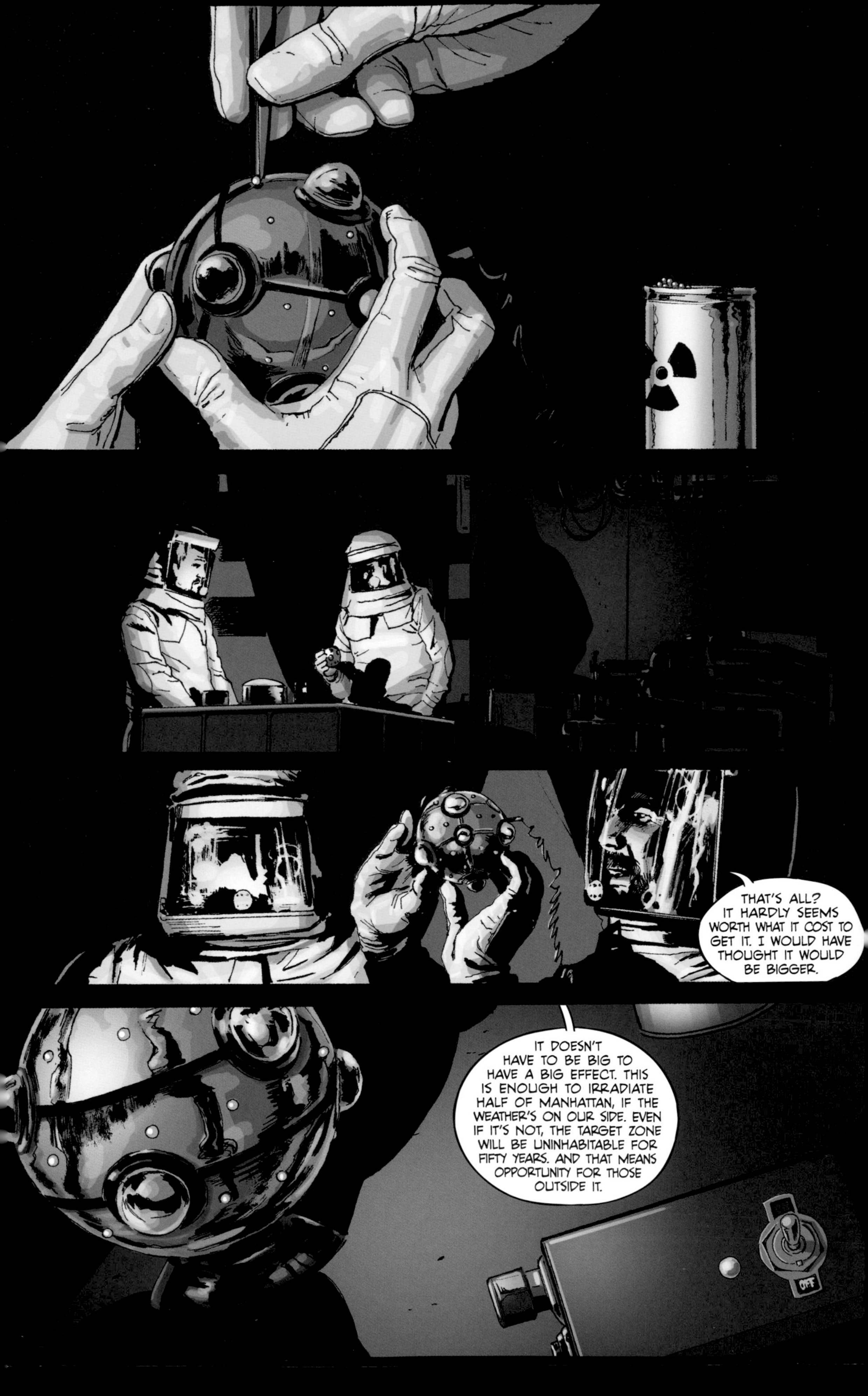
THAT'S ALL? IT HARDLY SEEMS WORTH WHAT IT COST TO GET IT. I WOULD HAVE THOUGHT IT WOULD BE BIGGER.
IT DOESN'T HAVE TO BE BIG TO HAVE A BIG EFFECT. THIS IS ENOUGH TO IRRADIATE HALF OF MANHATTAN, IF THE WEATHER'S ON OUR SIDE. EVEN IF IT'S NOT, THE TARGET ZONE WILL BE UNINHABITABLE FOR FIFTY YEARS. AND THAT MEANS OPPORTUNITY FOR THOSE OUTSIDE IT.
OFF

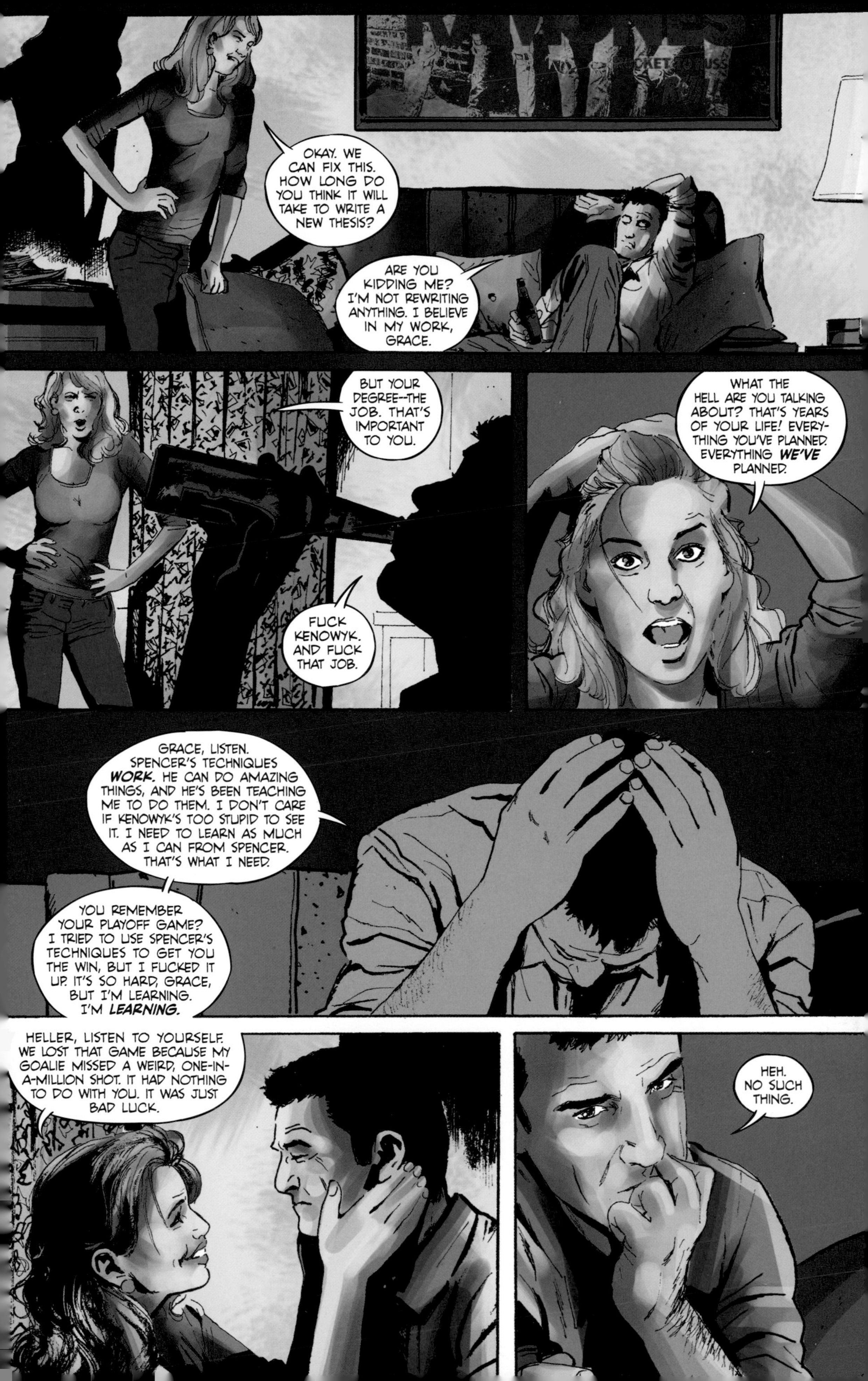
OKAY. WE CAN FIX THIS. HOW LONG DO YOU THINK IT WILL TAKE TO WRITE A NEW THESIS?
ARE YOU KIDDING ME? I'M NOT REWRITING ANYTHING. I BELIEVE IN MY WORK, GRACE.
BUT YOUR DEGREE--THE JOB. THAT'S IMPORTANT TO YOU.
FUCK KENOWYK. AND FUCK THAT JOB.
WHAT THE HELL ARE YOU TALKING ABOUT? THAT'S YEARS OF YOUR LIFE! EVERYTHING YOU'VE PLANNED. EVERYTHING WE'VE PLANNED.
GRACE, LISTEN. SPENCER'S TECHNIQUES WORK. HE CAN DO AMAZING THINGS, AND HE'S BEEN TEACHING ME TO DO THEM. I DON'T CARE IF KENOWYK'S TOO STUPID TO SEE IT. I NEED TO LEARN AS MUCH AS I CAN FROM SPENCER. THAT'S WHAT I NEED.
YOU REMEMBER YOUR PLAYOFF GAME? I TRIED TO USE SPENCER'S TECHNIQUES TO GET YOU THE WIN, BUT I FUCKED IT UP. IT'S SO HARD, GRACE, BUT I'M LEARNING. I'M LEARNING.
HELLER, LISTEN TO YOURSELF. WE LOST THAT GAME BECAUSE MY GOALIE MISSED A WEIRD, ONE-IN-A-MILLION SHOT. IT HAD NOTHING TO DO WITH YOU. IT WAS JUST BAD LUCK.
HEH. NO SUCH THING.

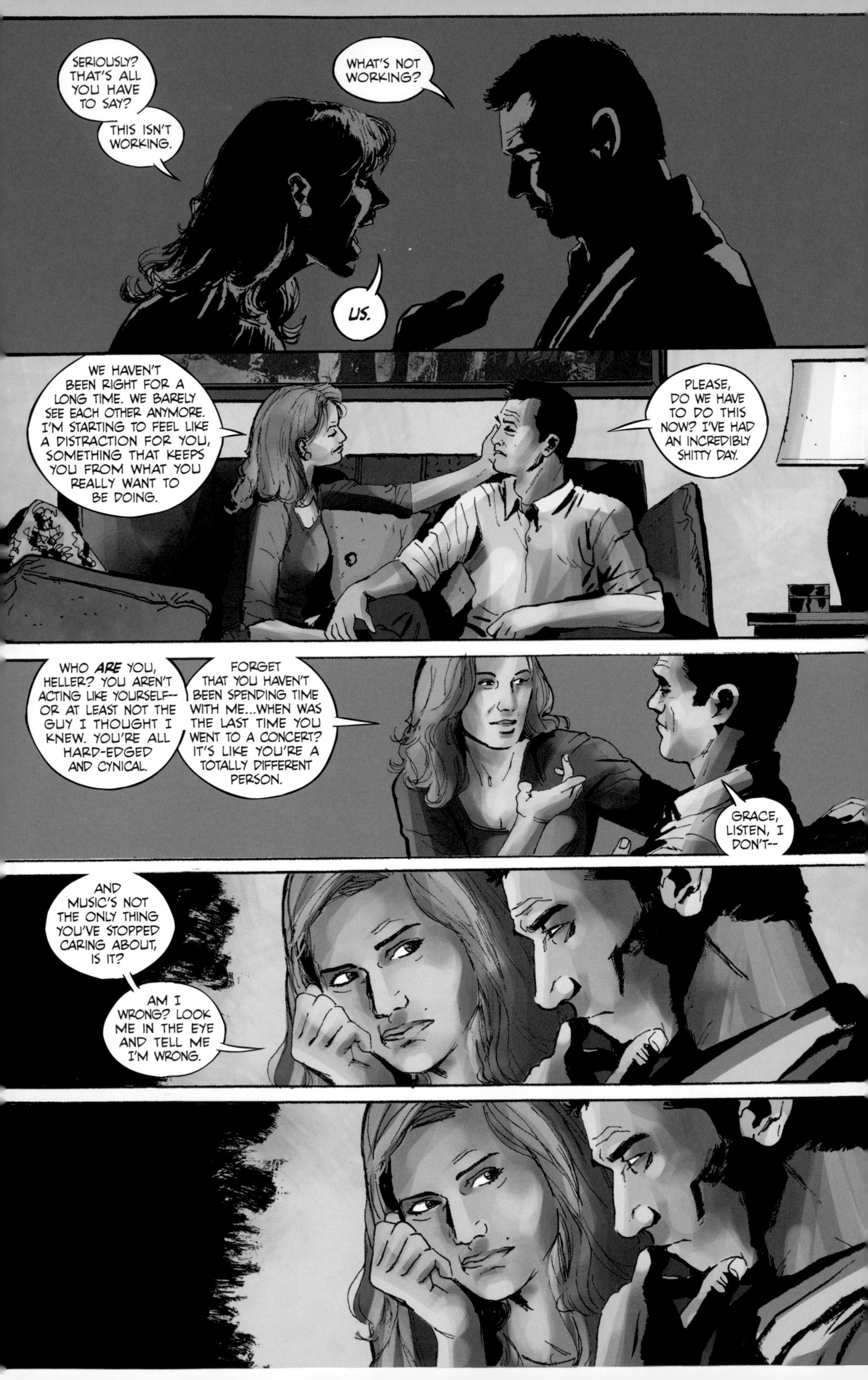
SERIOUSLY? THAT'S ALL YOU HAVE TO SAY?
WHAT'S NOT WORKING?
THIS ISN'T WORKING.
US.
WE HAVEN'T BEEN RIGHT FOR A LONG TIME. WE BARELY SEE EACH OTHER ANYMORE. I'M STARTING TO FEEL LIKE A DISTRACTION FOR YOU, SOMETHING THAT KEEPS YOU FROM WHAT YOU REALLY WANT TO BE DOING.
PLEASE, DO WE HAVE TO DO THIS NOW? I'VE HAD AN INCREDIBLY SHITTY DAY.
WHO ARE YOU, HELLER? YOU AREN'T ACTING LIKE YOURSELF-- OR AT LEAST NOT THE GUY I THOUGHT I KNEW. YOU'RE ALL HARD-EDGED AND CYNICAL.
FORGET THAT YOU HAVEN'T BEEN SPENDING TIME WITH ME...WHEN WAS THE LAST TIME YOU WENT TO A CONCERT? IT'S LIKE YOU'RE A TOTALLY DIFFERENT PERSON.
GRACE, LISTEN, I DON'T--
AND MUSIC'S NOT THE ONLY THING YOU'VE STOPPED CARING ABOUT, IS IT?
AM I WRONG? LOOK ME IN THE EYE AND TELL ME I'M WRONG.

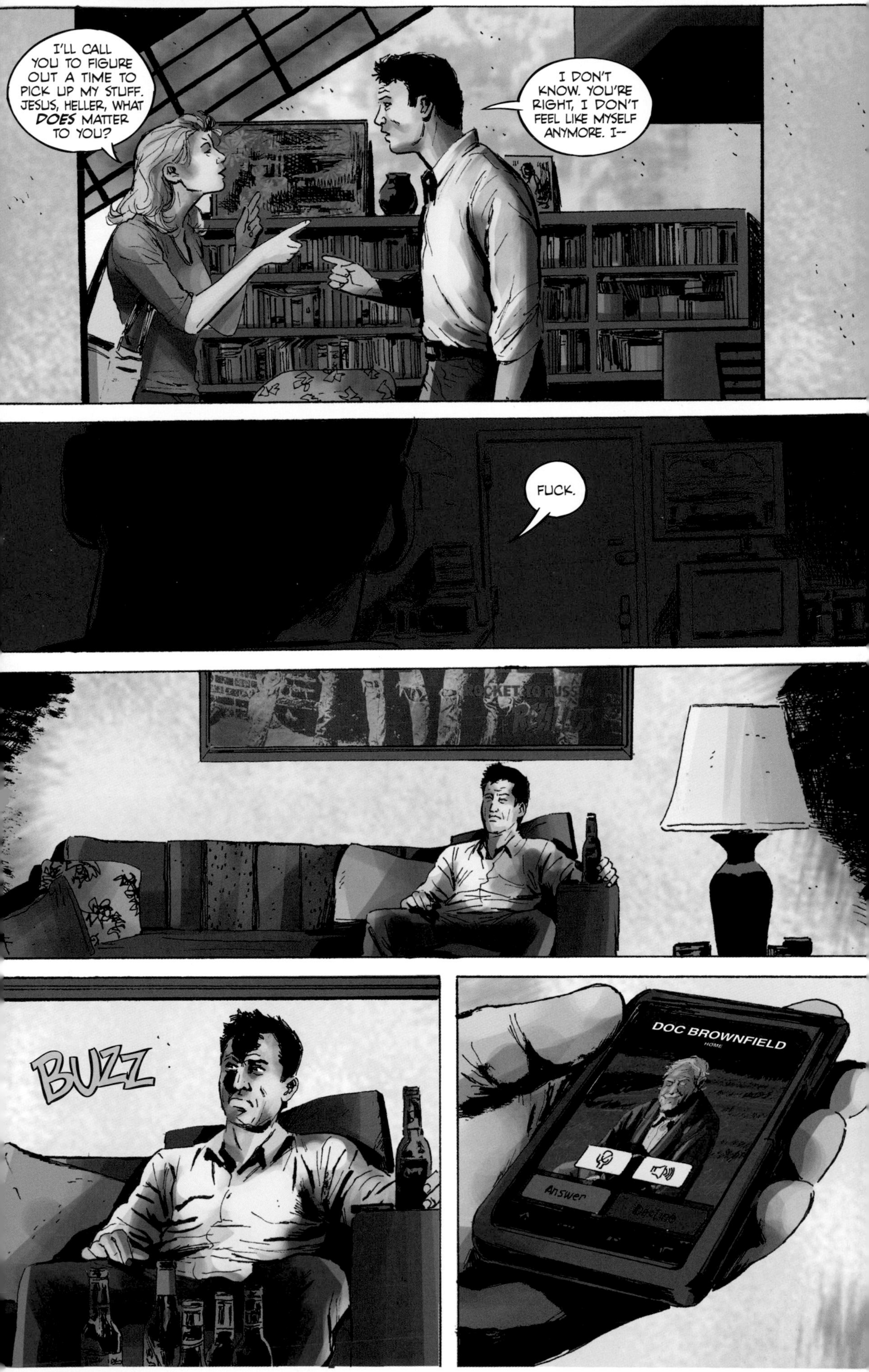
I'LL CALL YOU TO FIGURE OUT A TIME TO PICK UP MY STUFF. JESUS, HELLER, WHAT *DOES* MATTER TO YOU?
I DON'T KNOW. YOU'RE RIGHT, I DON'T FEEL LIKE MYSELF ANYMORE. I--
FUCK.
BUZZ
DOC BROWNFIELD
HOME
Answer

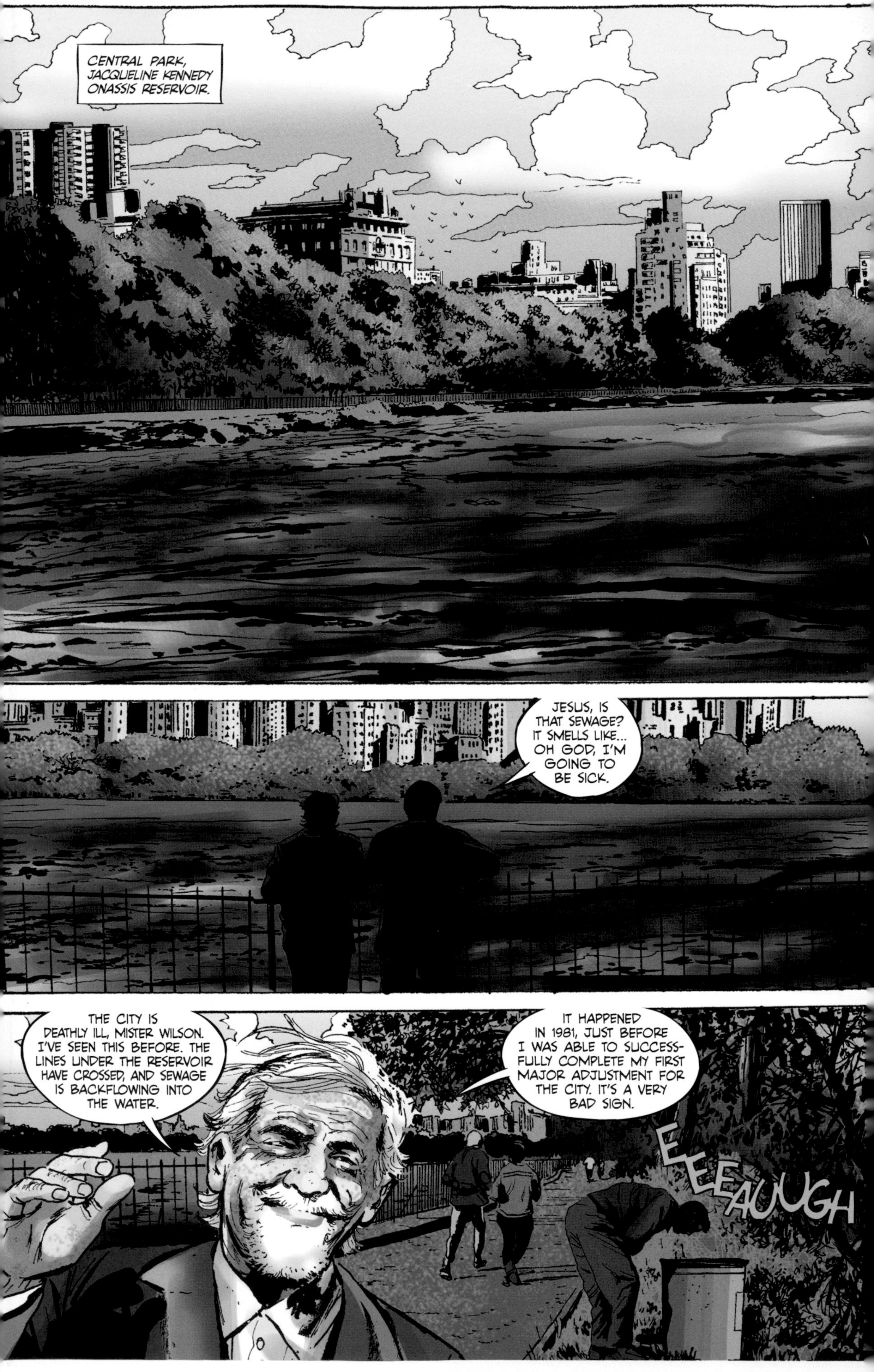
CENTRAL PARK, JACQUELINE KENNEDY ONASSIS RESERVOIR.
JESUS, IS THAT SEWAGE? IT SMELLS LIKE... OH GOD, I'M GOING TO BE SICK.
THE CITY IS DEATHLY ILL, MISTER WILSON. I'VE SEEN THIS BEFORE. THE LINES UNDER THE RESERVOIR HAVE CROSSED, AND SEWAGE IS BACKFLOWING INTO THE WATER.
IT HAPPENED IN 1981, JUST BEFORE I WAS ABLE TO SUCCESSFULLY COMPLETE MY FIRST MAJOR ADJUSTMENT FOR THE CITY. IT'S A VERY BAD SIGN.
EEEEAUUGH

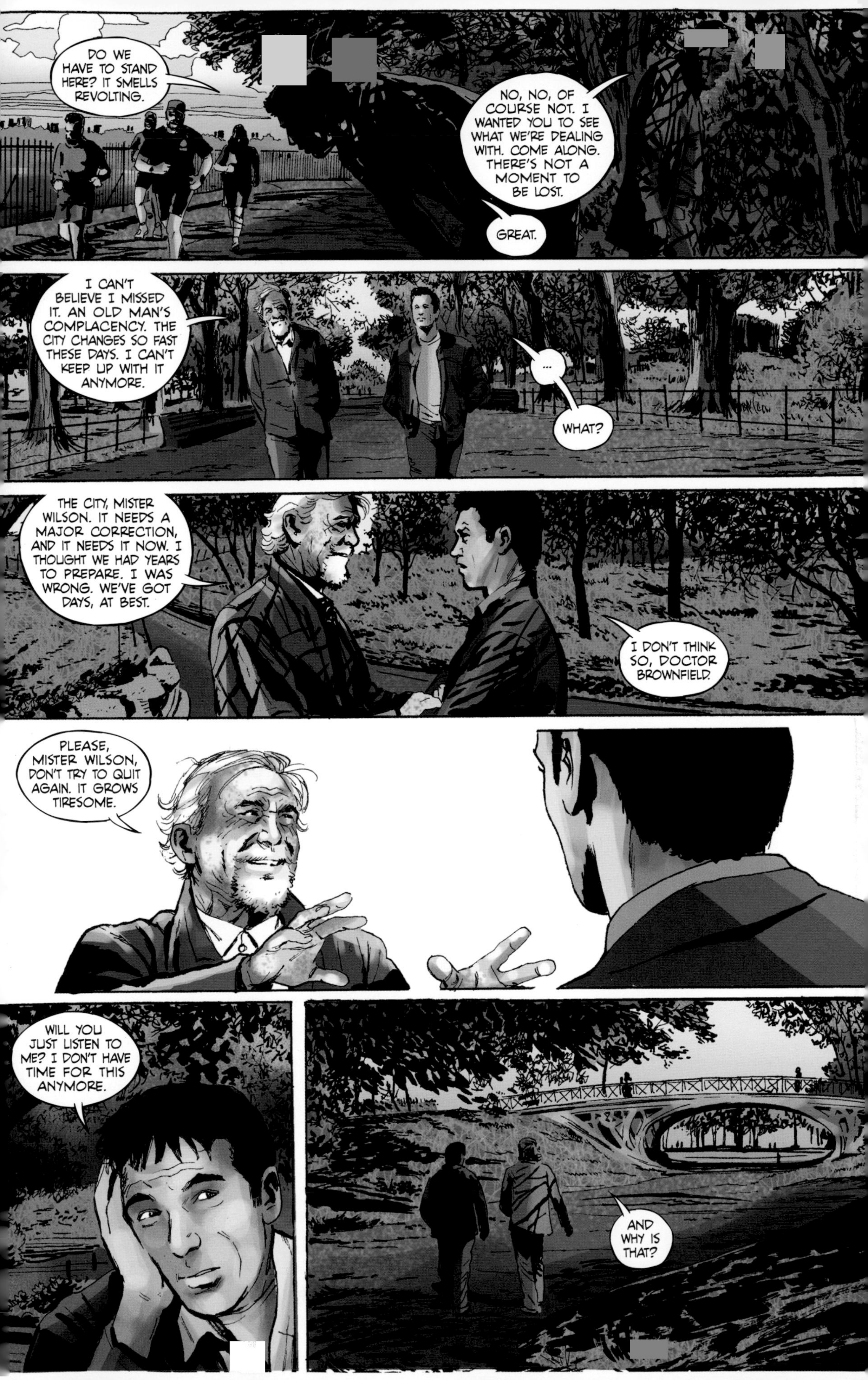
DO WE HAVE TO STAND HERE? IT SMELLS REVOLTING.
NO, NO, OF COURSE NOT. I WANTED YOU TO SEE WHAT WE'RE DEALING WITH. COME ALONG. THERE'S NOT A MOMENT TO BE LOST.
GREAT.
I CAN'T BELIEVE I MISSED IT. AN OLD MAN'S COMPLACENCY. THE CITY CHANGES SO FAST THESE DAYS. I CAN'T KEEP UP WITH IT ANYMORE.
...
WHAT?
THE CITY, MISTER WILSON. IT NEEDS A MAJOR CORRECTION, AND IT NEEDS IT NOW. I THOUGHT WE HAD YEARS TO PREPARE. I WAS WRONG. WE'VE GOT DAYS, AT BEST.
I DON'T THINK SO, DOCTOR BROWNFIELD.
PLEASE, MISTER WILSON, DON'T TRY TO QUIT AGAIN. IT GROWS TIRESOME.
WILL YOU JUST LISTEN TO ME? I DON'T HAVE TIME FOR THIS ANYMORE.
AND WHY IS THAT?

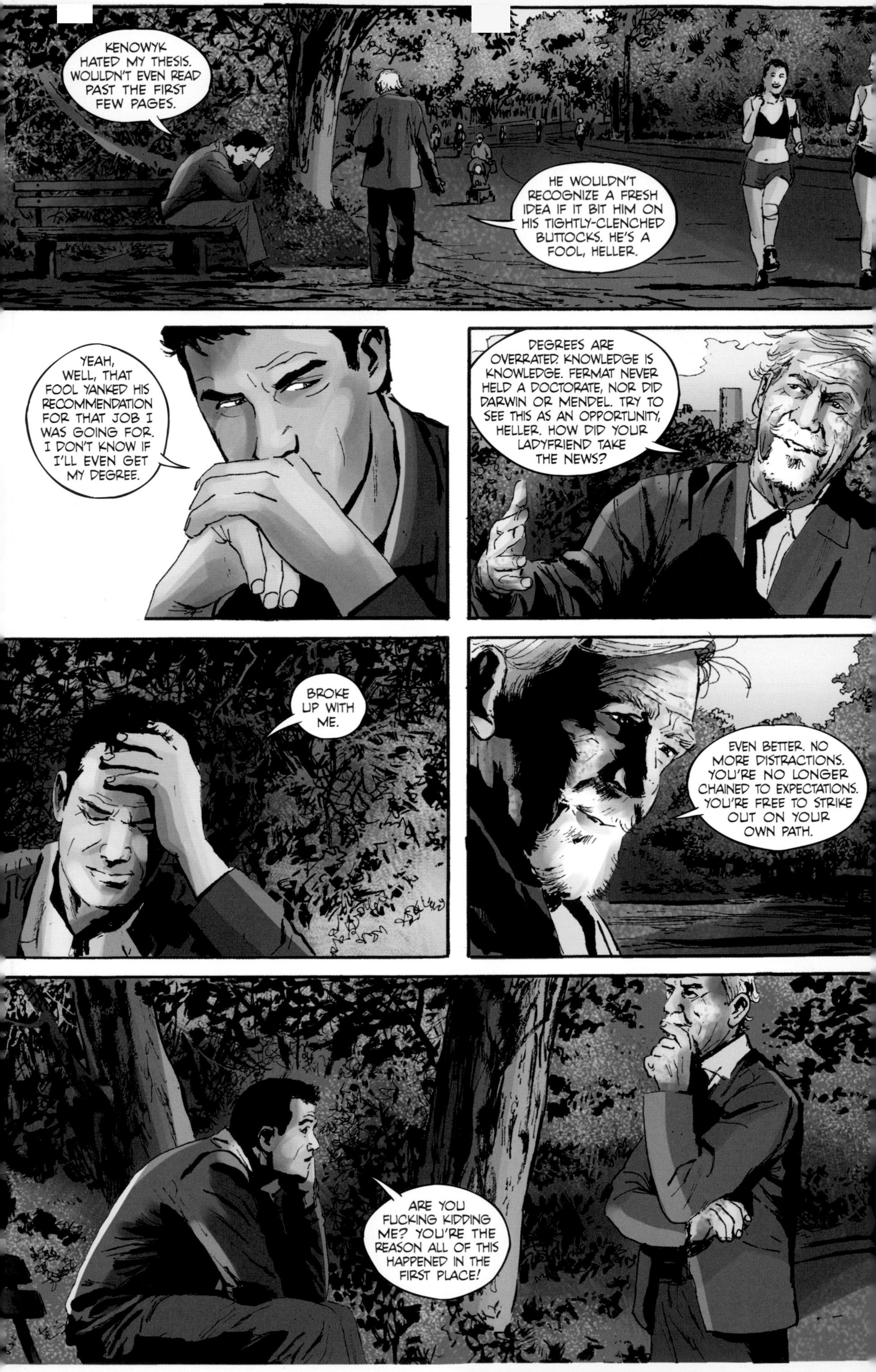
KENOWYK HATED MY THESIS. WOULDN'T EVEN READ PAST THE FIRST FEW PAGES.
HE WOULDN'T RECOGNIZE A FRESH IDEA IF IT BIT HIM ON HIS TIGHTLY-CLENCHED BUTTOCKS. HE'S A FOOL, HELLER.
YEAH, WELL, THAT FOOL YANKED HIS RECOMMENDATION FOR THAT JOB I WAS GOING FOR. I DON'T KNOW IF I'LL EVEN GET MY DEGREE.
DEGREES ARE OVERRATED. KNOWLEDGE IS KNOWLEDGE. FERMAT NEVER HELD A DOCTORATE, NOR DID DARWIN OR MENDEL. TRY TO SEE THIS AS AN OPPORTUNITY, HELLER. HOW DID YOUR LADYFRIEND TAKE THE NEWS?
BROKE UP WITH ME.
EVEN BETTER. NO MORE DISTRACTIONS. YOU'RE NO LONGER CHAINED TO EXPECTATIONS. YOU'RE FREE TO STRIKE OUT ON YOUR OWN PATH.
ARE YOU FUCKING KIDDING ME? YOU'RE THE REASON ALL OF THIS HAPPENED IN THE FIRST PLACE!

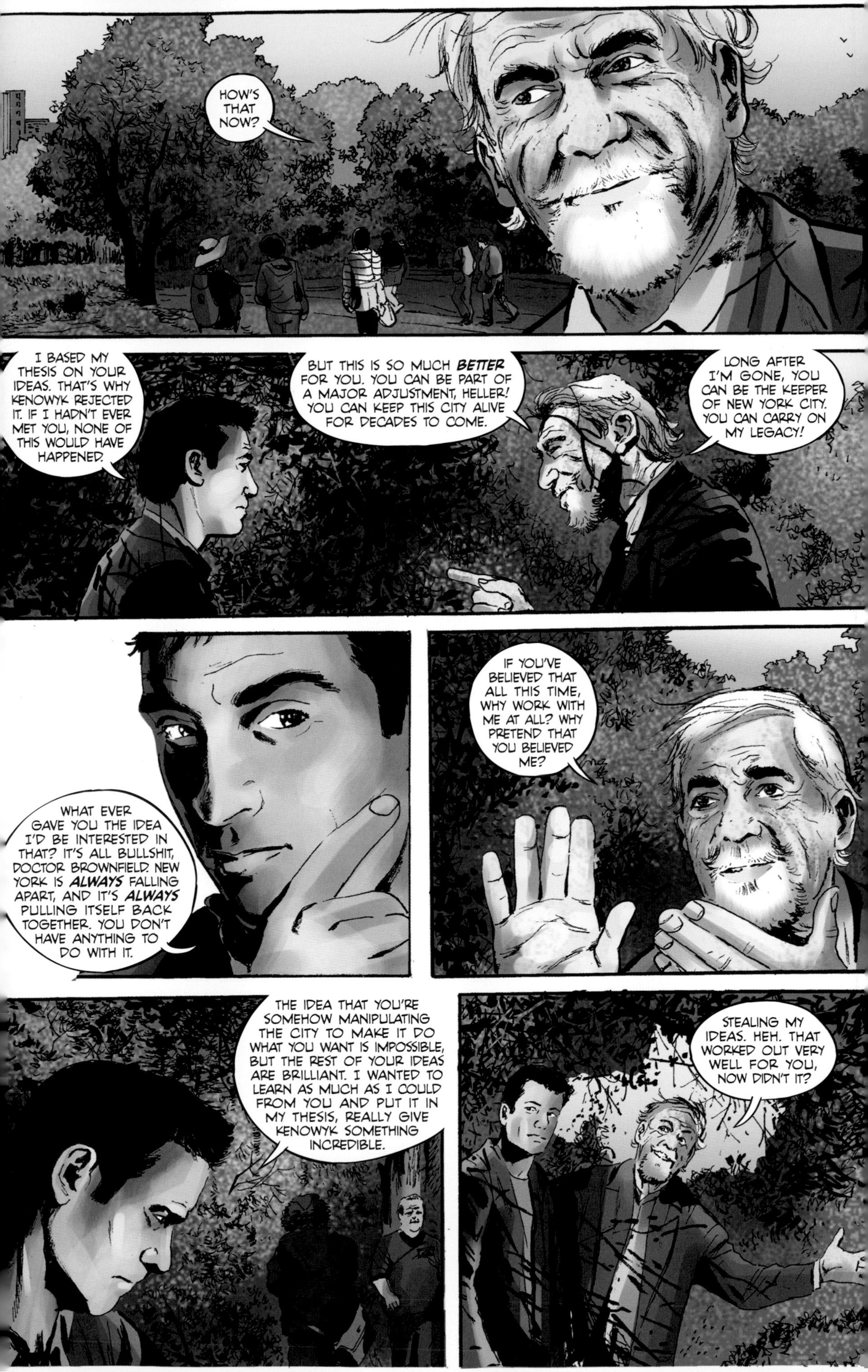
HOW'S THAT NOW?
I BASED MY THESIS ON YOUR IDEAS. THAT'S WHY KENOWYK REJECTED IT. IF I HADN'T EVER MET YOU, NONE OF THIS WOULD HAVE HAPPENED.
BUT THIS IS SO MUCH BETTER FOR YOU. YOU CAN BE PART OF A MAJOR ADJUSTMENT, HELLER! YOU CAN KEEP THIS CITY ALIVE FOR DECADES TO COME.
LONG AFTER I'M GONE, YOU CAN BE THE KEEPER OF NEW YORK CITY. YOU CAN CARRY ON MY LEGACY!
WHAT EVER GAVE YOU THE IDEA I'D BE INTERESTED IN THAT? IT'S ALL BULLSHIT, DOCTOR BROWNFIELD. NEW YORK IS ALWAYS FALLING APART, AND IT'S ALWAYS PULLING ITSELF BACK TOGETHER. YOU DON'T HAVE ANYTHING TO DO WITH IT.
IF YOU'VE BELIEVED THAT ALL THIS TIME, WHY WORK WITH ME AT ALL? WHY PRETEND THAT YOU BELIEVED ME?
THE IDEA THAT YOU'RE SOMEHOW MANIPULATING THE CITY TO MAKE IT DO WHAT YOU WANT IS IMPOSSIBLE, BUT THE REST OF YOUR IDEAS ARE BRILLIANT. I WANTED TO LEARN AS MUCH AS I COULD FROM YOU AND PUT IT IN MY THESIS, REALLY GIVE KENOWYK SOMETHING INCREDIBLE.
STEALING MY IDEAS. HEH. THAT WORKED OUT VERY WELL FOR YOU, NOW DIDN'T IT?

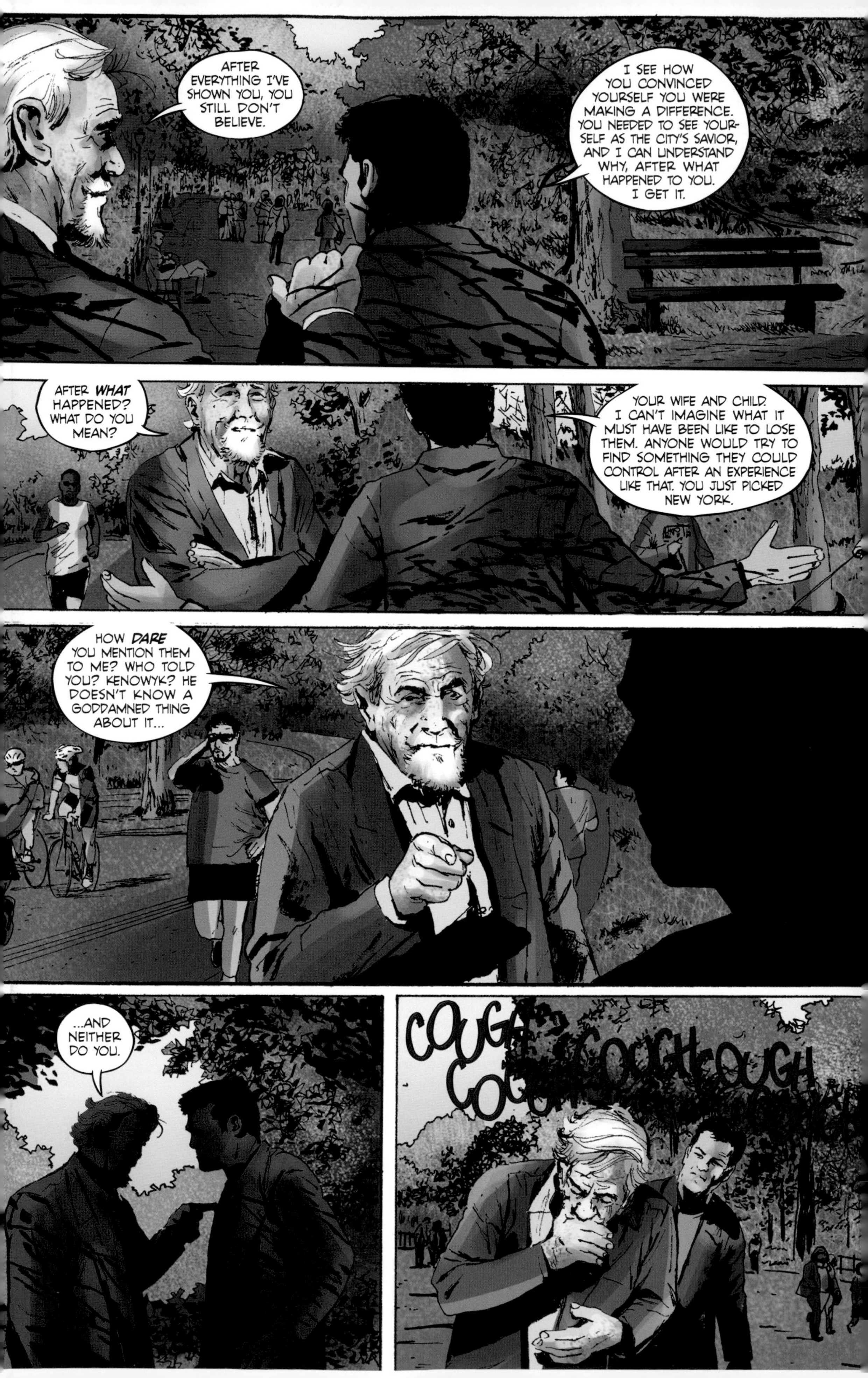
AFTER EVERYTHING I'VE SHOWN YOU, YOU STILL DON'T BELIEVE.
I SEE HOW YOU CONVINCED YOURSELF YOU WERE MAKING A DIFFERENCE. YOU NEEDED TO SEE YOURSELF AS THE CITY'S SAVIOR, AND I CAN UNDERSTAND WHY, AFTER WHAT HAPPENED TO YOU. I GET IT.
AFTER WHAT HAPPENED? WHAT DO YOU MEAN?
YOUR WIFE AND CHILD. I CAN'T IMAGINE WHAT IT MUST HAVE BEEN LIKE TO LOSE THEM. ANYONE WOULD TRY TO FIND SOMETHING THEY COULD CONTROL AFTER AN EXPERIENCE LIKE THAT. YOU JUST PICKED NEW YORK.
HOW DARE YOU MENTION THEM TO ME? WHO TOLD YOU? KENOWYK? HE DOESN'T KNOW A GODDAMNED THING ABOUT IT...
...AND NEITHER DO YOU.
COUGH COUGHCOUGH

IT'S NOT SUPPOSED TO BE THIS WAY. YOU'RE SUPPOSED TO TAKE OVER FOR ME ONCE I'M GONE. DON'T YOU UNDERSTAND? WE DIDN'T MEET BY ACCIDENT.

I HAVE TO GO, DOCTOR BROWNFIELD. I THINK IT'S BEST IF WE GO OUR SEPARATE WAYS. IF YOU CAN, TRY TO LET ALL THIS GO AND LIVE THE REST OF YOUR LIFE. YOU'VE GIVEN THE CITY THIRTY YEARS--IT WILL SURVIVE WITHOUT YOU.

WHAT IS THIS?

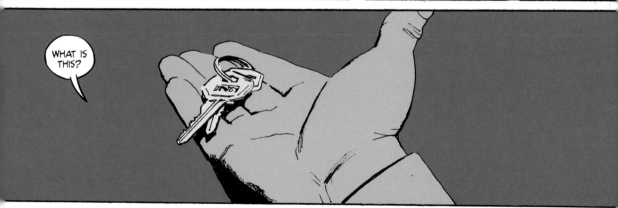

GO TO MY APARTMENT. LOOK AT THE MODEL. CHECK MY RESULTS. IF YOU STILL DON'T AGREE THAT NEW YORK'S IN DESPERATE SHAPE, THEN FINE, TO HELL WITH YOU. BUT HELLER, I'M NOT SURE I CAN DO THIS ALONE.

I'M OLD, AND THESE MAJOR ADJUSTMENTS TAKE SO MUCH FROM ME.

PLEASE, HELLER. FOR THE SAKE OF THE TIME WE'VE SPENT TOGETHER. WHAT CAN IT HURT JUST TO LOOK?

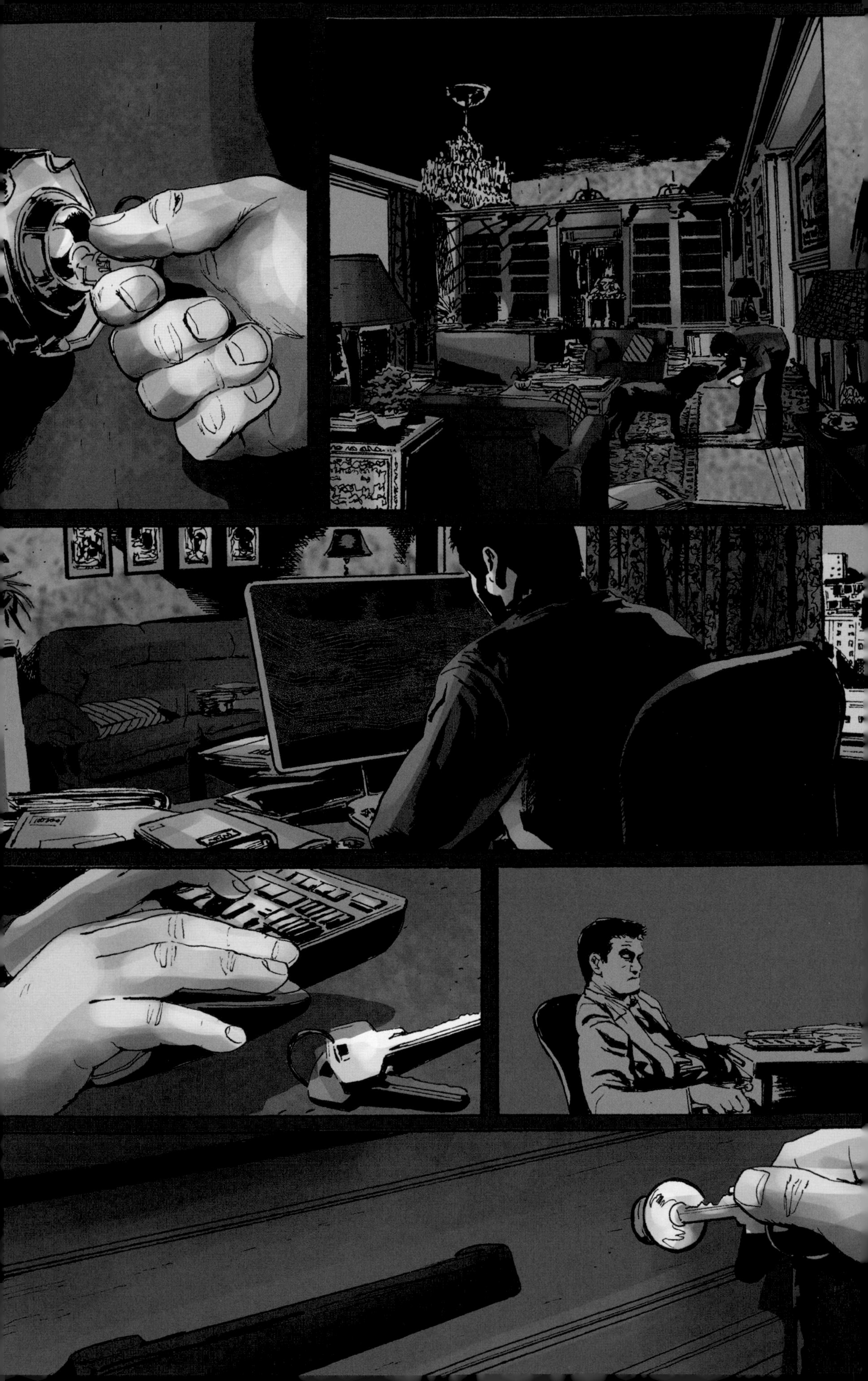

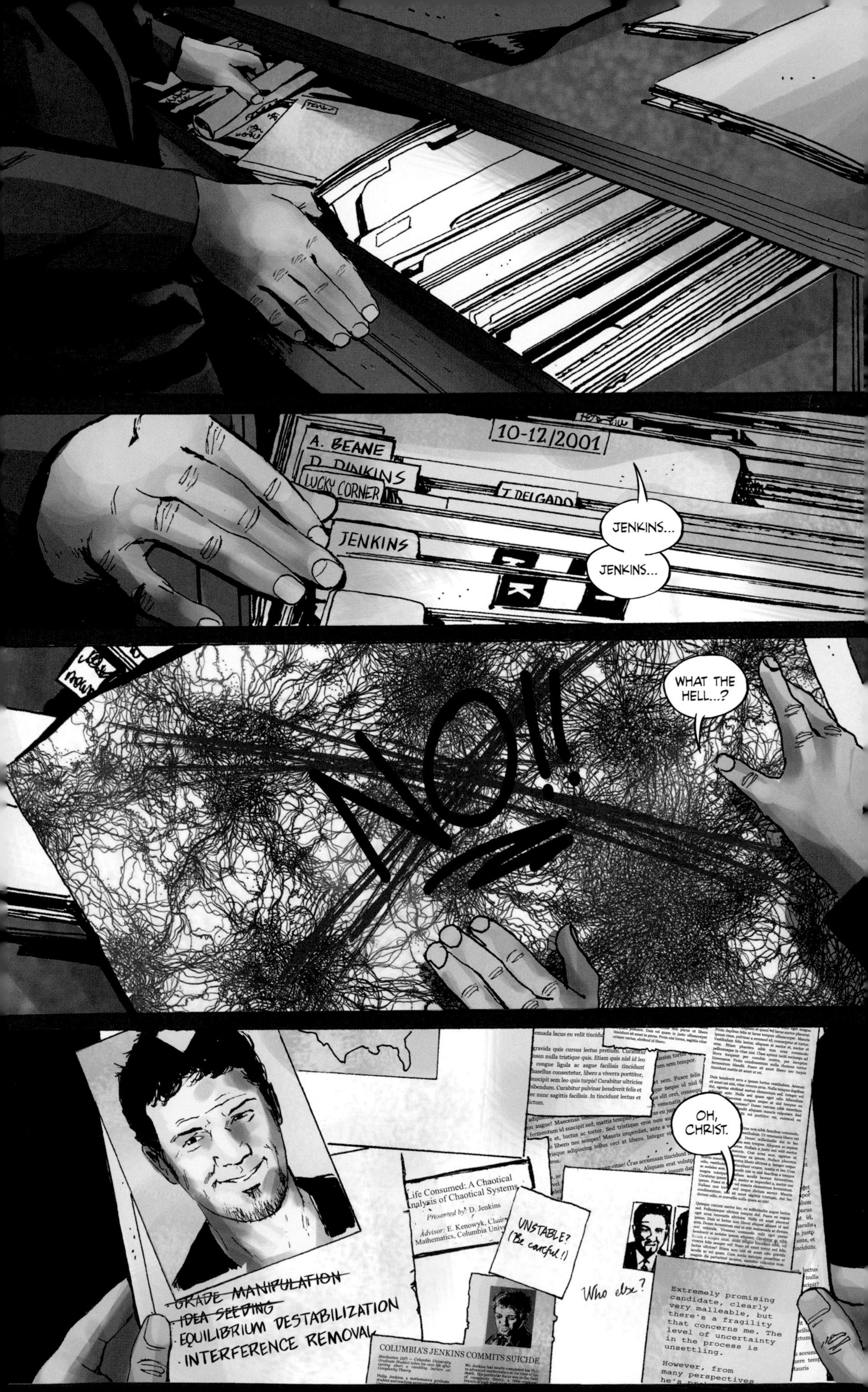
10-12/2001
A. BEANE
D. DINKINS
LUCKY CORNER
J. DELGADO
JENKINS
JENKINS...
JENKINS...
WHAT THE HELL...?
NO!!
OH, CHRIST.
~~GRADE MANIPULATION~~
~~IDEA SEEDING~~
· EQUILIBRIUM DESTABILIZATION
· INTERFERENCE REMOVAL
Life Consumed: A Chaotical Analysis of Chaotical Systems
Presented by: D. Jenkins
Advisor: E. Kenowyk, Chair
Mathematics, Columbia Unive
UNSTABLE? (Be careful!)
Who else?
Extremely promising candidate, clearly very malleable, but there's a fragility that concerns me. The level of uncertainty in the process is unsettling.
However, from many perspectives
COLUMBIA'S JENKINS COMMITS SUICIDE

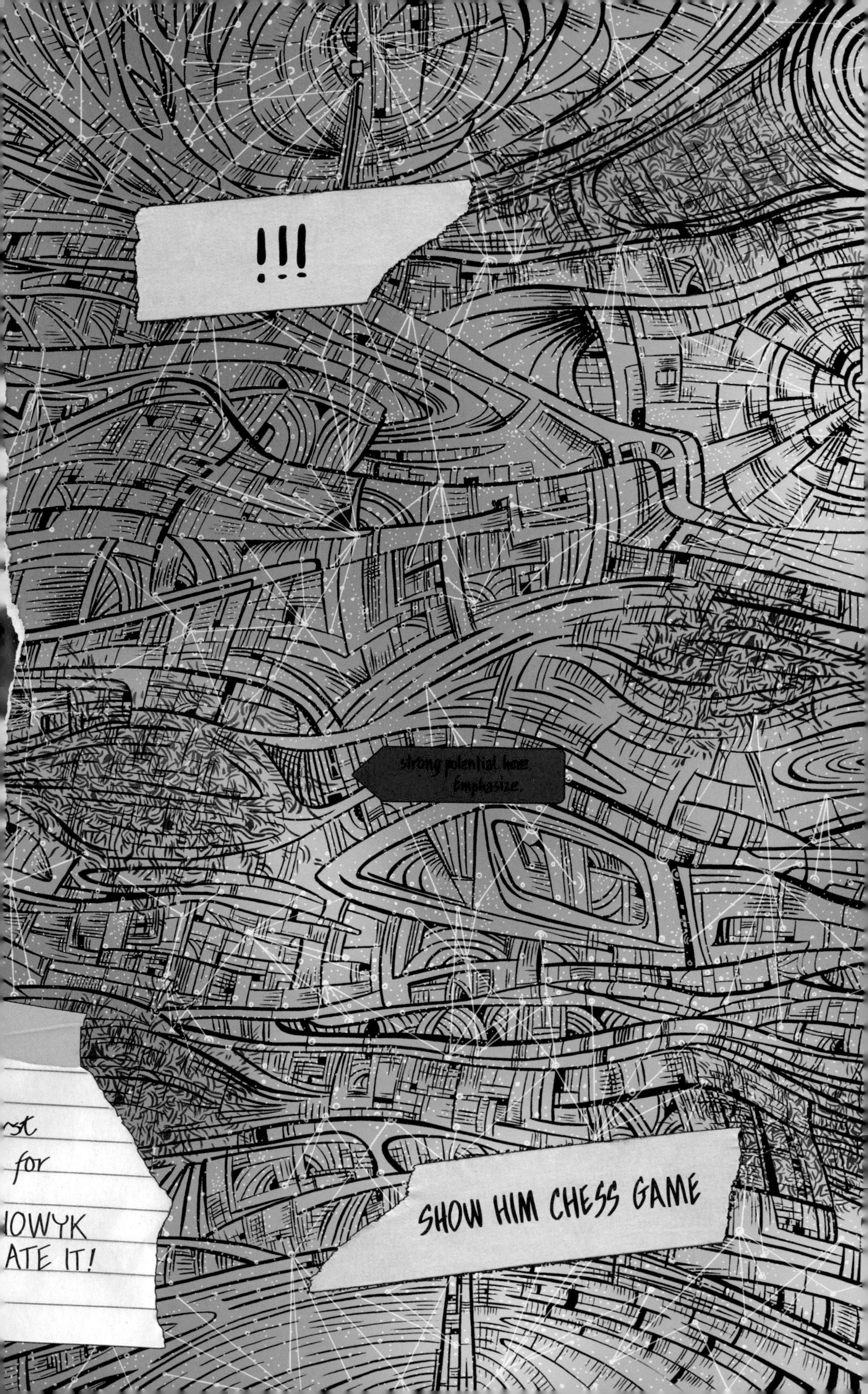
!!!
strong potential here.
Emphasize.
for
IOWYK
ATE IT!
SHOW HIM CHESS GAME

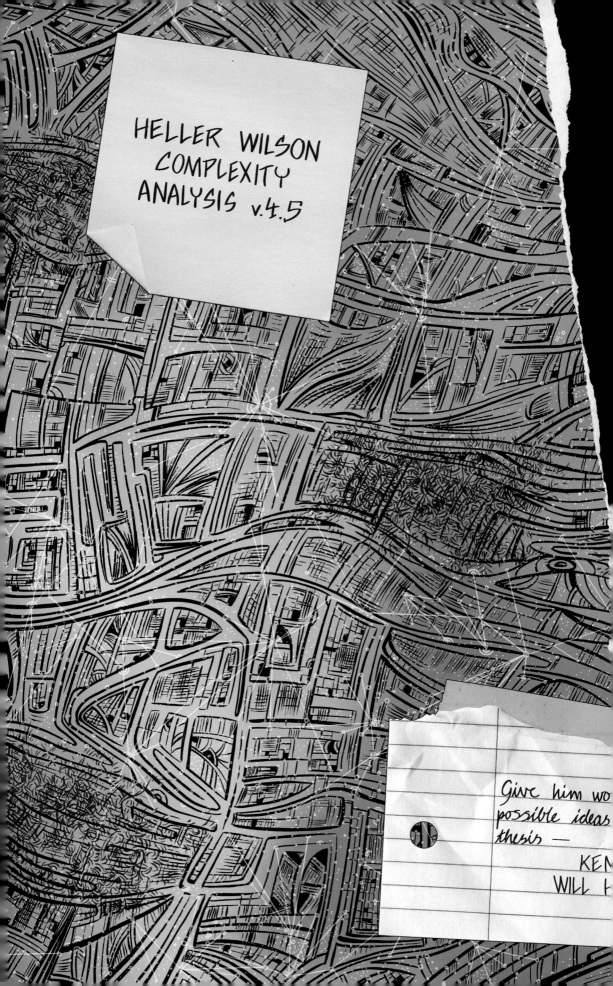

HELLER WILSON
COMPLEXITY
ANALYSIS v.4.5

Give him wo
possible ideas
thesis —
KEN
WILL H

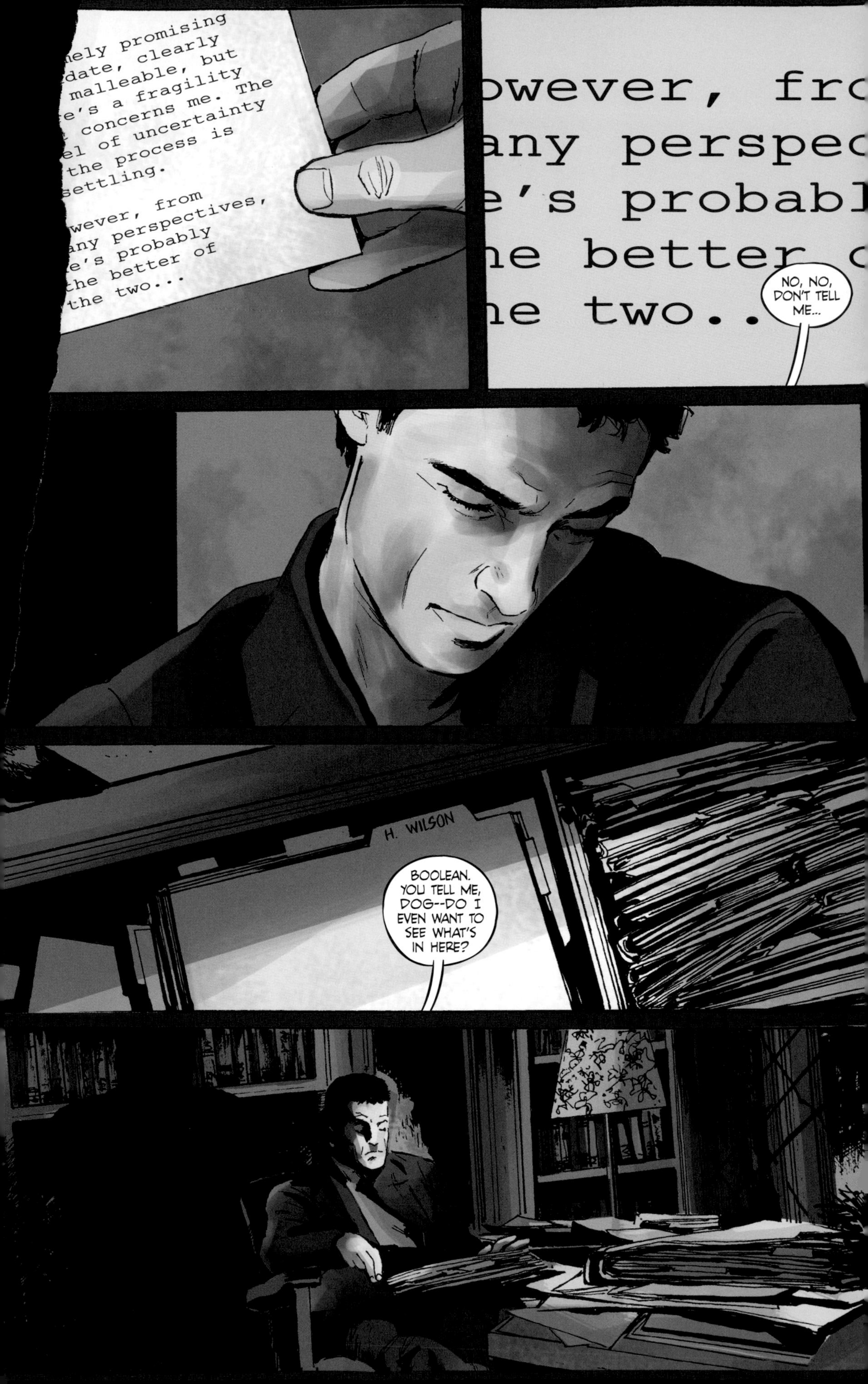

nely promising
date, clearly
malleable, but
e's a fragility
concerns me. The
el of uncertainty
the process is
settling.
wever, from
any perspectives,
e's probably
the better of
the two...
owever, fro
any perspec
e's probabl
he better o
he two...
NO, NO, DON'T TELL ME...
H. WILSON
BOOLEAN. YOU TELL ME, DOG--DO I EVEN WANT TO SEE WHAT'S IN HERE?

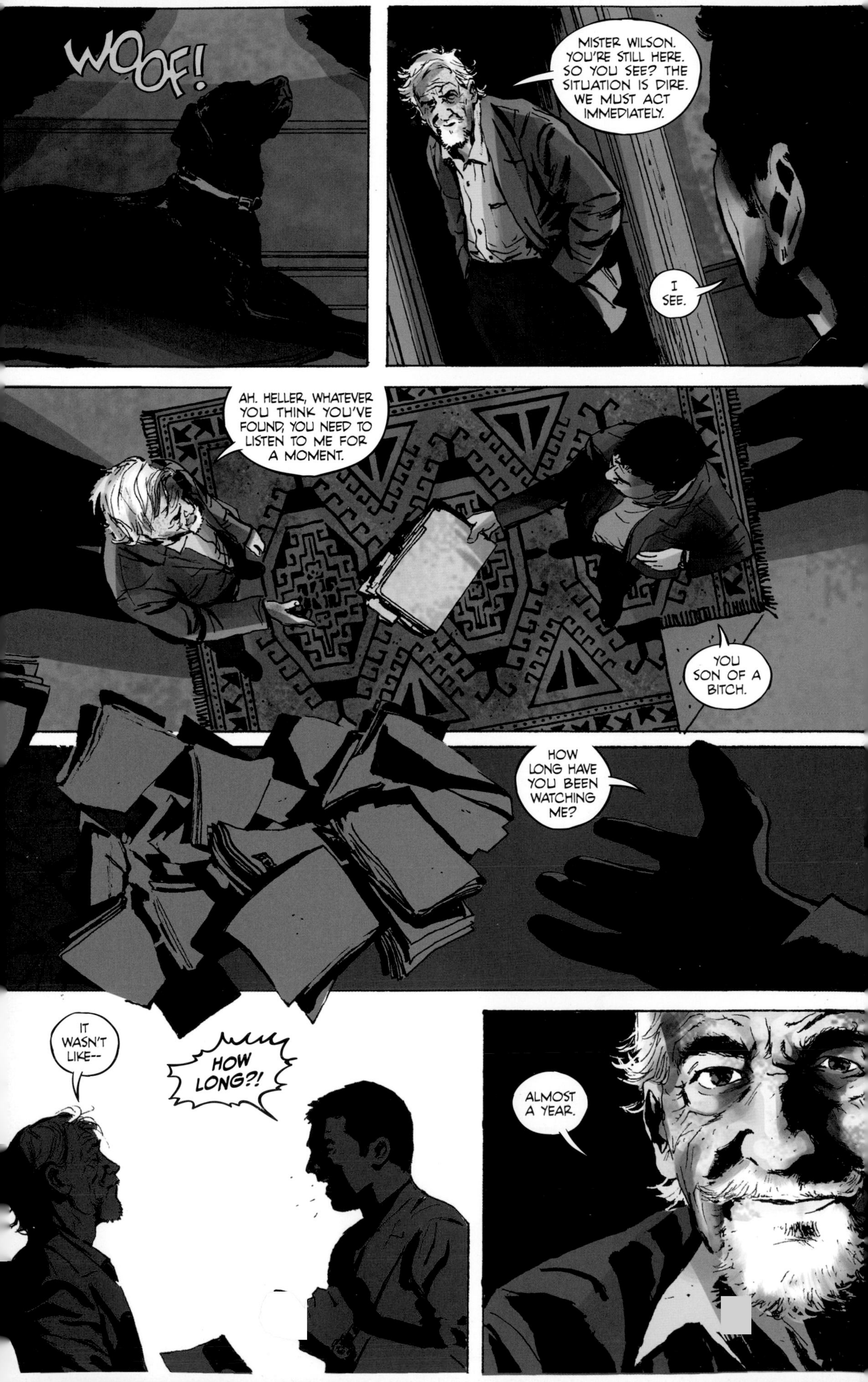
WOOF!
MISTER WILSON. YOU'RE STILL HERE. SO YOU SEE? THE SITUATION IS DIRE. WE MUST ACT IMMEDIATELY.
I SEE.
AH. HELLER, WHATEVER YOU THINK YOU'VE FOUND, YOU NEED TO LISTEN TO ME FOR A MOMENT.
YOU SON OF A BITCH.
HOW LONG HAVE YOU BEEN WATCHING ME?
IT WASN'T LIKE--
HOW LONG?!
ALMOST A YEAR.

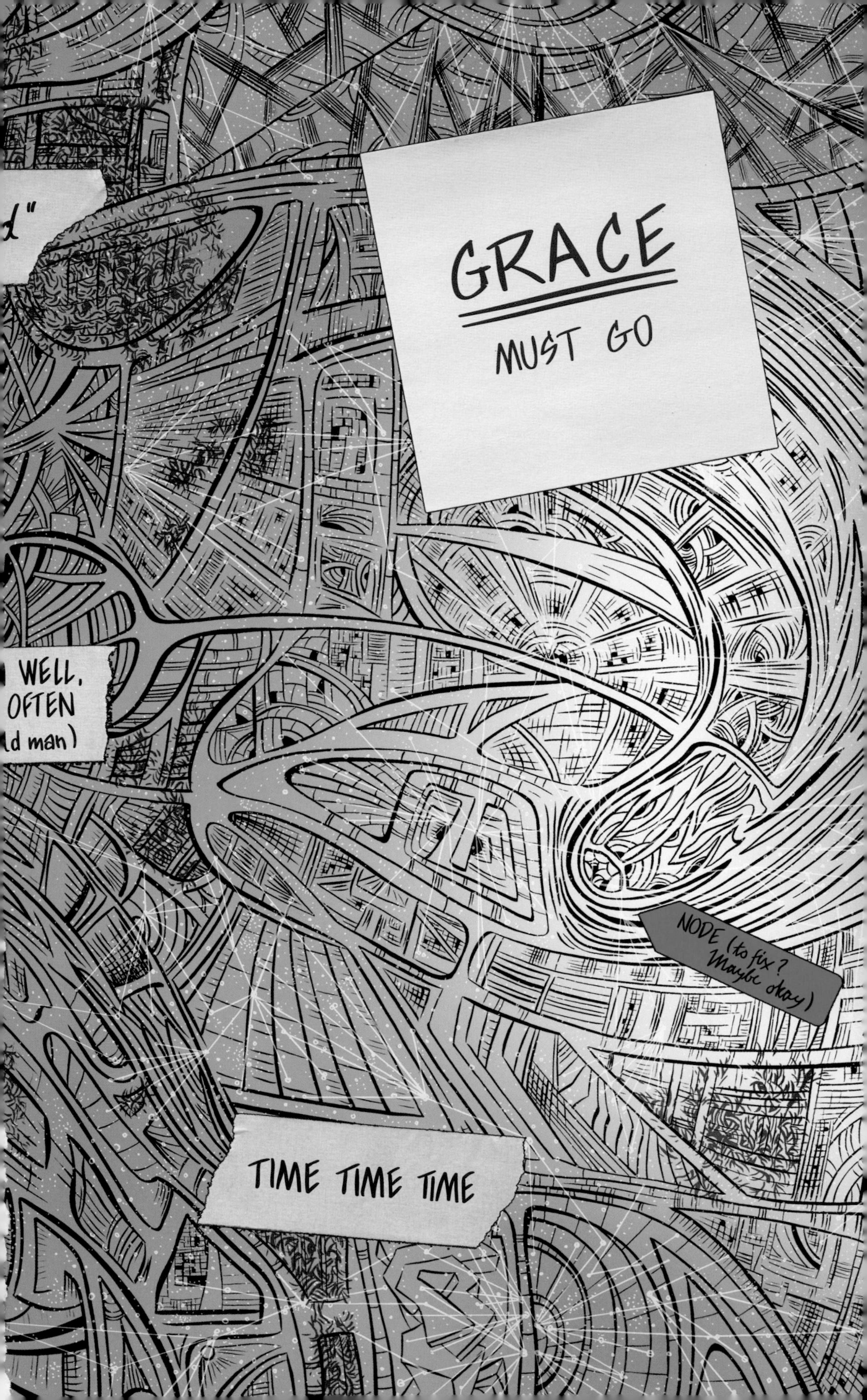
GRACE
MUST GO
WELL,
OFTEN
NODE (to fix? Maybe okay)
TIME TIME TIME

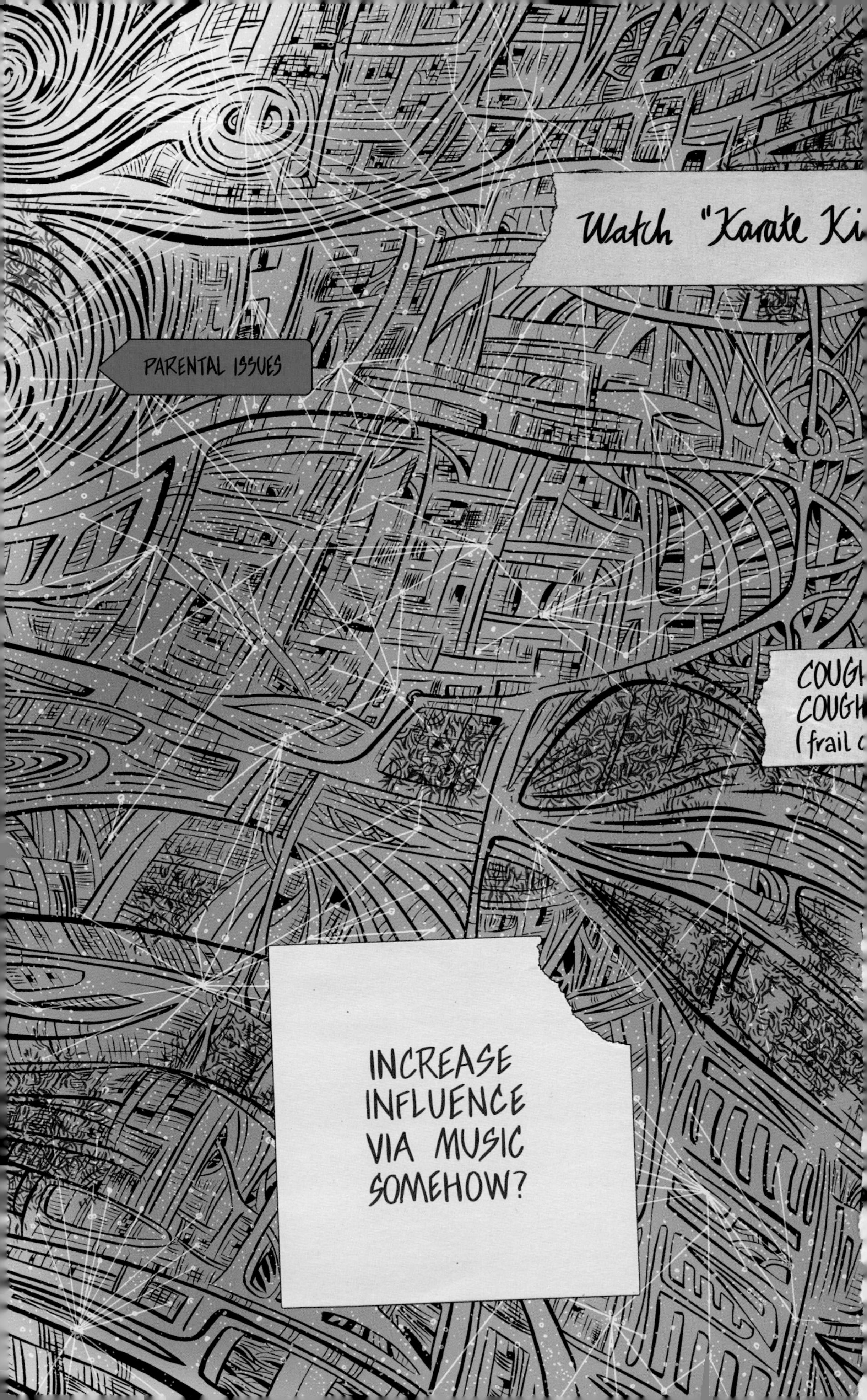
Watch "Karate Ki
PARENTAL ISSUES
COUGH
COUGH
(frail c
INCREASE INFLUENCE VIA MUSIC SOMEHOW?

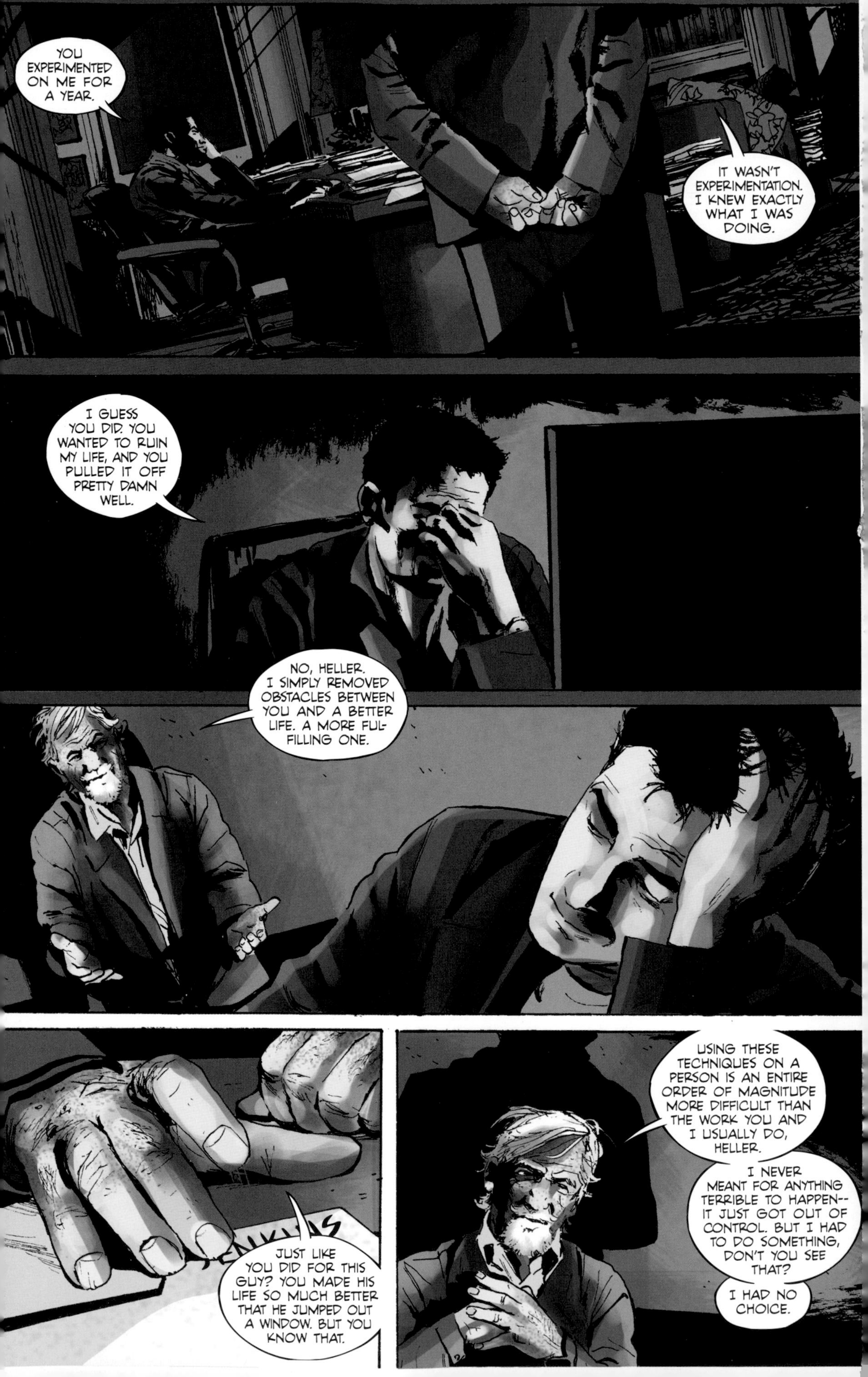
YOU EXPERIMENTED ON ME FOR A YEAR.
IT WASN'T EXPERIMENTATION. I KNEW EXACTLY WHAT I WAS DOING.
I GUESS YOU DID. YOU WANTED TO RUIN MY LIFE, AND YOU PULLED IT OFF PRETTY DAMN WELL.
NO, HELLER. I SIMPLY REMOVED OBSTACLES BETWEEN YOU AND A BETTER LIFE. A MORE FUL-FILLING ONE.
JUST LIKE YOU DID FOR THIS GUY? YOU MADE HIS LIFE SO MUCH BETTER THAT HE JUMPED OUT A WINDOW. BUT YOU KNOW THAT.
USING THESE TECHNIQUES ON A PERSON IS AN ENTIRE ORDER OF MAGNITUDE MORE DIFFICULT THAN THE WORK YOU AND I USUALLY DO, HELLER.
I NEVER MEANT FOR ANYTHING TERRIBLE TO HAPPEN-- IT JUST GOT OUT OF CONTROL. BUT I HAD TO DO SOMETHING, DON'T YOU SEE THAT?
I HAD NO CHOICE.

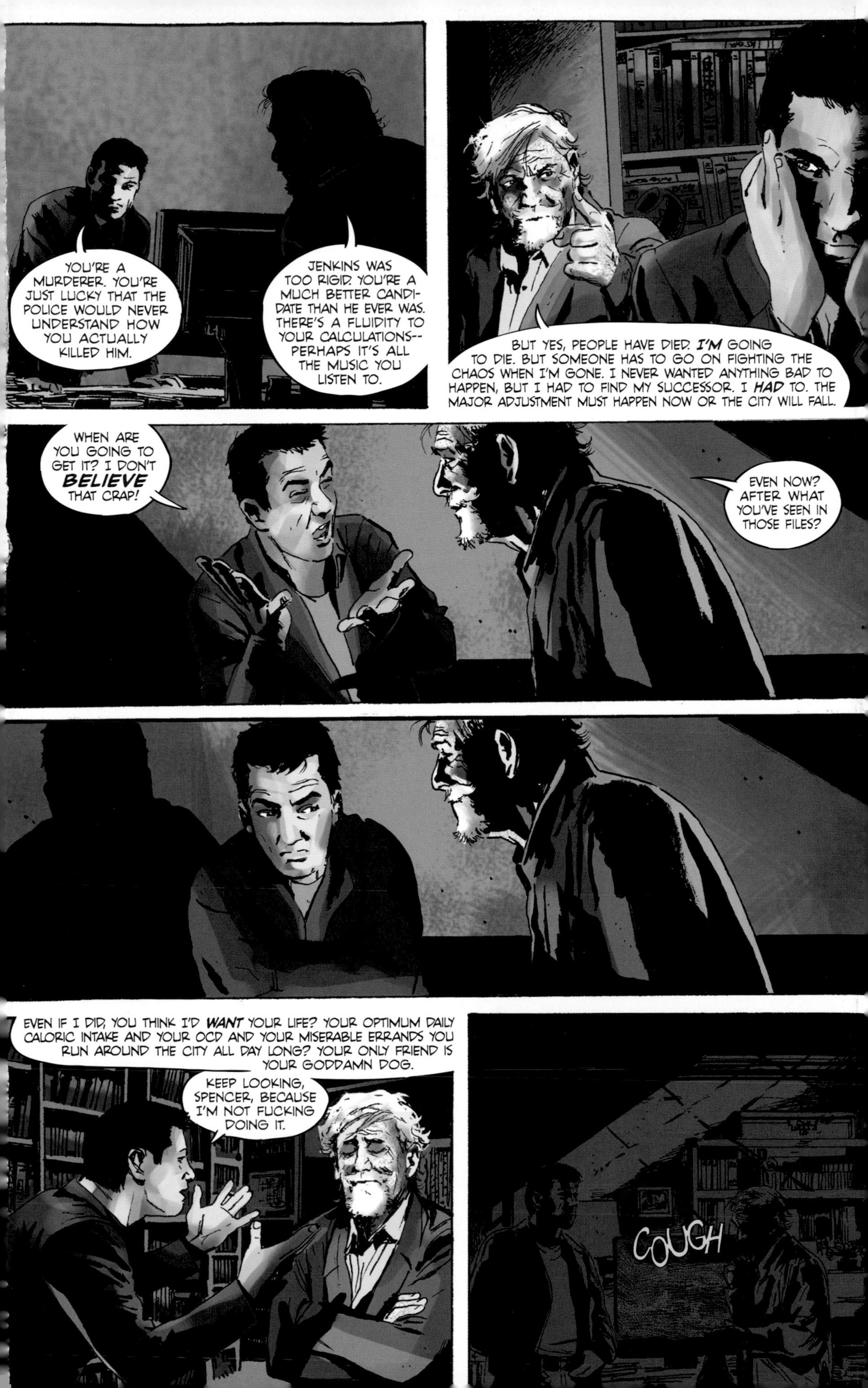
YOU'RE A MURDERER. YOU'RE JUST LUCKY THAT THE POLICE WOULD NEVER UNDERSTAND HOW YOU ACTUALLY KILLED HIM.
JENKINS WAS TOO RIGID. YOU'RE A MUCH BETTER CANDIDATE THAN HE EVER WAS. THERE'S A FLUIDITY TO YOUR CALCULATIONS-- PERHAPS IT'S ALL THE MUSIC YOU LISTEN TO.
BUT YES, PEOPLE HAVE DIED. *I'M* GOING TO DIE. BUT SOMEONE HAS TO GO ON FIGHTING THE CHAOS WHEN I'M GONE. I NEVER WANTED ANYTHING BAD TO HAPPEN, BUT I HAD TO FIND MY SUCCESSOR. I *HAD* TO. THE MAJOR ADJUSTMENT MUST HAPPEN NOW OR THE CITY WILL FALL.
WHEN ARE YOU GOING TO GET IT? I DON'T **BELIEVE** THAT CRAP!
EVEN NOW? AFTER WHAT YOU'VE SEEN IN THOSE FILES?
EVEN IF I DID, YOU THINK I'D *WANT* YOUR LIFE? YOUR OPTIMUM DAILY CALORIC INTAKE AND YOUR OCD AND YOUR MISERABLE ERRANDS YOU RUN AROUND THE CITY ALL DAY LONG? YOUR ONLY FRIEND IS YOUR GODDAMN DOG.
KEEP LOOKING, SPENCER, BECAUSE I'M NOT FUCKING DOING IT.
COUGH

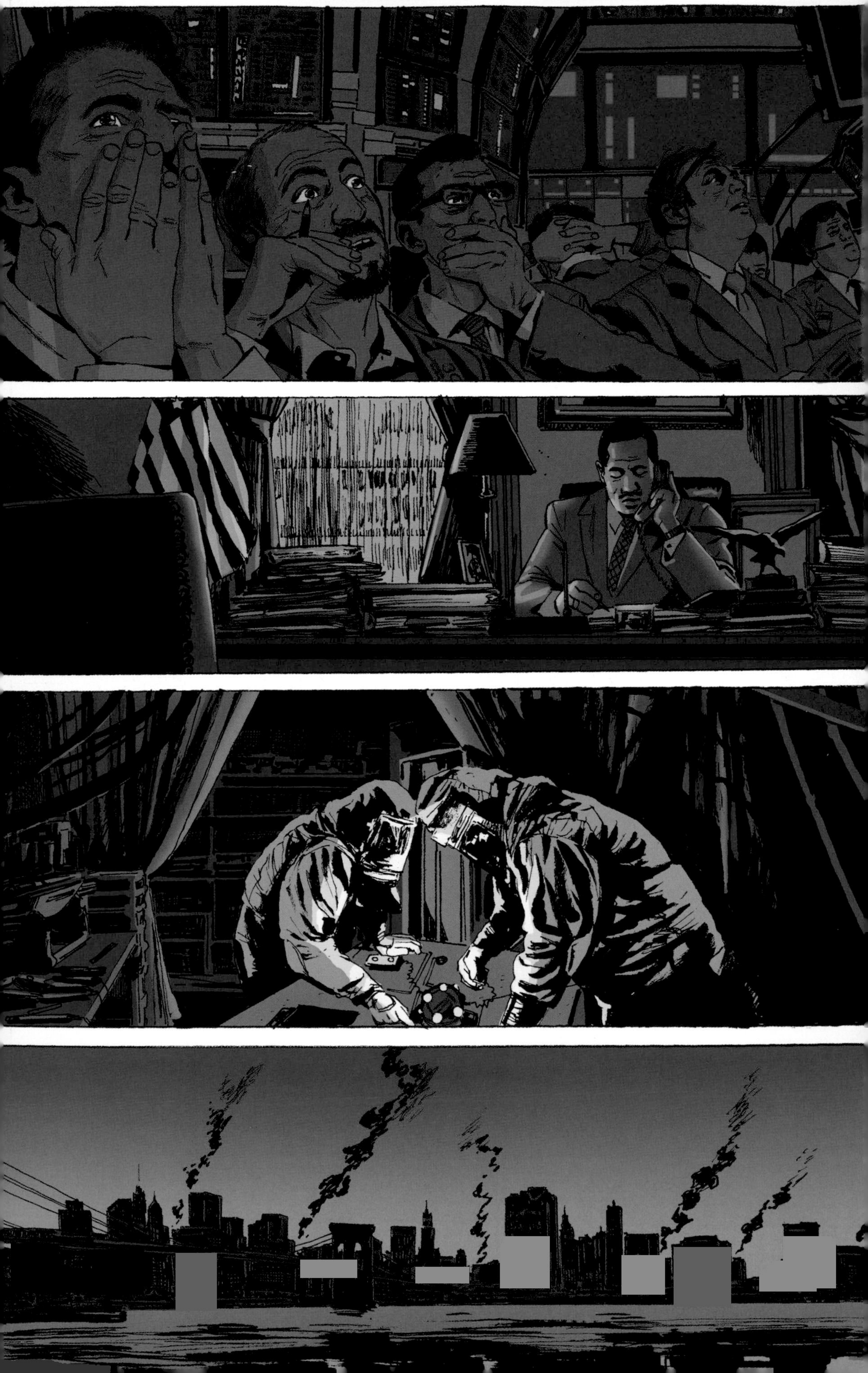

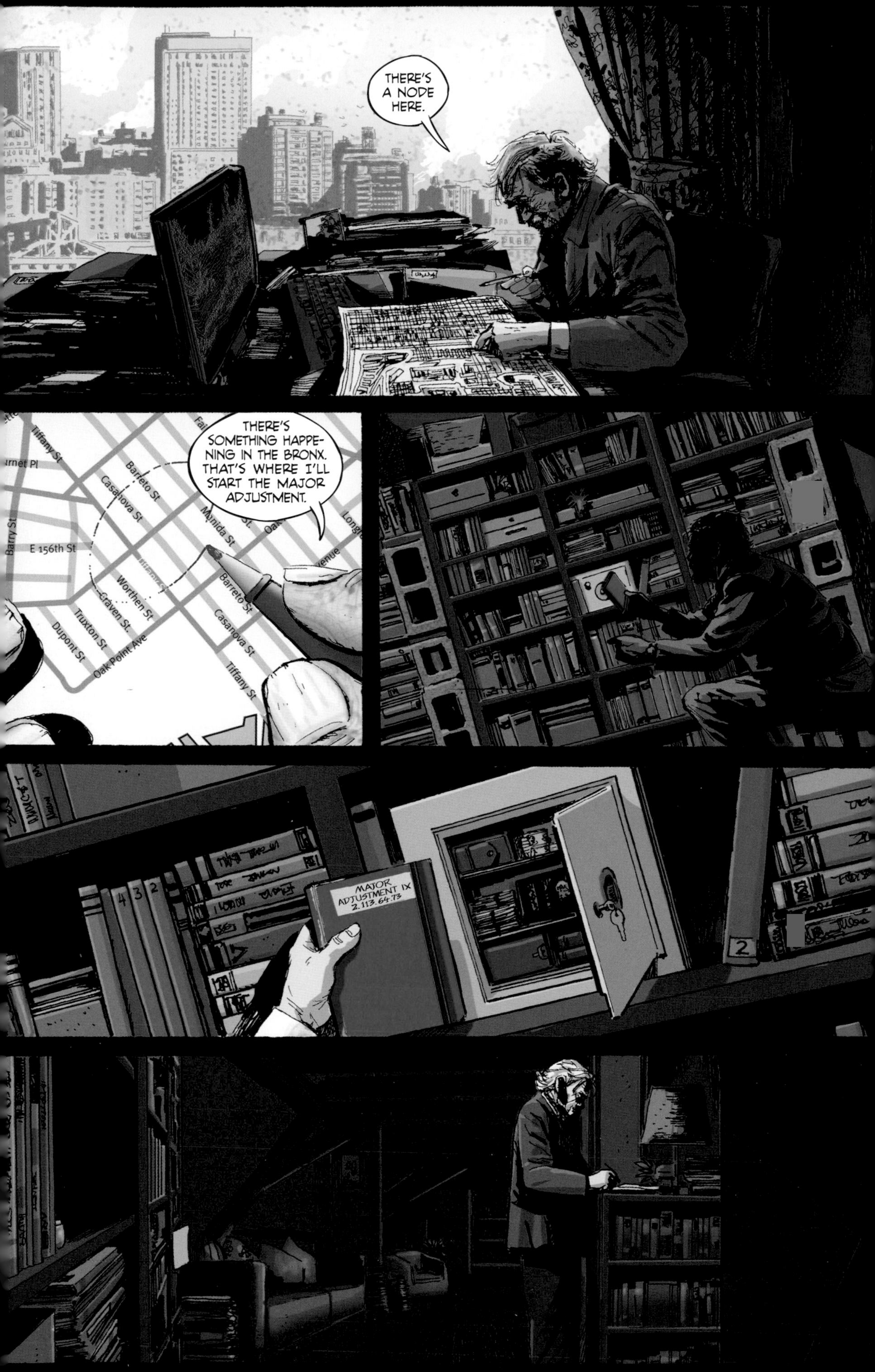
THERE'S A NODE HERE.
THERE'S SOMETHING HAPPENING IN THE BRONX. THAT'S WHERE I'LL START THE MAJOR ADJUSTMENT.
Tiffany St
Barry St
E 156th St
Barreto St
Casanova St
Manida St
Worthen St
Craven St
Truxton St
Dupont St
Oak Point Ave
Barreto St
Casanova St
Tiffany St
MAJOR ADJUSTMENT IX 2.113.64.73

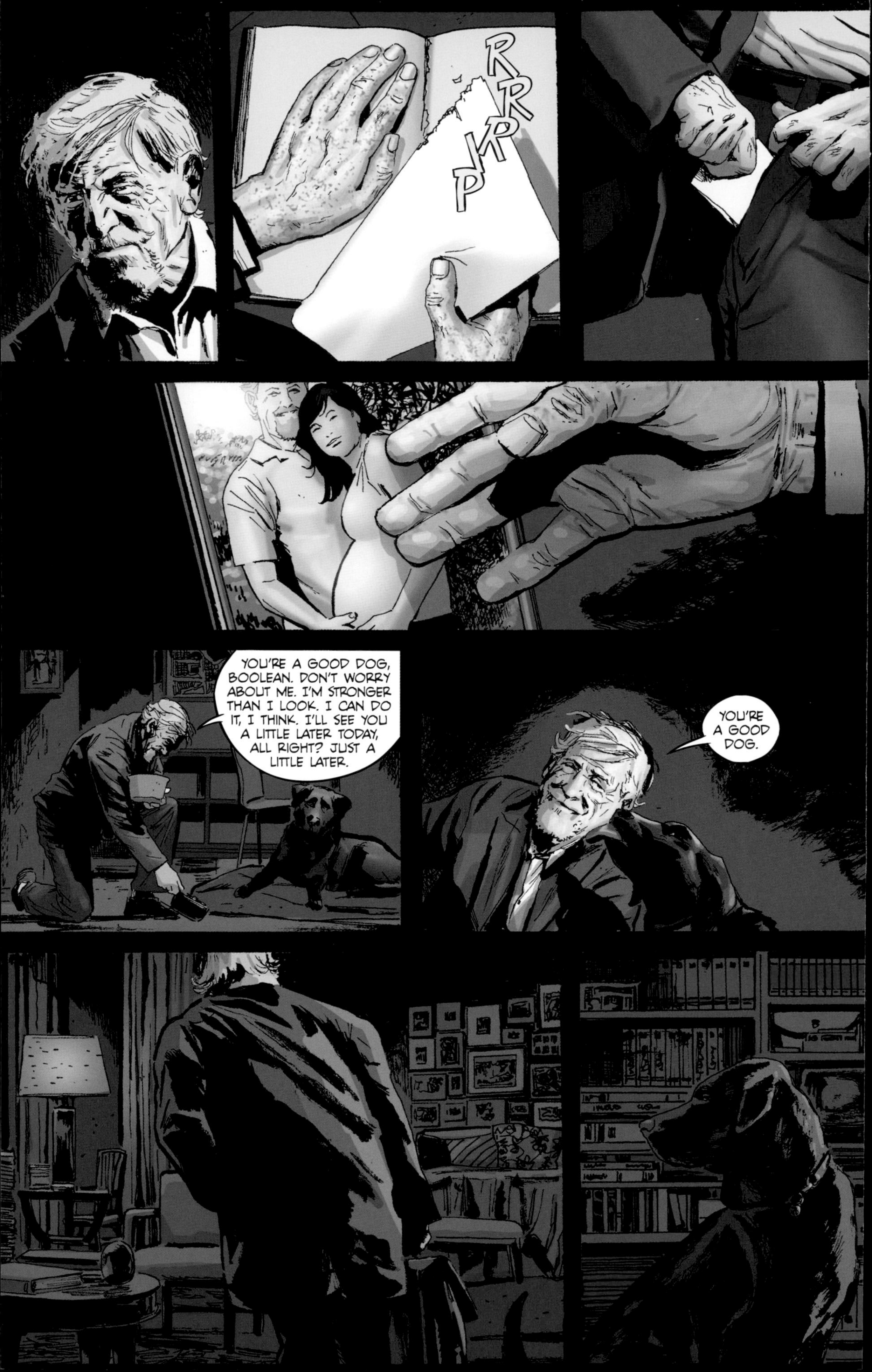
RRRP
YOU'RE A GOOD DOG, BOOLEAN. DON'T WORRY ABOUT ME. I'M STRONGER THAN I LOOK. I CAN DO IT, I THINK. I'LL SEE YOU A LITTLE LATER TODAY, ALL RIGHT? JUST A LITTLE LATER.
YOU'RE A GOOD DOG.

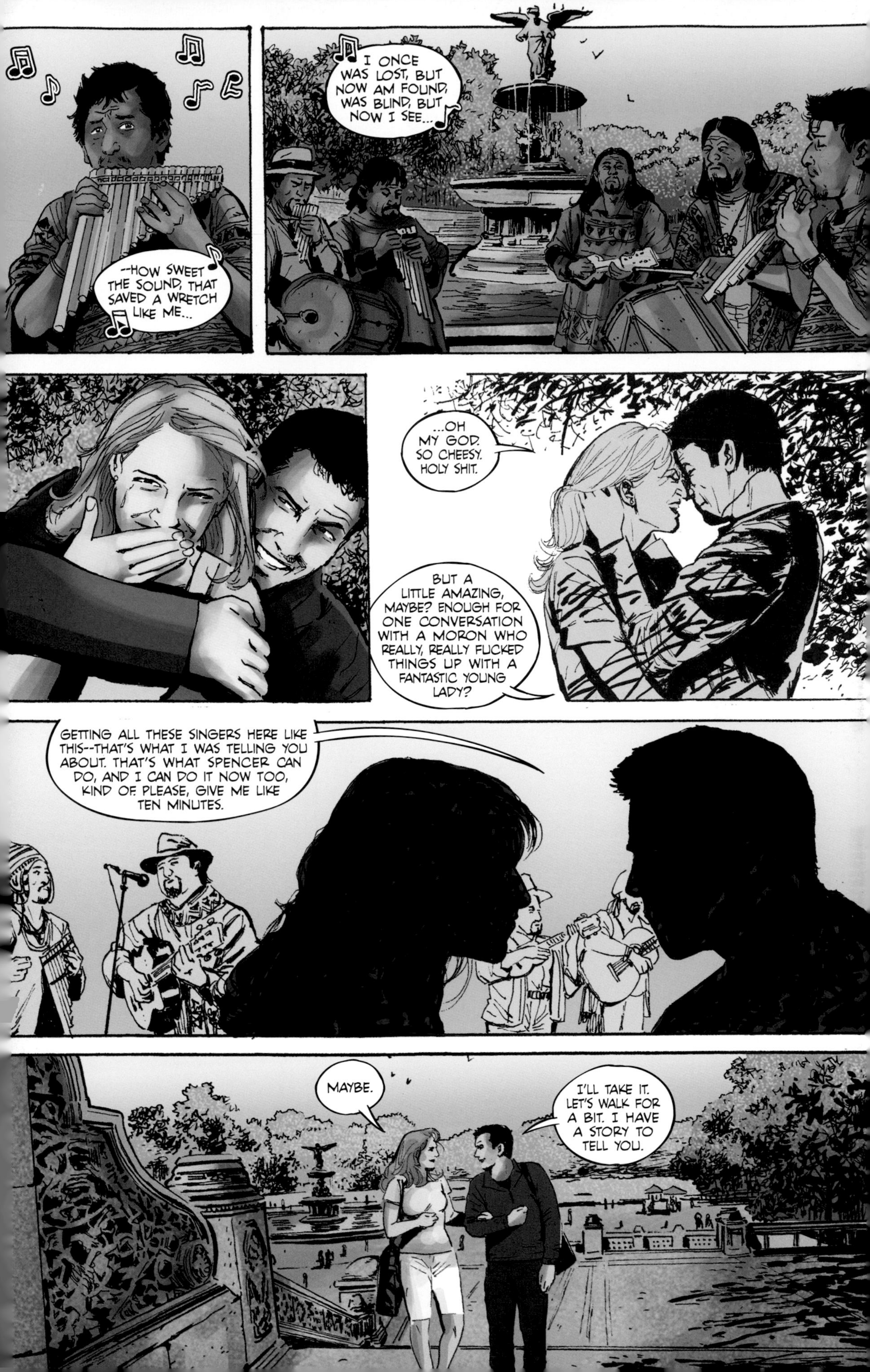
--HOW SWEET THE SOUND, THAT SAVED A WRETCH LIKE ME...
I ONCE WAS LOST, BUT NOW AM FOUND, WAS BLIND, BUT NOW I SEE...
...OH MY GOD. SO CHEESY. HOLY SHIT.
BUT A LITTLE AMAZING, MAYBE? ENOUGH FOR ONE CONVERSATION WITH A MORON WHO REALLY, REALLY FUCKED THINGS UP WITH A FANTASTIC YOUNG LADY?
GETTING ALL THESE SINGERS HERE LIKE THIS--THAT'S WHAT I WAS TELLING YOU ABOUT. THAT'S WHAT SPENCER CAN DO, AND I CAN DO IT NOW TOO, KIND OF. PLEASE, GIVE ME LIKE TEN MINUTES.
MAYBE.
I'LL TAKE IT. LET'S WALK FOR A BIT. I HAVE A STORY TO TELL YOU.

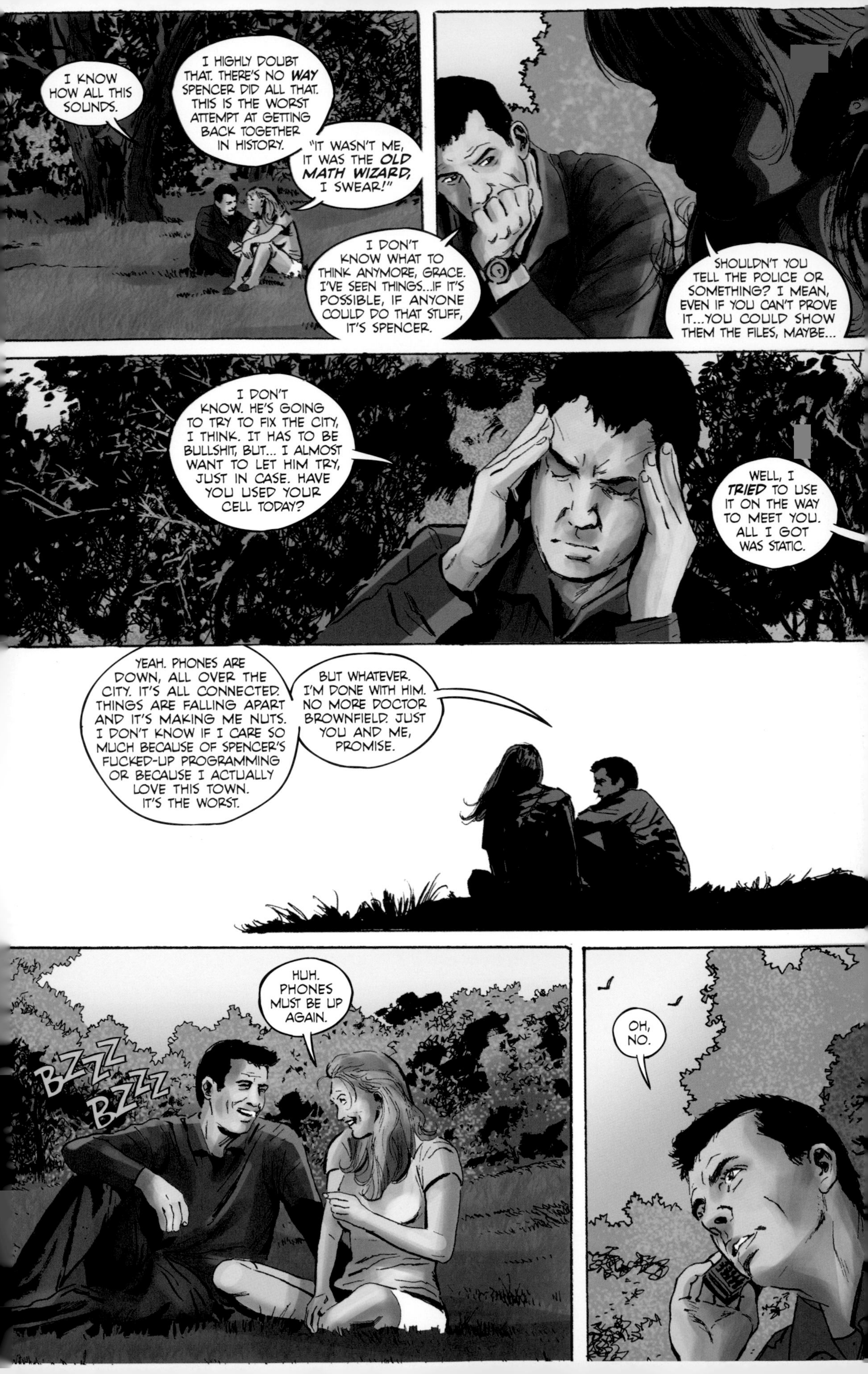
I KNOW HOW ALL THIS SOUNDS.
I HIGHLY DOUBT THAT. THERE'S NO *WAY* SPENCER DID ALL THAT. THIS IS THE WORST ATTEMPT AT GETTING BACK TOGETHER IN HISTORY.
"IT WASN'T ME, IT WAS THE *OLD MATH WIZARD,* I SWEAR!"
I DON'T KNOW WHAT TO THINK ANYMORE, GRACE. I'VE SEEN THINGS...IF IT'S POSSIBLE, IF ANYONE COULD DO THAT STUFF, IT'S SPENCER.
SHOULDN'T YOU TELL THE POLICE OR SOMETHING? I MEAN, EVEN IF YOU CAN'T PROVE IT...YOU COULD SHOW THEM THE FILES, MAYBE...
I DON'T KNOW. HE'S GOING TO TRY TO FIX THE CITY, I THINK. IT HAS TO BE BULLSHIT, BUT... I ALMOST WANT TO LET HIM TRY, JUST IN CASE. HAVE YOU USED YOUR CELL TODAY?
WELL, I *TRIED* TO USE IT ON THE WAY TO MEET YOU. ALL I GOT WAS STATIC.
YEAH. PHONES ARE DOWN, ALL OVER THE CITY. IT'S ALL CONNECTED. THINGS ARE FALLING APART AND IT'S MAKING ME NUTS. I DON'T KNOW IF I CARE SO MUCH BECAUSE OF SPENCER'S FUCKED-UP PROGRAMMING OR BECAUSE I ACTUALLY LOVE THIS TOWN. IT'S THE WORST.
BUT WHATEVER. I'M DONE WITH HIM. NO MORE DOCTOR BROWNFIELD. JUST YOU AND ME, PROMISE.
BZZZ BZZZ
HUH. PHONES MUST BE UP AGAIN.
OH, NO.

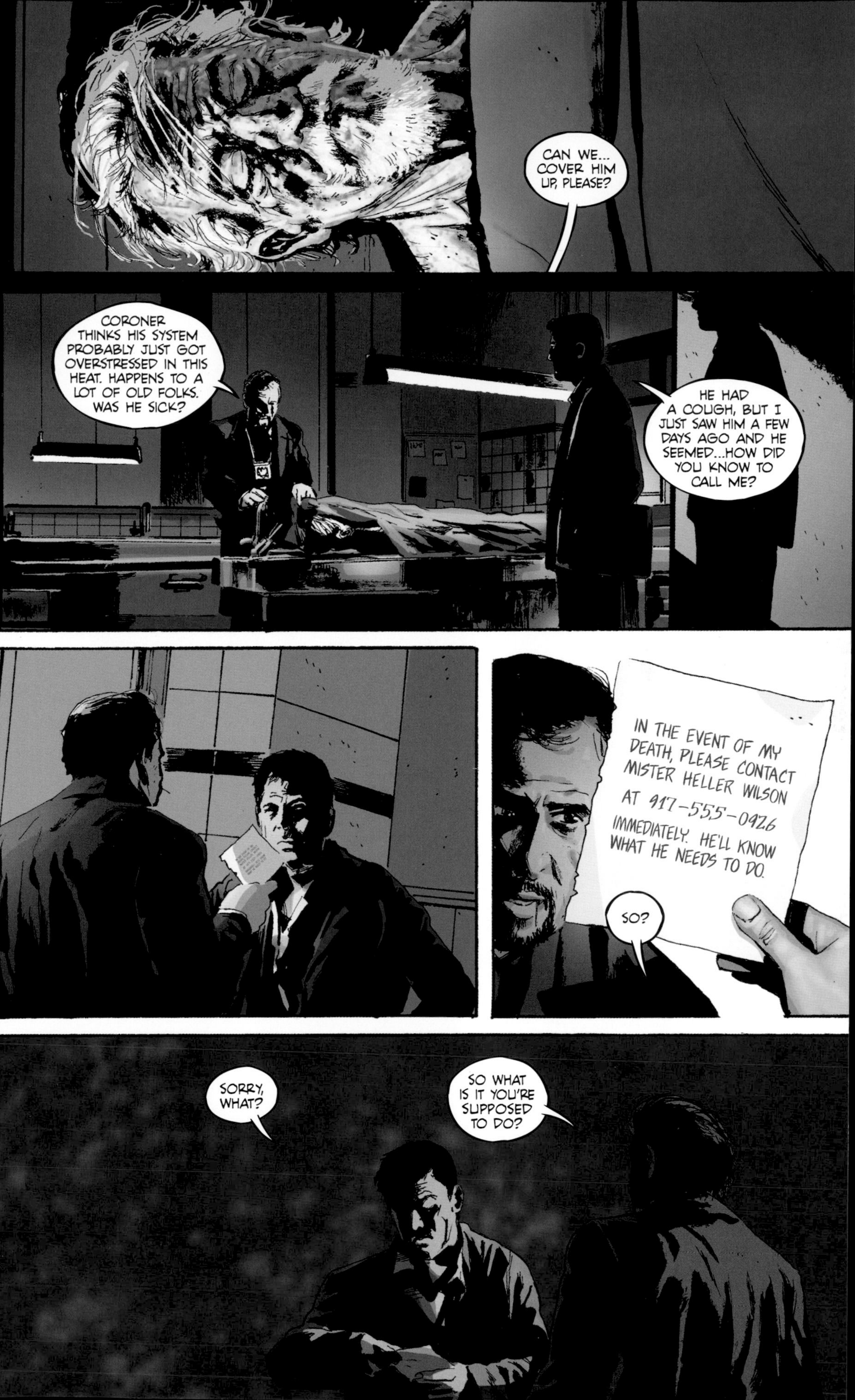
CAN WE... COVER HIM UP, PLEASE?
CORONER THINKS HIS SYSTEM PROBABLY JUST GOT OVERSTRESSED IN THIS HEAT. HAPPENS TO A LOT OF OLD FOLKS. WAS HE SICK?
HE HAD A COUGH, BUT I JUST SAW HIM A FEW DAYS AGO AND HE SEEMED...HOW DID YOU KNOW TO CALL ME?
IN THE EVENT OF MY DEATH, PLEASE CONTACT MISTER HELLER WILSON
AT 917-555-0926
IMMEDIATELY. HE'LL KNOW WHAT HE NEEDS TO DO.
SO?
SORRY, WHAT?
SO WHAT IS IT YOU'RE SUPPOSED TO DO?

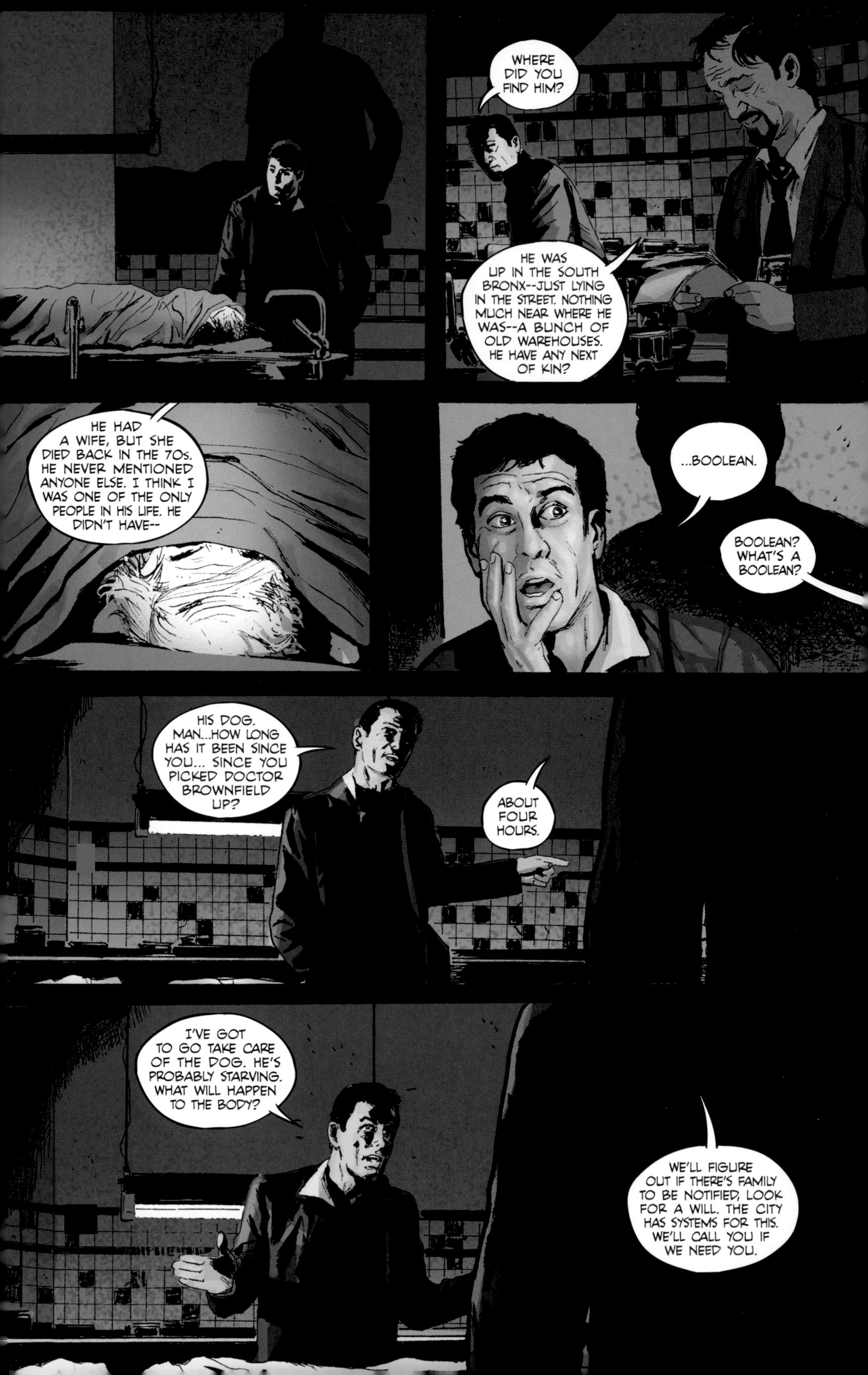
WHERE DID YOU FIND HIM?
HE WAS UP IN THE SOUTH BRONX--JUST LYING IN THE STREET. NOTHING MUCH NEAR WHERE HE WAS--A BUNCH OF OLD WAREHOUSES. HE HAVE ANY NEXT OF KIN?
HE HAD A WIFE, BUT SHE DIED BACK IN THE 70s. HE NEVER MENTIONED ANYONE ELSE. I THINK I WAS ONE OF THE ONLY PEOPLE IN HIS LIFE. HE DIDN'T HAVE--
...BOOLEAN.
BOOLEAN? WHAT'S A BOOLEAN?
HIS DOG. MAN...HOW LONG HAS IT BEEN SINCE YOU... SINCE YOU PICKED DOCTOR BROWNFIELD UP?
ABOUT FOUR HOURS.
I'VE GOT TO GO TAKE CARE OF THE DOG. HE'S PROBABLY STARVING. WHAT WILL HAPPEN TO THE BODY?
WE'LL FIGURE OUT IF THERE'S FAMILY TO BE NOTIFIED, LOOK FOR A WILL. THE CITY HAS SYSTEMS FOR THIS. WE'LL CALL YOU IF WE NEED YOU.

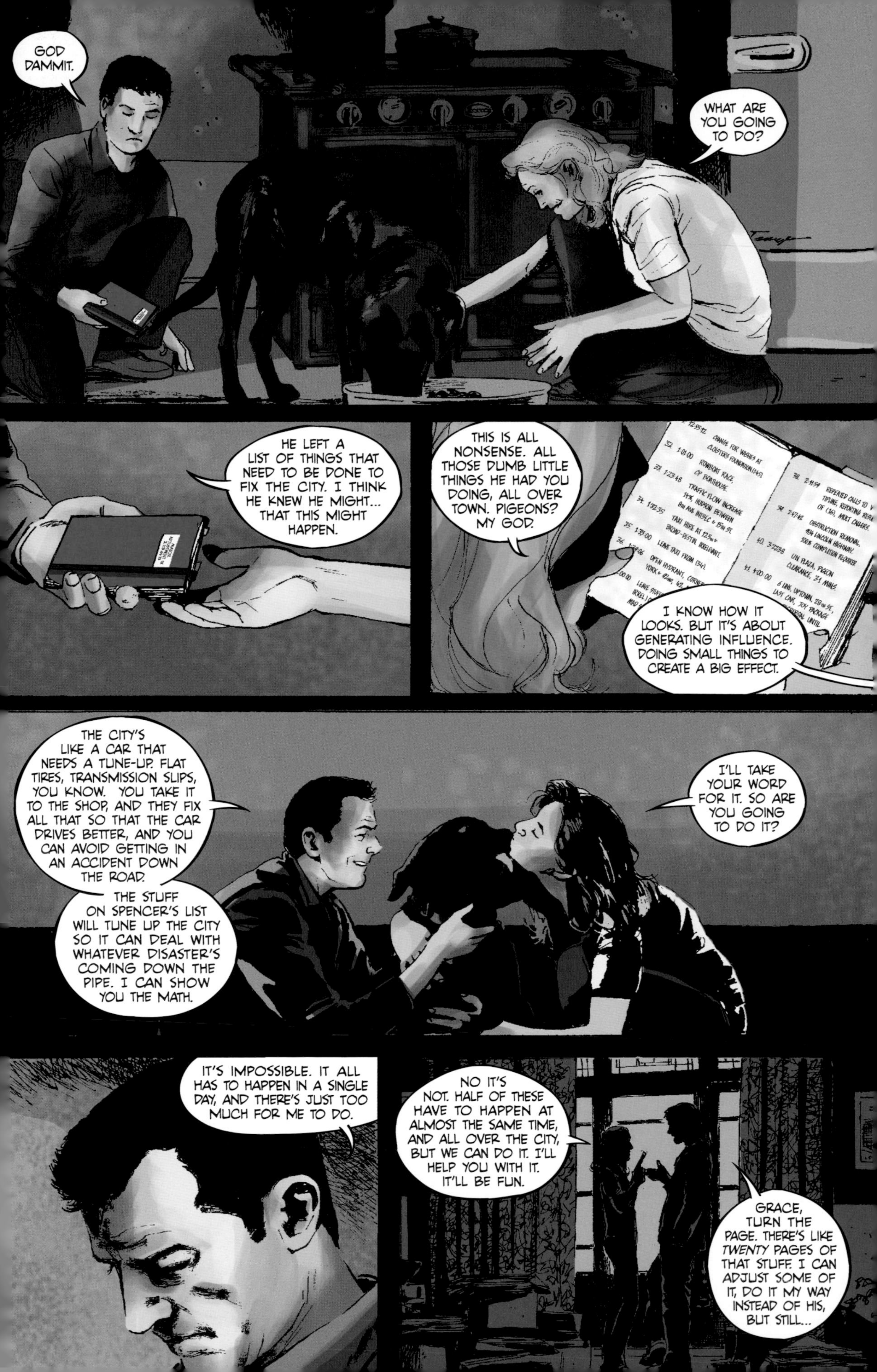
GOD DAMMIT.
WHAT ARE YOU GOING TO DO?
HE LEFT A LIST OF THINGS THAT NEED TO BE DONE TO FIX THE CITY. I THINK HE KNEW HE MIGHT... THAT THIS MIGHT HAPPEN.
THIS IS ALL NONSENSE. ALL THOSE DUMB LITTLE THINGS HE HAD YOU DOING, ALL OVER TOWN. PIGEONS? MY GOD.
I KNOW HOW IT LOOKS. BUT IT'S ABOUT GENERATING INFLUENCE. DOING SMALL THINGS TO CREATE A BIG EFFECT.
THE CITY'S LIKE A CAR THAT NEEDS A TUNE-UP. FLAT TIRES, TRANSMISSION SLIPS, YOU KNOW. YOU TAKE IT TO THE SHOP, AND THEY FIX ALL THAT SO THAT THE CAR DRIVES BETTER, AND YOU CAN AVOID GETTING IN AN ACCIDENT DOWN THE ROAD.
THE STUFF ON SPENCER'S LIST WILL TUNE UP THE CITY SO IT CAN DEAL WITH WHATEVER DISASTER'S COMING DOWN THE PIPE. I CAN SHOW YOU THE MATH.
I'LL TAKE YOUR WORD FOR IT. SO ARE YOU GOING TO DO IT?
IT'S IMPOSSIBLE. IT ALL HAS TO HAPPEN IN A SINGLE DAY, AND THERE'S JUST TOO MUCH FOR ME TO DO.
NO IT'S NOT. HALF OF THESE HAVE TO HAPPEN AT ALMOST THE SAME TIME, AND ALL OVER THE CITY, BUT WE CAN DO IT. I'LL HELP YOU WITH IT. IT'LL BE FUN.
GRACE, TURN THE PAGE. THERE'S LIKE *TWENTY* PAGES OF THAT STUFF. I CAN ADJUST SOME OF IT, DO IT MY WAY INSTEAD OF HIS, BUT STILL...

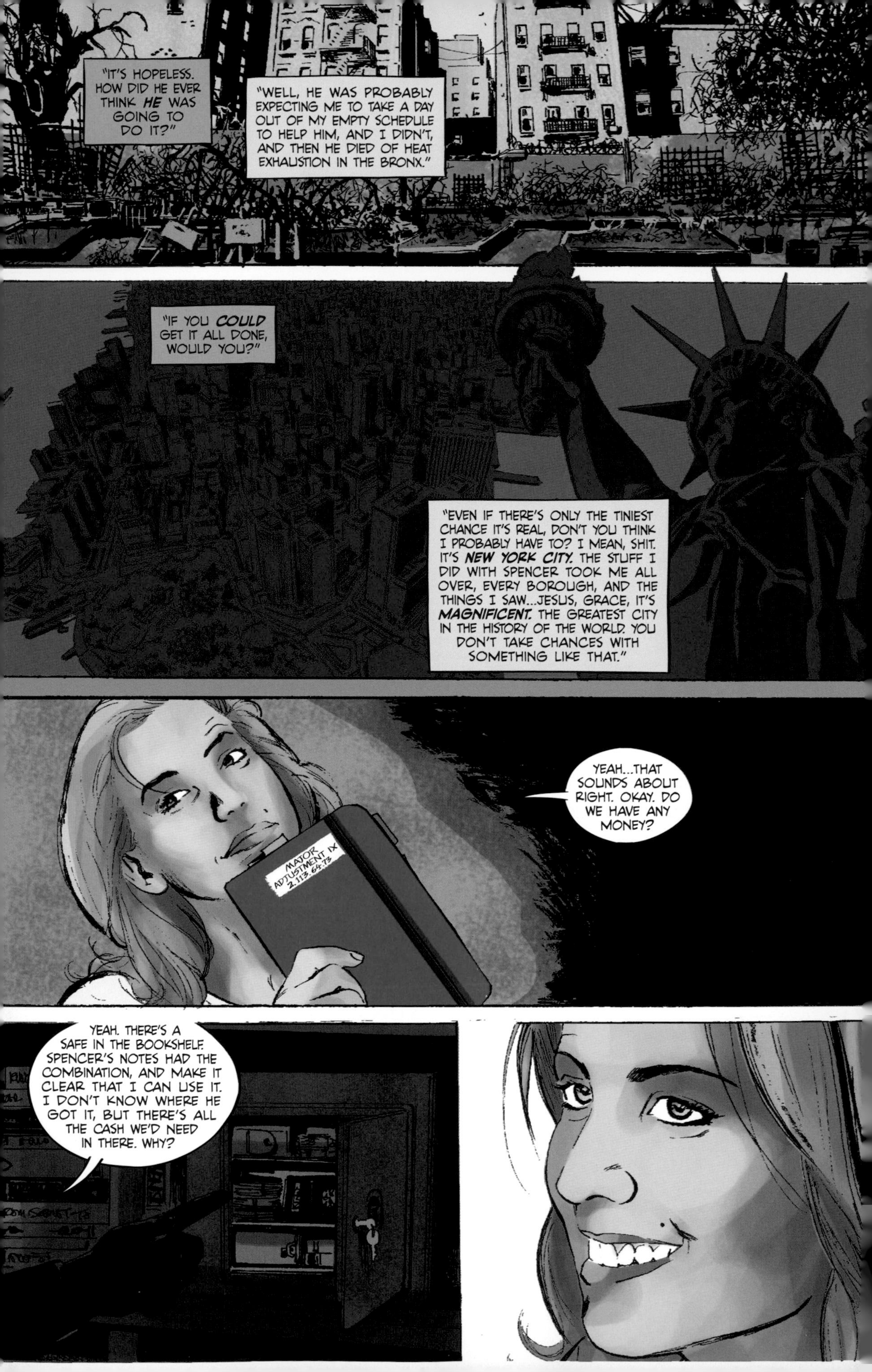
"IT'S HOPELESS. HOW DID HE EVER THINK HE WAS GOING TO DO IT?"
"WELL, HE WAS PROBABLY EXPECTING ME TO TAKE A DAY OUT OF MY EMPTY SCHEDULE TO HELP HIM, AND I DIDN'T, AND THEN HE DIED OF HEAT EXHAUSTION IN THE BRONX."
"IF YOU COULD GET IT ALL DONE, WOULD YOU?"
"EVEN IF THERE'S ONLY THE TINIEST CHANCE IT'S REAL, DON'T YOU THINK I PROBABLY HAVE TO? I MEAN, SHIT. IT'S NEW YORK CITY. THE STUFF I DID WITH SPENCER TOOK ME ALL OVER, EVERY BOROUGH, AND THE THINGS I SAW...JESUS, GRACE, IT'S MAGNIFICENT. THE GREATEST CITY IN THE HISTORY OF THE WORLD. YOU DON'T TAKE CHANCES WITH SOMETHING LIKE THAT."
MAJOR ADJUSTMENT IX 2.113.64.73
YEAH...THAT SOUNDS ABOUT RIGHT. OKAY. DO WE HAVE ANY MONEY?
YEAH. THERE'S A SAFE IN THE BOOKSHELF. SPENCER'S NOTES HAD THE COMBINATION, AND MAKE IT CLEAR THAT I CAN USE IT. I DON'T KNOW WHERE HE GOT IT, BUT THERE'S ALL THE CASH WE'D NEED IN THERE. WHY?

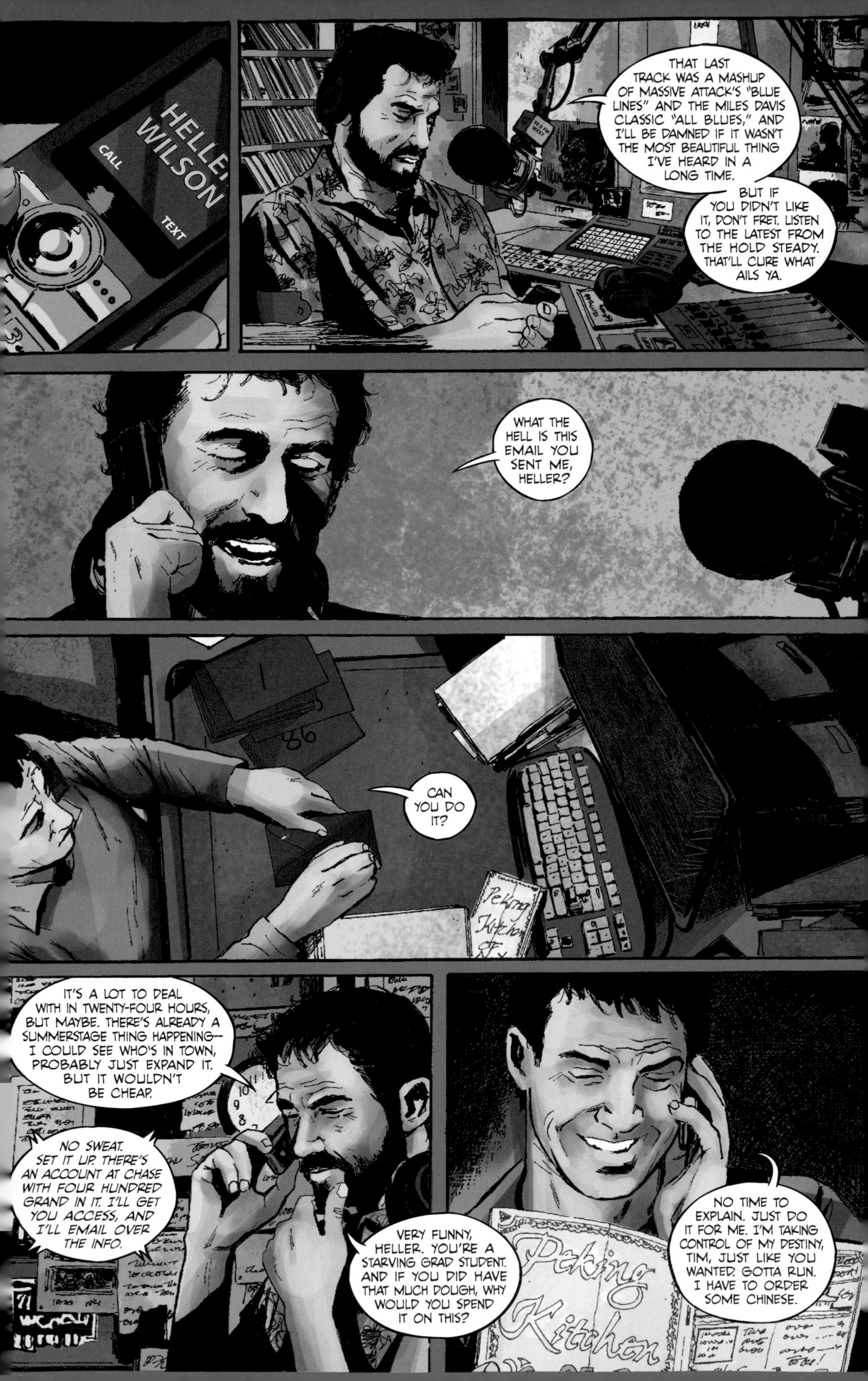
HELLER WILSON
CALL
TEXT
THAT LAST TRACK WAS A MASHUP OF MASSIVE ATTACK'S "BLUE LINES" AND THE MILES DAVIS CLASSIC "ALL BLUES," AND I'LL BE DAMNED IF IT WASN'T THE MOST BEAUTIFUL THING I'VE HEARD IN A LONG TIME.
BUT IF YOU DIDN'T LIKE IT, DON'T FRET. LISTEN TO THE LATEST FROM THE HOLD STEADY. THAT'LL CURE WHAT AILS YA.
WHAT THE HELL IS THIS EMAIL YOU SENT ME, HELLER?
CAN YOU DO IT?
IT'S A LOT TO DEAL WITH IN TWENTY-FOUR HOURS, BUT MAYBE. THERE'S ALREADY A SUMMERSTAGE THING HAPPENING-- I COULD SEE WHO'S IN TOWN, PROBABLY JUST EXPAND IT. BUT IT WOULDN'T BE CHEAP.
NO SWEAT. SET IT UP. THERE'S AN ACCOUNT AT CHASE WITH FOUR HUNDRED GRAND IN IT. I'LL GET YOU ACCESS, AND I'LL EMAIL OVER THE INFO.
VERY FUNNY, HELLER. YOU'RE A STARVING GRAD STUDENT. AND IF YOU DID HAVE THAT MUCH DOUGH, WHY WOULD YOU SPEND IT ON THIS?
NO TIME TO EXPLAIN. JUST DO IT FOR ME. I'M TAKING CONTROL OF MY DESTINY, TIM, JUST LIKE YOU WANTED. GOTTA RUN. I HAVE TO ORDER SOME CHINESE.
Peking Kitchen

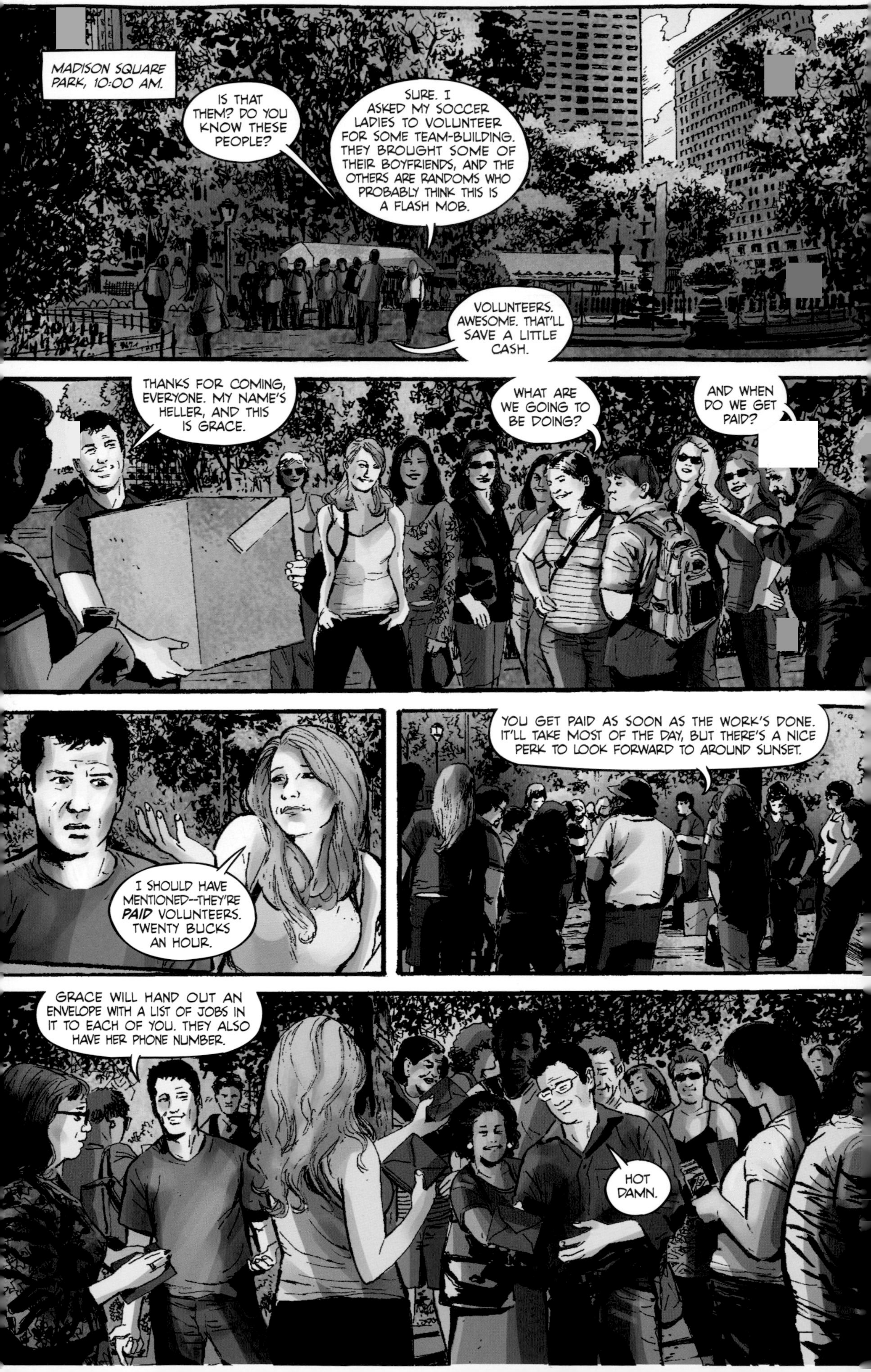
MADISON SQUARE PARK, 10:00 AM.
IS THAT THEM? DO YOU KNOW THESE PEOPLE?
SURE. I ASKED MY SOCCER LADIES TO VOLUNTEER FOR SOME TEAM-BUILDING. THEY BROUGHT SOME OF THEIR BOYFRIENDS, AND THE OTHERS ARE RANDOMS WHO PROBABLY THINK THIS IS A FLASH MOB.
VOLUNTEERS. AWESOME. THAT'LL SAVE A LITTLE CASH.
THANKS FOR COMING, EVERYONE. MY NAME'S HELLER, AND THIS IS GRACE.
WHAT ARE WE GOING TO BE DOING?
AND WHEN DO WE GET PAID?
I SHOULD HAVE MENTIONED--THEY'RE *PAID* VOLUNTEERS. TWENTY BUCKS AN HOUR.
YOU GET PAID AS SOON AS THE WORK'S DONE. IT'LL TAKE MOST OF THE DAY, BUT THERE'S A NICE PERK TO LOOK FORWARD TO AROUND SUNSET.
GRACE WILL HAND OUT AN ENVELOPE WITH A LIST OF JOBS IN IT TO EACH OF YOU. THEY ALSO HAVE HER PHONE NUMBER.
HOT DAMN.

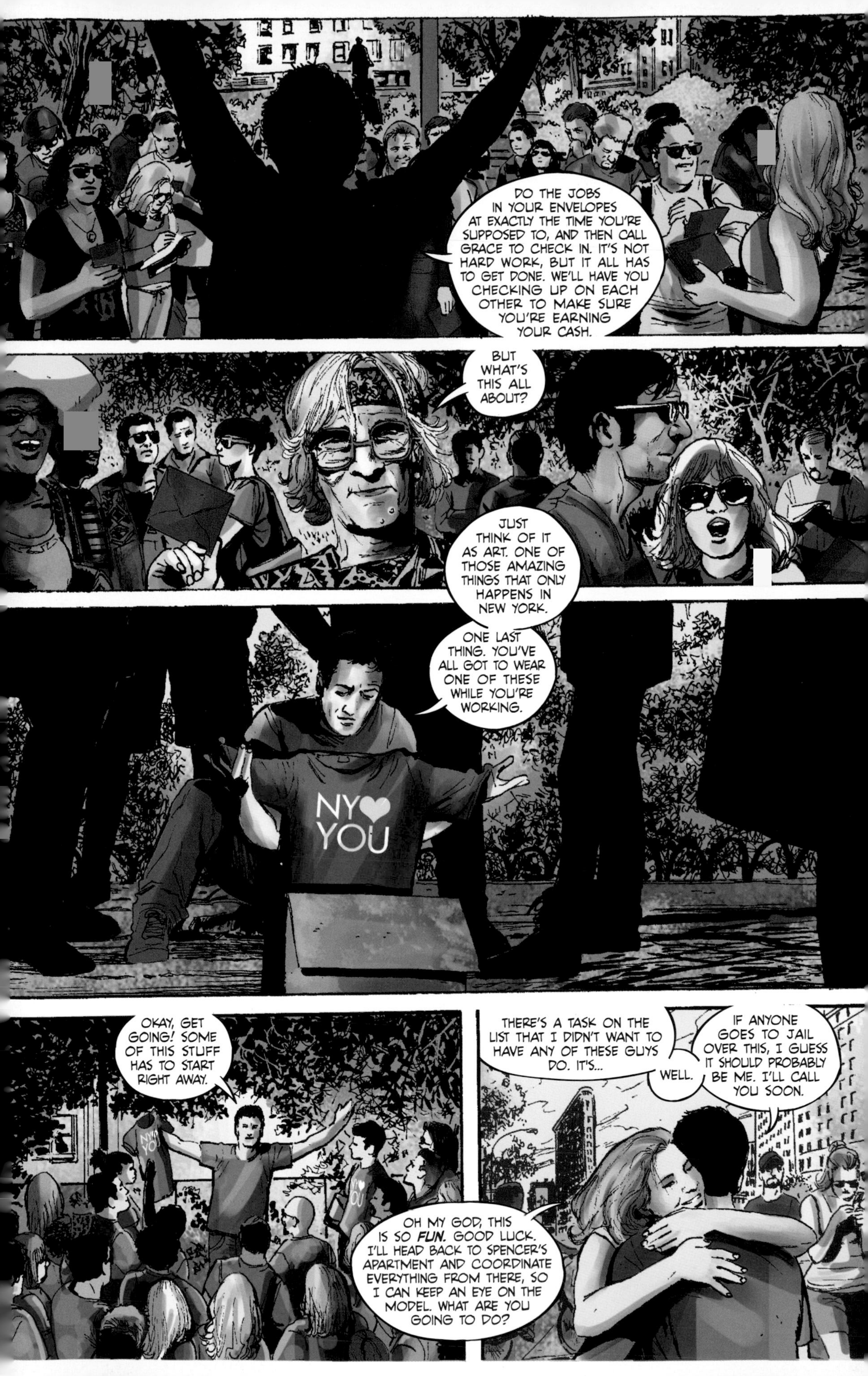
DO THE JOBS IN YOUR ENVELOPES AT EXACTLY THE TIME YOU'RE SUPPOSED TO, AND THEN CALL GRACE TO CHECK IN. IT'S NOT HARD WORK, BUT IT ALL HAS TO GET DONE. WE'LL HAVE YOU CHECKING UP ON EACH OTHER TO MAKE SURE YOU'RE EARNING YOUR CASH.
BUT WHAT'S THIS ALL ABOUT?
JUST THINK OF IT AS ART. ONE OF THOSE AMAZING THINGS THAT ONLY HAPPENS IN NEW YORK.
ONE LAST THING. YOU'VE ALL GOT TO WEAR ONE OF THESE WHILE YOU'RE WORKING.
NY♥ YOU
OKAY, GET GOING! SOME OF THIS STUFF HAS TO START RIGHT AWAY.
THERE'S A TASK ON THE LIST THAT I DIDN'T WANT TO HAVE ANY OF THESE GUYS DO. IT'S...
WELL.
IF ANYONE GOES TO JAIL OVER THIS, I GUESS IT SHOULD PROBABLY BE ME. I'LL CALL YOU SOON.
OH MY GOD, THIS IS SO *FUN.* GOOD LUCK. I'LL HEAD BACK TO SPENCER'S APARTMENT AND COORDINATE EVERYTHING FROM THERE, SO I CAN KEEP AN EYE ON THE MODEL. WHAT ARE YOU GOING TO DO?

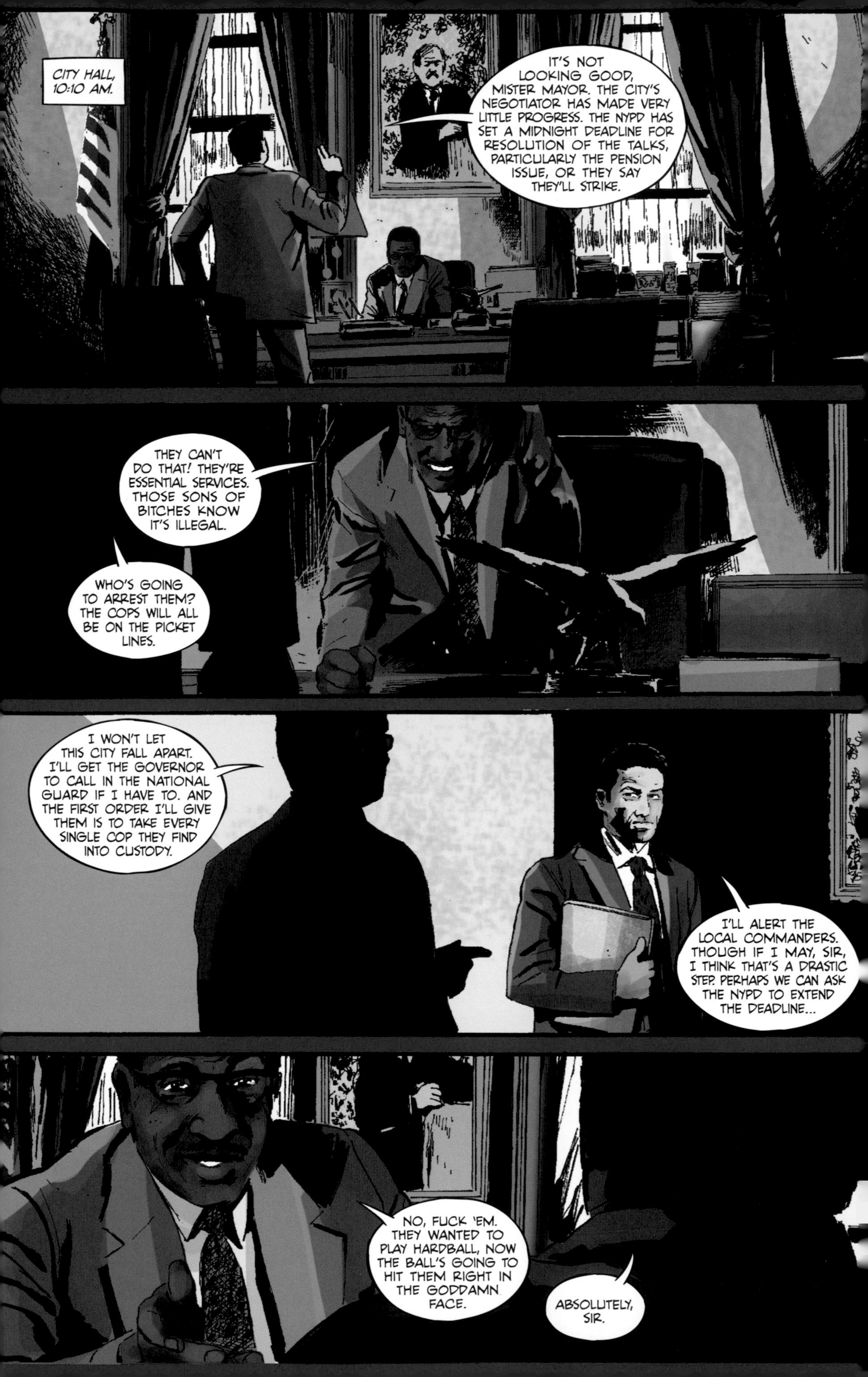
CITY HALL, 10:10 AM.
IT'S NOT LOOKING GOOD, MISTER MAYOR. THE CITY'S NEGOTIATOR HAS MADE VERY LITTLE PROGRESS. THE NYPD HAS SET A MIDNIGHT DEADLINE FOR RESOLUTION OF THE TALKS, PARTICULARLY THE PENSION ISSUE, OR THEY SAY THEY'LL STRIKE.
THEY CAN'T DO THAT! THEY'RE ESSENTIAL SERVICES. THOSE SONS OF BITCHES KNOW IT'S ILLEGAL.
WHO'S GOING TO ARREST THEM? THE COPS WILL ALL BE ON THE PICKET LINES.
I WON'T LET THIS CITY FALL APART. I'LL GET THE GOVERNOR TO CALL IN THE NATIONAL GUARD IF I HAVE TO. AND THE FIRST ORDER I'LL GIVE THEM IS TO TAKE EVERY SINGLE COP THEY FIND INTO CUSTODY.
I'LL ALERT THE LOCAL COMMANDERS. THOUGH IF I MAY, SIR, I THINK THAT'S A DRASTIC STEP. PERHAPS WE CAN ASK THE NYPD TO EXTEND THE DEADLINE...
NO, FUCK 'EM. THEY WANTED TO PLAY HARDBALL, NOW THE BALL'S GOING TO HIT THEM RIGHT IN THE GODDAMN FACE.
ABSOLUTELY, SIR.

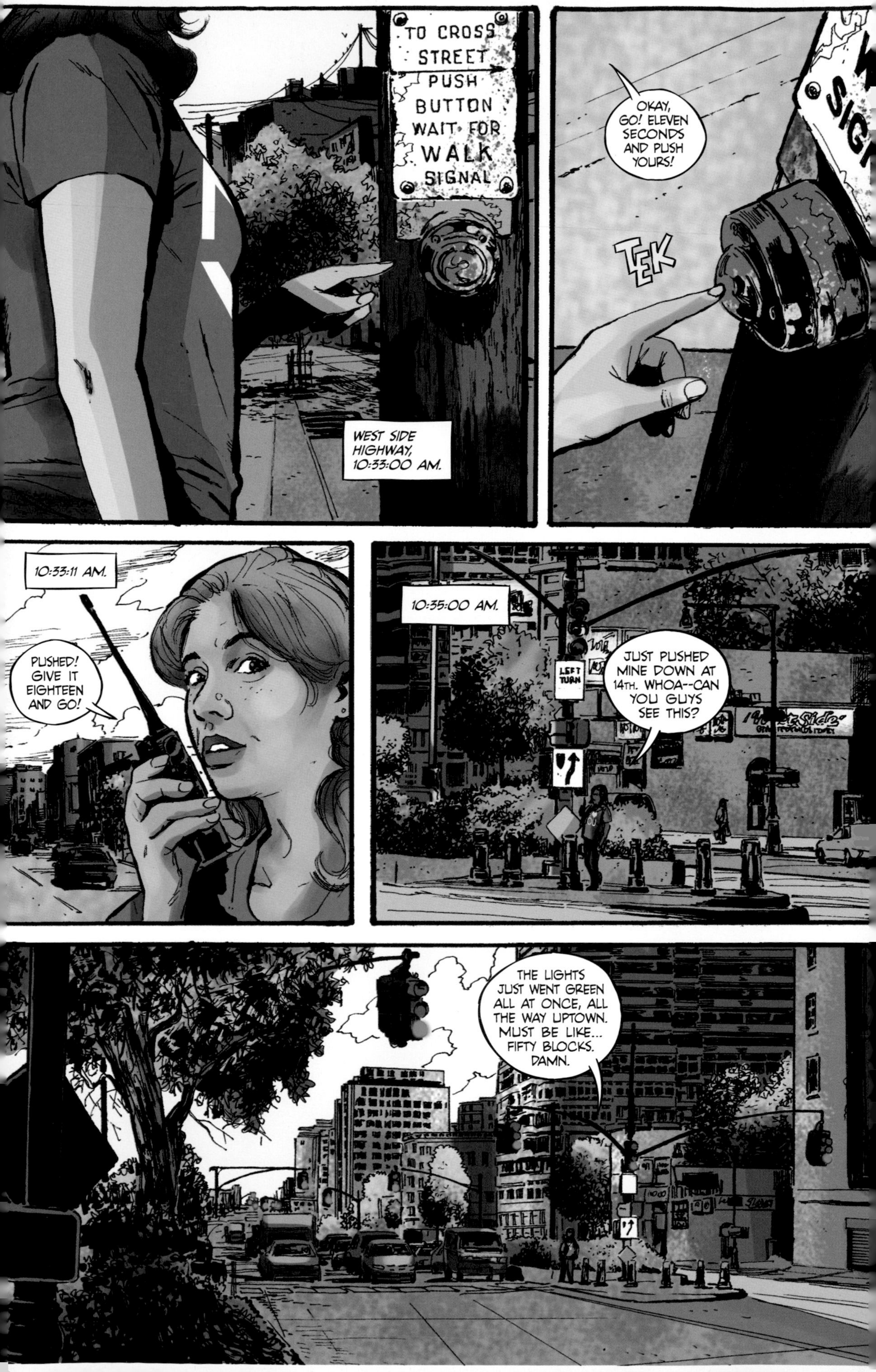
TO CROSS STREET PUSH BUTTON WAIT FOR WALK SIGNAL
WEST SIDE HIGHWAY, 10:33:00 AM.
OKAY, GO! ELEVEN SECONDS AND PUSH YOURS!
TEK
10:33:11 AM.
PUSHED! GIVE IT EIGHTEEN AND GO!
10:35:00 AM.
LEFT TURN
JUST PUSHED MINE DOWN AT 14TH. WHOA--CAN YOU GUYS SEE THIS?
THE LIGHTS JUST WENT GREEN ALL AT ONCE, ALL THE WAY UPTOWN. MUST BE LIKE... FIFTY BLOCKS. DAMN.

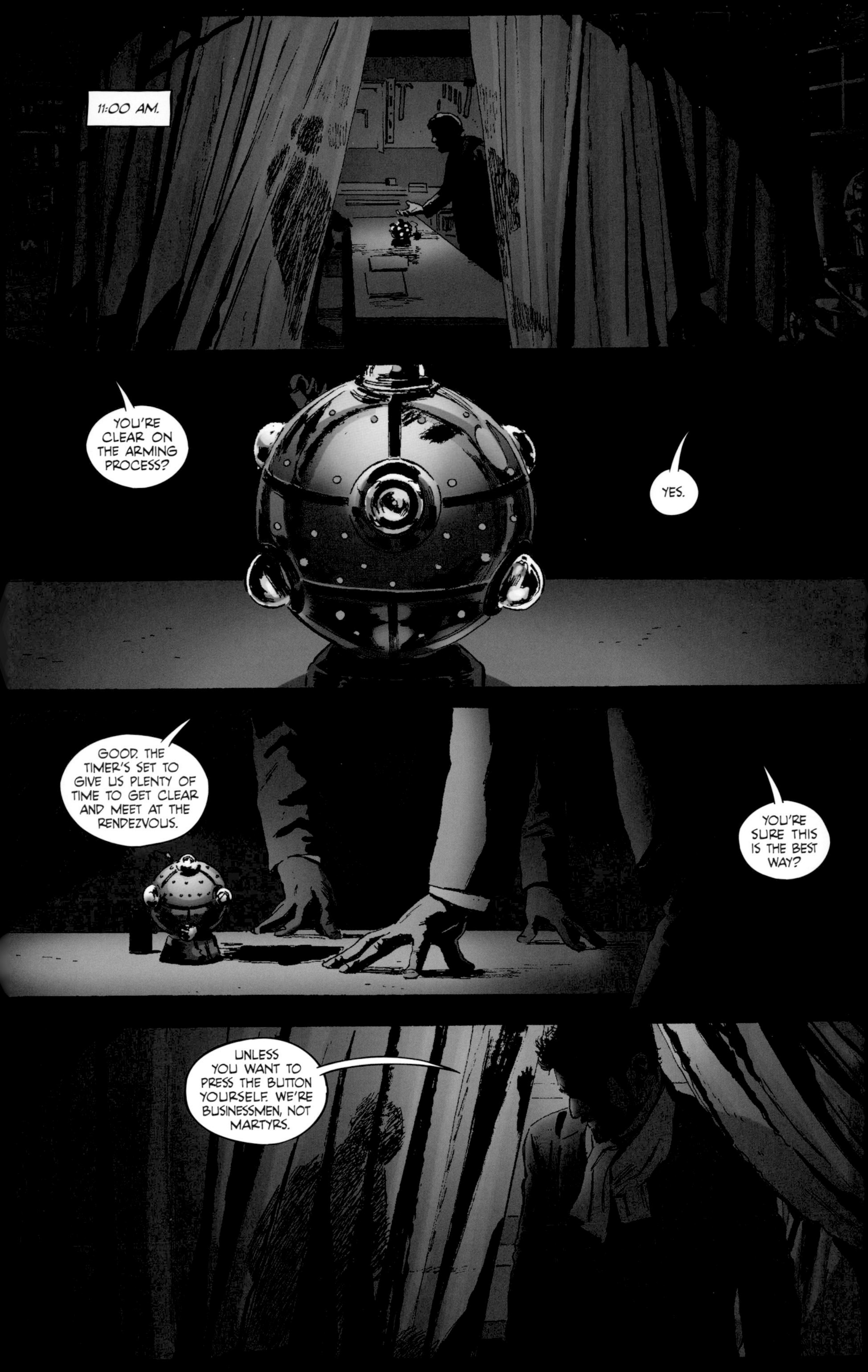
11:00 AM.
YOU'RE CLEAR ON THE ARMING PROCESS?
YES.
GOOD. THE TIMER'S SET TO GIVE US PLENTY OF TIME TO GET CLEAR AND MEET AT THE RENDEZVOUS.
YOU'RE SURE THIS IS THE BEST WAY?
UNLESS YOU WANT TO PRESS THE BUTTON YOURSELF. WE'RE BUSINESSMEN, NOT MARTYRS.

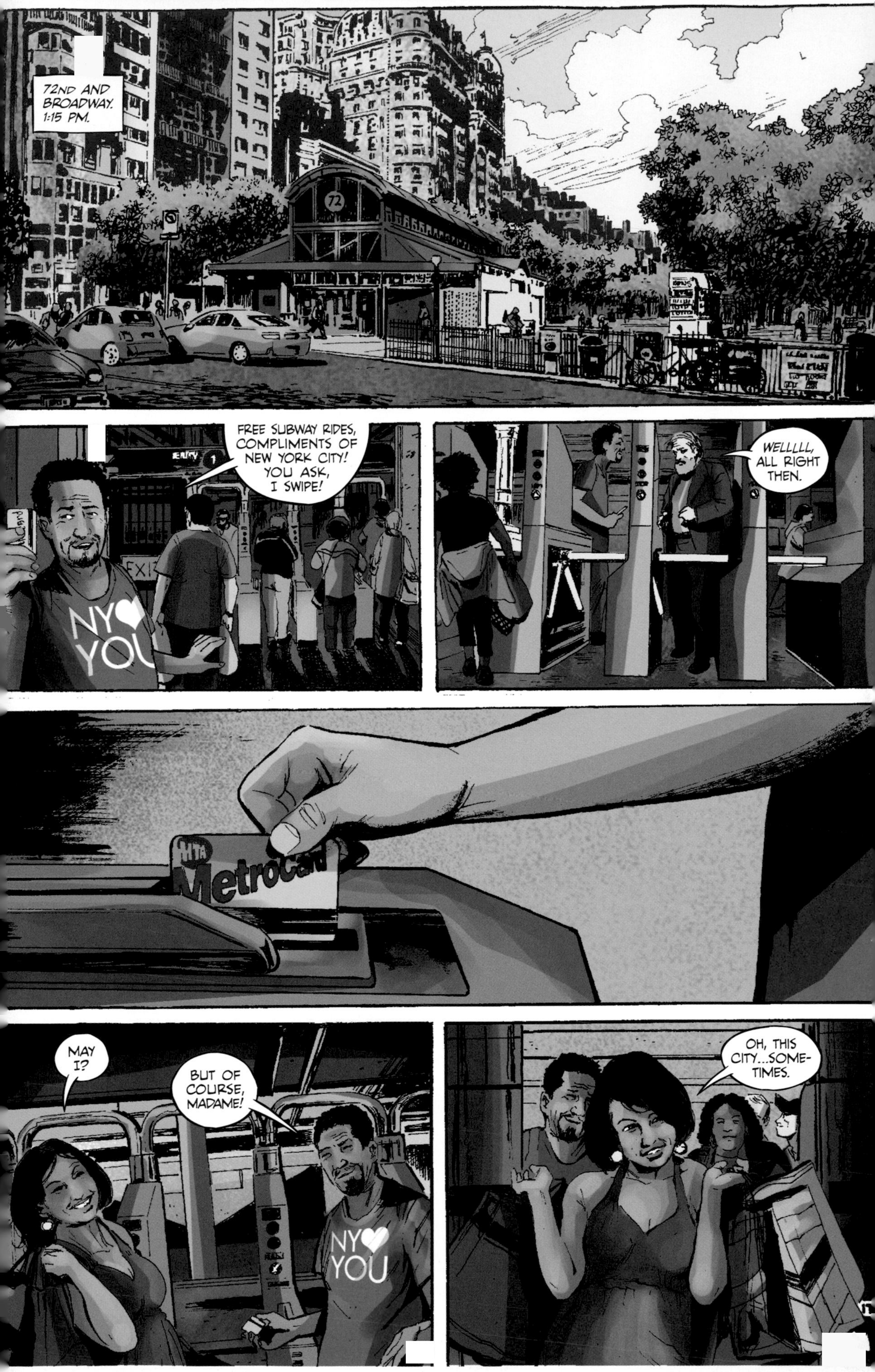
72ND AND BROADWAY. 1:15 PM.
FREE SUBWAY RIDES, COMPLIMENTS OF NEW YORK CITY! YOU ASK, I SWIPE!
WELLLLL, ALL RIGHT THEN.
MetroCard
MAY I?
BUT OF COURSE, MADAME!
OH, THIS CITY...SOME-TIMES.

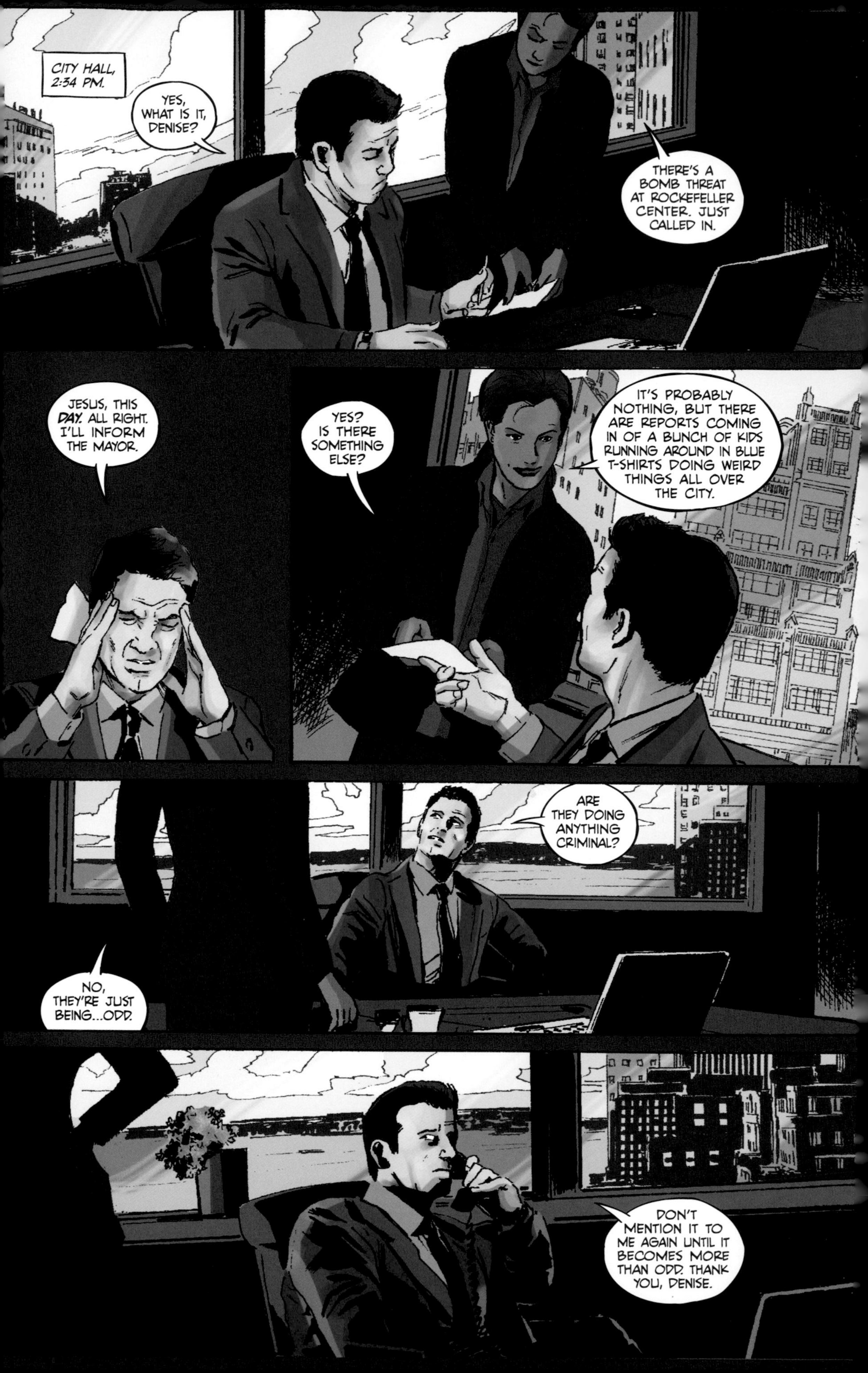
CITY HALL, 2:34 PM.
YES, WHAT IS IT, DENISE?
THERE'S A BOMB THREAT AT ROCKEFELLER CENTER. JUST CALLED IN.
JESUS, THIS DAY. ALL RIGHT. I'LL INFORM THE MAYOR.
YES? IS THERE SOMETHING ELSE?
IT'S PROBABLY NOTHING, BUT THERE ARE REPORTS COMING IN OF A BUNCH OF KIDS RUNNING AROUND IN BLUE T-SHIRTS DOING WEIRD THINGS ALL OVER THE CITY.
ARE THEY DOING ANYTHING CRIMINAL?
NO, THEY'RE JUST BEING...ODD.
DON'T MENTION IT TO ME AGAIN UNTIL IT BECOMES MORE THAN ODD. THANK YOU, DENISE.

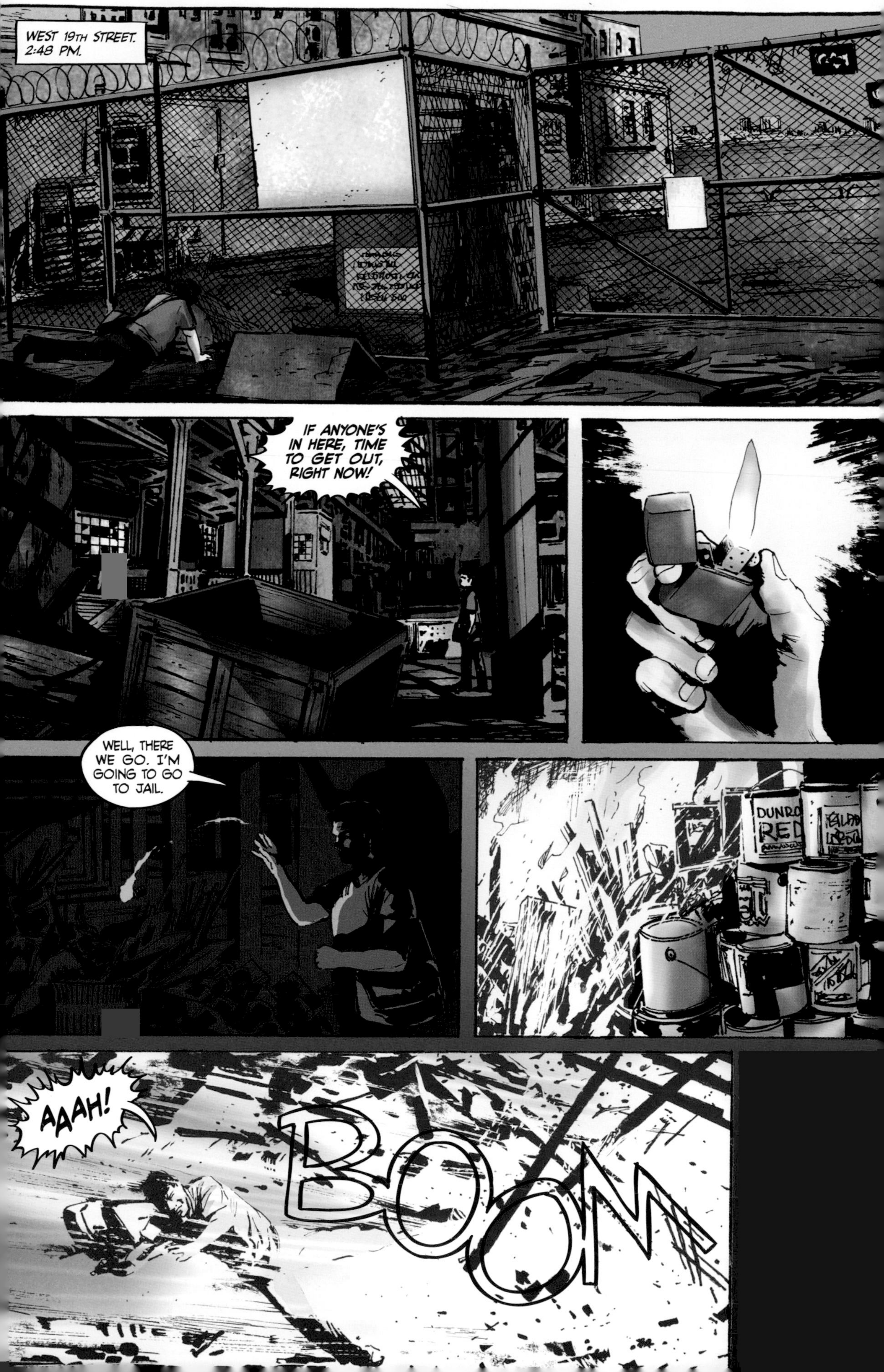
WEST 19TH STREET.
2:48 PM.
IF ANYONE'S IN HERE, TIME TO GET OUT, RIGHT NOW!
WELL, THERE WE GO. I'M GOING TO GO TO JAIL.
AAAH!
BOOM

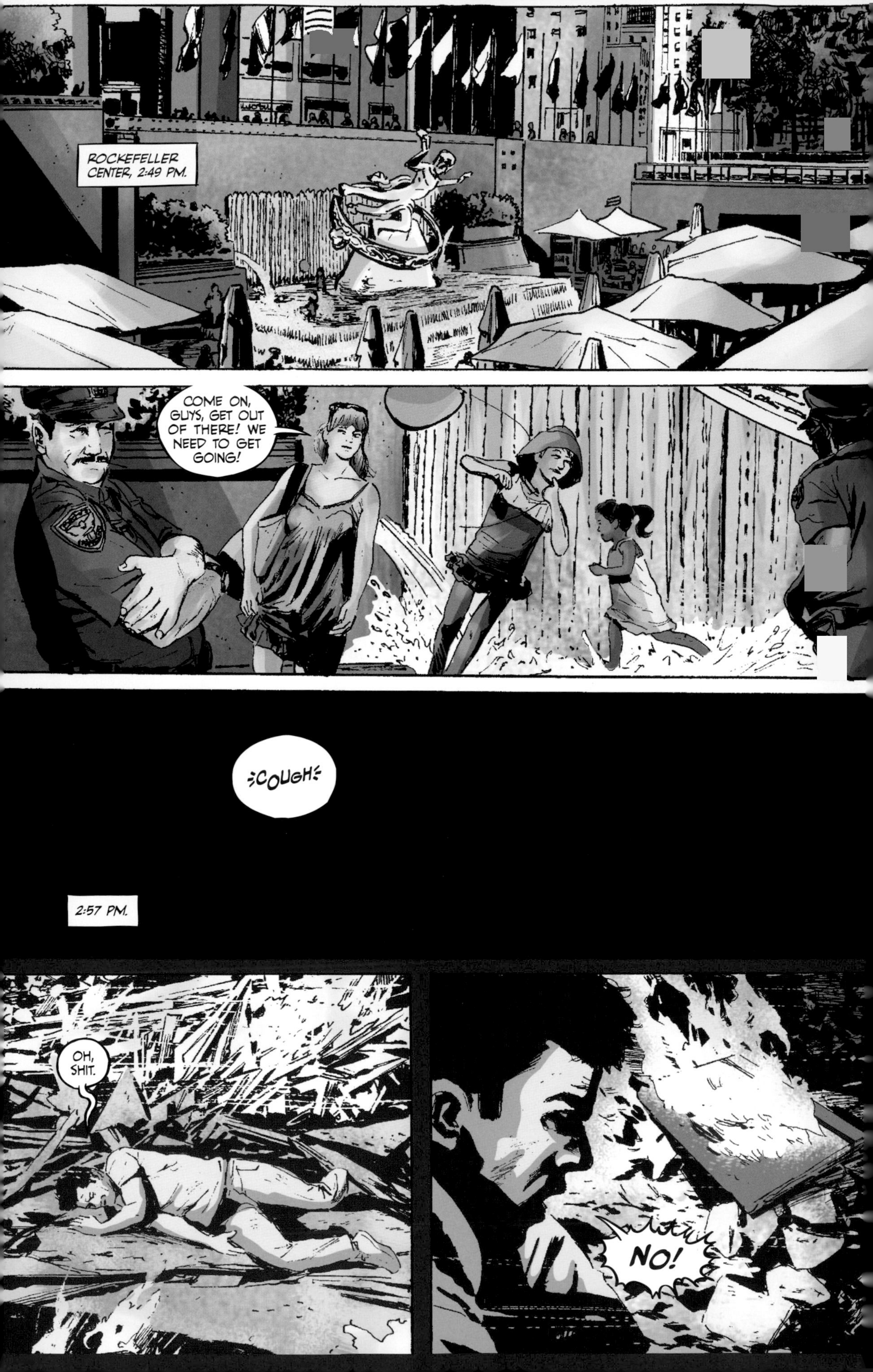
ROCKEFELLER CENTER, 2:49 PM.
COME ON, GUYS, GET OUT OF THERE! WE NEED TO GET GOING!
COUGH
2:57 PM.
OH, SHIT.
NO!

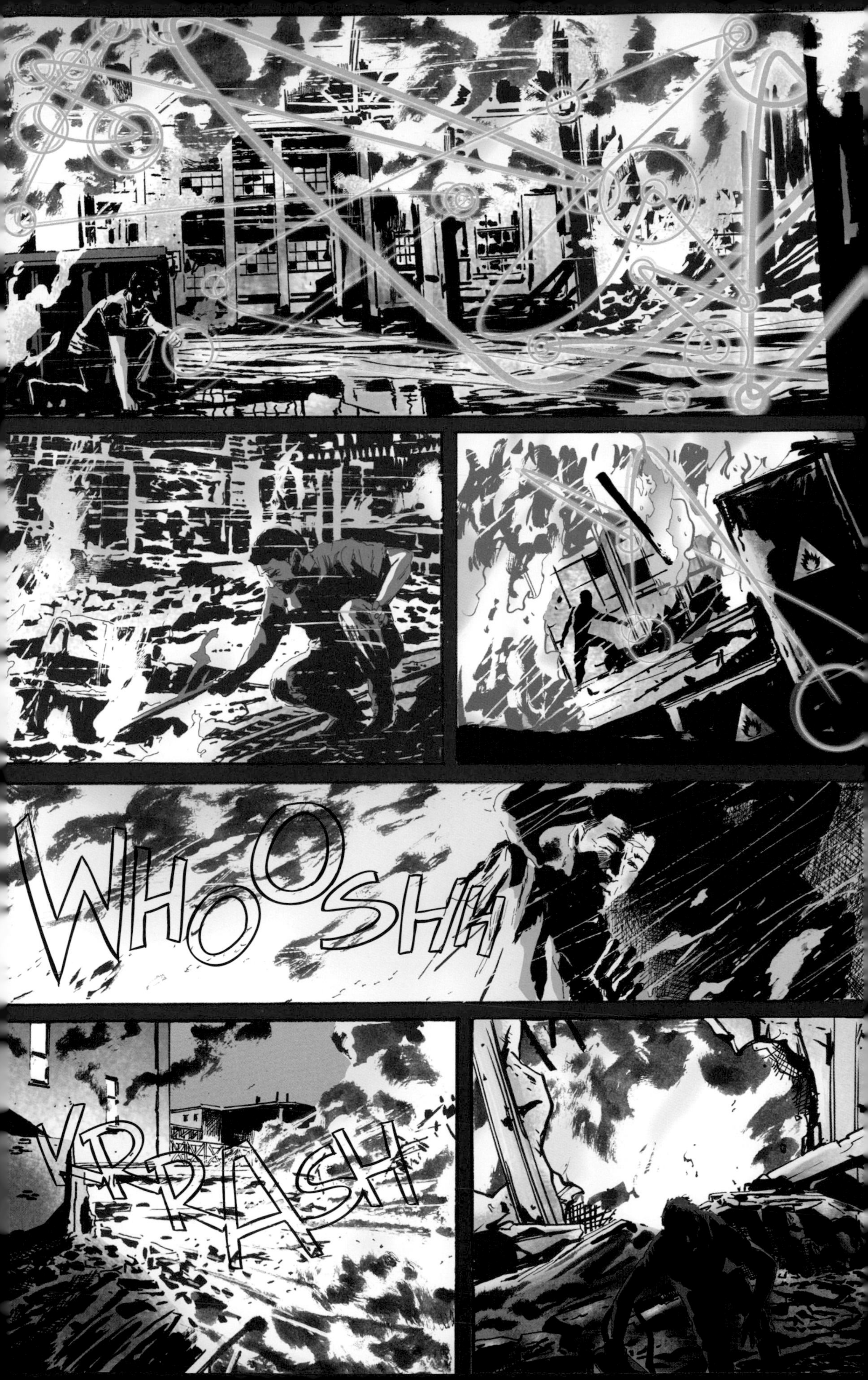
WHOOOSHH
VRRASH

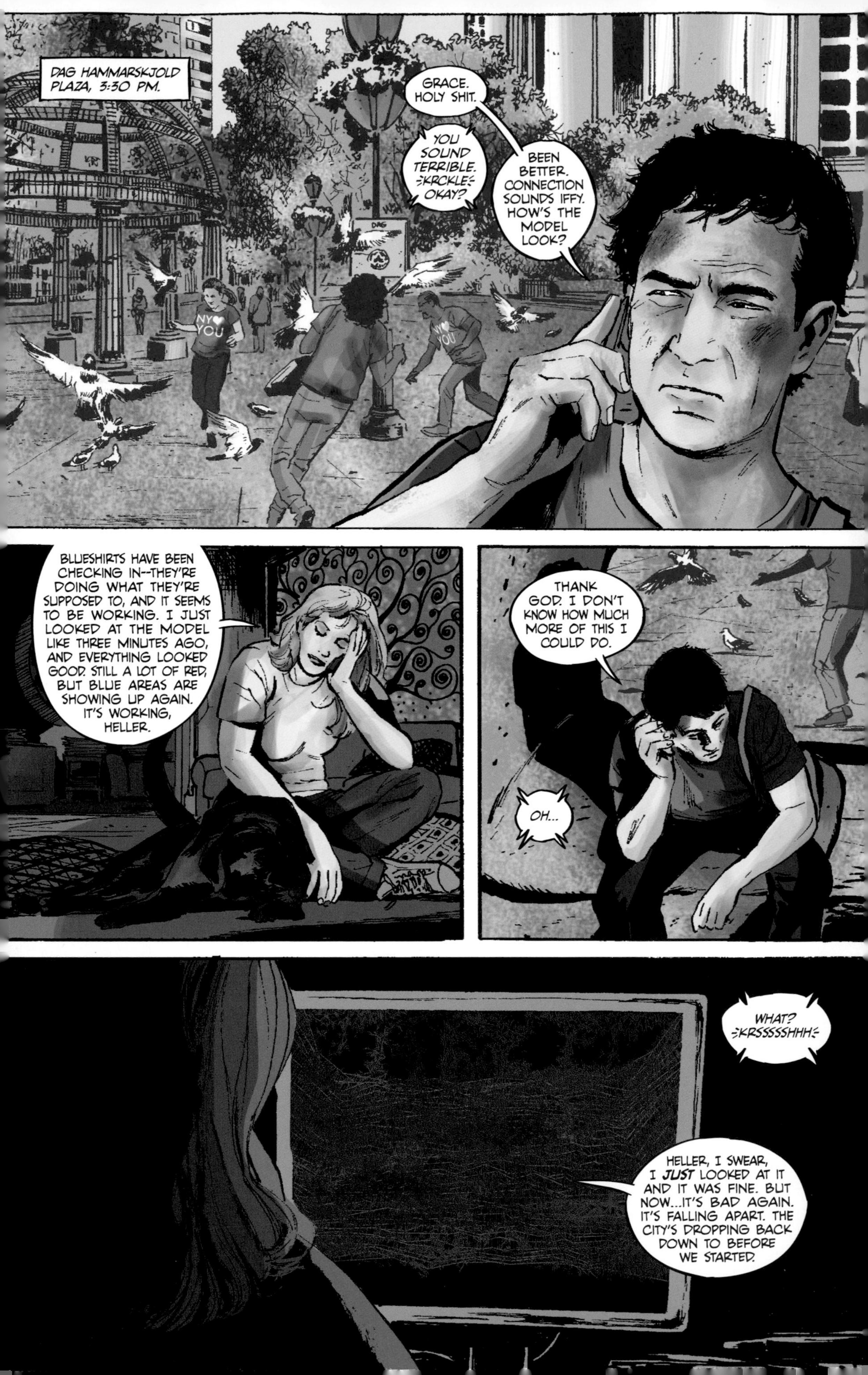
DAG HAMMARSKJOLD PLAZA, 3:30 PM.
GRACE. HOLY SHIT.
YOU SOUND TERRIBLE. ≶KRCKLE≶ OKAY?
BEEN BETTER. CONNECTION SOUNDS IFFY. HOW'S THE MODEL LOOK?
NY♥ YOU
BLUESHIRTS HAVE BEEN CHECKING IN--THEY'RE DOING WHAT THEY'RE SUPPOSED TO, AND IT SEEMS TO BE WORKING. I JUST LOOKED AT THE MODEL LIKE THREE MINUTES AGO, AND EVERYTHING LOOKED GOOD. STILL A LOT OF RED, BUT BLUE AREAS ARE SHOWING UP AGAIN. IT'S WORKING, HELLER.
THANK GOD. I DON'T KNOW HOW MUCH MORE OF THIS I COULD DO.
OH...
WHAT? ≶KRSSSSSHHH≶
HELLER, I SWEAR, I ***JUST*** LOOKED AT IT AND IT WAS FINE. BUT NOW...IT'S BAD AGAIN. IT'S FALLING APART. THE CITY'S DROPPING BACK DOWN TO BEFORE WE STARTED.

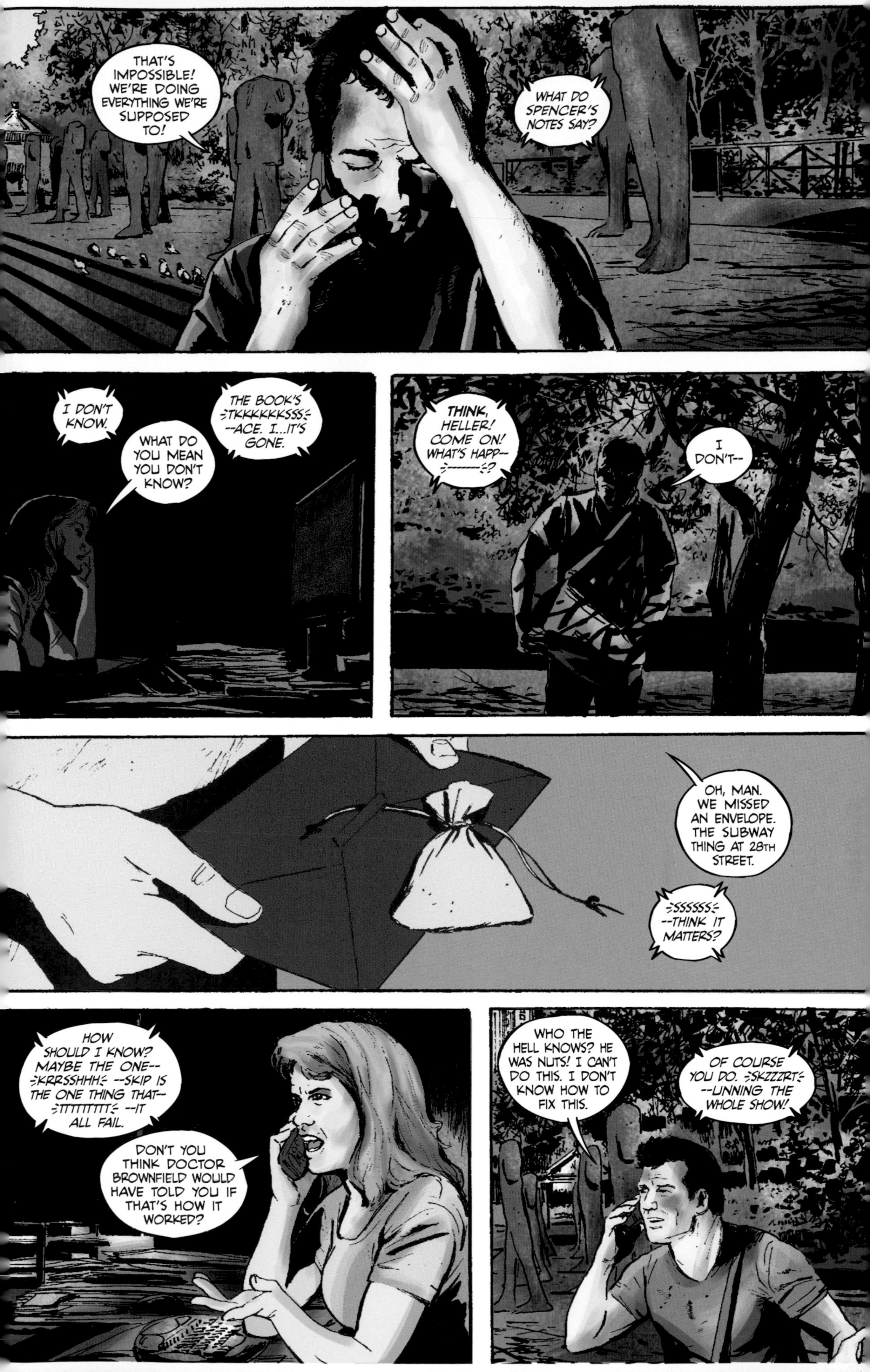
THAT'S IMPOSSIBLE! WE'RE DOING EVERYTHING WE'RE SUPPOSED TO!
WHAT DO SPENCER'S NOTES SAY?
I DON'T KNOW.
WHAT DO YOU MEAN YOU DON'T KNOW?
THE BOOK'S =TKKKKKKSSS= --ACE. I...IT'S GONE.
THINK, HELLER! COME ON! WHAT'S HAPP-- =-------=?
I DON'T--
OH, MAN. WE MISSED AN ENVELOPE. THE SUBWAY THING AT 28TH STREET.
=SSSSSS= --THINK IT MATTERS?
HOW SHOULD I KNOW? MAYBE THE ONE-- =KRRSSHHH= --SKIP IS THE ONE THING THAT-- =TTTTTTTTT= --IT ALL FAIL.
DON'T YOU THINK DOCTOR BROWNFIELD WOULD HAVE TOLD YOU IF THAT'S HOW IT WORKED?
WHO THE HELL KNOWS? HE WAS NUTS! I CAN'T DO THIS. I DON'T KNOW HOW TO FIX THIS.
OF COURSE YOU DO. =SKZZZRT= --UNNING THE WHOLE SHOW!

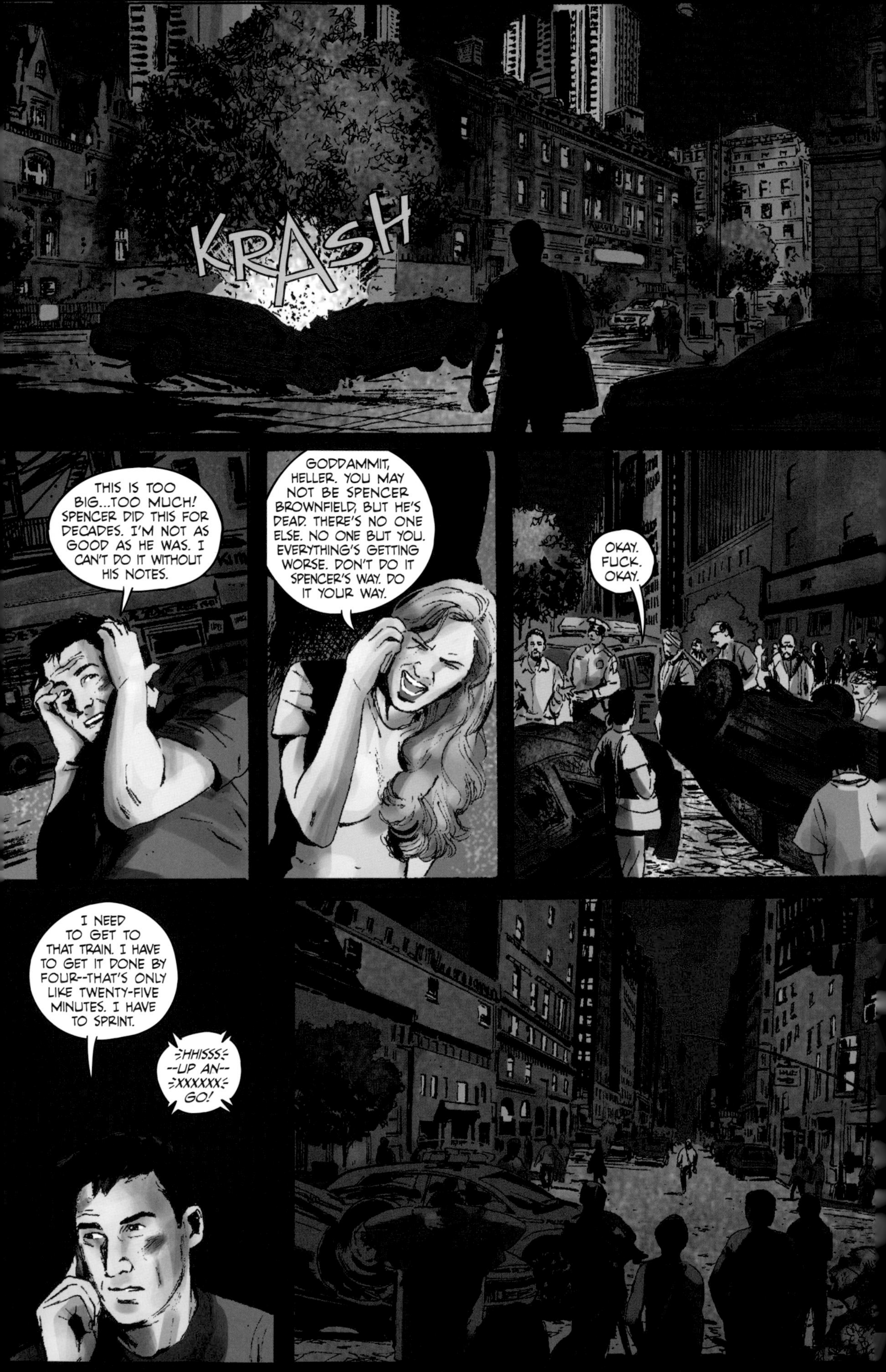
KRASH
THIS IS TOO BIG...TOO MUCH! SPENCER DID THIS FOR DECADES. I'M NOT AS GOOD AS HE WAS. I CAN'T DO IT WITHOUT HIS NOTES.
GODDAMMIT, HELLER. YOU MAY NOT BE SPENCER BROWNFIELD, BUT HE'S DEAD. THERE'S NO ONE ELSE. NO ONE BUT YOU. EVERYTHING'S GETTING WORSE. DON'T DO IT SPENCER'S WAY. DO IT YOUR WAY.
OKAY. FUCK. OKAY.
I NEED TO GET TO THAT TRAIN. I HAVE TO GET IT DONE BY FOUR--THAT'S ONLY LIKE TWENTY-FIVE MINUTES. I HAVE TO SPRINT.
HHISSS --UP AN-- XXXXXX GO!

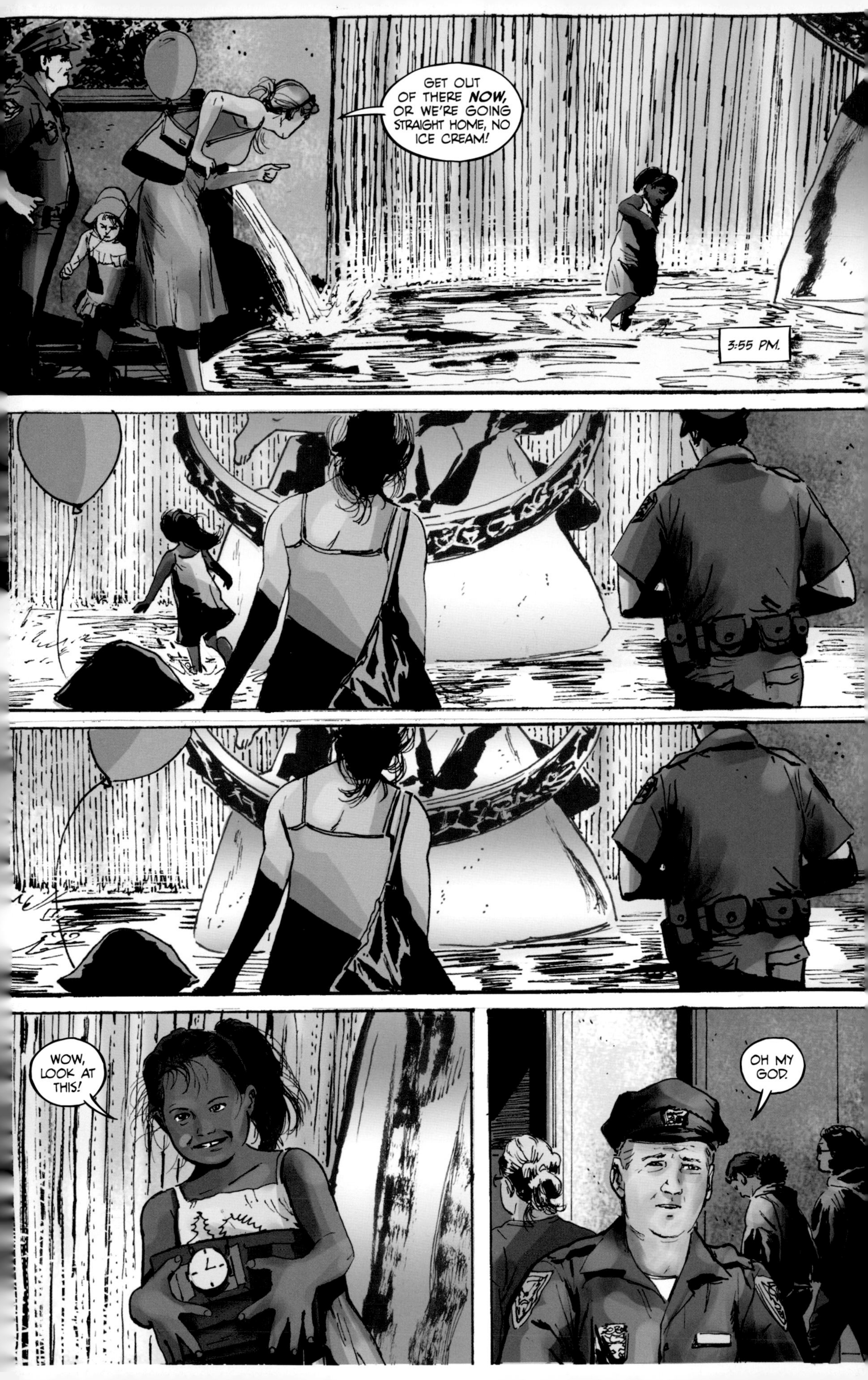
GET OUT OF THERE NOW, OR WE'RE GOING STRAIGHT HOME, NO ICE CREAM!
3:55 PM.
WOW, LOOK AT THIS!
OH MY GOD.

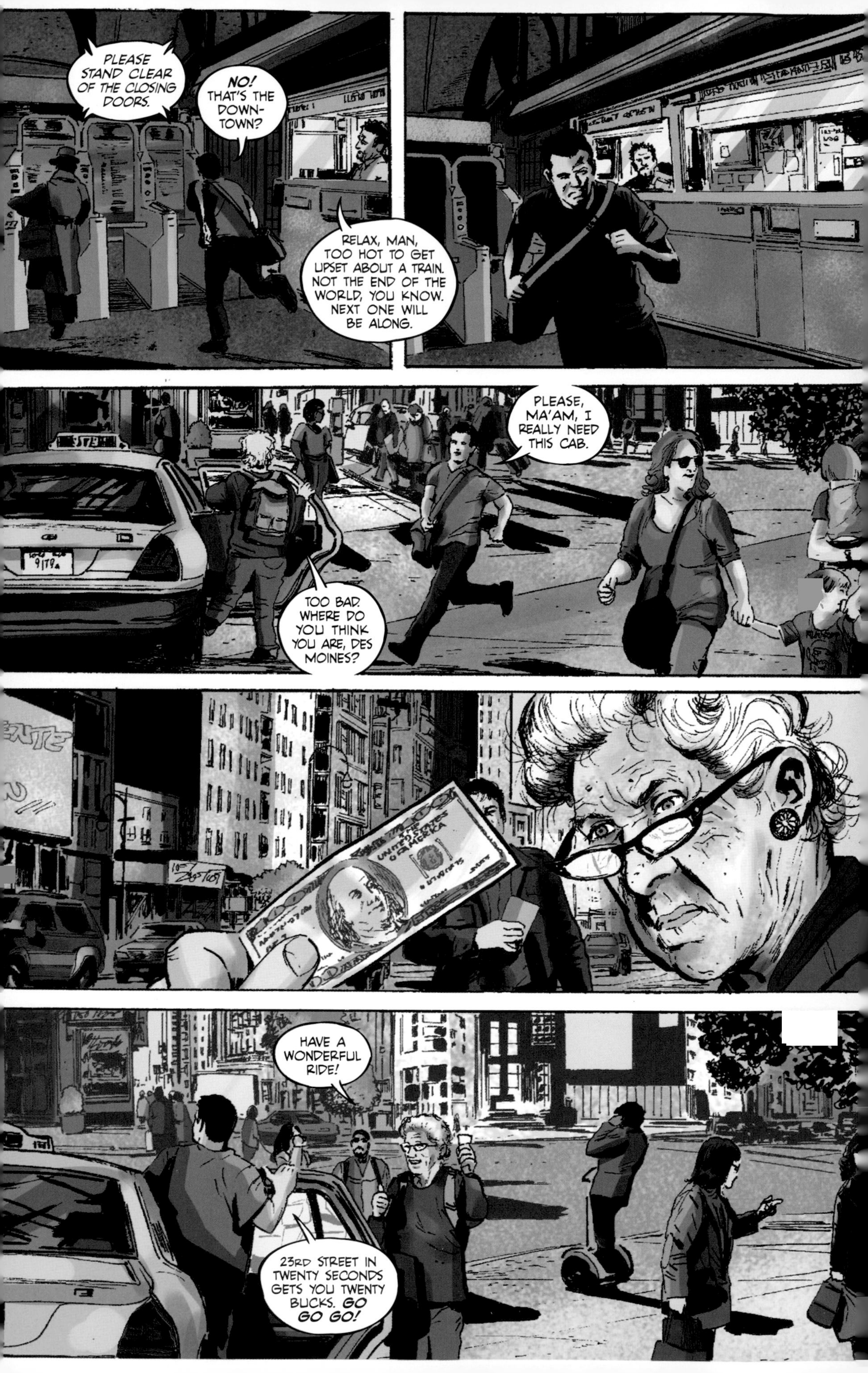
PLEASE STAND CLEAR OF THE CLOSING DOORS.
NO! THAT'S THE DOWN-TOWN?
RELAX, MAN, TOO HOT TO GET UPSET ABOUT A TRAIN. NOT THE END OF THE WORLD, YOU KNOW. NEXT ONE WILL BE ALONG.
PLEASE, MA'AM, I REALLY NEED THIS CAB.
TOO BAD. WHERE DO YOU THINK YOU ARE, DES MOINES?
HAVE A WONDERFUL RIDE!
23RD STREET IN TWENTY SECONDS GETS YOU TWENTY BUCKS. GO GO GO!

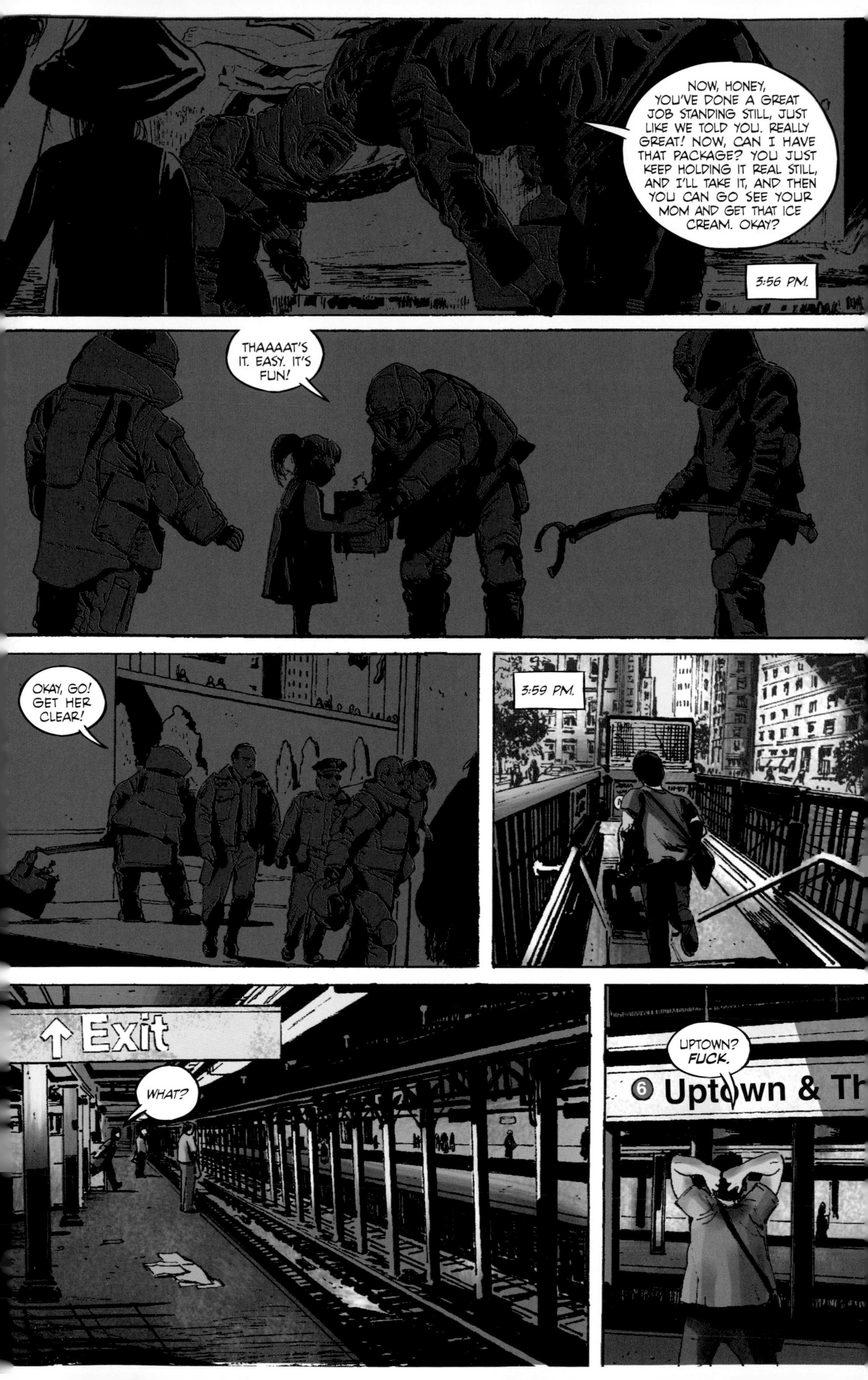
NOW, HONEY, YOU'VE DONE A GREAT JOB STANDING STILL, JUST LIKE WE TOLD YOU. REALLY GREAT! NOW, CAN I HAVE THAT PACKAGE? YOU JUST KEEP HOLDING IT REAL STILL, AND I'LL TAKE IT, AND THEN YOU CAN GO SEE YOUR MOM AND GET THAT ICE CREAM. OKAY?
3:56 PM.
THAAAAT'S IT. EASY. IT'S FUN!
OKAY, GO! GET HER CLEAR!
3:59 PM.
Exit
WHAT?
UPTOWN? FUCK.
6 Uptown & Th

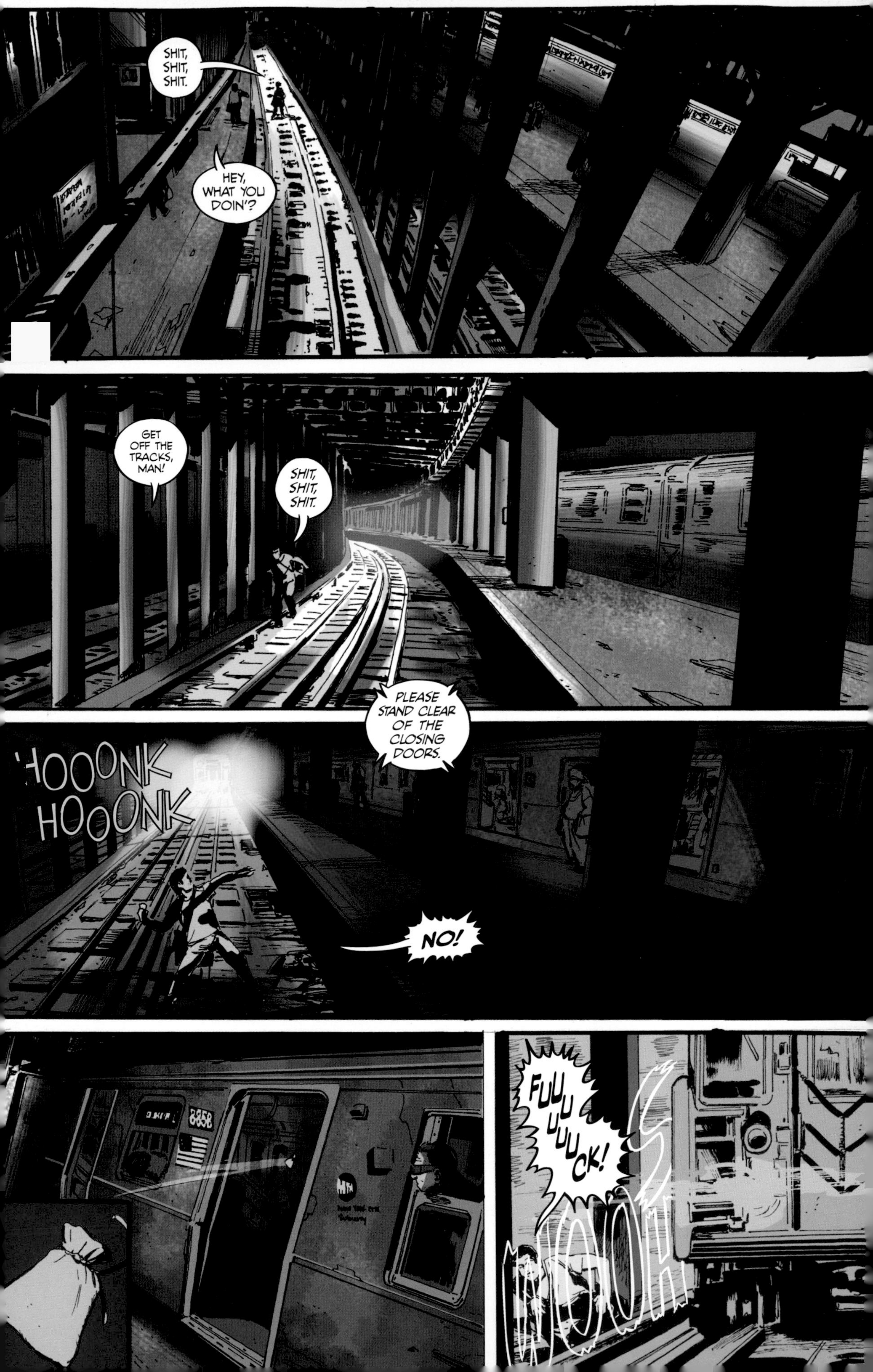
SHIT, SHIT, SHIT.
HEY, WHAT YOU DOIN'?
GET OFF THE TRACKS, MAN!
SHIT, SHIT, SHIT.
PLEASE STAND CLEAR OF THE CLOSING DOORS.
HOOONK HOOONK
NO!
8858
FUUUUUUCK!
WOOOOH

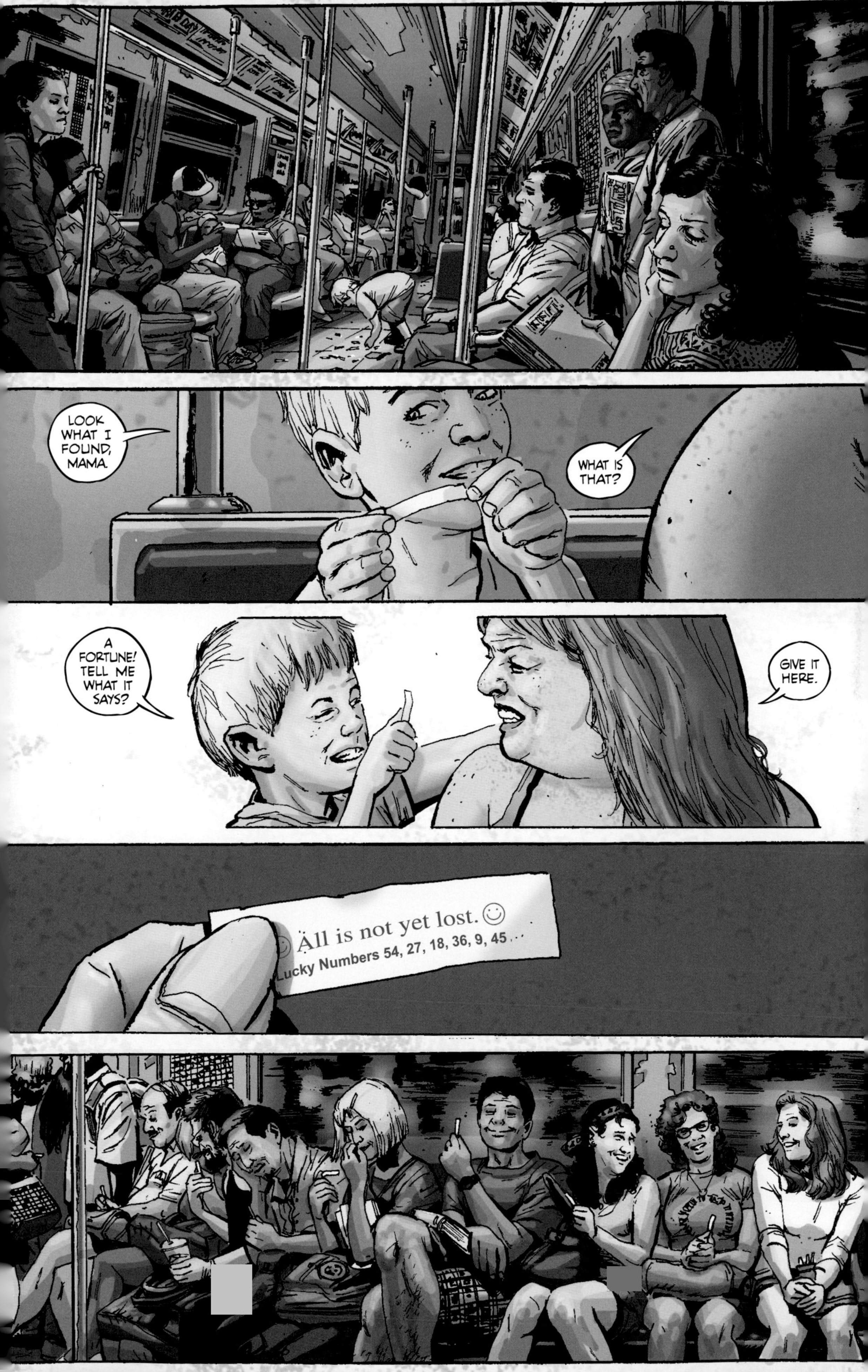
LOOK WHAT I FOUND, MAMA.
WHAT IS THAT?
A FORTUNE! TELL ME WHAT IT SAYS?
GIVE IT HERE.
All is not yet lost.
Lucky Numbers 54, 27, 18, 36, 9, 45...

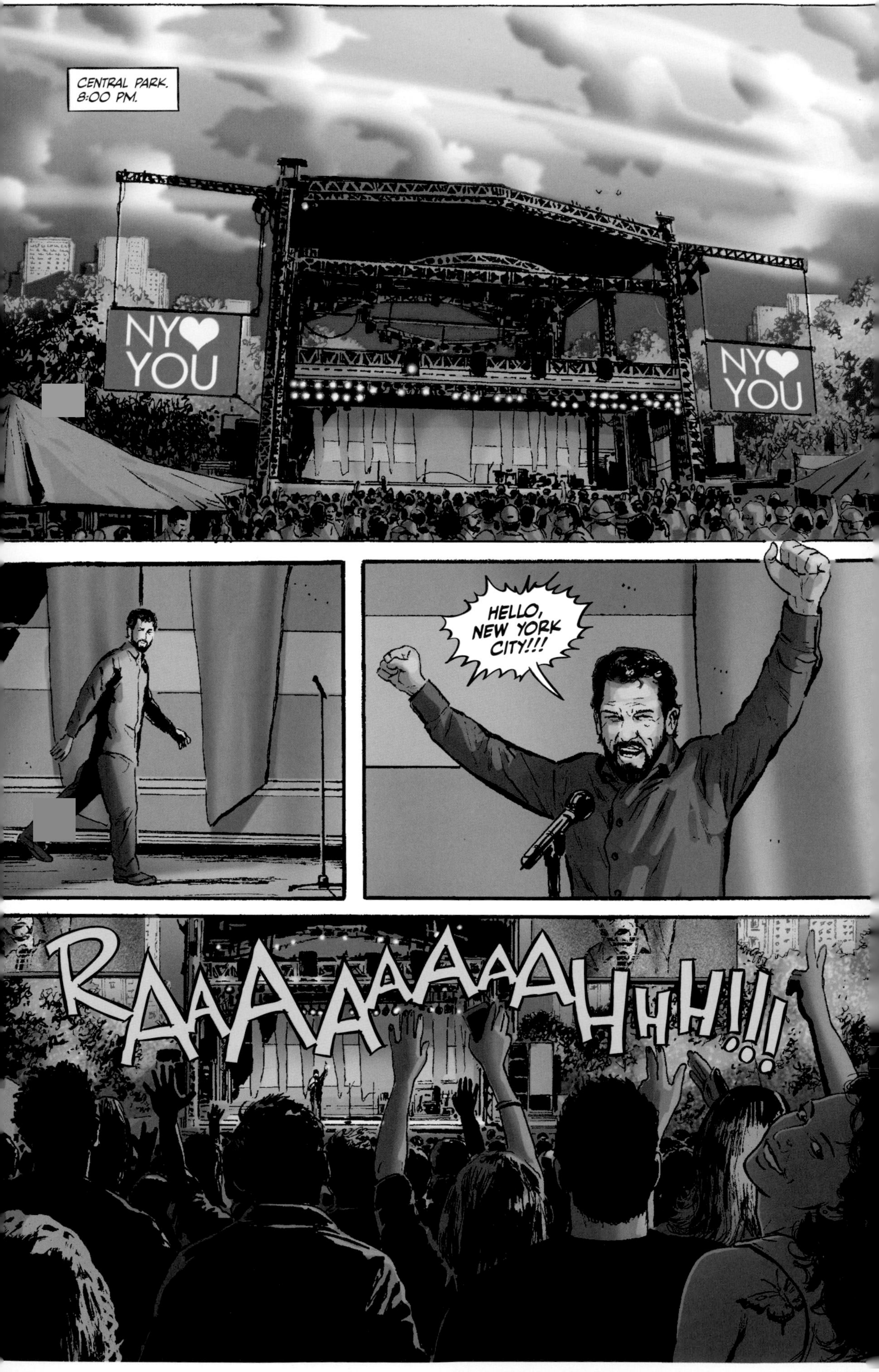
CENTRAL PARK.
8:00 PM.
NY YOU
NY YOU
HELLO, NEW YORK CITY!!!
RAAAAAAAAHHH!!!

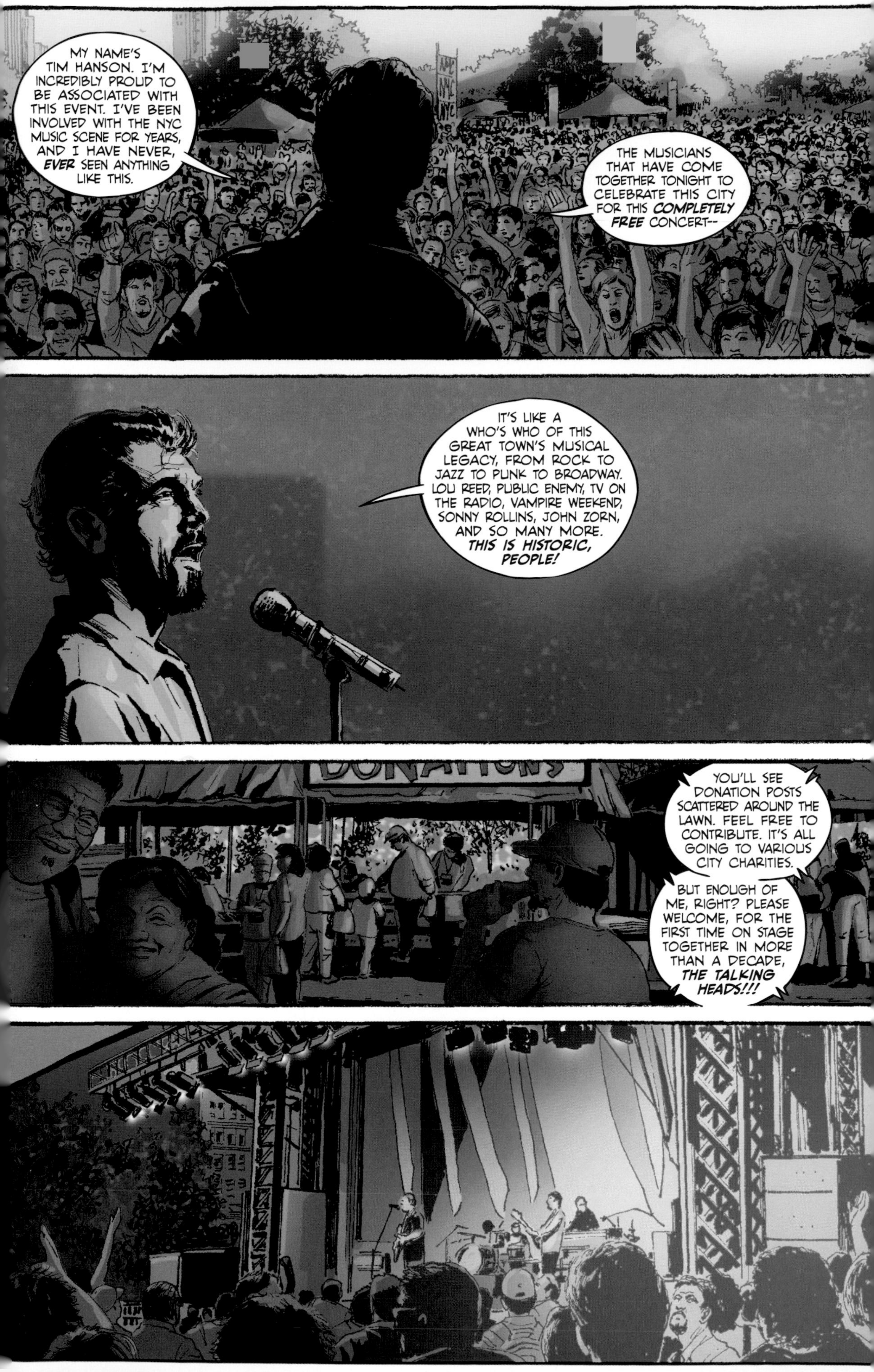
MY NAME'S TIM HANSON. I'M INCREDIBLY PROUD TO BE ASSOCIATED WITH THIS EVENT. I'VE BEEN INVOLVED WITH THE NYC MUSIC SCENE FOR YEARS, AND I HAVE NEVER, *EVER* SEEN ANYTHING LIKE THIS.
THE MUSICIANS THAT HAVE COME TOGETHER TONIGHT TO CELEBRATE THIS CITY FOR THIS *COMPLETELY FREE* CONCERT--
IT'S LIKE A WHO'S WHO OF THIS GREAT TOWN'S MUSICAL LEGACY, FROM ROCK TO JAZZ TO PUNK TO BROADWAY. LOU REED, PUBLIC ENEMY, TV ON THE RADIO, VAMPIRE WEEKEND, SONNY ROLLINS, JOHN ZORN, AND SO MANY MORE. *THIS IS HISTORIC, PEOPLE!*
DONATIONS
YOU'LL SEE DONATION POSTS SCATTERED AROUND THE LAWN. FEEL FREE TO CONTRIBUTE. IT'S ALL GOING TO VARIOUS CITY CHARITIES.
BUT ENOUGH OF ME, RIGHT? PLEASE WELCOME, FOR THE FIRST TIME ON STAGE TOGETHER IN MORE THAN A DECADE, *THE TALKING HEADS!!!*

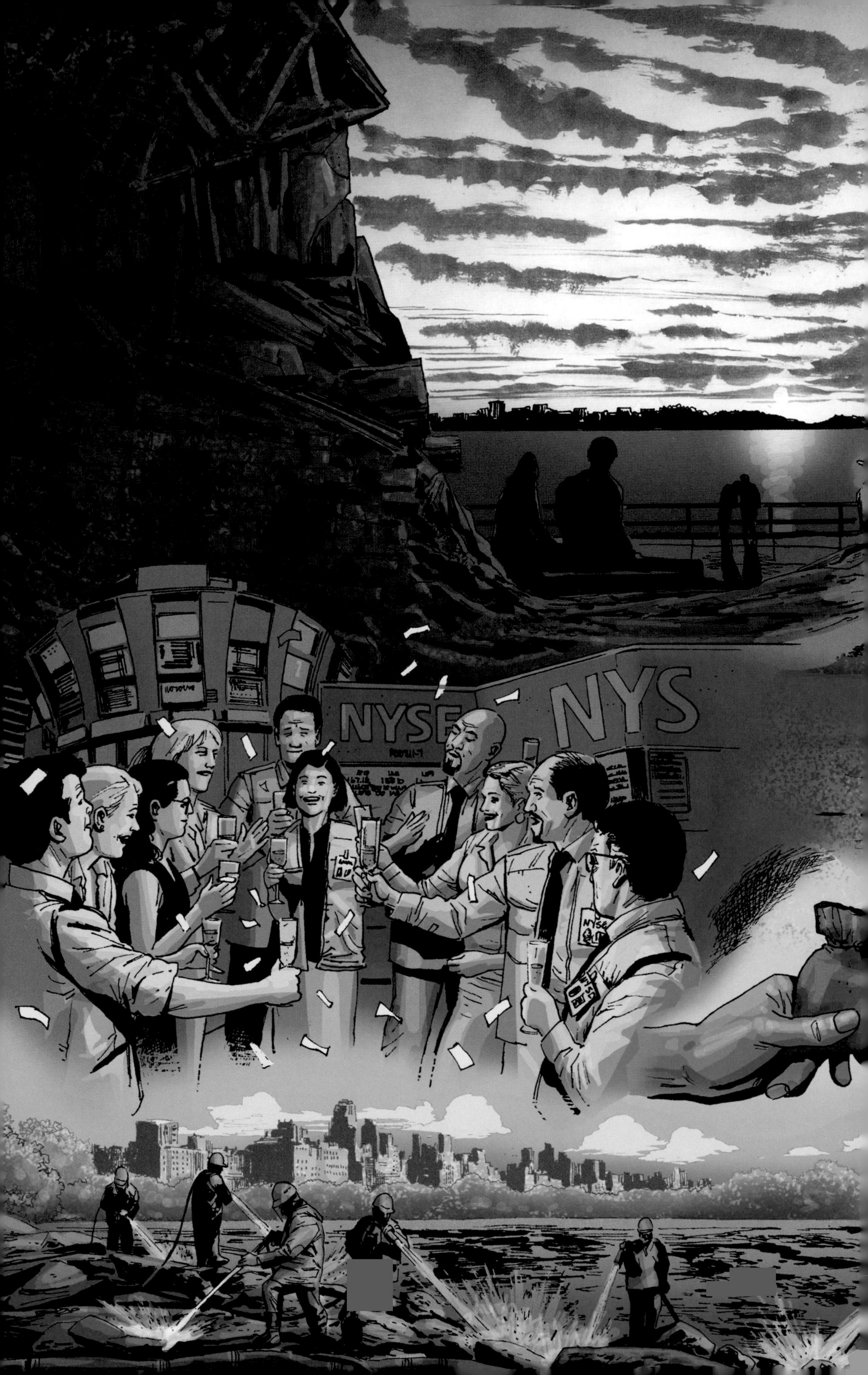
NYSE
NYS

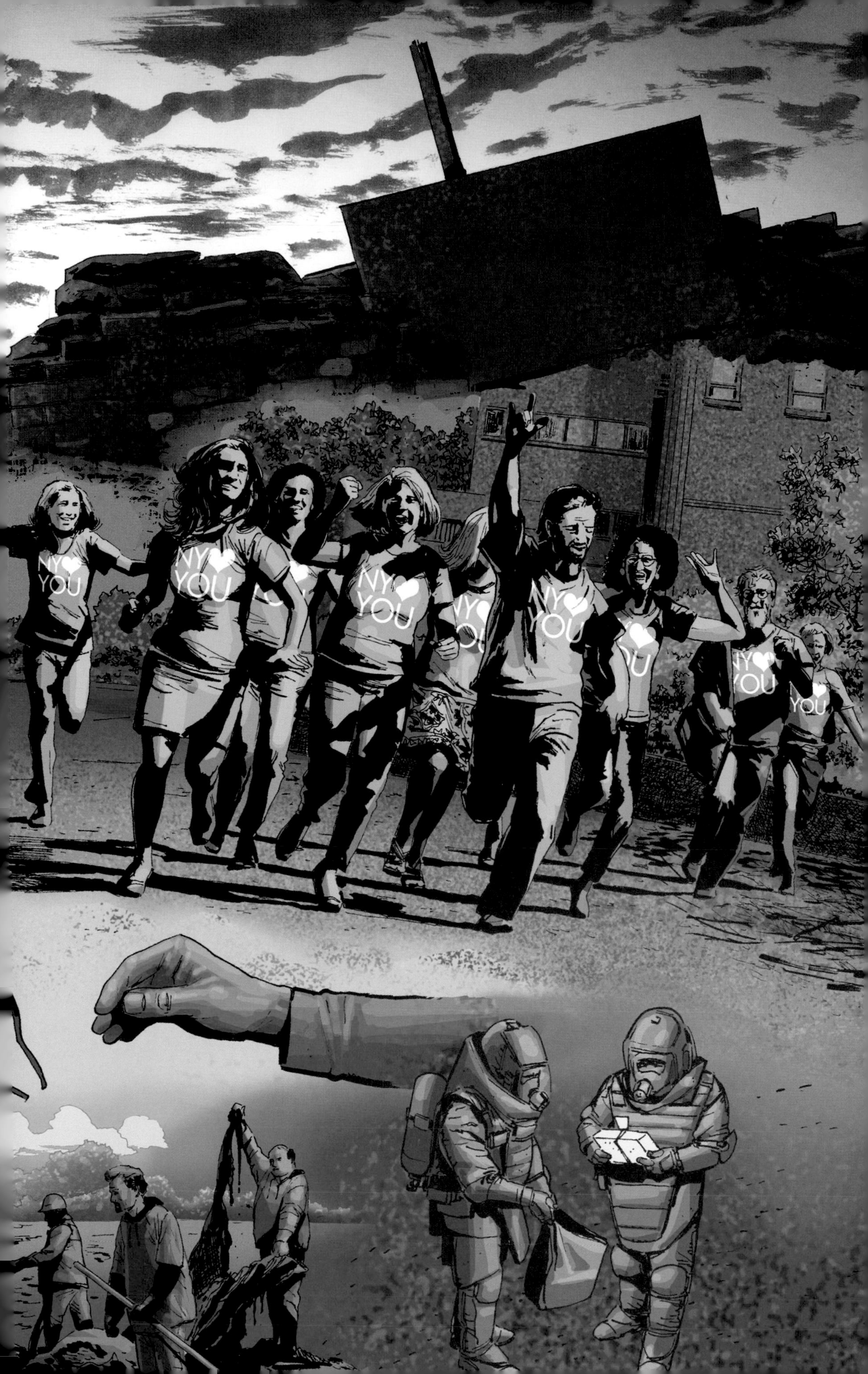
NY ♥ YOU

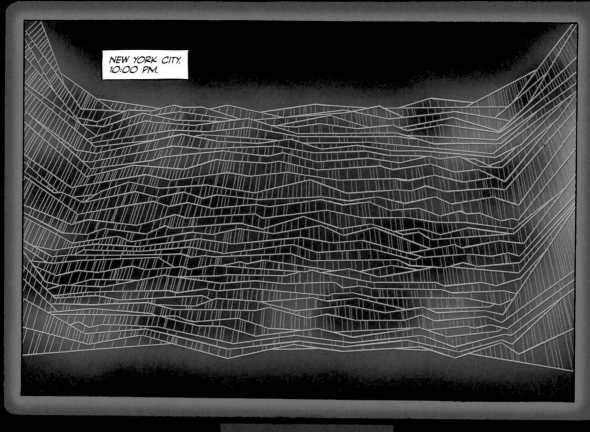

NEW YORK CITY.
10:00 PM.

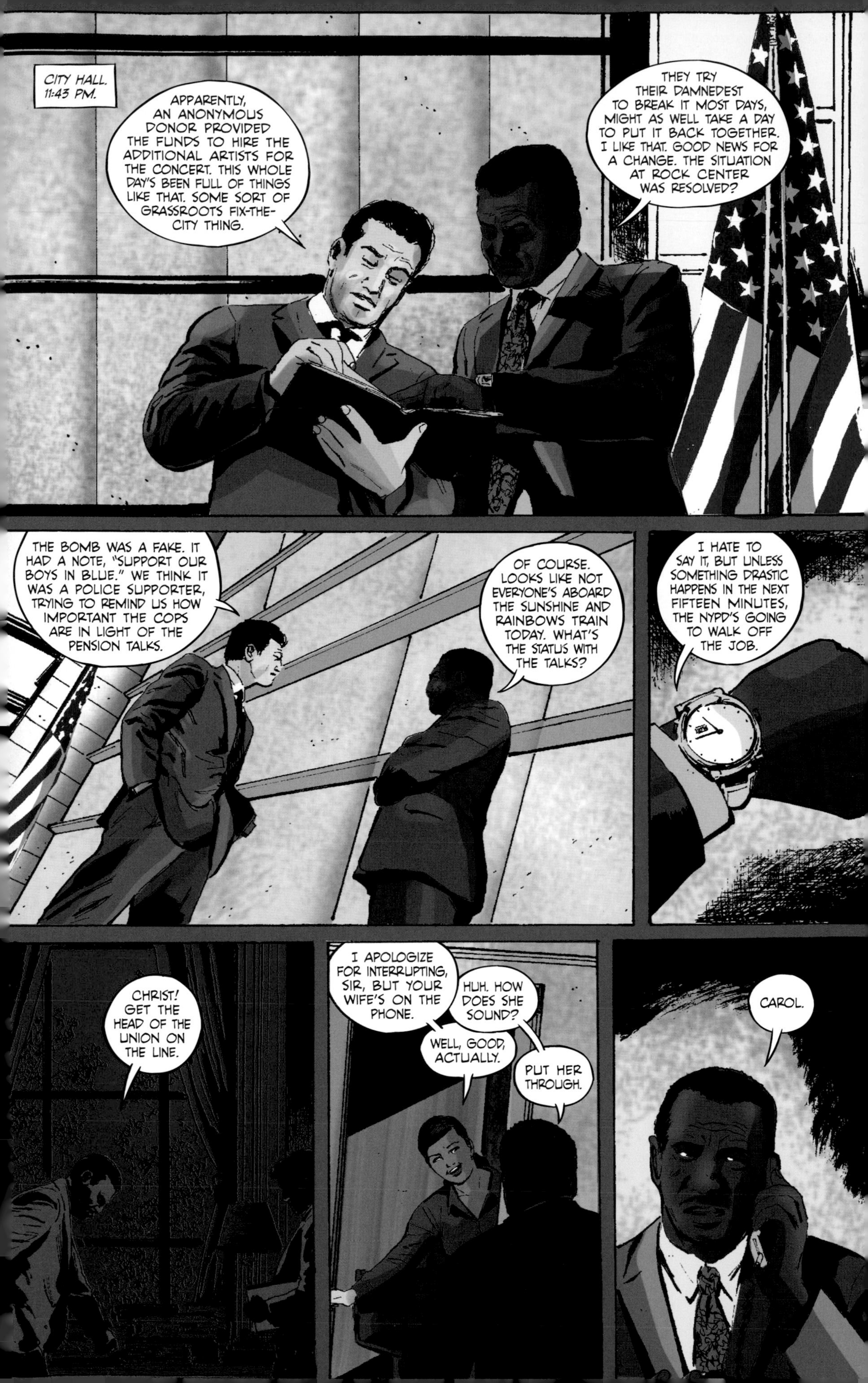
CITY HALL. 11:43 PM.
APPARENTLY, AN ANONYMOUS DONOR PROVIDED THE FUNDS TO HIRE THE ADDITIONAL ARTISTS FOR THE CONCERT. THIS WHOLE DAY'S BEEN FULL OF THINGS LIKE THAT. SOME SORT OF GRASSROOTS FIX-THE-CITY THING.
THEY TRY THEIR DAMNEDEST TO BREAK IT MOST DAYS, MIGHT AS WELL TAKE A DAY TO PUT IT BACK TOGETHER. I LIKE THAT. GOOD NEWS FOR A CHANGE. THE SITUATION AT ROCK CENTER WAS RESOLVED?
THE BOMB WAS A FAKE. IT HAD A NOTE, "SUPPORT OUR BOYS IN BLUE." WE THINK IT WAS A POLICE SUPPORTER, TRYING TO REMIND US HOW IMPORTANT THE COPS ARE IN LIGHT OF THE PENSION TALKS.
OF COURSE. LOOKS LIKE NOT EVERYONE'S ABOARD THE SUNSHINE AND RAINBOWS TRAIN TODAY. WHAT'S THE STATUS WITH THE TALKS?
I HATE TO SAY IT, BUT UNLESS SOMETHING DRASTIC HAPPENS IN THE NEXT FIFTEEN MINUTES, THE NYPD'S GOING TO WALK OFF THE JOB.
CHRIST! GET THE HEAD OF THE UNION ON THE LINE.
I APOLOGIZE FOR INTERRUPTING, SIR, BUT YOUR WIFE'S ON THE PHONE.
HUH. HOW DOES SHE SOUND?
WELL, GOOD, ACTUALLY.
PUT HER THROUGH.
CAROL.

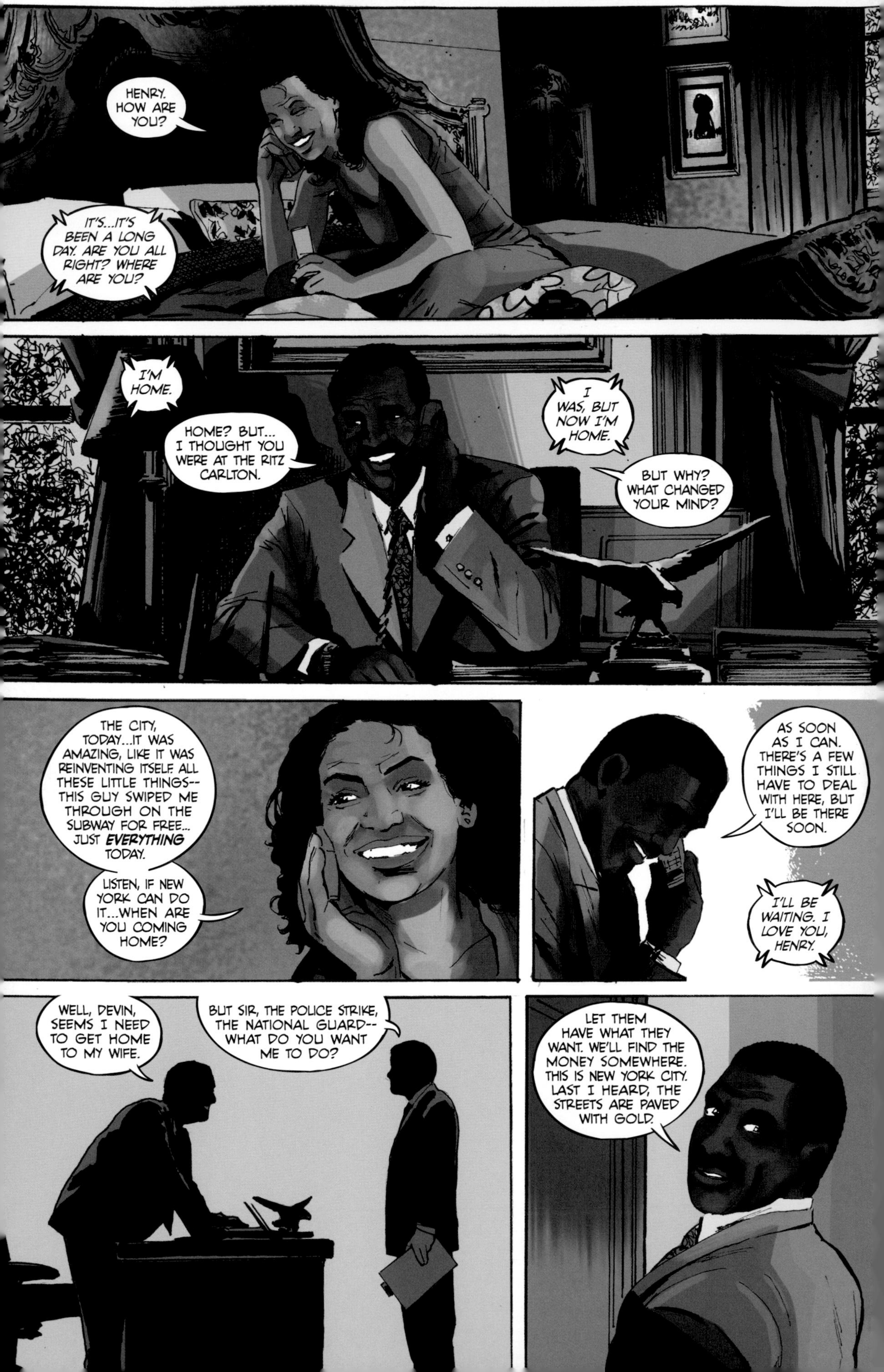
HENRY. HOW ARE YOU?
IT'S...IT'S BEEN A LONG DAY. ARE YOU ALL RIGHT? WHERE ARE YOU?
I'M HOME.
HOME? BUT... I THOUGHT YOU WERE AT THE RITZ CARLTON.
I WAS, BUT NOW I'M HOME.
BUT WHY? WHAT CHANGED YOUR MIND?
THE CITY, TODAY...IT WAS AMAZING, LIKE IT WAS REINVENTING ITSELF. ALL THESE LITTLE THINGS--THIS GUY SWIPED ME THROUGH ON THE SUBWAY FOR FREE... JUST **EVERYTHING** TODAY.
LISTEN, IF NEW YORK CAN DO IT...WHEN ARE YOU COMING HOME?
AS SOON AS I CAN. THERE'S A FEW THINGS I STILL HAVE TO DEAL WITH HERE, BUT I'LL BE THERE SOON.
I'LL BE WAITING. I LOVE YOU, HENRY.
WELL, DEVIN, SEEMS I NEED TO GET HOME TO MY WIFE.
BUT SIR, THE POLICE STRIKE, THE NATIONAL GUARD--WHAT DO YOU WANT ME TO DO?
LET THEM HAVE WHAT THEY WANT. WE'LL FIND THE MONEY SOMEWHERE. THIS IS NEW YORK CITY. LAST I HEARD, THE STREETS ARE PAVED WITH GOLD.

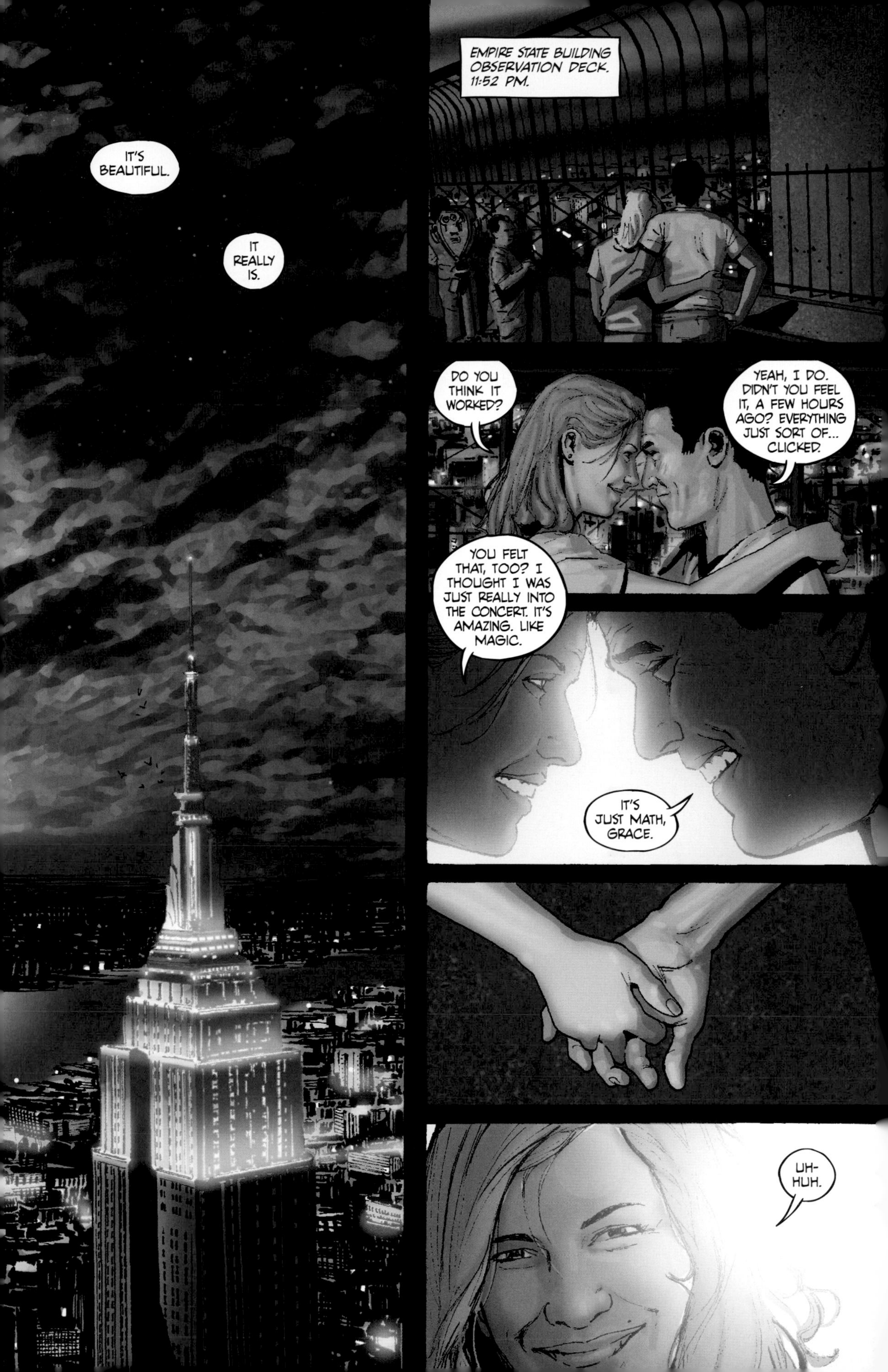
IT'S BEAUTIFUL.
IT REALLY IS.
EMPIRE STATE BUILDING OBSERVATION DECK. 11:52 PM.
DO YOU THINK IT WORKED?
YEAH, I DO. DIDN'T YOU FEEL IT, A FEW HOURS AGO? EVERYTHING JUST SORT OF... CLICKED.
YOU FELT THAT, TOO? I THOUGHT I WAS JUST REALLY INTO THE CONCERT. IT'S AMAZING. LIKE MAGIC.
IT'S JUST MATH, GRACE.
UH-HUH.

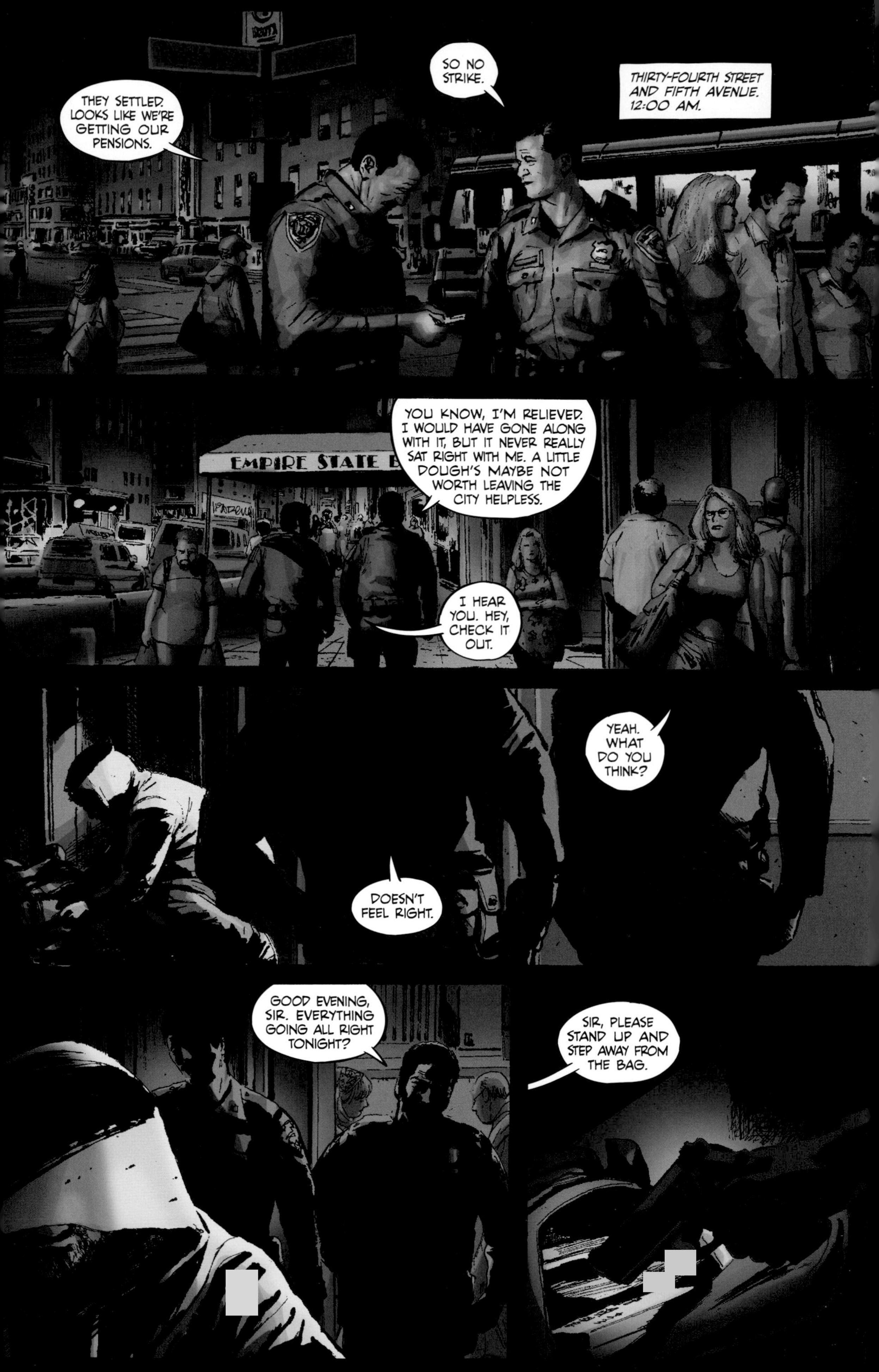
THIRTY-FOURTH STREET AND FIFTH AVENUE. 12:00 AM.
THEY SETTLED. LOOKS LIKE WE'RE GETTING OUR PENSIONS.
SO NO STRIKE.
EMPIRE STATE B
YOU KNOW, I'M RELIEVED. I WOULD HAVE GONE ALONG WITH IT, BUT IT NEVER REALLY SAT RIGHT WITH ME. A LITTLE DOUGH'S MAYBE NOT WORTH LEAVING THE CITY HELPLESS.
I HEAR YOU. HEY, CHECK IT OUT.
YEAH. WHAT DO YOU THINK?
DOESN'T FEEL RIGHT.
GOOD EVENING, SIR. EVERYTHING GOING ALL RIGHT TONIGHT?
SIR, PLEASE STAND UP AND STEP AWAY FROM THE BAG.

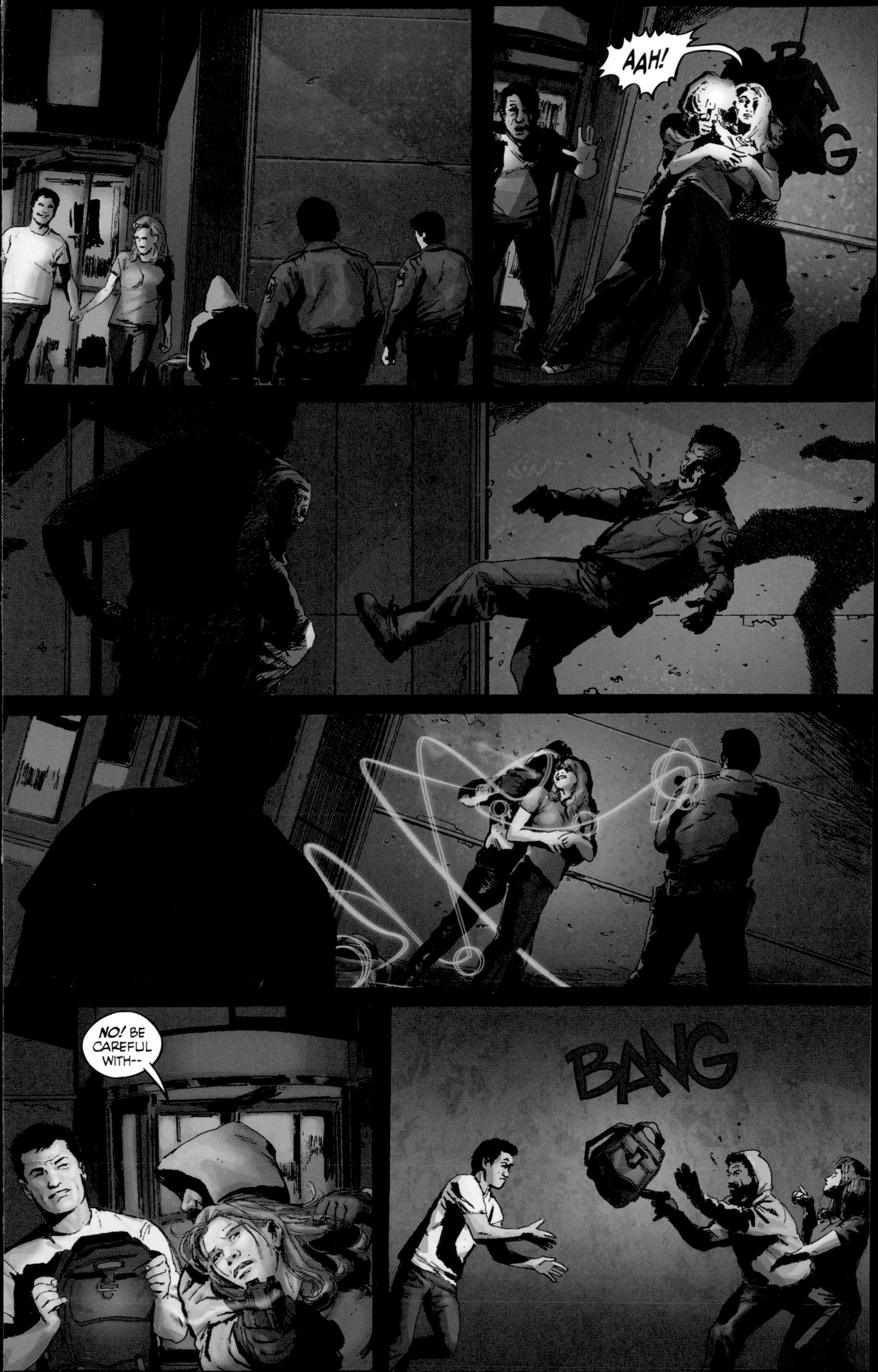
AAH!
BANG
NO! BE CAREFUL WITH--
BANG

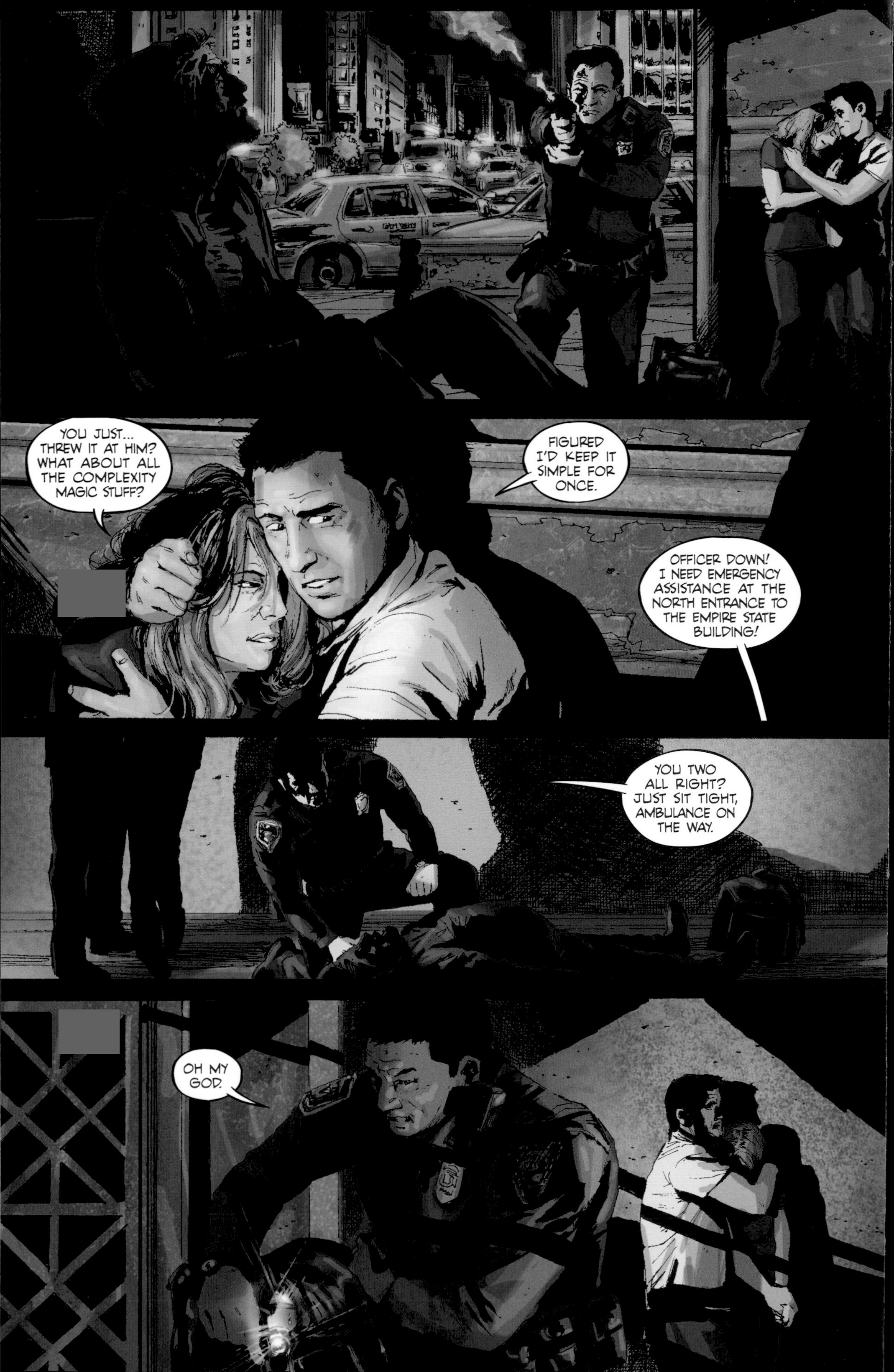
YOU JUST... THREW IT AT HIM? WHAT ABOUT ALL THE COMPLEXITY MAGIC STUFF?
FIGURED I'D KEEP IT SIMPLE FOR ONCE.
OFFICER DOWN! I NEED EMERGENCY ASSISTANCE AT THE NORTH ENTRANCE TO THE EMPIRE STATE BUILDING!
YOU TWO ALL RIGHT? JUST SIT TIGHT, AMBULANCE ON THE WAY.
OH MY GOD.

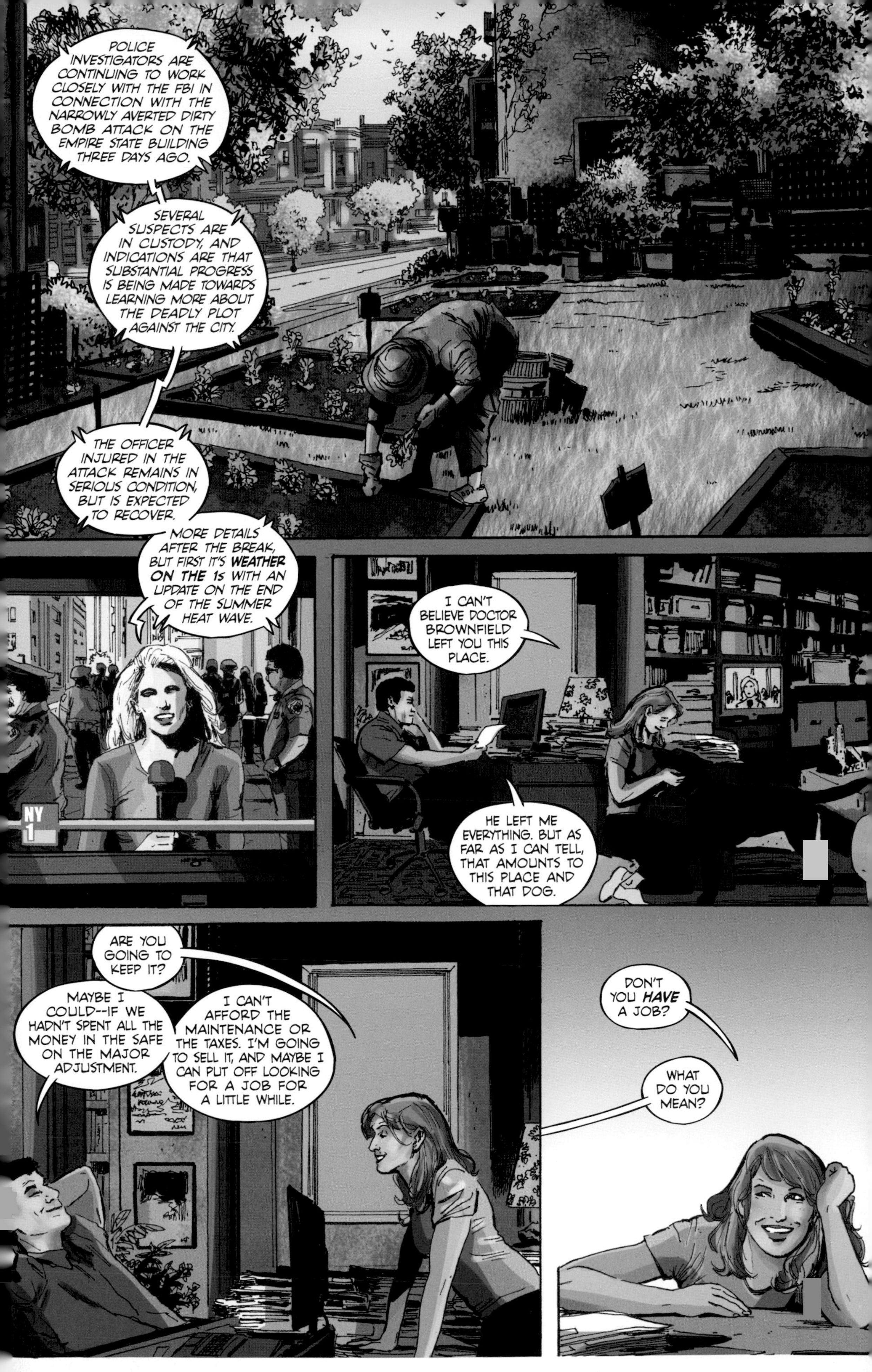
POLICE INVESTIGATORS ARE CONTINUING TO WORK CLOSELY WITH THE FBI IN CONNECTION WITH THE NARROWLY AVERTED DIRTY BOMB ATTACK ON THE EMPIRE STATE BUILDING THREE DAYS AGO.
SEVERAL SUSPECTS ARE IN CUSTODY, AND INDICATIONS ARE THAT SUBSTANTIAL PROGRESS IS BEING MADE TOWARDS LEARNING MORE ABOUT THE DEADLY PLOT AGAINST THE CITY.
THE OFFICER INJURED IN THE ATTACK REMAINS IN SERIOUS CONDITION, BUT IS EXPECTED TO RECOVER.
MORE DETAILS AFTER THE BREAK, BUT FIRST IT'S **WEATHER ON THE 1s** WITH AN UPDATE ON THE END OF THE SUMMER HEAT WAVE.
NY 1
I CAN'T BELIEVE DOCTOR BROWNFIELD LEFT YOU THIS PLACE.
HE LEFT ME EVERYTHING. BUT AS FAR AS I CAN TELL, THAT AMOUNTS TO THIS PLACE AND THAT DOG.
ARE YOU GOING TO KEEP IT?
I CAN'T AFFORD THE MAINTENANCE OR THE TAXES. I'M GOING TO SELL IT, AND MAYBE I CAN PUT OFF LOOKING FOR A JOB FOR A LITTLE WHILE.
MAYBE I COULD--IF WE HADN'T SPENT ALL THE MONEY IN THE SAFE ON THE MAJOR ADJUSTMENT.
DON'T YOU ***HAVE*** A JOB?
WHAT DO YOU MEAN?

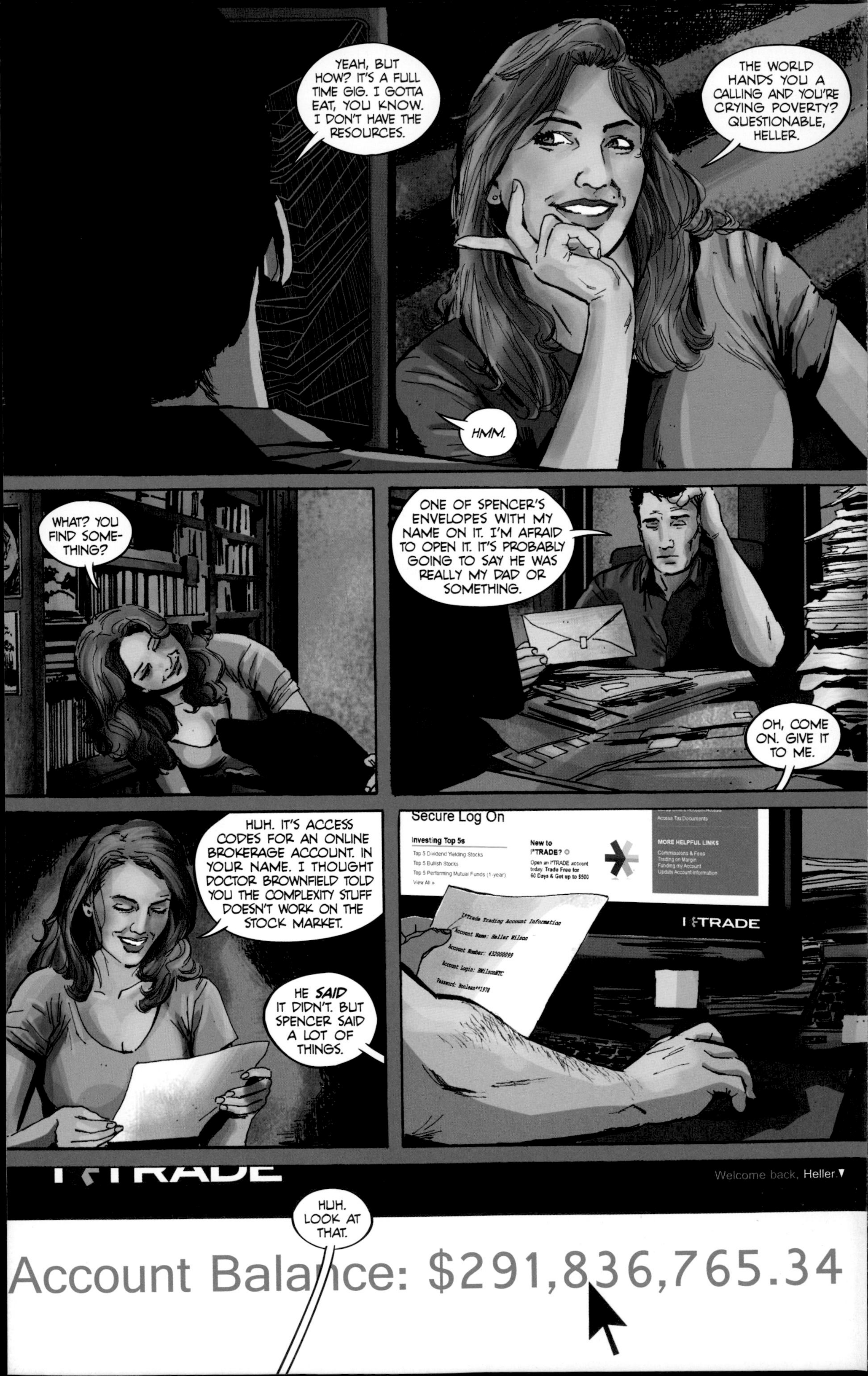

YEAH, BUT HOW? IT'S A FULL TIME GIG. I GOTTA EAT, YOU KNOW. I DON'T HAVE THE RESOURCES.
THE WORLD HANDS YOU A CALLING AND YOU'RE CRYING POVERTY? QUESTIONABLE, HELLER.
HMM.
WHAT? YOU FIND SOME-THING?
ONE OF SPENCER'S ENVELOPES WITH MY NAME ON IT. I'M AFRAID TO OPEN IT. IT'S PROBABLY GOING TO SAY HE WAS REALLY MY DAD OR SOMETHING.
OH, COME ON. GIVE IT TO ME.
HUH. IT'S ACCESS CODES FOR AN ONLINE BROKERAGE ACCOUNT. IN YOUR NAME. I THOUGHT DOCTOR BROWNFIELD TOLD YOU THE COMPLEXITY STUFF DOESN'T WORK ON THE STOCK MARKET.
HE *SAID* IT DIDN'T. BUT SPENCER SAID A LOT OF THINGS.
Secure Log On
Investing Top 5s
Top 5 Dividend Yielding Stocks
Top 5 Bullish Stocks
Top 5 Performing Mutual Funds (1-year)
View All »
New to I*TRADE?
Open an I*TRADE account today. Trade Free for 60 Days & Get up to $500
Access Tax Documents
MORE HELPFUL LINKS
Commissions & Fees
Trading on Margin
Funding my Account
Update Account Information
I*Trade Trading Account Information
Account Name: Heller Wilson
Account Number: 432000099
Account Login: HWilsonNYC
Password: Boolean**1978
I*TRADE
Welcome back, Heller.
HUH. LOOK AT THAT.
Account Balance: $291,836,765.34

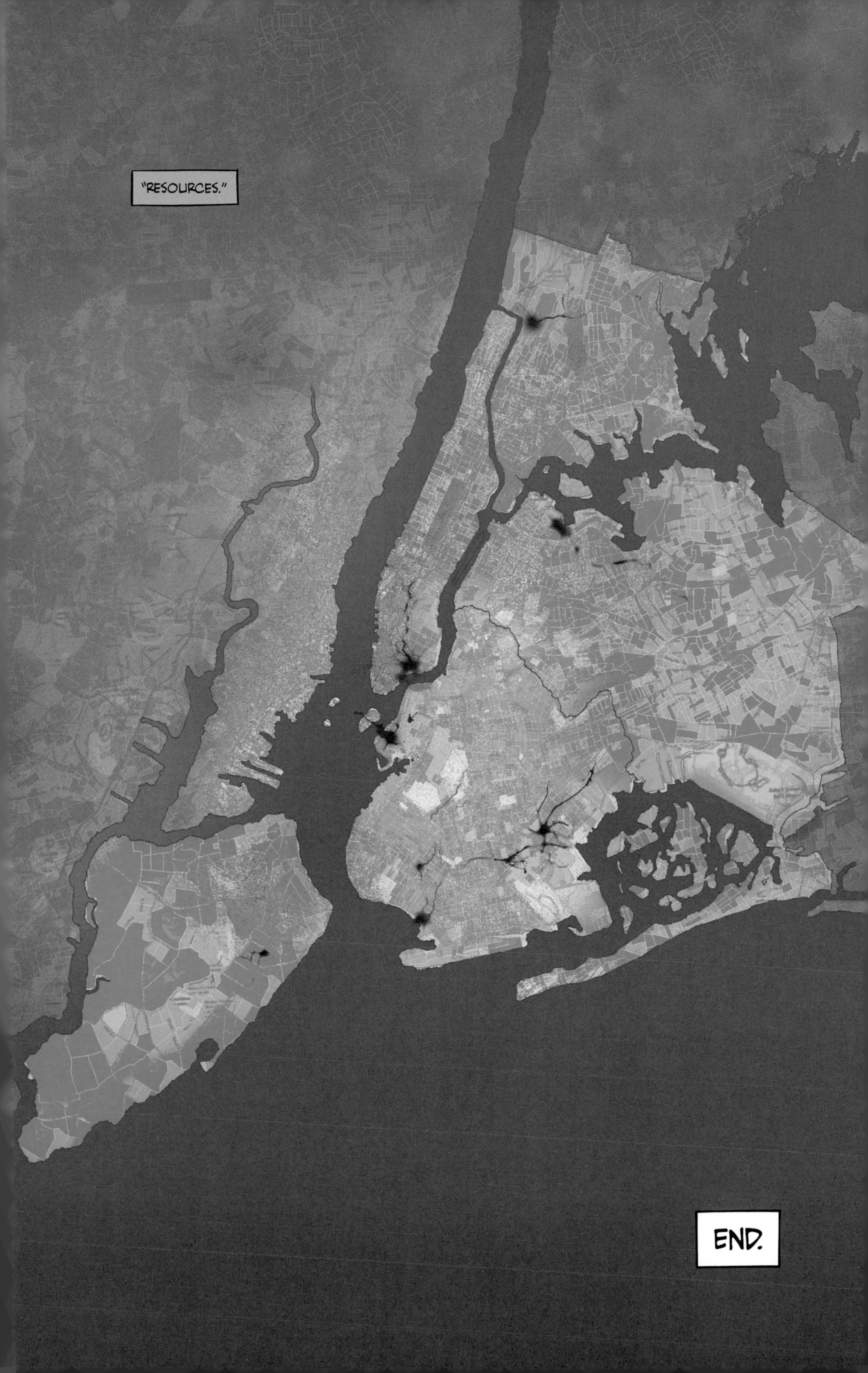
"RESOURCES."
END.

DR. BROWNFIELD'S NOTEBOOK MAPS

I began the **Strange Attractors** project by focusing on the maps the reader first sees in Dr. Spencer Brownfield's notebook on page 30. The maps needed to feel hand-drawn but also methodical and scientific. The process to create them was organic in that Charles Soule would convey a visual reference he had in mind (e.g., the chaos of tangled wires) and—after gathering my own visual inspiration—I would create very rough thumbnail sketches. Influences for the maps ranged from constellations, planetary orbits, and city subway maps, to topographic renderings and aerial photos of highways. I created the artwork methodically, but also organically, using rulers and drawing freehand, approaching them as an aerial map of a city randomly populated with people, their connections and bursts of chaos.

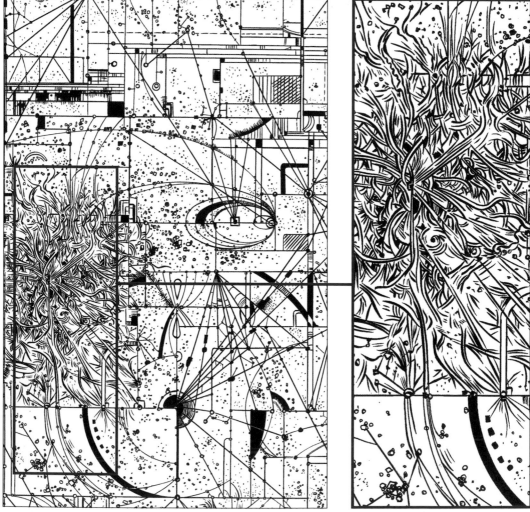

Sample Notebook Map (Detail)

Map Chaos (Sub-Detail)

WORDS AND ILLUSTRATIONS BY ROBERT SAYWITZ

COMPUTER MAPS

The computer maps were a different type of challenge from the hand-drawn, in that they needed to have the same sense of complexity and chaos, but rendered as if a computer program were translating Dr. Brownfield's notebook through a three-dimensional software program. My initial inspiration came from 3D modeling images of wireframe interior spaces and topographic maps. I then drew an underlying city grid—which remained the same in all the computer maps—though shown in varying degrees of chaos. Once the grid was inked, I scanned and colorized it with neon blue and placed it on a black background for better legibility and to give it a technical feel. I took inspiration from rock and ice formations, stalactites, cacti, and imagining how towering sculptures compiled of jagged pieces of glass might look.

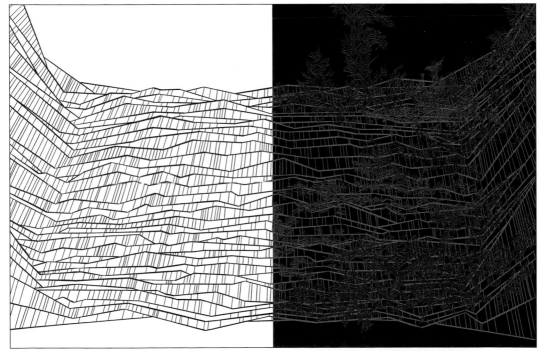

Underlying Grid Drawing and Final Color Version

Sample Chaos Drawing

Sample Chaos Drawing (Detail)

JENKINS MAP

When it came time to focus on the Jenkins map, the challenge was to take the approach I used with the New York City complexity maps and use it to create a map of a person. I would eventually have to do this for the main character, Heller—as a four-page foldout—but this was different, since Jenkins commits suicide in the beginning of the story. Given this narrative, Charles wanted me to create the most beautiful and simultaneously ugly map possible. It had to show the complexity of a man under serious duress, which ultimately sends him down a path of self-destruction. For visual references, Charles suggested I look at images of tangled clumps of knotted hair and—if I could stomach it—images of skin diseases and "rat kings" (if you don't know what a "rat king" is, search online and beware). I also took some inspiration from lightning storms, how electricity travels across multiple nodes and what that might look like when out of control. The colors—like the art itself—needed to be very macabre, but beautiful.

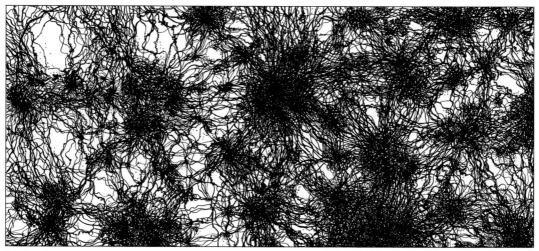

Ink Drawing (Detail)

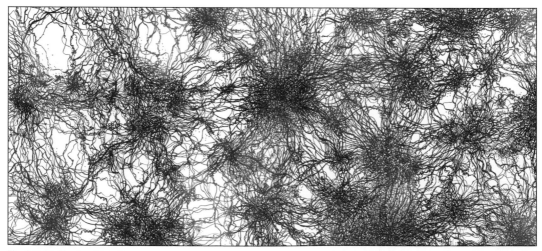

Final Color Version (Detail)

HELLER MAP

The goal here was to show a complexity map of the story's hero—illustrating his underlying physical structure, interconnected moving parts and various areas of emotional chaos. I began with a background landscape resembling a hybrid of robotic innards and a vast futuristic highway system. Once Charles and I agreed upon the concept, I taped four pages of bristol paper together and created the structural layer of artwork as if it were one giant canvas stretched out to 44″ wide by 17″ tall. On separate sheets of bristol, overlaid on a light table, I drew connector lines and dots. On a third sheet, I charted the areas of chaos and, after inking, combined each layer together on the computer for the final colorization process.

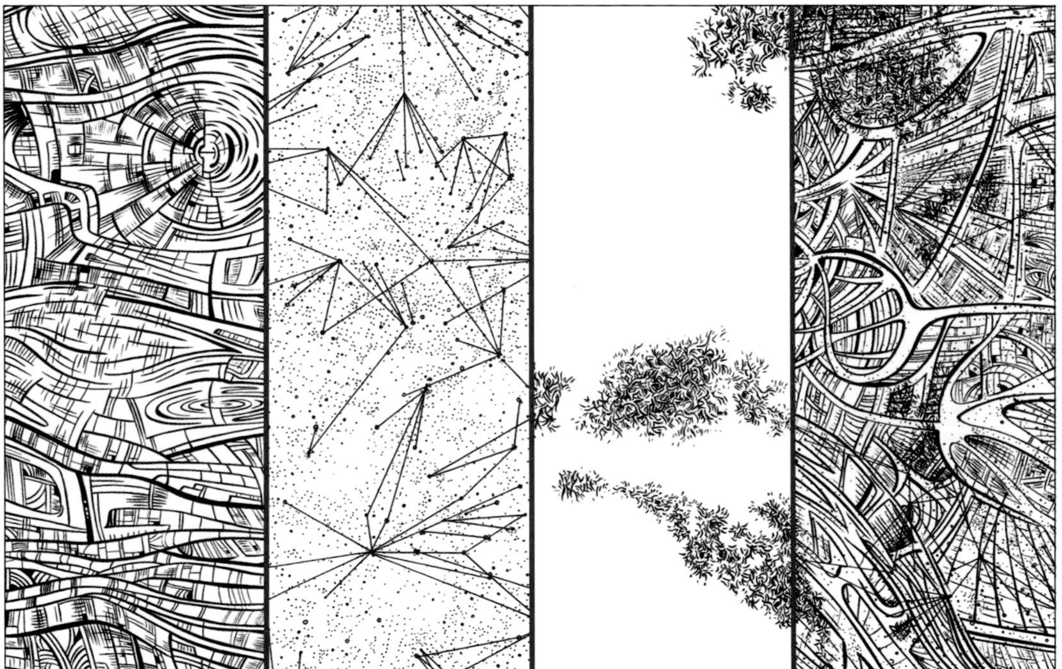

Structural Layer **Connector Layer** **Chaos Layer** **Final Version**

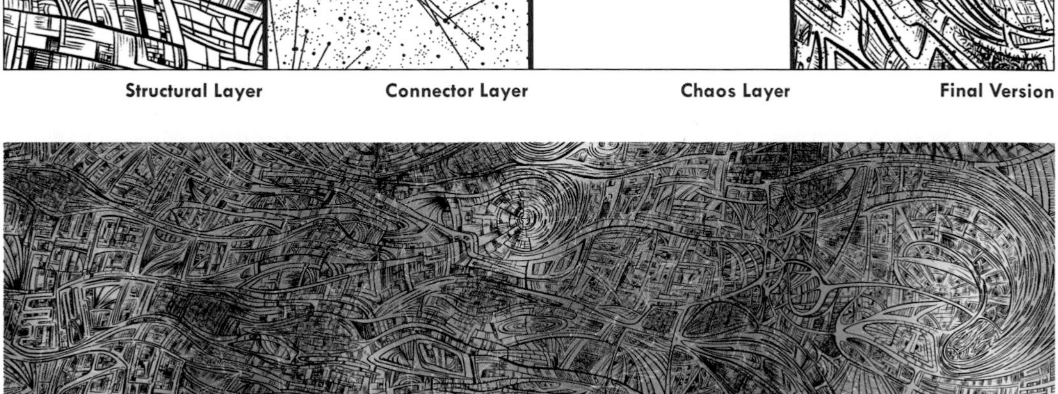

Final Color Version

ABOUT THE AUTHORS

CHARLES SOULE **WRITER**

Charles is based in Brooklyn, and has lived in New York City for more than fifteen years. He loves the city, and finds it hard to imagine ever living anywhere else. He is the author of *27* from Image/Shadowline, *Letter 44* from Oni Press, and the acclaimed OGN series *Strongman*, from SLG Publishing.

GREG SCOTT **ILLUSTRATOR**

Greg is a self-taught artist who loves staying home in Staten Island, drawing, doing whatever he can to never work a 9 to 5 job again. *Strange Attractors* was the hardest (in the best way) drawing job he's ever worked, a labor of love and a tribute to the greatest city in the world.

ART LYON **COLORS**

Art was born in the heart of an exploding sun and can see what you're doing from a trillion miles away. To distract himself from all that, he colors comics at his home in Bloomington, Indiana, USA, where he lives with his lovely and talented wife, two remarkable children, one dog, two geriatric cats, a kitten, and too, too many comic books.

MATTHEW PETZ **COLORS**

Matthew is a Brooklyn-based illustrator who has worked for DC Comics, Random House and MTV. He also has an unhealthy knowledge of giant monsters, and a penchant for drawing otters with turtle helmets.

ROBERT SAYWITZ **COMPLEXITY MAPS**

Robert is a Brooklyn-based artist whose work ranges from fine art painting, to graphic novel and children's book illustration, to music, film, theater design, and branding, always with strong storytelling as a primary goal. Robert creates narratives in the form of graphic novels, art books, and original works on canvas and paper—his work has been exhibited at various art spaces and galleries in New York. To see more of Robert's work, visit **rsaywitz.com**.

THOMAS MAUER **LETTERS**

Thomas, since jumping ship from a life as a historian, has worked as a letterer, designer, art director, and editor for a wide variety of publishers. He has had a hand in a number of Harvey and Eisner Award-nominated and -winning titles, including Image Comics' **POPGUN** anthology series and the webcomic *The Guns of Shadow Valley*.